A Voyage to Terra Australis

UNDERTAKEN FOR THE PURPOSE OF COMPLETING THE DISCOVERY OF THAT VAST COUNTRY, AND PROSECUTED IN THE YEARS 1801, 1802 AND 1803, IN HIS MAJESTY'S SHIP THE INVESTIGATOR, AND SUBSEQUENTLY IN THE ARMED VESSEL PORPOISE AND CUMBERLAND SCHOONER.

WITH AN ACCOUNT OF THE SHIPWRECK OF THE PORPOISE, ARRIVAL OF THE CUMBERLAND AT MAURITIUS, AND IMPRISONMENT OF THE COMMANDER DURING SIX YEARS AND A HALF IN THAT ISLAND.

Volume One

By Matthew Flinders

Commander of the Investigator

Published by Pantianos Classics

ISBN-13: 978-1979090391

First published in 1814

Contents

Preface

The publication in 1814 of a voyage commenced in 1801, and of which all the essential parts were concluded within three years, requires some explanation. Shipwreck and a long imprisonment prevented my arrival in England until the latter end of 1810; much had then been done to forward the account, and the charts in particular were nearly prepared for the engraver; but it was desirable that the astronomical observations, upon which so much depended, should undergo a re-calculation, and the lunar distances have the advantage of being compared with the observations made at the same time at Greenwich; and in July 1811, the necessary authority was obtained from the Board of Longitude. A considerable delay hence arose, and it was prolonged by the Greenwich observations being found to differ so much from the calculated places of the sun and moon, given in the Nautical Almanacks of 1801, 2 and 3, as to make considerable alterations in the longitudes of places settled during the voyage; and a reconstruction of all the charts becoming thence indispensable to accuracy, I wished also to employ in it corrections of another kind, which before had been adopted only in some particular instances.

A variety of observations with the compass had shown the magnetic needle to differ from itself sometimes as much as six, and even seven degrees, in or very near the same place, and the differences appeared to be subject to regular laws; but it was so extraordinary in the present advanced state of navigation, that they should not have been before discovered and a mode of preventing or correcting them ascertained, that my deductions, and almost the facts were distrusted; and in the first construction of the charts I had feared to deviate much from the usual practice. Application was now made to the Admiralty for experiments to be tried with the compass on board different ships; and the results in five cases being conformable to one of the three laws before deduced, which alone was susceptible of proof in England, the whole were adopted without reserve, and the variations and bearings taken throughout the voyage underwent a systematic correction. From these causes the reconstruction of the charts could not be commenced before 1813, which, when the extent of them is considered, will explain why the publication did not take place sooner; but it is hoped that the advantage in point of accuracy will amply compensate the delay.

Besides correcting the lunar distances and the variations and bearings, there are some other particulars, both in the account of the voyage and in the Atlas, where the practice of former navigators has not been strictly followed. Latitudes, longitudes, and bearings, so important to the seaman and uninteresting to the general reader, have hitherto been interwoven in the text; they are here commonly separated from it, by which the one will be enabled to find them more readily, and the other perceive at a glance what may be passed. I heard it declared that a man who published a quarto volume without an index ought to be set in the pillory, and being unwilling to incur the full rigour of this sentence, a running title has been affixed to all the pages; on one side is expressed the country or coast, and on the opposite the particular part where the ship is at anchor or which is the immediate subject of examination; this, it is hoped, will answer the main purpose of an index, without swelling the volumes. Longitude is one of the most essential, but at the same time least certain data in hydrography; the man of science therefore requires something more than the general result of observations before giving his unqualified assent to their accuracy, and the progress of knowledge has of late been such, that a commander now wishes to know the foundation upon which he is to rest his confidence and the safety of his ship; to comply with this laudable desire, the particular results of the observations by which the most important points on each coast are fixed in longitude, as also the means used to obtain them, are given at the end of the volume wherein that coast is described., as being there of most easy reference.

The deviations in the Atlas from former practice, or rather the additional marks used, are intended to make the charts contain as full a journal of the voyage as can be conveyed in this form; a chart is the seaman's great, and often sole guide, and if the information in it can be rendered more complete without introducing confusion, the advantage will be admitted by those who are not opposers of all improvement. In closely following a track laid down upon a chart, seamen often run at night, unsuspicious of danger if none be marked; but some parts of that track were run in the night also, and there may consequently be rocks or shoals, as near even as half a mile, which might prove fatal to them; it therefore seems proper that night tracks should be distinguished from those of the day, and they are so in this Atlas, I believe, for the first time. A distinction is made between the situations at noon where the latitude was observed, and those in which none could be obtained; and the positions fixed in longitude by the time keepers are also marked in the track, as are the few points where a latitude was obtained from the moon.

It has appeared to me, that to show the direction and strength of the winds, with the kind of weather we had when running along these coasts, would be an useful addition to the charts; not only as it would enable those who may navigate by them alone to form a judgment of what is to be expected at the same season, but also that it may be seen how far circumstances prevented several parts of the coast being laid down so correctly as others. This has been done by single arrows, wherever they could be marked without confusion; they are more or less feathered, proportionate to the strength of wind intended to be expressed, and the arrows themselves give the direction. Under each is a short or abridged word, denoting the weather; when this weather prevailed in a more than usual degree a line is drawn under the word, and when in an excessive degree there are two lines. Single arrows being thus appropriated to the winds, the tides and currents are shown by double arrows, between which is usually marked the rate per hour.

On the land, the shading of the hills gives a general idea of their elevation, and it has been assisted by saying how far particular hills and capes are visible from a ship's deck in fine weather; this will be useful to a seaman on first making the land, be a better criterion to judge of its height, and those hills not so marked may be more nearly estimated by comparison. Behind different parts of the coast is given a short description of their appearance, which it is conceived will be gratifying to scientific, and useful to professional men. The capes and hills whose positions are fixed by cross bearings taken on shore or from well ascertained points in the track, as also the stations whence bearings were observed with a theodolite, have distinguishing marks; which, with all others not before in common use, are explained.

To have laid down no more than the lands and dangers seen in the Investigator and other vessels under my command, would have left several open spaces, and obliged the seaman to have recourse to other charts where the difference of positions might have perplexed; the discoveries and examinations of former navigators which come within the sphere of each sheet, are therefore incorporated with, or added to mine, but so marked as to be distinctly known. In making the combination, alterations in their longitudes were frequently necessary to agreement; and that they might be made with every regard to accuracy, the charts of the former discoveries were compared with the astronomical observations, narratives, or manuscript journals, when such could be had, and the alterations introduced where there seemed to be the best authority. This has been done with the charts of the east coast of New South Wales, published by Mr. Dalrymple from the manuscripts, as it should appear, of captain Cook; and since it may be thought presumptuous in me to have made alterations in any work of so great a master, this case is selected for a more particular explanation.

Time keepers were in their infancy in 1768, when captain Cook sailed upon his first voyage, and he was not then furnished with them; his longitude was therefore regulated only by occasional observations of lunar distances and some few of Jupiter's satellites, which even in the present improved state of instruments and tables, require to be connected by time keepers before satisfactory conclusions can be drawn. Errors of greater or less magnitude were thence unavoidable; at Cape Gloucester, where I quitted the East Coast, my longitude was 20½' greater than captain Cook's chart--at Cape York where the survey was again resumed, it was 58½; and to incorporate the intermediate parts, it was necessary not only to carry his scale of longitude 20½' more west, but also to reduce the extent of the coast. The chart was compared with the narrative and chart in Hawkesworth, and the log book of the Endeavour with them all; when it was found that reductions might be made in various places upon one or more of the above authorities, for differences between them were frequent and sometimes considerable, and in one instance alone a reduction of 12' in the chart was obtained. It is said in Hawkesworth (III, 202), "As soon as we got within side the reef (through Providential Channel) we anchored in nineteen fathom;" and afterwards (p. 204), that the channel, "bore E. N. E. distant ten or twelve miles." In the first chart the distance is 14½ miles, and nearly the same in that which accompanies the narrative; but in the log book it is said to be 2½ miles only, which corresponds with having anchored as soon as they got within the reef, and has been adopted. In some cases it was not easy to make a choice between these different authorities; but I have commonly followed the narrative and log book when they were found to specify with precision, and they generally produced such corrections to the chart as brought the longitudes of places nearer to my positions. Captain Cook's track in Plates XI. XII. and XIII. is laid down afresh from the log book; and many soundings, with some other useful particulars not to be found in the original chart, are introduced, for the benefit of any navigator who may follow the same route.

The reconstruction of the charts in the Atlas was done upon various scales, but that no error might escape unseen, the least was of ten inches to a degree of longitude; they were then reduced by Mr. Thomas Arrowsmith to four inches, this being thought sufficiently large for a general sailing scale; and each reduced sheet was scrupulously compared by me with the original before it went into the engravers hands, and the proof impressions with the drawing until no errors were found. To those who may read this voyage with a view to geographical information, a frequent reference to the Atlas is earnestly recommended; for many particulars are there marked which it would have been tedious to describe, and should any thing appear obscure in the narrative the charts will generally afford an elucidation.

From the general tenour of the explanations here given, it will perhaps be inferred that the perfection of the Atlas has been the principal object of concern; in fact, having no pretension to authorship, the writing of the narrative, though by much the most troublesome part of my labour, was not that upon which any hope of reputation was founded; a polished style was therefore not attempted, but some pains have been taken to render it clearly intelligible. The first quire of my manuscript was submitted to the judgment of a few literary friends, and I hope to have profited by the corrections they had the kindness to make; but finding these to bear more upon redundancies than inaccuracy of expression, I determined to confide in the indulgence of the public, endeavour to improve as the work advanced, and give my friends no further trouble. Matter, rather than manner, was the object of my anxiety; and if the reader shall be satisfied with the selection and arrangement, and not think the information destitute of such interest as might be expected from the subject, the utmost of my hopes will be accomplished.

N.B. *Throughout this narrative the variation has been allowed upon the bearings, and also in the direction of winds, tides, etc.; the whole are therefore to be considered with reference to the true poles of the earth, unless it be otherwise particularly expressed; and perhaps in some few cases of the ship's head when variations are taken, where the expression by compass, or magnetic, may have been omitted.*

Introduction

The voyages which had been made, during the seventeenth and eighteenth centuries, by Dutch and by English navigators, had successively brought to light various extensive coasts in the southern hemisphere, which were thought to be united; and to comprise a land, which must be nearly equal in magnitude to the whole of Europe. To this land, though known to be separated from all other great portions of the globe, geographers were disposed to give the appellation of Continent: but doubts still existed, of the continuity of its widely extended shores; and it was urged, that, as our knowledge of some parts was not founded upon well authenticated information, and we were in total ignorance of some others, these coasts might, instead of forming one great land, be no other than parts of different large islands.

The establishment, in 1788, of a British colony on the easternmost, and last discovered, of these new regions, had added that degree of interest to the question of their continuity, which a mother country takes in favour, even, of her outcast children, to know the form, extent, and general nature of the land, where they may be placed. The question had, therefore, ceased to be one in which geography was alone concerned: it claimed the paternal consideration of the father of all his people, and the interests of the national commerce seconded the call for investigation.

Accordingly, the following voyage was undertaken by command of HIS MAJESTY, in the year 1801; in a ship of 334 tons, which received the appropriate name of the INVESTIGATOR; and, besides great objects of clearing up the doubt respecting the unity of these southern regions, and of opening therein fresh sources to commerce, and new ports to seamen, it was intended, that the voyage should contribute to the advancement of natural knowledge in various branches; and that some parts of the neighbouring seas should he visited, wherein geography and navigation had still much to desire.

The vast regions to which this voyage was principally directed, comprehend, in the western part, the early discoveries of the Dutch, under the name of NEW HOLLAND; and in the east, the coasts explored by British navigators, and named NEW SOUTH WALES. It has not, however, been unusual to apply the first appellation to both regions; but to continue this, would be almost as great an injustice to the British nation, whose seamen have had so large a share in the discovery, as it would be to the Dutch, were New South Wales to be so extended. This appears to have been felt by a neighbouring, and even rival, nation; whose writers commonly speak of these countries under the general term of Terres Australes. In fact, the original name, used by the Dutch themselves until some time after Tasman's second voyage, in 1644, was Terra Australis, or Great South Land; and when it was displaced by New Holland, the new term was applied only to the parts lying westward of a meridian line, passing through Arnhem's Land on the north., and near the isles of St. Francis and St. Peter, on the south: all to the eastward, including the shores of the Gulph of Carpentaria, still remained as Terra Australis. This appears from a chart published by THEVENOT, in 1663; which, he says, "was originally taken from that done in inlaid work, upon the pavement of the new Stadt-House at Amsterdam."[2] The same thing is to be inferred from the notes of Burgomaster WITSEN, in 1705; of which there will be occasion to speak in the sequel.

It is necessary, however, to geographical precision, that so soon as New Holland and New South Wales were known to form one land, there should be a general name applicable to the whole; and this essential point having been ascertained in the present voyage, with a degree of certainty sufficient to authorise the measure, I have, with the concurrence of opinions entitled to deference, ventured upon the re-adoption of the original TERRA AUSTRALIS; and of this term I shall hereafter make use, when speaking of New Holland and New South Wales, in a collective sense; and when using it in the most extensive signification, the adjacent isles, including that of Van Diemen, must be understood to be comprehended.

There is no probability, that any other detached body of land, of nearly equal extent, will ever be found in a more southern latitude; the name Terra Australis will, therefore, remain descriptive of the geographical importance of this country, and of its situation on the globe: it has antiquity to recommend it; and, having no reference to either of the two claiming nations, appears to be less objectionable than any other which could have been selected.[2]

In dividing New South Wales from New Holland, I have been guided by the British patent to the first governor of the new colony, at Port Jackson. In this patent, a meridian, nearly corresponding to the ancient line of separation, between New Holland and Terra Australis, has been made the western limit of New South Wales; and is fixed at the longitude of 135° east, from the meridian of Greenwich. From hence, the British territory extends eastward, to the islands of the Pacific, or Great Ocean: its northern limit is at Cape York; and the extremity of the southern Van Diemen's Land, is its opposite boundary.

The various discoveries which had been made upon the coasts of Terra Australis, antecedently to the present voyage, are of dates as widely distant, as are the degrees of confidence to which they are respectively entitled; the accounts, also, lie scattered through various books in different languages; and many are still in manuscript. It has, therefore, been judged, that a succinct history of these discoveries would be acceptable to the public; and would form an appropriate introduction to a voyage, whose principal object was to complete what they had left unfinished. Such a history will not only, it is hoped, be found interesting, but, from the occasions it will furnish to point out what remained to be done at the beginning of the nineteenth century, will satisfy a question which may be asked: Why it should have been thought necessary to send another expedition to explore the coasts of a country, concerning which it has been said, near thirty years ago--"It is no longer a doubt, that we have now a full knowledge of the whole circumference of this vast body of land, this fifth part of the world."[3] An expression, which the learned writer could have intended to apply only to the general extent of the new continent, and not to the particular formation of every part of the coasts; since the chart, which accompanies the voyage of which he was writing the introduction, represents much of the south coast, as being totally unknown.

In tracing a historical sketch of the previous discoveries, I shall not dwell upon such as depend upon conjecture and probability, but come speedily to those, for which there are authentic documents. In this latter, and solely important, class, the articles extracted from voyages, which are in the hands of the public, will be abridged to their leading heads; and the reader referred, for the details, to the original works; but in such articles as have either not appeared before, or but very imperfectly, in an English dress, as also in those extracted from unpublished manuscripts, a wider range will be taken: in these, so far as the documents go, on the one hand, and the limits of an introduction can allow, on the other, no interesting fact will be omitted.

Conformably to this plan, no attempt will be made to investigate the claims of the Chinese to the earliest knowledge of Terra Australis; which some, from the chart of Marco Polo, have thought they possessed. Nor yet will much be said upon the plea advanced by the Abbé PRÉVOST,[4] and after him by the President DEBROSSES,[5] in favour of Paulmier de Gonneville, a French captain; for whom they claim the honour of having discovered Terra Australis, in 1504. It is evident from the proofs they adduce, that it was not to any part of this country, but to Madagascar, that Gonneville was driven; and from whence he brought his prince Essomeric, to Normandy.

Within these few years, however, two curious manuscript charts have been brought to light; which have favoured an opinion, that Terra Australis had really been visited by Europeans, nearly a century before any authentic accounts speak of its discovery. One of these charts is in French, without date; and from its almost exact similitude, is probably either the original, or a copy of the other, which is in English; and bears, with the date 1542, a dedication to the KING OF ENGLAND.[6] In it, an extensive country is marked to the southward of the Moluccas, under the name of GREAT JAVA; which agrees nearer with the position and extent of Terra Australis, than with any other land; and the direction given to some parts of the coast, approaches too near to the truth, for the whole to have been marked from conjecture alone. But, combining this with the exaggerated extent of Great Java in a southern direction, and the animals and houses painted upon the shores, such as have not been any where seen in Terra Australis, it should appear to have been partly formed from vague information, collected, probably, by the early Portuguese navigators, from the eastern nations; and that conjecture has done the rest. It may, at the same time, be admitted, that a part of the west and north-west coasts, where the coincidence of form is most striking, might have been seen by the Portuguese themselves, before the year 1540, in their voyages to, and from, India.

But quitting those claims to original discovery, in which conjecture bears so large a share, we come to such as are supported by undeniable documents. Before entering upon these, it is proper to premise, that, instead of following precisely the order of time, these discoveries will be classed under the heads of the different coasts upon which they were made: an arrangement which will obviate the confusion that would arise from being carried back from one coast to another, as must, of necessity, be the case, were the chronological order to be strictly followed.

The discoveries made in Terra Australis, prior to the Investigator's voyage, will, therefore, be divided into four Sections, under the following heads: 1. The NORTH COAST; 2. The WESTERN COASTS; 3. The SOUTH COAST; and, 4. The EAST COAST with VAN DIEMEN'S LAND. But the articles in the fourth Section, being numerous and more extensive, will be divided into two parts: PART I. will contain the early discoveries, and such of the later, as were made independently of the British colony in New South Wales; and PART II. those which were made in vessels sent from that colony; and which may be considered as a consequence of its establishment.

Notes

[1] "La carte que l'on a mise icy, tire sa première origine de celle que l'on a fait tailler de piéces rapportées, sur le pavé de la nouvelle Maison-de-Ville d'Amsterdam." Rélations de divers Voyages curieux.--Avis.

[2] *Had I permitted myself any innovation upon the original term, it would have been to convert it into AUSTRALIA; as being more agreeable to the ear, and an assimilation to the names of the other great portions of the earth.*
[3] *Cook's third Voyage, Introduction. p. xv.*
[4] *Histoire générale des Voyages. Tome XVI. (à la Haye) p. 7-14.*
[5] *Histoire des Navigations aux Terres Australes. Tome I. p. 102-120.*
[6] *A more particular account of these charts, now in the British Museum, will be found in Captain Burney's "History of Discoveries in the South Sea." Vol. I. p. 379-383. An opinion is there expressed concerning the early discoveries in these regions, which is entitled to respectful attention.*

Prior Discoveries in Terra Australis

Section I - North Coast

PRELIMINARY REMARKS

The late Hydrographer to the Admiralty, ALEXANDER DALRYMPLE, Esq., in his curious Collection concerning PA-PUA, published, with a translation, a paper which furnishes more regular and authentic accounts of the early Dutch discoveries in the East, than any thing with which the public was before acquainted. This interesting paper was procured by the Right Hon. Sir Joseph Banks; and is a copy of the instructions to commodore ABEL JANSZ TASMAN, for his second voyage of discovery: It is dated January 29, 1644, from the Castle of Batavia, and signed by the governor-general ANTONIO VAN DIEMEN, and by Vander Lyn, Maatsuyker, Schouten, and Sweers, members of the council. The instructions are prefaced with a recital, in chronological order, of the previous discoveries of the Dutch, whether made from accident or design, in NOVA GUINEA, and the Great SOUTH LAND; and from this account, combined with a passage from Saris,* it appears, that--

THE DUYFHEN. 1606.

On the 18th of November 1605, the Dutch yacht, the Duyfhen, was dispatched from Bantam to explore the islands of New Guinea; and that she sailed along, what was thought to be, the west side of that country, to 13¾° of south latitude. "This extensive country was found, for the greatest part, desert; but, in some places, inhabited by wild, cruel, black savages; by whom some of the crew were murdered. For which reason they could not learn anything of the land, or waters, as had been desired of them; and, from want of provisions and other necessaries, they were obliged to leave the discovery unfinished: The furthest point of the land, in their map, was called Cape KEER-WEER," or Turn-again. (ATLAS, Pl. I.)

The course of the Duyfhen, from New Guinea, was southward, along the islands on the west side of Torres' Strait, to that part of Terra Australis, a little to the west and south of Cape York; but all these lands were thought to be connected, and to form the west coast of New Guinea. Thus, without being conscious of it, the commander of the Duyfhen made the first authenticated discovery of any part of the great South Land, about the month of March 1606; for it appears, that he had returned to Banda in, or before, the beginning of June, of that year.

TORRES 1606

LUIS VAES DE TORRES, a Spanish navigator, was the next person who saw Terra Australis; and it is remarkable, that it was near the same place, and in the same year; and that he had as little knowledge of the nature of his discovery, as had the Duyfhen.

Torres was second in command to Pedro Fernandez de Quiros; when he sailed with three vessels, from the port of Callao in Peru, in the year 1605. One of the purposes of their expedition was to search for the TIERRA AUSTRAL; a continent which was supposed to occupy a considerable portion of that part of the southern hemisphere lying westward of America.

After the discovery of several islands, Quiros came to a land which he named AUSTRALIA DEL ESPIRITU SANTO, supposing it to be a part of the great Southern Continent; but this, on his separation from the admiral, Torres found could be no other than an island; and then continued his course westward, in prosecution of the research.

About the month of August 1606, and in latitude 11½° south, he fell in with a coast, which he calls "the beginning of New Guinea;" and which appears to have been the south-eastern part of the land, afterwards named Louisiade, by Mons. DE BOUGAINVILLE, and now known to be a chain of islands. Unable to pass to windward of this land, Torres bore away along its south side; and gives, himself, the following account of his subsequent proceedings.

"We went along 300 leagues of coast, as I have mentioned, and diminished the latitude 2½°, which brought us into 9°. From hence we fell in with a bank of from 3 to 9 fathoms, which extends along the coast above 180 leagues. We went over it along the coast to 7½ S. latitude, and the end of it is in 5°. We could not go further on for the many shoals and great currents, so we were obliged to sail S. W. in that depth to 11°. S. latitude. There is all over it an archipelago of islands without number, by which we passed, and at the end of the 11th degree, the bank became shoaler. Here were very large islands, and there appeared more to the southward: they were inhabited by black people, very corpulent, and naked: their arms were lances, arrows, and clubs of stone ill fashioned. We could not get any of their arms. We caught in all this land 20 persons of different nations, that with them we might be able to give a better account to Your Majesty. They give much notice of other people, although as yet they do not make themselves well understood. "We were upon this bank two months, at the end of which time we found ourselves in 25 fathoms, and in 5° S. latitude, and 10 leagues from the coast. And having gone 480 leagues, here the coast goes to the N. E. I did not reach it, for the bank became very shallow. So we stood to the north."[1]

It cannot be doubted, that the "very large islands" seen by Torres, at the 11th degree of south latitude, were the hills of Cape York; or that his two months of intricate navigation were employed in passing the strait which divides Terra Australis and New Guinea. But the account of this and other discoveries, which Torres himself addressed to the King of Spain, was so kept from the world, that the existence of such a strait was generally unknown, until 1770; when it was again discovered and passed by our great circumnavigator Captain Cook.

Torres, it should appear, took the precaution to lodge a copy of his letter in the archives of Manila; for, after that city was taken by the British forces, in 1762, Mr. Dalrymple found out, and drew from oblivion, this interesting document of early discovery; and, as a tribute due to the enterprising Spanish navigator, he named the passage TORRES' STRAIT; and the appellation now generally prevails.

ZEACHEN. 1618.

ZEACHEN is said to have discovered the land of Arnhem and the northern Van Diemen's Land, in 1618; and he is supposed, from the first name, to have been a native of Arnhem, in Holland; and that the second was given in honour of the governor-general of the Indies.[2] But there are two important objections to the truth of this vague account: first, no mention is made of Zeachen in the recital of discoveries which preface the instructions to Tasman; nor is there any, of the North Coast having been visited by the Dutch, in that year: secondly, it appears from Valentyn's lives of the governors of Batavia, that Van Diemen was not governor-general until January 1, 1636.

CARSTENS. 1623.

The second expedition, mentioned in the Dutch recital, for the discovery of the Great South Land, "was undertaken in a yacht, in the year 1617, with little success;" and the journals and remarks were not to be found. In January 1623, the yachts Pera and Arnhem, under the command of JAN CARSTENS, were despatched from Amboina, by order of His Excellency Jan Pieterz Coen. Carstens, with eight of the Arnhem's crew, was treacherously murdered by the natives of New Guinea; but the vessels prosecuted the voyage, and discovered "the great islands ARNHEM and the SPULT."[3] They were then "untimely separated," and the Arnhem returned to Amboina. The Pera persisted; and "sailed along the south coast of New Guinea, to a flat cove, situate in 10° south latitude; and ran along the West Coast of this land to Cape Keer-Weer; from thence discovered the coast further southward, as far as 17°, to STATEN RIVER. From this place, what more of the land could be discerned, seemed to stretch westward:" the Pera then returned to Amboina. "In this discovery were found, every where, shallow water and barren coasts; islands altogether thinly peopled by divers cruel, poor, and brutal nations; and of very little use to the (Dutch East-India) Company."

POOL. PIETERSEN. 1636.

GERRIT TOMAZ POOL was sent, in April 1636, from Banda, with the yachts Klyn Amsterdam and Wezel, upon the same expedition as Carstens; and, at the same place, on the coast of New Guinea, he met with the same fate. Nevertheless "the voyage was assiduously continued under the charge of the supra-cargo Pieterz Pietersen; and the islands Key and Arouw visited. By reason of very strong eastwardly winds, they could not reach the west coast of New Guinea (Carpentaria); but shaping their course very near south, discovered the coast of Arnhem, or Van Diemen's Land, in 11° south latitude; and sailed along the shore for 120 miles (30 mijlen), without seeing any people, but many signs of smoke."

TASMAN. 1644.

This is all that appears to have been known of the North Coast, when ABEL JANSZ TASMAN sailed upon his second voyage, in 1644; for the instructions to him say, that after quitting "Point Ture, or False Cape, situate in 8° on the south coast of New Guinea, you are to continue eastward, along the coast, to 9° south latitude; crossing prudently the Cove at that place. Looking about the high islands or Speult's River, with the yachts, for a harbour; despatching the tender De Braak, for two or three days into the Cove, in order to discover whether, within the GREAT INLET, there be not to be found an entrance into the South Sea.[4] From this place you are to coast along the west coast of New Guinea. (Carpentaria,) to the furthest discoveries in 17° south latitude; following the coast further, as it may run, west or southward."

"But it is to be feared you will meet, in these parts, with the south-east trade winds; from which it will be difficult to keep the coast on board, if stretching to the south-east; but, notwithstanding this, endeavour by all means to proceed; that we may be sure whether this land is divided from the Great Known SOUTH CONTINENT, or not."

The Dutch had, by this time, acquired some knowledge of a part of the south coast of Terra Australis; of the west coast; and of a part of the north-west; and these are the lands meant by "the Great Known South Continent." Arnhem's, and the northern Van Diemen's Lands, on the North Coast, are not included in the expression; for Tasman was directed "from De Witt's Land (on the North-west Coast,) to run across, very near eastward, to complete the discovery of Arnhem's and Van Diemen's Lands; and to ascertain perfectly, whether these lands are not one and the same island."

It is a great obstacle to tracing correctly the progress of early discovery in Terra Australis, that no account of this voyage of Tasman has ever been published; nor is any such known to exist. But it seems to have been the general opinion, that he sailed round the Gulph of Carpentaria; and then westward, along Arnhem's and the northern Van Diemen's Lands; and the form of these coasts in Thevenot's chart of 1663, and in those of most succeeding geographers, even up to the end of the eighteenth century, is supposed to have resulted from this voyage. The opinion is strengthened by finding the names of Tasman, and of the governor-general and two of the council, who signed his instructions, applied to places at the head of the Gulph; as is also that of Maria, the daughter of the governor, to whom our navigator is said to have been attached. In the notes, also, of Burgomaster Witsen, concerning the inhabitants of NOVA GUINEA and HOLLANDIA NOVA, as extracted by Mr. Dalrymple; Tasman is mentioned amongst those, from whom his information was drawn.

THREE DUTCH VESSELS. 1705.

The President De Brosses[5] gives, from the miscellaneous tracts of Nicolas Struyck, printed at Amsterdam, 1753, the following account of another, and last voyage of the Dutch, for the discovery of the North Coast.

"March 1, 1705, three Dutch vessels were sent from Timor, with order to explore the north coast of New Holland, better than it had before been done. They carefully examined the coasts, sand banks, and reefs. In their route to it, they did not meet with any land, but only some rocks above water, in 11° 52' south latitude:" (probably the south part of the great Sahul Bank; which, according to captain Peter Heywood, who saw it in 180l, lies in 11° 40'.) "They saw the west coast of New Holland 4° to the eastward of the east point of Timor. From thence they continued their route towards the north; and passed a point, off which lies a bank of sand above water, in length more than five German miles of fifteen to a degree. After which, they made sail to the east, along the coast of New Holland; observing every thing with care, until they came to a gulph, the head of which they did not quite reach. I (Struyck) have seen a chart made of these parts."

What is here called the West, must have been the North-west Coast; which the vessels appear to have made somewhat to the south of the western Cape Van Diemen. The point which they passed, was probably this same Cape itself; and in a chart, published by Mr. Dalrymple, Aug. 27, 1783, from a Dutch manuscript (possibly a copy of that which Struyck had seen), a shoal, of thirty geographic miles in length, is marked as running off, from it; but incorrectly, according to Mr. Mc. Cluer. The gulph here mentioned, was probably a deep bay in Arnhem's Land; for had it been the Gulph of Carpentaria, some particular mention of the great change in the direction of the coast, would, doubtless, have been made.

From this imperfect account of the voyage of these three vessels, very little satisfactory information is obtained; and this, with some few exceptions, is the case with all the accounts of the early Dutch discoveries; and has usually been attributed to the monopolizing spirit of their East-India Company, which induced it to keep secret, or to destroy, the journals.

COOK. 1770.

The north coast of Terra Australis does not appear to have been seen by any succeeding navigator, until the year 1770; when our celebrated captain JAMES COOK passed through Endeavour's Strait, between Cape York and the Prince of Wales' Islands; and besides clearing up the doubt which, till then, existed, of the actual separation of Terra Australis from New Guinea, his more accurate observations enabled geographers to assign something like a true place to the former discoveries of the Dutch, in these parts. Captain Cook did not land upon the main; but, at Possession Island, he saw ten natives: "Nine of them were armed with such lances as we had been accustomed to see, and the tenth had a bow, and a bundle of arrows, which we had never seen in the possession of the natives of this country before."[6]

Mc. CLUER. 1791.

At the end of the year 1791, lieutenant JOHN Mc. CLUER of the Bombay marine, in returning from the examination of the west side of New Guinea, made the Land of Arnhem, in longitude 135¼°, east of Greenwich. He then sailed westward, along the shore, to 129° 55'; when the coast was found to take a southern direction. The point of turning is placed in 11° 15' south latitude; and is, doubtless, the Cape Van Diemen of the old charts, and the west extremity of the north coast of Terra Australis.

It does not appear that any other account has been given of this navigation, than the chart published by Mr. Dalrymple, in 1792. According to it, though lieutenant Mc. Cluer constantly had soundings, in from 7 to 40 fathoms; yet he was generally at such a distance from the land, that it was not often seen; and, consequently, he was unable to identify the particular points. No landing seems to have been effected upon the main; but some service was rendered to navigation, by ascertaining the positions of several small islands, shoals, and projecting parts of the coast; and in conferring a certain degree of authenticity upon the discoveries of the early Dutch navigators.

Lieutenant Mc. Cluer is the last person, who can strictly be said to have added to our knowledge of the north coast of Terra Australis, previously to the time in which the voyage of the Investigator was planned; but several navigators had followed captain Cook through Torres' Strait, and by considerably different routes: these it will be proper to notice; as their discoveries are intimately connected with the present subject.

BLIGH. 1789.

After the mutineers of the Bounty had forced their commander, lieutenant (now rear-admiral) WILLIAM BLIGH, to embark in the launch, near the island Tofoa; he steered for Coepang, a Dutch settlement, at the south-west end of Timor. In the way, he made the east coast of New South Wales, in about 12½° of South latitude; and, sailing northward, passed round Cape York and the Prince of Wales' Islands.

It was not to be supposed, that captain Bligh, under the circumstances of extreme distress, of fatigue, and difficulty of every kind, could do much for navigation and geography; yet, he took views and made such observations and notes, as enabled him to construct a chart of his track, and of the lands and reefs seen from the launch. And as captain Bligh passed to the north of the Prince of Wales' Islands, whereas captain Cook had passed to the south, his interesting narrative, with the accompanying chart, made an useful addition to what little was yet known of Torres'Strait.[7]

EDWARDS. 1791.

CAPTAIN (now admiral) EDWARD EDWARDS of HIS Majesty's frigate Pandora, on his return from the island Taheity,[8] made the reefs of Torres' Strait, on Aug. 25; in about the latitude 10° south, and two degrees of longitude to the east of Cape York. Steering from thence westward, he fell in with three islands, rather high, which he named MURRAY'S; lying in latitude 9° 57' south, and longitude 143° 42' east;[9] and some canoes, with two masts, were seen running within side of the reef which lay between the islands and the ship. This reef was of considerable extent; and, during the whole of August 26, captain Edwards ran along it to the southward, without finding any passage through. On the 27th, the search was continued, without success; but on the 28th, a boat was despatched to examine an opening in the reef; and the ship stood off and on, waiting the result. At five in the evening, the boat made a signal for a passage being found; but fearing to venture through, so near sunset, without more particular information, captain Edwards called the boat on board. In the mean time, a current, or tide, set the Pandora upon the reef; and, after beating there till ten o'clock, she went over it into deep water; and sunk in 15 fathoms, at daylight of the 29th.

A dry sand bank was perceived within the opening, at the distance of four miles; and thither the boats repaired with the remaining officers and people; thirty-nine men having lost their lives in this melancholy disaster. This opening was ascertained to lie in latitude 11° 24' and longitude 143° 38'; and is represented as very practicable for ships. Not being able to save any thing from the wreck, captain Edwards, almost destitute of provisions and water, set sail on Aug. 30, with his squadron of four boats; and steered for the north-east part of Terra Australis. No reefs, or other dangers, appear to have been encountered in the way to the coast; but in the course northward, along it, some islands and reefs were seen. From one part of the coast, two canoes with three black men in each, paddled hard after the boats; but though they waved and made many signs, it was not thought prudent to wait for them. At one of the York Isles, the natives, for some trifling presents, filled a keg of water for captain Edwards; but refused to bring down any more; and, soon afterward, they let fly a shower of arrows amongst the unfortunate sufferers. Happily no person was wounded; and the aggressors were put to flight, by a volley of musketry.

At the Prince of Wales' Islands, good water was found; and much alleviated the distress of captain Edwards and his people. They heard here the howling of wolves, (probably of wild dogs,) and "discovered a morai, or rather heap of bones. There were amongst them two human skulls, the bones of some large animals, and some turtle bones. They were heaped together in the form of a grave; and a long paddle, supported at each end by a bifurcated branch of a tree, was laid horizontally along it. Near to this, there were marks of a fire having been recently made; and the ground about was much footed and worn."[10]

A few small oysters, a harsh austere fruit, resembling a plum, and a small berry of a similar taste to the plum, were all that could be found for food.

"There is a large sound formed here, to which," says Mr. Hamilton, "we gave the name of Sandwich's Sound; and commodious anchorage for shipping in the bay, to which we gave the name of Woy's Bay, in which there is from five to seven fathoms all round. Near the centre of the sound is a small, dark-coloured, rocky island."

Sept. 2. In the afternoon, captain Edwards passed out to the northward, with his little squadron, from amongst the Prince of Wales' Islands; and the same evening, by steering westward, cleared all the islands and reefs of Torres' Strait: on the 14th he reached Timor.

The track and discoveries of the Pandora, in Plate XIII. are taken from a chart published in 1798, by Mr. Dalrymple, upon the authority of one constructed by lieutenant Hayward; but it does not contain the track of the boats after the loss of the Pandora. This chart, and the account given by Mr. Hamilton, which, though more than sufficiently explicit upon some points, is very defective in what concerns navigation and geography; are all that appears to have been published of this voyage.

BLIGH and PORTLOCK. 1792.

Neither the great extent of the reefs, to the eastward of Cape York, nor the loss of the Pandora, were known in 1792; when captain WILLIAm BLIGH came a second time to Torres' Strait, with His Majesty's ship Providence, and the brig Assistant commanded by lieutenant (now captain) NATHANIEL PORTLOCK. The objects of his mission were, to transport the bread-fruit plant from Taheity to the West Indies; and, in his way, to explore a new passage through the Strait; in both of which he was successful.

A chart of the discoveries made in Torres' Strait, was lodged, by captain Bligh, in the Admiralty Office; and is incorporated with other authorities, in Plate XIII. of the accompanying Atlas. No account of this voyage having yet been published; it is conceived, that the following brief relation of the passage through the strait, will be acceptable to the nautical reader; and, having had the honour to serve in the expedition, I am enabled to give it from my own journal, with the sanction of captain Bligh.

Aug. 31. Latitude at noon 9° 25' south; longitude from fifteen sets of distances of the sun west, and star east, of the moon, taken on the 24th, 25th, and 26th, preceding, 145° 22' and by time keepers, 145° 23' east. No land seen since passing Louisiade the preceding day; but many birds and fish, and much rock weed. At dusk, having steered W. ¼ S. 27 miles, breakers were seen ahead, at the distance of two miles; and the vessels hauled to the wind: no bottom at 94 fathoms.

Sept. 1. They bore away W. by S.; but hauled up gradually to South, on account of the breakers; and not being able to weather them, tacked to the N. E. At noon, latitude 9° 37' south, longitude by time keepers, 144° 59' east: part of the reef, which was named after captain Portlock, seen in the N. N. W. from the mast head. At four o'clock, the vessels edged away round the north end of Portlock's Reef, which, at dusk, bore South, about two leagues; and the wind was then hauled for the night.

Sept. 2. The breakers bore South, four or five miles; and captain Bligh steered westward: the Assistant leading. At noon, the latitude being 9° 26', longitude, by time keepers, 144° 23', other breakers were seen ahead, and the vessels hauled the wind to the southward; but finding another reef in that direction, with a dry bank upon it, they tacked to the N. E. at half past one; and got ground, for the first time, in 64 fathoms, coral bottom. During the following night, they stood off and on, constantly getting soundings.

No breakers were in sight in the morning of Sept. 3. At seven, a boat was sent ahead; and the vessels bore away after her to the N. W., in order to try the New-Guinea side of the Strait. At noon, their course was interrupted by a reef, which was named Bonds Reef, extending from W. N. W. to North, and distant four or five miles: observed latitude 9° 6', longitude 144° 13'. The north side of the Strait being judged impracticable, the wind was again hauled to the southward; and, at dusk, the vessels anchored in 37 fathoms, fine grey sand; five or six miles north of a reef, upon which was a dry bank, called Anchor Key. An island of considerable height, bearing S. W. by W. ten leagues, was then seen from the mast head: Captain Bligh gave it the name of Darnley's Island; and to the space between Portlock's and Bond's Reefs, by which the vessels had entered the Strait, that of Bligh's Entrance.

Sept. 4. A boat was sent to the S. S. W., and the vessels followed. Other high lands (Murray's Isles) were seen to the southward; and a reef with a sand bank on it, to the west. At noon, the latitude was 9° 32' south, and longitude 143° 59' east: Darnley's Island bore S. 74° to 82° W., four leagues; and the largest of Murray's Isles, S. 13° to 21° E.: the western reef was about three miles distant, but nothing was visible ahead in the S. by W. At four o'clock, the vessels anchored in 21 fathoms, sandy bottom; with Darnley's Island bearing N. 60° W., three leagues. Betwixt a sand-bank, called Canoe Key, which bore S. 60° W., two leagues, and a reef lying in the W. by S., there appeared to be a passage, which the boats were sent to examine.

On the 5th, boats were again sent to sound the passage. Several large sailing canoes were seen; and the cutter making the signal for assistance, the pinnace was sent to her, well manned and armed. On the return of the boats in the afternoon, it appeared, that, of four canoes which used their efforts to get up to the cutter, one succeeded. There were in it fifteen Indians, black, and quite naked; and they made signs which were interpreted to be amicable. These signs the officer imitated; but not thinking it prudent to go so near as to take a green cocoa-nut, which was held up to him, he continued rowing for the ship. A man, who was sitting upon the shed erected in the centre of the canoe, then said something to those below; and immediately they began to string their bows. Two of them had already fitted arrows, when the officer judged it necessary to fire in his own defence. Six muskets were discharged; and the Indians fell flat into the bottom of the canoe, all except the man on the shed: the seventh musket was fired at him, and he fell also. During this time, the canoe dropped astern; and the three others having joined her, they all gave chase to the cutter, trying to cut her off from the ship; in which they would probably have succeeded, had not the pinnace arrived, at that juncture, to her assistance. The Indians then hoisted their sails, and steered for Darnley's Island.

No boats could have been manoeuvred better, in working to windward, than were these long canoes by the naked savages. Had the four been able to reach the cutter, it is difficult to say, whether the superiority of our arms would have been equal to the great difference of numbers; considering the ferocity of these people, and the skill with which they seemed to manage their weapons.

September 6. Two boats were sent ahead; and the vessels followed them, between Canoe Key and the reef lying from it half a mile to the north. After running twelve miles beyond this narrow pass, they anchored in 13 fathoms; the latitude being 9° 37', and longitude 143° 41'. In the afternoon, they proceeded five miles further, to the N. N. W.; and Darnley's Island then bore S. 74° to 55° E. two leagues: except on the north side, this island appeared to be surrounded with reefs and sand banks to a considerable distance. In sailing from Canoe Key, the vessels had left, on the larbord hand, a long chain of reefs and banks; at the north-west end of which, were three low, woody islands: the nearest of these, bearing S. 41° W. two or three miles from the anchorage, was named Nepean Island. The view to the northward, from W. by N. to E. by S., was free from dangers; but in every other direction there were reefs, islands, or dry banks.

This day, several canoes from Darnley's Island came off to both vessels. On approaching, the Indians clapped upon their heads, and exclaimed Whou! Whou! Whoo! repeatedly, with much vehemence; at the same time, they held out arrows and other weapons, and asked for toore-tooree! by which they meant iron.[11] After much difficulty, they were persuaded to come along-side; and two men ventured into the ship. They had bushy hair--were rather stout made--and nearly answered the description given of the natives of New Guinea.[12] The cartilage, between the nostrils, was cut away in both these people; and the lobes of their ears slit, and stretched to a great length, as had before been observed in a native of the Fejee Islands. They had no kind of clothing; but wore necklaces of cowrie shells, fastened to a braid of fibres; and some of their companions had pearl-oyster shells hung round their necks. In speaking to each other, their words seemed to be distinctly pronounced.

Their arms were bows, arrows, and clubs, which they bartered for every kind of iron work with eagerness; but appeared to set little value on any thing else. The bows are made of split bamboo; and so strong, that no man in the ship could bend one of them. The string is a broad slip of cane, fixed to one end of the bow; and fitted with a noose, to go over the other end, when strung. The arrow is a cane of about four feet long, into which a pointed piece of the hard, heavy, casuarina wood, is firmly and neatly fitted; and some of them were barbed. Their clubs are made of the casuarina, and are powerful weapons. The hand part is indented, and has a small knob, by which the firmness of the grasp is much assisted; and the heavy end is usually carved with some device: One had the form of a parrot's head, with a ruff round the neck; and was not ill done.

Their canoes are about fifty feet in length, and appear to have been hollowed out of a single tree; but the pieces which form the gunwales, are planks sewed on with the fibres of the cocoa nut, and secured with pegs. These vessels are low, forward, but rise abaft; and, being narrow, are fitted with an outrigger on each side, to keep them steady. A raft, of greater breadth than the canoe, extends over about half the length; and upon this is fixed a shed or hut, thatched with palm leaves. These people, in short, appeared to be dextrous sailors and formidable warriors; and to be as much at ease in the water, as in their canoes.

Sept. 7. The boats having found deep water round the north end of the three low islands, the vessels followed them; but anchored again, soon after noon, in latitude 9° 31', and longitude 143° 31'; being sheltered by the two western islands, named Stephens' and Campbell's, and the reefs which surround them. There were then no less than eight islands in sight, at different distances; though none further to the westward than W. S. W. All these, except Darnley's Island, first seen, were small, low, and sandy; but generally well covered with wood in the central parts.

On the 8th, the vessels steered westward, with the usual precautions. No land, or other obstruction, had been seen in that quarter; but, at ten o'clock, they were forced to haul the wind to the southward, their course being impeded by reefs; upon one of which, was Pearce's sandy Key. At noon, they had anchored in 15 fathoms, under the lee of Dalrymple's Island, the westernmost before seen; but two other islands were then visible in the S. by W.; and reefs extended from N.4°, to S. 55° W., at the distance of three or four miles. The latitude here was 9° 37'; and longitude, from six sets of distances of the sun and moon, 143° 31'; but, by the time-keepers, 143° 15' east.

Several canoes were lying upon the shore of Dalrymple's Island; but no natives could he distinguished from the ships. When the boats returned, however, from sounding, in the afternoon, they came out upon the beach; waving green branches and clapping upon their heads, in token of friendship. Boats were afterwards sent to them, and were amicably received; the natives running into the water to meet them, and some getting into one of the boats. They eagerly asked for toore-tooree; and gave in exchange some ornaments of shells, and a kind of plum somewhat resembling a jambo. When the boats pushed off from the shore, the natives followed into the water, and appeared anxious to detain them; but offered no violence. A moderately-sized dog, of a brown, chestnut colour, was observed amongst the party.

Sept. 9. The vessels steered after the boats, between the cluster of islands to the southward, and an extensive reef to the west; with soundings from 15 to 10 fathoms. At noon, the latitude was 9° 48', longitude by timekeepers 143° 6'; and two other islands came in sight to the westward. Before two o'clock, an extensive reef, partly dry, to which the name of Dungeness was given, made it necessary to heave to, until the boats had time to sound; after which, captain Bligh bore away along the north side of the reef, and anchored a mile from it, in 17 fathoms, hard bottom. In this situation, Dungeness Island, which is low and very woody, bore N. 64° to 87° W. three miles; and a small sandy isle, named Warriors Island, N. 6° to 1° W. four miles: this last appeared to stand upon the great western reef, and was surrounded with dry sands. Besides these, there were other low isles, called the Six Sisters, in sight, to the south-east; and a long, flat island, bearing S. 33° to 46° W. over the dry Dungeness Reef; in the west, also, there were islands visible, at a greater distance, and much higher, than the others. The Strait, instead of becoming clearer, seemed to be more and more embarrassed with dangers, as the vessels proceeded westward. The latitude of this anchorage was 9° 50½' south, and the longitude 142° 55' east.

Sept. 10. The boats sounded the channel to the north-west, between Dungeness and Warriors Islands; and finding sufficient water, the vessels got under way, at noon, to follow them. There were many natives collected upon the shore of Dungeness Island, and several canoes from Warriors Island were about the brig. Presently, captain Portlock made the signal for assistance; and there was a discharge of musketry and some guns, from his vessel and from the boats. Canoes were also coming towards the Providence; and when a musket was fired at the headmost, the natives set up a great shout, and paddled forward in a body; nor was musketry sufficient to make them desist. The second great gun, loaded with round and grape, was directed at the foremost of eight canoes, full of men; and the round shot, after raking the whole length, struck the high stem. The Indians leaped out, and swam towards their companions; plunging constantly, to avoid the musket balls which showered thickly about them. The squadron then made off, as fast as the people could paddle without showing themselves; but afterwards rallied at a greater distance, until a shot, which passed over their heads, made them disperse, and give up all idea of any further attack.

In passing the deserted canoe, one native was observed still sitting in it. The other canoes afterwards returned to him; and, with glasses, signals were perceived to be made by the Indians, to their friends on Dungeness Island, expressive, as was thought, of grief and consternation.

No arrows fell on board the Providence; but three men were wounded in the Assistant, and one of them afterwards died: The depth to which the arrows penetrated into the decks and sides of the brig, was represented to be truly astonishing.

The vessels passed between Dungeness and Warriors Islands, with from 19 to 13 fathoms; and anchored, at four o'clock, under the lee of Dungeness Island and Reef. The passage to the westward then appeared clearer; three high islands, bearing from S. 60° W. three leagues, to N. 76° W. five leagues, forming the sole visible obstructions.

Sept. 11. Captain Bligh proceeded on his course to the W. N. W., and passed two islands, to which the descriptive names of Turtle-backed Island and the Cap were given; and, soon after noon, the vessels anchored in 7 fathoms, soft bottom. There was a dry sand bearing N. 63° W. two or three miles; between which, and the third high island, called The Brothers, bearing S. 55° to 69° W. three miles, it was judged necessary for the boats to sound, before proceeding further. This anchorage was in latitude 9° 43', and longitude 142° 40'; and, besides the islands already mentioned, there was in sight a mountainous island, to which the name of Banks was given, bearing S. 43° W., twelve or thirteen leagues; also Burke's Island, S. 13° W. eight or ten leagues; and Mount Cornwallis, on another island, N. 29° W. six or eight leagues; and from behind this last, to N. 7° W., there extended a level land, which was supposed to be a part of the coast of NEW GUINEA.

Sept. 12. The vessels followed the boats to the westward; but were interrupted by reefs, and obliged to anchor again before noon. The water had shoaled gradually, and there was then only 6 fathoms: the bottom a coarse, coral sand. Two other islands were then in sight: a low one, named Turn-again Island, bore N. 53° W. about four leagues; and Jervis' Island, which is rather high, S. 48° W. nine leagues. A reef, with a dry sand upon it, extended from S. 7° E. to 62° W. four or five miles; another was distant three miles to the west; and a third bore N. 18° W. five miles. The latitude of the anchorage was 9° 41' south, and longitude 142° 24' east.

A fresh gale from south-east did not allow the Providence and Assistant to proceed onward for three days. In the mean time, the passage between the reefs to the N. W., was sounded by the boats; and found to contain about 5 fathoms, regularly, upon hard ground. They were also sent to examine the passage round the southern reefs; and this being deeper, with a superior bottom, it was chosen as the preferable route.

Sept. 16. The vessels passed to windward of the southern reef; and steered south-westward, as it trended, in from 7 to 5 fathoms water, until half past noon; when they anchored in latitude 10° 3', and longitude, by time-keeper, 142° 14'. The sole direction in which the eye could range without being obstructed, was that whence the vessels had come; every where else the view was arrested by rocks, banks, and islands. The most extensive of these, was Banks' Island, extending from S. 14° E. to 62° W., two or three leagues; with a high hill upon it named Mount Augustus, which bore S. 4° E:[13] Another large island, named Mulgrave's, extended from behind the last to a cluster of rocks, whose extreme bore W. 5° N. The nearest land, bearing S. 24° E., one mile and a half, was the north-westernmost of three small isles; and to this, the second lieutenant was sent, for the purpose of taking possession of all the islands seen in the Strait, for HIS BRITANNIC MAJESTY GEORGE III., with the ceremonies used on such occasions: the name bestowed upon the whole was CLARENCE'S ARCHIPELAGO.

North Possession Island was found to be little else than a mass of rocks surrounded by a reef; but it was covered with a variety of trees and shrubs. Amongst them was a cluster of cocoa-nut trees, bearing a small, but delicious, fruit; and the tree bearing a plum, such as had been seen at Dalrymple's Island. Besides these, the botanists found the peeha and nono of Taheity; and two new plants, of the size of the common mulberry. One, of the class polyadelphia, bears a scarlet, bell-shaped flower, large as the China rose; the other was a species of erythrina, bearing clusters of butterfly-shaped flowers, of a light yellow, tinged with purple: both were entirely destitute of leaves, and their woods remarkably brittle.

There did not appear to be any fixed inhabitants upon Possession Island; but from a fire which had been recently extinguished, and the shells and bones of turtle scattered around, it was supposed to have been visited not many days before. The bushes were full of small, green ants; which proved exceedingly troublesome to those who had sufficient hardihood to penetrate their retreats. Another, and larger species of ant, was black; and made its nest by bending and fixing together the leaves, in a round form, so as to be impenetrable to the wet. These, and a small kind of lizard, were all the animals found upon the island.

Sept. 17. The boats led to the westward, steering for a passage between Mulgrave's and Jervis' Islands; but seeing it full of rocks and shoals, the vessels anchored a little within the entrance, in 10 fathoms, coarse ground; until the boats should sound ahead. The latitude here was 10° 2', and longitude 142° 03'. The flood tide, from the E. N. E., was found to set through between the islands, at the rate of four miles an hour; and the breeze being fresh, and bottom bad, the situation was considered to be very unsafe.

Whilst the boats were sounding, several Indians in three canoes, were perceived making towards them; but on a swivel shot being fired over their heads, they returned to Mulgrave's Island, on the south side of the passage. On the signal being made for good anchorage further on, the Assistant led to the W. by S.; but on reaching the boats, the bottom was found much inferior to what had been imagined; the approach of night, however, obliged captain Bligh to anchor, soon afterward, in 8 fathoms.

In this situation, the vessels were so closely surrounded with rocks and reefs, as scarcely to have swinging room; the bottom was rocky; the wind blowing a fresh gale; and a tide running between four and five knots an hour. This anxious night was, however, passed without accident; and next morning, Sept. 18, the route was continued through the passage, between reefs and rocks, which, in some places, were not three quarters of a mile asunder: the smallest depth was 4 fathoms.

On clearing this dangerous pass, which captain Bligh named, Bligh's Farewell, he anchored in 6 fathoms, sandy bottom; the wind blowing strong at S. E. with thick weather. The latitude here was 10° 5', and longitude 141° 56'. From north nearly, round by the east, to S. 8° E., there was a mass of islands, rocks, and reefs, at various distances; but in the western half of the compass, no danger was visible; and as far as three miles to the W. N. W., the boats found good soundings in 6 and 7 fathoms.

Sept. 19. The wind moderated; and the vessels steered W. by S. until noon, with a depth gradually increasing from 6 to 8 fathoms. The latitude was then 10° 8½' south longitude, by time keeper, 141° 31' east, and no land was in sight; nor did any thing more obstruct captain Bligh and his associate, in their route to the island Timor.

Thus was accomplished, in nineteen days, the passage from the Pacific, or Great Ocean, to the Indian Sea; without other misfortune than what arose from the attack of the natives, and some damage done to the cables and anchors. Perhaps no space of 3½° in length, presents more dangers than Torres' Strait; but, with caution and perseverance, the captains Bligh and Portlock proved them to be surmountable; and within a reasonable time: how far it may be advisable to follow their track through the Strait, will appear more fully hereafter.

In the Voyage to the South Seas in H. M. ship Bounty, page 220, captain Bligh says, "I cannot with certainty reconcile the situation of some parts of the coast (near Cape York) that I have seen, to his (captain Cook's) survey;" and from the situation of the high islands on the west side of the Strait, which had been seen from the Bounty's launch, and were now subjected to the correction of the Providence's time-keepers; he was confirmed in the opinion, that some material differences existed in the positions of the lands near Cape York.

BAMPTON and ALT. 1793.

The last passage known to have been made through Torres' Strait, previously to the sailing of the Investigator, was by Messieurs WILLIAM BAMPTON and MATTHEW B. ALT, commanders of the ships Hormuzeer and Chesterfield. Their discoveries were made public, in two charts, by Mr. Dalrymple, in 1798 and 1799; and from them, and captain Bampton's manuscript journal, the south coast of New Guinea, and most of the reefs and islands near it, are laid down in Plate XIII.; after having been adjusted to the observations of captain Bligh, and to those subsequently made by me in the Investigator and Cumberland. The journal was obtained through the kindness of Mr. Arrowsmith; and, though no courses and distances be given, and the differences from the charts be sometimes considerable, it is yet so interesting in many points, that I have judged the following abridgement would be acceptable, as well to the general, as to the nautical, reader.

The Hormuzeer and Chesterfield sailed together from Norfolk Island; with the intention of passing through Torres' Strait, by a route which the commanders did not know to have been before attempted. June 20, 1793, in the evening, being in latitude 10° 24' south, and longitude 144° 14' east (by captain Bampton's chart), a dry reef was seen extending from W. ½ S. to N. W. by W., distant four or five miles, and breakers from the mast head at N. by E. ½ E. An island (Murray's), which appeared to be large and woody, was also seen, and bore N. W. ½ W. The ships got ground in 60 fathoms, and hauled the wind to the eastward, till midnight; when, having no bottom at 70 fathoms, they lay to, till morning.

June 21. The Hormuzeer's long boat was sent ahead; and, at ten o'clock, the ships bore away northward. At noon, the latitude was 9° 30'. The course was altered, at three, to the north-west; and at dusk, they hove to, for the night: soundings from 70 to 56 fathoms. The same course being resumed on the 22nd, the latitude, at noon, was 8° 48'; and the depth 30 fathoms, on a bottom of sand, mud, and shells. From noon to five p.m., when they anchored, the ships appear to have steered W. by S. The land had been seen at one o'clock; and at two, the water had shoaled suddenly, from 30 to 10 fathoms, and afterwards diminished to 5, which continued to the place of anchorage. The land was part of the coast of NEW GUINEA; and the extremes were set at W. by N. ½ N. and N. W. ½ N., six or seven leagues, (in the chart, miles.) The flood tide here, set two miles per hour, towards the land; and the rise, by the lead line, was nine feet.

June 23. The ships got under way with the weather, or ebb, tide, a little before noon: latitude 8° 52'. At four o'clock, the wind blew strong at south-east, with thick weather, and they anchored in 9 fathoms, blue mud; having made a course of E. N. E. nearly parallel to the coast. They remained here till the next afternoon; when the Hormuzeer having parted her cable, both ships stood to the north-eastward, along the land, until midnight; at which time they wore to the south-west, in 30 fathoms. At daylight of the 25th, the depth had decreased to 16 fathoms; and they stretched north-eastward again, with little variation in the soundings. The latitude, at noon, was 8° 10'; and the ships continued their course upon a wind, keeping as much to the east as possible; and the soundings having increased to 30 fathoms, at dusk, they hove to; but stretched off, at midnight, on coming into 10 fathoms. In the morning of June 26, they were standing to the eastward; but the wind becoming light at nine o'clock, Mr. Bampton anchored in 9 fathoms, on a muddy bottom, in latitude 7° 55' south. The coast of New Guinea was then seen to extend from N. N. W. ½ W. to E. N. E.; and the south end of a reef, running off from the western extreme, bore W. by S. ½ S., two leagues.

The land here forms a large, unsheltered bay; and an opening nearly at the head, bearing N. ½ E., appeared like the entrance of a considerable river; but an officer, who was sent in a boat to sound, saw breakers stretching across. The soundings were regular, from 9 to 6 fathoms, within a mile or two of the shore; when there was only twelve feet; and the surf which rolled in, made it impossible to land. The country round the bay is described as level and open, and of an agreeable aspect. On the return of the boat the ships weighed, and stretched southward until June 27, at noon. The latitude was then 9° 1'; and a sand bank was seen from the mast head, bearing S. W. ½ W. They then wore to the north-eastward; and continued upon that course until the 28th, at dusk; when the land of New Guinea being in sight as far as E. by N., the same, apparently, which had been set from the anchorage on the 26th, they stretched off till two in the morning and then in again, towards the land.

Captain Bampton had followed the coast of New Guinea thus far, in the hope of finding a passage to the northward, between it and Louisiade; but the trending of the land so far to the east, and the difficulty of weathering it, from the current being adverse, obliged him to give up that hope. A consultation was then held; and a determination made to attempt the passage through the middle of Torres' Strait.

At the time the ships hauled their wind to the southward, the latitude was 8° 3'; the longitude, from three distances of the sun and moon, 145° 23'; and the depth of water 40 fathoms, on a muddy bottom. They had no soundings from that time to July 1, at one a.m.; when there was 35 fathoms. At daylight, land, which was the Darnley's Island of captain Bligh, bore S. W. by S. seven or eight leagues; a dry sand was seen in the W. N. W., (probably W. S. W.); and a reef, which appears to have been that of Anchor Key, was six or seven miles distant in the S. E. At four in the afternoon, when Darnley's Island bore W. by N. ½ N. five leagues, and Murray's Island S. E. ½ E. (probably S. S. E. ½ E.) the ships anchored in 22 fathoms, marly bottom; and the boats were sent towards the first Island to sound, and see if it were inhabited. The latitude observed at this anchorage, was 9° 40' south, and longitude from three distances of the sun and moon 142° 58' 30" east.

July 2. The boats returned. Between the ships and the island, they had passed over five different reefs, separated by narrow channels of 11 to 14 fathoms deep. The natives of the island came down in considerable numbers; and exchanged some bows and arrows, for knives and other articles. They were stout men; and somewhat above the common size of Europeans. Except in colour, which was not of so deep a cast, they bore much resemblance to the natives of Port Jackson; and had scars raised upon their bodies in the same manner. The men were entirely naked; but the women, who kept at a distance and appeared small in size, wore an apron of leaves, reaching down, to the knee. Many cocoa-nut trees were seen in the lower parts of the island.

When the boats returned, they were followed by four canoes. One of them went along-side of the Chesterfield; and an Indian ventured on board, on a sailor going into the canoe, as a hostage for him. Most of these people had their ears perforated. The hair was generally cut short; but some few had it flowing loose. It is naturally black; but from being rubbed with something, it had a reddish, or burnt appearance. These Indians, so far as they could he understood, represented their island to abound in refreshments; and it was, therefore, determined to send another boat to make further examination.

July 3. Mr. Shaw, chief mate of the Chesterfield, Mr. Carter, and captain Hill of the New-South-Wales corps, who was a passenger, went away armed, with five seamen in a whale boat; and were expected to return on the following day; but the 4th, 5th, and 6th, passed, without any tidings of them; although many signal guns had been fired.

On the 7th, two boats, manned and armed, under the command of Mr. Dell, chief mate of the Hormuzeer, were sent in search of the whale boat. On reaching the island, Mr. Dell heard conch shells sounding in different parts; and saw eighty or ninety armed natives upon the shore. To the inquiries, by signs, after the missing boat, they answered that she was gone to the westward; but none of them would venture near; nor did they pay attention to a white handkerchief which was held up, and had before been considered a signal of peace.

As the boats proceeded in their search, round the island, the natives followed along the shore, with increasing numbers. One man, who was rubbed with something blue, and appeared to be a chief, had a small axe in his hand; which was known, from the red helve, to have belonged to Mr. Shaw. On reaching the bay in the north-west side of the island, Mr. Dell remarked that the natives disappeared; all except about thirty, who were very anxious in persuading him to land. They brought down women; and made signs, that the boat and people whom he sought, were a little way up in the island. He, however, rowed onward; when the beach was immediately crowded with people, who had been lying in ambush, expecting him to land.

After having gone entirely round the island, and seen nothing of the object of his research, Mr. Dell returned to the first cove; where a great concourse of natives, armed with bows, arrows, clubs, and lances, were assembled at the outskirt of the wood. By offering knives and other things, a few were induced to approach the boat; and the coxswain seized one of them by the hair and neck, with the intention of his being taken off to the ships, to give an account of the missing boat and people. A shower of arrows instantly came out of the wood; and a firing was commenced, which killed one Indian, and wounded some others. In the mean time, the coxswain found it impossible to keep the man, from his hair and body being greased; and the boat's crew was too much occupied to assist him.

July 8. The two commanders having heard the report of Mr. Dell, proceeded with the ships, round the northern reefs and sand banks, to the bay on the north-west side of Darnley's Island, which was named Treacherous Bay. On the 9th, in the afternoon, they anchored with springs on the cables, in 13 fathoms, sand, mud, and shells; the extremes of the island bearing E. ½ N. to S. W. by S., and the nearest part distant a quarter of a mile. A boat was sent on shore; and returned, at sunset, with a few cocoa nuts; but without having seen any of the inhabitants.

July 10. An armed party of forty-four men landed from the ships, under the command of Mr. Dell. After hoisting the union jack, and taking possession of this, and the neighbouring islands and coast of New Guinea, in the name of His Majesty, they examined the huts, and found the great coats of captain Hill, Mr. Carter, and Mr. Shaw; with several other things which had belonged to them, and to the boats' crew; so that no doubt was entertained of their having been murdered. In the evening, the party arrived from making the tour of the island; having burnt and destroyed one-hundred-and-thirty-five huts; sixteen canoes, measuring from fifty to seventy feet in length; and various plantations of sugar-cane. The natives appeared to have retired to the hills in the centre of the island; as not one of them could be discovered.

Darnley's Island was judged to be about fifteen miles in circumference. It is variegated with hills and plains; and the richness of the vegetation bespoke it to be very fertile; it appeared, however, to be scantily supplied with fresh water, there being only one small place where it was found near the shore. The plantations of the natives, which were extensive and numerous in the plains, contained yams, sweet potatoes, plantains, and sugar canes, inclosed within neat fences of bamboo; and cocoa-nut trees were very abundant particularly near the habitations. The hills, which mostly occupy the middle of the island, were covered with trees and bushes of a luxuriant growth; and upon different parts of the shores, the mangrove was produced in great plenty.

The habitations of the Indians were generally placed at the heads of the small coves; and formed into villages of ten or twelve huts each, inclosed within a bamboo fence of, at least, twelve feet high. The hut much resembles a haycock, with a pole driven through it; and may contain a family of six or eight people. The covering is of long grass, and cocoa leaves. The entrance is small; and so low, that the inhabitants must creep in and out; but the inside was was clean and neat; and the pole that supports the roof, was painted red, apparently with ochre.

In each of the huts, and usually on the right hand side going in, were suspended two or three human skulls; and several strings of hands, five or six on a string. These were hung round a wooden image, rudely carved into the representation of a man, or of some bird; and painted and decorated in a curious manner: the feathers of the Emu or Cassuary generally formed one of the ornaments. In one hut, containing much the greater number of skulls, a kind of gum was found burning before one of these images. This hut was adjoining to another, of a different form, and much more capacious than any of the others. The length was thirty feet, by fifteen in breadth; and the floor was raised six feet from the ground. The hut was very neatly built of bamboo, supported by long stakes, and thatched with cocoa leaves and dried grass. It was judged to be the residence of the chief of the island; and was the sole hut in which there were no skulls or hands; but the adjoining one had more than a double proportion. The corpse of a man, who had been shot, was found disposed of in the following manner. Six stakes were driven into the ground; about three feet from each other, and six feet high. A platform of twigs was worked upon them, at the height of five feet; and upon this, the body was laid, without covering; but the putrid state of the corpse, did not allow of a close inspection.

Upon the reefs which surround the island, square places, of about fifty feet every way, were formed, by piling up stones of two or three feet high. The tide flows over these; and, on the ebb, the Indians go down and take out the fish. On all parts of the reefs, there were bamboos set up, with pendants of dried leaves; but whether they were intended as beacons for the canoes, or to point out the boundaries of each fishery, could not be ascertained.

The description of the canoes is nearly the same as that given in the voyage of Bligh and Portlock; but Mr. Bampton says, "some of them were ingeniously carved and painted, and had curious figures at each end." The weapons of these people are bows, arrows, clubs of about four feet long, and spears and lances of various kinds, made of black., hard, wood. Some of the lances were jagged, from the sharp point to a foot upward; and most of them were neatly carved. The sole quadrupeds seen, were rats, mice, and lizards; which, when the huts were set on fire, ran from them in great numbers. Land birds were numerous in all parts of the island; and upon the reefs were many curlews, large yellow-spotted plover, king's fishers, sand pipers, red bills, and gulls.

Captain Bampton lays down Darnley's Island, which the natives call WAMVAX, in latitude 9° 39' 30" south, and longitude 142° 59' 15" east; but in his chart, the centre is placed in 9° 34' south., and 143° 1' east. He much regretted that he could not land again, to examine the interior parts of this fine island; but his long boat having drifted out of sight, without water, provisions, or compass, it was judged necessary for the ships to weigh, and look after her.

July 11. The Hormuzeer stood to the northward, with soundings of 15 to 19 fathoms. After three hours run, with a fresh breeze, a reef and sand bank were seen ahead, and the ship was veered to the south-west. Another reef and bank were descried, soon afterward, in the west; and, at the same time, a signal for seeing the long boat was made by the Chesterfield. In the afternoon, the boat was picked up, and both ships anchored under Stephens' Island.

An armed party was immediately sent on shore, to obtain intelligence if possible, of the lost whale boat. The natives were assembled in hostile array, upon the hills, sounding their conchs; but, after lancing a few arrows, they fled. Several were wounded by the shots fired in return; but they succeeded in escaping to a canoe at the back of the island, and getting off; all except one boy, who was taken unhurt.[14] In the huts, which were burnt, several things were found; and amongst them, a sheet of copper which belonged to the Chesterfield.

July 12. Stephens' Island was traversed all over; and a spike nail, with the king's broad arrow upon it, was brought on board, and excited many conjectures as to whence it came.[15] The plantations, huts, images, skulls, and hands, were found similar to those of Darnley's Island. Amongst the trees, there was one resembling an almond, the nuts of which were good. The cocoa nut grows abundantly; especially in the south-eastern part, where the trees formed a continued grove. The sole quadruped seen, except rats, was a pretty animal of the opossum tribe. It was found in a cage; and had probably been brought, either from New Guinea, or New South Wales.[16]

July 13. A boat was sent to Campbell's Island; but it did not contain either plantations, cocoa-nut trees, or fixed inhabitants. This, as also Stephens' and Nepean's Islands, are mostly low and sandy; and surrounded with extensive reefs, upon which, it was thought, the Indians pass from one island to the other, at low water.

In the afternoon, the ships proceeded to the westward; but meeting with many reefs, they hauled more to the north, and discovered Bristow Island, lying close to the coast of New Guinea. Their attempts to find a passage here, were fruitless; and after incurring much danger, and the Chesterfield getting aground, they returned to their former anchorage, in the evening of July 21.

Two canoes immediately came off from Stephens' Island; and one of the natives remained on board the Hormuzeer till eight o'clock. He seemed to be without fear; and when inquiry was made after the lost boat and people, he pointed to a whale boat, and made signs that such an one had been at Darnley's Island; and that six of the people were killed.[17] Many presents were made to this man; and he was clothed, and sent on shore in one of the boats.

July 22. The ships' crews beginning to feel the want of fresh water, people were sent on shore to dig a well; and the natives, though they still appeared shy and suspicious, gave them some assistance. On the 24th, the boats had discovered a passage to the south-westward; and as the well produced little water, and no provision could be obtained, it was determined to proceed onward, through the Strait, without further delay.

They weighed the same afternoon; and anchored, at dusk, in 14 fathoms; Campbell's Island bearing N. E. by E. to E. by N. ¾ N.; and many other small isles being in sight to the south-west and southward. Next day, the 25th, they steered S. by W. ½ W., from seven in the morning to six in the evening; when they anchored in 17 fathoms, having islands in sight nearly all round: the nearest at the distance of five or six miles. These islands were small; but inhabitants were seen on the greater number; and two canoes went off to the Chesterfield.

July 26. The ships proceeded westward, very slowly; the wind being at south-west. In the morning of the 27th, they were at anchor in 11 fathoms; Dungeness Island bearing W. by N. to N. W. by W. ½ W., about six miles; and Warriors Island N. N. W. ½ W. eight miles. Mr. Dell had passed the preceding night upon one of the Six Sisters, which was called Dove Island, bearing from the ship, S. S. E. six miles. A fire on the beach, with two fish broiling upon it, bespoke the presence of inhabitants; but on searching the island over, none could be discovered: it was thought that they had fled to a larger island, it being connected with this by a reef, which dries at low water. Mr. Dell had a seine with him, and caught a dozen fine fish; but the object of remaining all night, that of taking turtle, did not succeed; although large shells of them were found upon the shore.

Dove Island is about one mile and a half in circumference; and covered with trees and shrubs, the fragrance of whose flowers perfumed the air. Amongst other birds, two beautiful doves were shot. The plumage of the body was green; the head, bill, and legs, red; the tail, and under sides of the wings, yellow. No huts, plantations, or other signs of fixed inhabitants were seen; nor was there any fresh water.

On the return of the boat, the vessels weighed; and the wind being at W. S. W., they worked through. between Dungeness and Warriors Islands, with the flood tide. They then anchored in 11 fathoms; the first Island bearing S. S. E. to S ½ W. three leagues, and the second E. by S. ½ S.

July 28. Having a fresh breeze at E. S. E., the long boat was sent ahead, and the ships followed, to the westward. They passed Turtle-backed Island, the Cap, and the Brothers, on one side, and Nichols' Key on the other: the soundings gradually shoaling from 12 to 7 fathoms. Upon the Cap, Mr. Bampton "saw a volcano burning with great violence," which induced him to give it the name of Fire Island; not knowing that it had before been named. At noon, the Brothers, with the Cap and Turtle-backed Island behind, bore S. E. by S. to S. ½ E. four miles; and Mount Cornwallis N. 16° W.

The water continued to shoal; and at three p.m., the ships anchored in 5 fathoms, sand, shells, and stones; the Brothers bearing E. by S. ¼ S. five leagues, and Mount Cornwallis N. by E. ¼ E. There were two large islands in sight in the S. S. W. ¼ W. to S. W. ¼ S., at the distance of eight or ten leagues; and many nearer reefs in the same direction.

July 29. The long boat was sent to sound in the north-west; and when the ebb tide slacked, the ships followed: wind at E. S. E. The soundings increased from 5 to 7 fathoms; and afterwards varied between these depths, until noon; when the latitude observed was 9° 42' south.[18] The Brothers then bore S. 64° E.; Mount Cornwallis N. 38° E; and a long, low island (Turn-again., of Bligh,) N. 35° to 58° W. At three p.m. the reefs were so numerous, that the ships were obliged to anchor, until the boats could sound for a passage: the depth here was 4½ fathoms, on a bottom of rotten stones and coral.

July 31. They weighed, and hauled the wind eastward, to pass round Turn-again Island; bearing away occasionally to avoid small reefs: the soundings 5½ to 4 fathoms. After passing round, they anchored in 5 fathoms; until the boats should sound between the reefs which appeared on every side: Turn-again Island then bore S. 56° to 83° W. about two leagues, Mount Cornwallis N. 56° E., the Brothers S. 50° E.; the latitude observed was 9° 32', and longitude from four sights of the sun and moon, 140° 58' east. Next afternoon, in proceeding to the north-westward, the Chesterfield struck upon a bank in eight feet water; but the coral giving way to the ship, she went over without injury. In the evening, they both anchored in 4½ fathoms, gravel and shells; Mount Cornwallis bearing E. ¼ S., and a long tract of land from N. W. by N. to N. E., at the distance of five or six leagues. Turn-again Island bore S. S. E. ¾ E. to S. ½ W., four miles; and thither the ships ran on Aug. 3, and anchored in 3¾ fathoms, fine sand, within a quarter of a mile of the shore; the extremes bearing S. 58° E. to 60° W. The purpose for which they came to this island, was to procure wood, water, and refreshments; during the time necessary for the boats to explore a passage through the innumerable reefs and banks, which occupy this part of the Strait.

Messieurs Bampton and Alt remained here seventeen days; being afraid to move with the strong south-east winds which blew during the greater part of the time. Turn-again Island is flat, low, and swampy; and about three miles in length, by half that space in breadth. (Mr. Bampton's chart makes it the double of these dimensions; and, generally, the islands in it exceed the description of the journal in about the same proportion: the journal seems to be the preferable authority.) The reefs which surround Turn-again Island, extend a great distance to the east and west; particularly in the latter direction, where there are many dry sand banks. The island is mostly over-run with mangroves; and at the top of the flood, the wood cutters were obliged to work in the water; and were, at all times, exceedingly annoyed with musketoes. The island is said, in the journal, to be in 9° 34; south and 140° 55' east; which is 3' to the south and 1° 24' west of its situation in the chart of captain Bligh.

No other refreshment than small quantities of fish, crabs, and shell-fish, being procurable here, the ships crews were further reduced in their short allowance. With respect to fresh water, their situation was still worse: None could be obtained upon Turn-again Island; and had not captain Bampton ingeniously contrived a still, their state would have been truly deplorable. He caused a cover, with a hole in the centre, to be fitted by the carpenter upon a large cooking pot; and over the hole he funded an inverted tea kettle, with the spout cut off. To the stump of the spout, was fitted a part of the tube of a speaking trumpet; and this was lengthened by a gun barrel, which passed through a cask of salt water, serving as a cooler. From this machine, good fresh water, to the amount of twenty-five to forty gallons per day, was procured; and obtained a preference to that contained in the few casks remaining in the Hormuzeer.

By Aug. 20., when the weather had become more moderate, the boats had sounded amongst the reefs in all directions; but there appeared to be no practicable passage out of this labyrinth, except to the north-west. In that direction the ships proceeded three hours, in from 6 to 3 fathoms. Next afternoon, they steered westward, with the flood tide; and again anchored in 3 fathoms, sand and gravel. The coast of New Guinea then extended from N. by E. ¼ E. to N. W. ¾ N.; and the north-west end of a long island, to which the name of Talbot was given, bore N. by E. ½ E. nine or ten miles.

Aug. 22, At day-light they followed the long boat to the westward., in soundings from 2½ to 4 fathoms. At seven o'clock, the Hormuzeer grounded in 2 fathoms; upon a bank whence Talbot's Island bore N. N. E. to E. N. E., eight or ten miles, and where the observed latitude was 9° 27' south. She remained upon this bank until the morning of the 24th; when Mr. Bampton got into a channel of 13 fathoms, which had been found by the boats, and the ship did not appear to have received other damage, than the loss of the false keel. The still continued to be kept at work, day and night.

Aug. 27. Messieurs Bampton and Alt proceeded onward in a track which had been sounded by the boats. At sunset, they came to, in 4 fathoms; the extremes of New Guinea then bearing N. W. by W. to N. E. by E., three or four leagues. Some further progress was made next morning; and at noon, when at anchor in 3¾ fathoms, and in latitude 9° 26½', an island was discovered bearing S. W. ¾ S. five or six leagues; which received, eventually, the name of DELIVER-ANCE ISLAND.

Aug. 29. The Hormuzeer grounded at low water; from which it appeared that the tide had fallen twelve feet, though then at the neaps. When the ship floated, they made sail to the westward; and deepened the water to 9 and 12 fathoms. At noon, it had again shoaled to 6; Deliverance Island bearing S. S. W. ½ W. nine or ten miles, and New Guinea N. W. to N. by E. ½ E. four or five leagues: latitude observed 9° 25' south. After proceeding a little further westward, they anchored in 5 fathoms.

Aug. 30. The soundings varied as before, between 4 and 10 fathoms: the bottom, rotten coral intermixed with sand. At noon, when the latitude was 9° 21', Deliverance Island was just in sight from the deck, in the S. E. by S.; and the extremes of New Guinea bore N. E. by E. to N. W. ½ W., ten or twelve miles.[19] In the afternoon, the depth again decreased to 4 fathoms, and obliged them to anchor until morning. On the 31st, the ships appear to have steered south-westward, leaving on the starbord hand a very extensive bank, on which the long boat had 2 fathoms water: the soundings from the Hormuzeer were from 3 to 7 fathoms. At noon, the latitude was 9° 27', and no land in sight. The soundings then increased gradually; and at sunset, no bottom could be found at 40 fathoms. A swell coming from S. S. W. announced an open sea in that direction; and that the dangers of Torres' Strait were, at length, surmounted. This passage of the Hormuzeer and Chesterfield in seventy-two days, with that made in nineteen, by the captains Bligh and Portlock, displayed the extraordinary dangers of the Strait; and appear to have deterred all other commanders from following them, up to the time of the Investigator. Their accounts confirm the truth of Torres having passed through it, by showing the correctness of the sketch contained in his letter to the King of Spain.

Conclusive Remarks

The sole remaining information, relative to the North Coast of Terra Australis, was contained in a note, transcribed by Mr. Dalrymple, from a work of burgomaster WITSEN upon the Migration of Mankind. The place of which the burgo-master speaks, is evidently on the coast of Carpentaria, near the head of the Gulph; but it is called New Guinea; and he wrote in 1705. The note is as follows; but upon whose authority it was given, does not appear:
"In 16° 10' south, longitude 159° 17'" (east of Teneriffe, or between 142° and 143° east of Greenwich,) "the people swam on board of a Dutch ship; and when they received a present of a piece of linen, they laid it upon their head in token of gratitude: Every where thereabout, all the people are malicious. They use arrows, and bows of such a length, that one end rests on the ground when shooting. They have also hazeygaeys and kalawaeys, and attacked the Dutch; but did not know the execution of the guns." On summing up the whole of the knowledge which had been acquired of the North Coast, it will appear, that natural history, geography, and navigation had still much to learn of this part of the world; and more particularly, that they required the accomplishment of the following objects:
1st. A general survey of TORRES' STRAIT. The navigation from the Pacific, or Great Ocean to all parts of India, and to the Cape of Good Hope, would be greatly facilitated, if a passage through the Strait, moderately free from danger, could be discovered; since five or six weeks of the usual route, by the north of New Guinea or the more eastern islands, would thereby be saved. Notwithstanding the great obstacles which navigators had encountered in some parts of the Strait, there was still room to hope, that an examination of the whole, made with care and perseverance, would bring such a passage to light. A survey of it was, therefore, an object much to be desired; not only for the merchants and seamen trading to these parts, but also from the benefits which would certainly accrue therefrom to general navigation and geography.
2nd. An examination of the shores of the GULPH OF CARPENTARIA. The real form of this gulph remained in as great doubt with geographers, as were the manner how, and time when it acquired its name.[20] The east side of the Gulph had been explored to the latitude of 17°, and many rivers were there marked and named; but how far the representation given of it by the Dutch was faithful--what were the productions, and what its inhabitants--were, in a great measure, uncertain. Or rather it was certain, that those early navigators did not possess the means of fixing the positions and forms of lands, with any thing like the accuracy of modern science; and that they could have known very little of the productions, or inhabitants. Of the rest of the Gulph no one could say, with any confidence, upon what authority its form had been given in the charts; so that conjecture, being at liberty to appropriate the Gulph of Carpentaria to itself, had made it the entrance to a vast arm of the sea, dividing Terra Australis into two, or more, islands.
3rd. A more exact investigation of the bays, shoals, islands, and coasts of ARNHEM'S, and the northern VAN DIEMEN'S, LANDS. The information upon these was attended with uncertainty; first, because the state of navigation was very low at the time of their discovery; and second, from want of the details and authorities upon which they had been laid down. The old charts contained large islands lying off the coast, under the names of T' Hoog Landt or Wessel's Eylandt, and Crocodils Eylanden; but of which little more was known than that, if they existed, they must lie to the eastward of 135° from Greenwich. Of the R. Spult, and other large streams represented to intersect the coast, the existence even was doubtful. That the coast was dangerous, and shores sandy, seemed to be confirmed by Mr McCluer's chart; and that they were peopled by "divers cruel, poor, and brutal nations," was certainly not improbable, but it rested upon very suspicious authority. The Instructions to Tasman. said, in 1644, "Nova Guinea has been found to be inhabited by cruel, wild, savages; and as it is uncertain what sort of people the inhabitants of the South Lands are, it may be presumed that they are also wild and barbarous savages, rather than a civilized people." This uncertainty, with respect to the natives of Arnhem's and the northern Van Diemen's Lands, remained, in a great degree, at the end of the eighteenth century.
Thus, whatever could bear the name of exact, whether in natural history, geography, or navigation, was yet to be learned of a country possessing five hundred leagues of sea-coast; and placed in a climate and neighbourhood, where the richest productions of both the vegetable and mineral kingdoms were known to exist. A voyage which should

have had no other view, than the survey of Torres' Strait and the thorough investigation of the North Coast of Terra Australis, could not have been accused of wanting an object worthy of national consideration.

Notes

[1] *See the letter of Torres, dated Manila, July 12, 1607, in Vol. II. Appendix, No I. to Burney's "History of Discoveries in the South Sea;" from which interesting work this sketch of Torres' voyage is extracted.*

[2] *Hist. des Navigations aux Terres Aust. Tome 1. p. 432.*

[3] *In the old charts, a river Spult is marked, in the western part of Arnhem's Land; and it seems probable, that the land in its vicinity is here meant by THE SPULT.*

[4] *The Great Inlet or Cove, where the passage was to be sought, is the north-west part of Torres' Strait. It is evident, that a suspicion was entertained, in 1644, of such a strait; but that the Dutch were ignorant of its having been passed. The "high islands" are those which lie in latitude 10°, on the west side of the strait. Speult's River appears to be the opening betwixt the Prince of Wales' Islands and Cape York; through which captain Cook afterwards passed, and named it Endeavour's Strait. This Speult's River cannot, I conceive, be the same with what was before mentioned under the name of THE SPULT.*

[5] *Hist. des Nav. aux Terres Aust. Tome I. page 439.*

[6] *Hawkesworth's Voyages, Vol. III. page 211.*

[7] *Bligh's "Voyage to the South Seas in H. M. Ship Bounty," page 218-221.*

[8] *Commonly written Otaheite; but the 0 is either an article or a preposition, and forms no part of the name: Bougainville writes it Taïti.*

[9] *In Plates I. and XIII. Murray's Islands are laid down according to their situations afterwards ascertained in the Investigator; and the reefs, seen by the Pandora, are placed in their relative positions to those islands.*

[10] *See "A Voyage round the World in H. M. frigate Pandora," by George Hamilton, Surgeon; page 123, et seq.*

[11] *The name for iron at Taheity, is eure-euree, or ooree, orj, according to Bougainville, aouri.*

[12] *See a Voyage to New Guinea, by Captain Thomas Forrest.*

[13] *This mountain, in latitude 10° 12' south, longitude 142° 13' east, was seen by captain Bligh from the Bounty's launch, and marked in his chart, (Voyage, etc. p. 220.) It appears to be the same island indistinctly laid down by captain Cook, in latitude 10° 10', longitude 141° 14'; and is, also, one of those, to which the term Hoge Landt is applied in Thevenot's chart of 1663.*

[14] *It does not appear in the journal, when, or where this boy was set on shore; nor is any further mention made of him.*

[15] *It had probably been obtained from the crews of either the Providence or Assistant; which had anchored under Stephens' Island, nine months before.*

[16] *Mr. Bampton's description of this animal is briefly as follows. Size and shape, of the opossum. Colour, yellowish white with brown spots. End of the tail, deep red: prehensile. Eyes, reddish brown: red when irritated. No visible ears. Used its paws in feeding: five nails to each. Habit, dull and slothful: not savage. Food, maize, boiled rice, meat, leaves, or any thing offered. Odour, very strong at times, and disagreeable.*

[17] *Captain Hill and four of the seamen were murdered by the natives. Messieurs Shaw and Carter were severely wounded; but with Ascott, the remaining seaman, they got into the boat, cut the grapnel rope, and escaped. They were without provisions or compass; and it being impossible to reach the ships, which lay five leagues to windward, they bore away to the west, through the Strait; in the hope of reaching Timor. On the tenth day, they made land; which proved to be Timor-laoet. They there obtained some relief to their great distress; and went on to an island called by the natives, Sarrett; where Mr. Carter died: Messieurs Shaw and Ascott sailed in a prow, for Banda, in the April following. See Collins' Account of the English Colony in New South Wales. Vol. I. page 464, 465.*

[18] *This latitude is from 4' to 6' more south than captain Bligh's positions; and the same difference occurs in all the observations, where a comparison can be made.*

[19] *Mr. Bampton's chart and journal are more at variance here than in the preceding parts of the Strait, and I have found it very difficult to adjust them.*

[20] *I am aware that the president de Brossed says, "This same year also (1628) CARPENTARIA was thus named by P. Carpenter, who discovered it when general in the service of the Dutch Company. He returned from India to Europe, in the month of June 1628, with five ships richly laden." (Hist. des Nav. aux Terres Aust. Tome I. 433). But the president here seems to give either his own, or the Abbé' Prevost's conjectures, for matters of fact. We have seen, that the coast called Carpentaria was discovered long before 1628; and it is, besides, little probable, that Carpenter should have been making discoveries with five ships richly laden and homeward bound. This name of Carpentaria does not once appear in Tasman's Instructions, dated in 1644; but is found in Thevenot's chart of 1663.*

Section II - Western Coasts

PRELIMINARY OBSERVATIONS.

Under the term WESTERN COASTS, is comprehended the space from the western extremity of the northern Van Diemen's Land to the North-west Cape of New Holland; and from thence, southward to Cape Leeuwin. The first is usually termed the North-west, and the second the West Coast: Taken together, they present an extent of shore of between seven and eight hundred leagues in length; lying in the fine climates comprised between the 11th and 35th degrees of south latitude.

HARTOG. 1616.

The recital of discoveries in Tasman's instructions speaks of the first knowledge gained of these coasts in the following terms: "In the years 1616, 1618, 1619, and 1622, the west coast of this Great unknown SOUTH LAND, from 35° to 22° south latitude, was discovered by outward-bound ships; and among them by the ship Endragt." The recital gives no further particulars; but from thence, and from a manuscript chart by Eessel Gerrits, 1627,[1] there seems to be sufficient authority for attributing the first authenticated discovery of any part of the Western Coasts to DIRK HARTOG, commander of the ship Endragt, outward-bound from Holland to India. He appears to have first seen the West Coast in latitude about 26½° south; and to have sailed northward along it, to about 23°; giving the name LANDT DE ENDRAGT, to the country so discovered. An important part of his discovery was Dirk Hartog's Road (at the entrance of a sound afterwards called Shark's Bay, by Dampier), lying a little south Of 25°. Upon one of the islands which form the road there was found, first in 1697, and afterwards in 1801, a plate of tin, bearing the following inscription. "Anno 1616, the 25th of October arrived here the ship Endragt of Amsterdam; the first merchant Gillis Miebais of Luik, Dirk Hartog of Amsterdam, captain. They sailed from hence for Bantam, the 27th Do." On the lower part, as far as could be distinguished in 1697, was cut with a knife, "The under merchant Jan Stins; chief mate Pieter Dookus of Bill. Ao. 1616."
The Mauritius, another outward-bound ship, appears to have made some further discovery upon the West Coast, in July 1618, particularly Of WILLEM'S RIVER, near the North-west Cape; but no further particulars are known.

EDEL. 1619.

In Campbell's edition of Harris' Voyages (p. 325), it is said, "The next year the LAND OF EDEL was found, and received its name from the discoverer.". The president De Brosses says nearly the same thing (Tome I. P. 432); whence, combining this with the Dutch recital and the chart of Eessel Gerritz, it should appear that J. DE EDEL commanded an outward-bound ship; and, in July 1619, accidentally fell in with that part of the West Coast to which his name is applied. The extent of Edel's discovery appears, from Thevenot's chart, to have been from about the latitude 29°, northward to 26½°, where the Land of Endragt commences; but in a chart of this coast, by Van Keulen, the name is extended southward to 32° 20', past the island Rottenest, which, according to Thevenot, should rather have been the discovery of the ship Leeuwin.
The great reef lying off the coast of Edel, called Houtman's Abrolhos, was discovered at the same time; probably by Edel, or by some ship in the same squadron.

THE LEEUWIN. 1622.

I do not find it any where said who commanded the Leeuwin, or Lioness; but it should appear, that this was also one of the outward-bound ships which fell in with the West Coast. In Thevenot's chart, Leeuwin's Land comprehends about ninety leagues of the south-west extremity of New Holland; and, from the latitude of 35°, extends northward to about 31°; but in later publications, it has been much restricted in its northern limit, apparently, upon the authority of Van Keulen.

THE VIANEN. 1628.

The next discovery upon the Western Coasts was that of the ship Vianen, one of the seven which returned to Europe under the command of the governor-general Carpenter. The Dutch recital speaks of this discovery in the following terms. The coast was seen "again accidentally in the year 1628, on the north side, in the latitude 21° south, by the ship Vianen, homeward bound from India; when they coasted two-hundred miles, without gaining any knowledge of this Great Country; only observing a foul and barren shore, green fields, and very wild, black, barbarous inhabitants." This was the part called DE WITT'S LAND; but whether the name were applied by the captain of the Vianen does not appear in the recital. De Brosses says, "William de Witt gave his own name to the country which he saw in 1628, to the north of Remessen's River; and which Viane, a Dutch captain, had, to his misfortune, discovered in the month of January in the same year; when he was driven upon this coast of De Witt, in 21° of latitude, and lost all his riches." The confusion that reigns in the president's account does not render it improbable, that the country might have received its name in the way he describes, and in the year 1628; for, in 1644, De Witt's Land is used as a known term for this part of the North-west Coast.

PELSERT. 1629.

Thus far, the parts of the Western Coasts have been distinguished by little else than the dates and limits of their discovery; for, in fact, this is all that has reached us from these early navigators. The following account is of a different character: it is extracted from the twenty-first piece in Thevenot's collection; and, in the table of contents, is said to be translated from the Dutch.

The Batavia, commanded by FRANCISCO PELSERT, struck, in the night of June 4, 1629, upon a reef, "called by our Flemings the Abrolhos or Rocks of Frederick Houtman," lying off the west coast of New Holland. At daylight, an island was seen about three leagues distant, and two islets, or rather rocks, somewhat nearer, to which the passengers and part of the crew were sent. There being no fresh water to be found upon these islands, Pelsert had a deck laid over one of the boats; and, on June 8, put to sea, in order to make search upon the opposite main land: his latitude, at noon, was 28° 13' south.

A short time after quitting the Abrolhos, captain Pelsert got sight of the coast, which, by estimation, bore N. by W. eight leagues from the place of shipwreck.[2] He had 25 to 30 fathoms, and stood off till midnight, when he again steered for the land; and in the morning of the 9th, it was four leagues off. He ran that day from five to seven leagues, sometimes to the north, sometimes to the west; the direction of the coast being N. by W.: it appeared to be rocky--without trees--and about the same height as the coast of Dover. A small, sandy bay was seen, into which Pelsert desired to enter; but finding too much surf, and the weather becoming bad, he was obliged to haul further off.

June 10. He kept in the same parallel, upon a wind; the weather being bad, and his boat very leaky. Next day, the wind was at W. S. W., and more moderate. He then steered north; for the sea was too high to approach the shore in safety. On the 12th, Pelsert observed the latitude to be 27°, and steered along the coast with a fair wind at S. E.; but the shore was too steep to admit of landing; neither could he find any bay or island to break off the sea. At a distance, the land seemed fertile and covered with plants. The latitude, on the 13th, was 25° 40', which showed a current setting to the northward. Here Pelsert found himself a-breast of an opening, where the coast trends to the north-east (apparently into Shark's Bay). The course this day was nearly north; the shore consisted of reddish rock, of an equal height; and there being no island in front, the waves, which broke high upon it, prevented landing.

June 14. The wind was at east; and at noon, the latitude was observed to be 24°. The tides (or rather the current) took the boat further to the north than was desired; for Pelsert then carried but little sail, in the hope to find a landing place without going further. Perceiving some smokes at a distance, he rowed towards them; but the shore proved to be steep, with many rocks, and the sea broke high against it. At length, six of his people leaped overboard, and with much labour and risk got through the surf, whilst the boat remained at anchor, in 25 fathoms. The sailors employed the rest of the day in seeking for water; and on looking about on every side, they saw four natives creeping towards them on their hands and feet. One of "our people" having appeared on an eminence, near them, the natives rose up and took to flight; so that those who were in the boat could see them distinctly. These men were wild, black, and altogether naked; not covering even those parts which almost all savages conceal.

The six sailors, losing all hope of finding water, swam back to the boat, wounded and bruised by the blows they had received from the waves and rocks. The anchor was then weighed, and Pelsert continued his course, under easy sail, along the coast; but keeping without side of the shoals. The 15th in the morning, they discovered a cape, off which lay a chain of rocks, running out four miles into the sea; and behind this was another reef, close to the shore. The water being tolerably still between them, Pelsert thought to pass through; but the reefs joined round further on, and obliged him to return. At noon, an opening was seen, where the water was smooth, and they went into it, but with considerable danger; for the depth was no more than two feet, and the bottom stony. On landing, the people dug holes in the sand; but the water which oozed in was salt. At length, fresh rain water was found in the cavities of the rocks, and afforded them great relief; for they had, hitherto, been confined to a pint of water each. They staid on shore that night, and collected full forty gallons. Ashes and the remains of cray fish were found; which showed that the natives had been there no long time before.

June 16. They sought to collect more water, but were unsuccessful; and none could be expected in the sandy, level country behind the coast. This plain was destitute of both grass and trees, and covered with ant hills so large, that they might have been taken for the houses of Indians. The quantity of flies was such, that the people had great difficulty in keeping them off. Eight savages, with with each a stick (probably a spear) in his hand, were seen at a distance. They came within musket shot; but on the Dutch sailors going towards them they took to flight.

Captain Pelsert, being at length convinced of the impossibility of procuring more water, determined to quit this coast. At noon, he got withoutside of the reef by a second opening more to the north; for, having observed the latitude to be 22° 17', his intention was to seek for the River of Jacob Remessens (near the North-west Cape); but the wind veering to north-east, he could no longer follow the direction of the coast. Considering, then, that he was more than four hundred miles from the place of shipwreck, and that scarcely water enough had been found for themselves, Pelsert resolved to make the best of his way to Batavia, to solicit assistance from the governor-general.

In the mean time, some one of the people left upon the islands of the Abrolhos thought of tasting the water in two holes, which, from its rising and falling with the tide, was believed to be salt; but, to their great surprise and joy, it was found good to drink, and never failed them afterwards.

On Pelsert's return to the Abrolhos in the yacht Sardam, he was under the necessity of executing some atrocious conspirators, and two were set on shore upon the opposite main land.[3] Tasman was directed by his instructions, in 1644, to "inquire at the continent thereabout, after two Dutchmen; who, having forfeited their lives, were put on shore by the commodore Francisco Pelsert, if still alive. In such case, you may make your inquiries of them about the situation of those countries; and if they entreat you to that purpose, give them passage hither."

TASMAN. 1644.

It is not from any direct information, that ABEL JANSZ TASMAN is placed as the next discoverer upon the western coasts of Terra Australis; for, as has been already observed, no account of his second voyage has ever been made public, or is any such known to exist. It is, however, supposed, with great probability of truth, that, after the examination of the North Coast, he pursued his course westward along the shore to the North-west Cape, conformably to his instructions; but that he did not go further southward along the Land of Endragt than to the tropic of Capricorn, where he quitted his examination, and returned to Batavia.

The chart published by Thevenot, in 1663, gives a form to the Western Coasts, and joins them to the northern Van Diemen's Land; but it is evident from Tasman's instructions, that the part between De Witt's Land and Cape Van Diemen was unknown to the Dutch government at Batavia in 1644. And since there is no account of its having been seen during the intermediate nineteen years, it may be concluded that the North-west Coast was first explored by him; and Dampier says (Vol. III. p. 96), that he had Tasman's chart of it; though none bearing his name can now be found.[4]

The notes of burgomaster Witsen show, that the North-west Coast was visited by Tasman; and as they give the earliest information of the inhabitants, and are curious in themselves, they are here transcribed from Mr. Dalrymple's Papua.

"In lat. 13° 8' S. lon. 146° 18'" (probably about 129½° east of Greenwich), "the coast is barren. The people are bad and wicked, shooting at the Dutch with arrows, without provocation, when they were coming on shore: It is here very populous."

"In 14° 58' S. lon. 138° 59' (about 125° east), the people are savage, and go naked: none can understand them."

"In HOLLANDIA NOVA,[5] in 17° 12' S. (lon. 121° or 122° east) Tasman found a naked, black people, with curly hair; malicious and cruel, using for arms, bows and arrows, hazeygaeys and kalawaeys. They once came to the number of fifty, double armed, dividing themselves into two parties, intending to have surprised the Dutch, who had landed twenty-five men; but the firing of guns frightened them so that they fled. Their prows are made of the bark of trees: their coast is dangerous: there are few vegetables: the people use no houses."

"In 19° 35' S. long. 134° (about 120°, apparently), the inhabitants are very numerous, and threw stones at the boats sent by the Dutch to the shore. They made fires and smoke all along the coast, which, it was conjectured, they did to give notice to their neighbours of strangers being upon the coast. They appear to live very poorly; go naked; eat yams and other roots."

DAMPIER. 1688.

The buccaneers with whom our celebrated navigator, WILLIAM DAMPIER, made a voyage round the world, came upon the north-west coast of Terra Australis, for the purposes of careening their vessel, and procuring refreshments. They made the land in the latitude of 16° 50', due south from a shoal whose longitude is now known to be 122¼° east. From thence, they ran along the shore, N. E. by E. twelve leagues, to a bay or opening, where a convenient place was found for their purpose. Dampier's description of the country and inhabitants of the place, where he remained from Jan. 5. to March 12., is contained in the account of his voyages, Vol. I. page 462 to 470; and renders it unnecessary to do more than to mark its coincidence or disagreement with what is said, in the above note from Tasman, of the inhabitants and country near the same part of the coast.

Dampier agrees in the natives being "a naked, black people, with curly hair," like that of the negroes; but he says they have "a piece of the rind of a tree tied like a girdle about their waists, and a handful of long grass, or three or four green boughs full of leaves, thrust under their girdle, to cover their nakedness." Also, "that the two fore teeth of the upper jaw are wanting in all of them, men and women, old and young: neither have they any beards;" which circumstances are not mentioned in the note from Tasman. Dampier did not see either bows or arrows amongst them; but says, "the men, at our first coming ashore, threatened us with their lances and swords; but they were frightened by firing one gun, which we did purposely to scar them." Of "their prows made of the bark of trees," he saw nothing. On the contrary, he "espied a drove of these men swimming from one island to another; for they have no boats, canoes, or bark logs." The English navigator is silent as to any dangers upon the twelve leagues of coast seen by him; but fully agrees in the scarcity of the vegetable productions, and in the circumstance of the natives using no houses.

VLAMING. 1696.

The relation of Willem DE VLAMING'S voyage to New Holland was published at Amsterdam in 1701; but not having been fortunate enough to procure it, I have had recourse to Valentyn, who, in his Description of Banda, has given what appears to be an abridgment of the relation. What follows is conformable to the sense of the translation which Dr. L. Tiarks had the goodness to make for me; and the reasons for entering more into the particulars of this voyage than usual are, the apparent correctness of the observations, and that no account of them seems to have been published in the English language.[6]

On Dec. 28, the ships got soundings in 48 fathoms, coral bottom; in latitude 31° 53', and longitude 133° 44' (east, apparently, from the Peak of Teneriffe, 16° 45' to the west of Greenwich); where the variation was observed to be 10° 28' west: they afterwards had 25 fathoms, on better ground. On the 29th, they anchored under the island Rottenest, which lies in lat. 31° 50', long. 134° 25';[7] and next day, a piece of wood, which had some time been fixed to the deck of a ship, was found upon the shore; but the nails were then rusted away. Fire wood was abundant here.

VLAMING. 1697.

Jan. 5. Vlaming went on shore (to the main coast), with eighty-eight armed men, and walked inland to the eastward. There were a few large, and some small trees, from which dropped a kind of gum-lac; but they found nothing which could be used as food: the birds were small cockatoos and green parrots, and both were very shy. At the end of three hours walk they came to a piece of water, which was salt, and upon the beach were footsteps of full-grown persons and of children. No men were seen, but they observed many smokes; and found three deserted huts, so low and ill-constructed as to be inferior to those of the Hottentots.

On the 6th, they divided themselves into three parties: one took to the north, another to the south, and the third went four miles east, more into the interior; but, except one or two decayed huts, they met with nothing. Being returned to the salt lake without finding fresh water, they dug a pit near the side of it, and obtained wherewith to relieve their thirst. The lake had fallen a foot, which showed it to have a communication with the sea; and they afterwards found the outlet, a little to the southward. No noxious animal of any kind was seen; and after remaining on shore all night, they returned on board on the 7th. The ships were then anchored nearer to the land, with the entrance of the lake or river bearing S. E. by E. The commodore afterwards went up this river, to the distance of fourteen or sixteen leagues, and caught some smelts, as also several black swans, of which two were taken alive to Batavia.[8]

Having clearly ascertained the latitude (of the ships at anchor, most probably,) to be 31° 43' south, and discovered a reef four geographic miles in length, and two miles from the shore, they sailed from thence on Jan. 13. The wind was from the southward; and whilst the ships steered N. by W., parallel to the coast, the boats ran along within them, to examine it more closely. On the 15th, the people from the boats reported that they had seen neither men nor animals, and very few trees; but had met with a reef near the shore, in 30° 17'; and many shoals, both under and above water. Fires upon the land were seen from all the ships in the night of Jan. 16; and next day, a boat was sent with armed people; but they returned with nothing, except some sea-mews which had been caught upon the islands and shoals lying along the coast. On the 18th, the ships were in latitude 30° 30', and found the variation to be 9° 21' west; and the 20th, some small islands were seen, and shrubs observed on the main land. On the 23rd, they were near a steep head, in 28° 8', and sent a boat to the shore; but the high surf prevented landing. People were perceived walking on the downs, but at too great a distance to distinguish more than that they were of the common stature, black, and naked.[9] The boat got on shore soon afterward, when some brackish water was found; and having landed again on the

27th, the people saw some huts, as also the footsteps of men, and some birds; but there was no other vegetation than small shrubs. Some very indifferent water was the sole useful thing met with, and it was too far off for any to be taken on board.

Jan. 30. The boats were again sent on shore, and discovered two inlets, of which the southernmost, in latitude 26° 16', was three miles in width. On Feb. 2, they found two other openings, very deep, one of which ran up northward, and the other to the east, far inland. They went eleven leagues up the first of these, and found that it had another communication with the sea, to the N. N. W.[10] On the 3rd, a boat brought the above account; and also, that the chief mate of the Geelvink had found a plate of tin, with an inscription commemorating the arrival and departure of Dirk Hartog. (See the inscription under the article Hartog, preceding.) This Road of Dirk Hartog's Bay, where the plate had been set up, is in 25° 24'; and the west variation was 8° 34'.

No mention is made by Valentyn of the ships entering the road, nor of their departure from it; but it should seem that they anchored on Feb. 4. On the 5th, commodore Vlaming and the commander of the Nyptang went with three boats to the shore, which proved to be an island. They found also a river, and went up it four or five leagues, amongst rocks and shoals; when they saw much water inland, as if the country were drowned, but no men, nor any thing for food; and, wherever they dug, the ground was salt. They afterwards came to another river, which they ascended about one league, and found it to terminate in a round basin, and to be entirely salt water. No men were seen, nor any animals, except divers which were very shy; and the country was destitute of grass and trees. Returning downward on the 10th, they saw footsteps of men and children, of the common size, and observed the point of entrance into the river to be of a very red sand.

The ships appear to have left Dirk Hartog's Road on Feb. 12. In the evening, the west variation was observed to be 7° 21'; am on the 13th, they saw a cliffy point from whence three shoals, connected by a reef, stretch out to the N. N. E. The shore here, in latitude 24° 42', lies S. by E. and N. by W. On the 16th, they passed round the point, and steered southward along the inner side of this land; and having doubled its south end, found that it was it was an island: their latitude was then 24° 54'.

Feb. 17. The variation was observed to be 5° west, in latitude 23° 59'. Eight miles south of this situation they saw a bay with a rugged point; but to the northward the land was low: the variation was 7° 3', in the evening. They discovered some reefs on the 19th, lying three geographic miles off shore; and also a point or cape (the North-west Cape) from which a reef extended two miles to the N. N. W. On the north side of this cape is a bay, where the Geelvink anchored; and a little further on (eastward), the other two vessels found an opening like a river, whose entrance was twelve miles wide. They went into it, but could no where find anchorage. The bay is called Willem's River; and the two vessels afterwards there joined the Geelvink: it is in 21° 28'. The same day it was determined to sail for Batavia, every thing having been done that the commodore's orders required; and, on the 21st, they departed accordingly.

Thus the West Coast, from the island Rottenest to the North-west Cape, was examined with care by Vlaming; and it is most probable, that the chart in Van Keulen, which Mr. Dalrymple republished, and was the best known at the end of the eighteenth century, resulted from this same voyage.

DAMPIER. 1699.

CAPTAIN WILLIAM DAMPIER visited, a second time, the western coasts of Terra Australis; being then sent out purposely for discovery, in his Majesty's ship the Roebuck.

In the night of Aug. 1, 1699, he struck soundings upon the northern part of the Abrolhos shoal, in latitude about 27° 40' south. Next morning he saw the main coast, and ran northward along it; discovering, in 26. 10', an opening two leagues wide, but full of rocks and foul ground. Aug. 6, he anchored (in Dirk Hartog's Road) at the entrance of a sound, which he named SHARK's BAY, in latitude 25° 5' south. He remained there eight days, examining the sound, cutting wood upon the islands, fishing, etc.; and gives a description of what was seen in his usually circumstantial manner.[11]

An animal found upon one of the islands is described as "a sort of raccoon, different from that of the West Indies, chiefly as to the legs; for these have very short fore legs; but go jumping upon them" (not upon the short fore, but the long hind, legs, it is to be presumed), "as the others do; and like them are very good meat." This appears to have been the small kangaroo, since found upon the islands which form the road; and if so, this description is probably the first ever made of that singular animal.

Leaving Shark's Bay on Aug. 14, captain Dampier steered northward, along the coast; but at too great a distance to make much observation upon it, until he got round the North-west Cape. On the 22nd, he saw an extensive cluster of islands; and anchored, in latitude 20° 21', under one of the largest, which he called Rosemary Island. This was near the southern part of De Witt's Land; but, besides an error in latitude of 40', he complains that, in Tasman's chart, "the shore is laid down as all along joining in one body, or continent, with some openings like rivers; and not like islands, as really they are."--"By what we saw of them, they must have been a range of islands, of about twenty leagues in length, stretching from E. N. E. to W. S. W.; and for ought I know, as far as to those of Shark's Bay; and to a considerable breadth also, for we could see nine or ten leagues in amongst them, towards the continent or main land of New Holland, if there be any such thing hereabouts: And by the great tides I met with awhile afterwards, more to the north-east, I had a strong suspicion that here might be a kind of archipelago of islands; and a passage, possibly, to the to the south of New Holland and New Guinea, into the great South Sea, eastward."

Not finding fresh water upon such of the islands as were visited that day, captain Dampier quitted his anchorage next morning, and "steered away E. N. E., coasting along as the land lies." He seems to have kept the land in sight, in the day time, at the distance of four to six leagues; but the shore being low, this was too far for him to be certain whether all was main land which he saw; and what might have been passed in the night was still more doubtful.

Aug. 30, being in latitude 18° 21', and the weather fair, captain Dampier steered in for the shore; and anchored in 8 fathoms, about three-and-half leagues off. The tide ran "very swift here; so that our nun-buoy would not bear above the water to be seen. It flows here, as on that part of New Holland I described formerly, about five fathoms."

He had hitherto seen no inhabitants; but now met with several. The place at which he had touched in the former voyage "was not above forty or fifty leagues to the north-east of this. And these were much the same blinking creatures (here being also abundance of the same kind of flesh flies teizing them), and with the same black skins, and hair frizzled, tall and thin, etc., as those were. But we had not the opportunity to see whether these, as the former, wanted two of their fore teeth." One of them, who was supposed to be a chief, "was painted with a circle of white paste or pigment about his eyes, and a white streak down his nose, from his forehead to the tip of it. And his breast, and some part of his arms, were also made white with the same paint."

Neither bows nor arrows were observed amongst these people: they used wooden lances, such as Dampier had before seen. He saw no houses at either place, and believed they had none; but "there were several things like haycocks, standing in the savannah; which, at a distance, we thought were houses, looking just like the Hottentots' houses at the Cape of Good Hope; but we found them to be so many rocks." [12]

The land near the sea-coast is described as equally sandy with the parts before visited, and producing, amongst its scanty vegetation, nothing for food. No stream of fresh water was seen, nor could any, fit to drink, be procured by digging.

Quitting this inhospitable shore, captain Dampier weighed his anchor on September 5, with the intention of seeking water and refreshments further on to the north-eastward. The shoals obliged him to keep at a considerable distance from the land; and finally, when arrived at the latitude 16° 9', to give up his project, and direct his course for Timor.

Conclusive Remarks

With the voyage of Dampier terminates the information gained of the Western Coasts, previously to the year 1801. Monsieur de St. Alouarn had, indeed, seen some points or islands, in the year 1772, when he commanded the French flûte Le Gros Ventre; but the particulars are not generally known, being, in all probability, of little importance.

The summary of the knowledge possessed by the public, and the objects to which investigation might be usefully directed in these parts of Terra Australis, were as follow. The outline of the north-west coast was known upon the authority, as generally believed, of Tasman; with some points corrected by Dampier. The accuracy of Tasman's chart was, however, very much called in doubt: instead of being a continued shore, as the Dutch chart represented it, Dampier found the southern parts of De Witt's Land to consist of a range of islands. And he gives it as his opinion, that the northern part of New Holland was separated from the lands to the southward, by a strait; "unless", says he, "the high tides and indraught thereabout should be occasioned by the mouth of some large river; which hath often low lands on each side of the outlet, and many islands and shoals lying at its entrance: but I rather thought it a channel, or strait, than a river." This opinion he supports by a fair induction from facts; and the opening of twelve miles wide, seen near the same place by Vlaming's two vessels, and in which they could find no anchorage, strongly corroborated Dampier's supposition.

Later information had demonstrated, that the supposed strait could not lead out into the Great Ocean, eastward, as the English navigator had conjectured; but it was thought possible, that it might communicate with the Gulph of Carpentaria, and even probable that a passage existed from thence to the unknown part of the South Coast, beyond the Isles of St. Francis and St. Peter.

But whether this opening were the entrance to a strait, separating Terra Australis into two or more islands, or led into a mediterranean sea, as some thought; or whether it were the entrance of a large river, there was, in either case, a great geographical question to be settled, relative to the parts behind Rosemary Island.

If Tasman's chart were defective at De Witt's Land, it was likely to be so in other parts of the same coast; where there was no account, or belief, that it had been examined by any other person further north than the latitude 16½°. An investigation of the whole North-west Coast, with its numerous islands and shoals, was, therefore, required, before it could enter into the present improved systems of geography and navigation.

The chart of the West Coast, as far south as Rottenest, was founded upon much better authority; but for its formation from thence to Cape Leeuwin there were no good documents. In this part, there was room even for discovery; and the whole coast required to be laid down with more accuracy than had been attainable by the Dutch navigators.

As to the soil and vegetable productions upon several points near the sea, from Rottenest, northward to 16½, there was tolerably good general information; the inhabitants, also, had been seen; and, at one place, communication with them had been obtained. The accounts did, certainly, not give any flattering prospect, that much interesting knowledge was likely to be acquired under these heads, unless a strait, or inland sea, were found; but the accounts were not only confined as to place, but, with the exception of Dampier's, were very imperfect; and the great extent of the coasts, in the richest climates of the world, excited hopes that a close investigation would not only be of advantage to natural history, but would bring to light something useful in the mineral or vegetable kingdoms.

In the case of penetrating the interior of Terra Australis, whether by a great river, or a strait leading to an inland sea, a superior country, and perhaps a different people, might be found, the knowledge of which could not fail to be very interesting, and might prove advantageous to the nation making the discovery.

Notes

[1] See Dalrymple's Collection concerning Papua, note, page 6.

[2] Thevenot says six miles, and does not explain what kind of miles they are; but it is most probable that he literally copies his original, and that they are Dutch miles of fifteen to a degree. Van Keulen, in speaking of Houtman's Abrolhos, says, page 19, "This shoal is, as we believe, 11 or 12 leagues (8 ä 9 mijlen) from the coast."

[3] For an account of the miseries and horrors which took place on the islands of the Abrolhos during the absence of Pelsert, the English reader is referred to Vol. I. p. 320 to 325 of Campbell's edition of Harris' Voyages; but the nautical details there given are very incorrect.

[4] The French editor of the Voyage de Découvertes aux Terres Australes, published in 1807, Vol. I. p. 128, attributes the formation of the North-west Coast in the common charts to the expedition of the three Dutch vessels sent from Timor in 1705. But this is a mistake. It is the chart of Thevenot, his countryman, published forty-two years previously to that expedition, which has been mostly followed by succeeding geographers.

[5] This expression indicates, that the before-mentioned places were not then included under the term NEW HOLLAND by Witsen: he wrote in 1705.

[6] The Abbé Prévost in his Hist. gen. des Voyages, Tome XVI. (à la Haye) p. 79-81, has given some account of Vlaming's voyage in French; but the observations on the coast between Shark's Bay and Willem's River are there wholly omitted.]

A Dutch ship, called the Ridderschap, having been missing from the time she had left the Cape of Good Hope, in 1684 or 1685, it was thought probable she might have been wrecked upon the GREAT SOUTH LAND, and that some of the crew might (in 1696) be still living. Accordingly, the commodore Willem de Vlaming, who was going out to India with the Geelvink, Nyptang, and Wezel, was ordered to make a search for them.

[7] The account in Van Keulen is somewhat different. He says "we steered for the Land of Endragt: and on Dec. 28, got soundings in 63 fathoms, sandy bottom. The ensuing day we had 30 fathoms, and the coast was then in sight. The Island Rottenest, in 32° south latitude, was the land we steered for; and we had from 30 to 10 fathoms, in which last we anchored on a sandy bottom."

[8] This appears to be the first mention made of the black swan: the river was named Black-Swan River.

[9] It was near this place that captain Pelsert put the two Dutch conspirators on shore in 1629. Vlaming appears to have passed within Houtman's Abrolhos without seeing them.

[10] These two openings, which in the original are called rivers, were nothing more than the entrance into Shark's Bay. A small island, lying a little within the entrance, probably made it be taken for two openings.]

[11] For the full account of Dampier's proceedings and observations, with views of the land, see his Voyages, Vol. III. page 81, et seq.

[12] Dampier could not have examined these rocks closely; for there can be little doubt that they were the ant hills described by Pelsert as being "so large., that they might have been taken for the houses of Indians."

Section III - South Coast

NUYTS. 1627.

No historical fact seems to be less disputed, than that the South Coast of New Holland was first discovered in January 1627: whether it were the 26th, according to De Hondt, or the 16th, as is expressed on Thevenot's chart, is of very little import. It is generally said, that the ship was commanded by PIETER NUYTS; but as Nuyts, on his arrival at Batavia, was sent ambassador to Japan, and afterwards made governor of Formosa, it seems more probable that he was a civilian, perhaps Company's first merchant on board, rather than captain of the ship: the land discovered has, however, always borne his name.

The Dutch recital says--"In the year 1627, the South Coast of the Great SOUTH LAND was accidentally discovered by the ship the Gulde Zeepaard, outward-bound from Fatherland, for the space of a thousand miles."

This discovery has always been considered as of importance. A memoir was published at Amsterdam in 1718, "to prove, that NUYTS' LAND, being in the fifth climate, between 34° and 36° of latitude; it ought to be, like all other countries so situated, one of the most habitable, most rich, and most fertile parts of the world."[1] The journal of this discovery seems to have been lost; or possibly was either suppressed or destroyed, according to what is thought to have been the Dutch policy of that time. It was, therefore, from the chart, and the above passage in the recital, alone, that any particulars could be drawn. If the extent of a thousand miles were taken to be in a straight line, and to commence at Cape Leeuwin, the end of Nuyts' Land would reach nearly to the longitude of 135° east of Greenwich; but if, as was probable, the windings of the shore were included, and a deduction made of one-sixth to one-seventh in the distance, then the Isles of St. Francis and St. Peter might be expected to be found between the 132nd and 133rd degrees of east longitude.

VANCOUVER. 1791.

With the exception of Mons. de St. Alouarn, who is said to have anchored near Cape Leeuwin in 1772, the south coast of Terra Australis, though occupying much attention from geographers, seems to have been left unvisited from 1627 to 1791. In this year, captain GEORGE VANCOUVER, being on his way to North-west America, made the South Coast on Sept. 26, at Cape Chatham, in latitude 35° 3' south, and longitude 116° 35' east, not many leagues beyond where Nuyts appears to have commenced his discovery. He sailed eastward, from thence, along the shore, till the 28th; when he anchored in a sound, to which was given the name of KING GEORGE THE III.

The country in the neighbourhood of the Sound, and of its two harbours, was found to be agreeably variegated in form; to be clothed with grass and wood; and, though generally more barren than fertile, yet affording many spots capable of cultivation. No considerable river was discovered; but fresh water was every where abundant for domestic purposes; and the climate was judged to be as healthy as the temperature was found to be agreeable. Kangaroos did not appear to be scarce; nor were the woods ill tenanted by the feathered tribes; and reptiles and other noxious animals were not numerous. Amongst the aquatic birds, black swans and wild ducks held a distinguished place; but, like the land animals, were very shy: sea and shell fish were in tolerable abundance.

None of the inhabitants were seen; but from the appearance of their deserted huts, they were judged to be the same miserable race as those of the North-west and East Coasts. No marks of canoes, nor the remains of fish, even shell fish, were found near their habitations; and this circumstance, with the shyness of the birds and quadrupeds, induced a belief that the natives depended principally upon the woods for their subsistence.

Captain Vancouver quitted King George's Sound on Oct. 11, and proceeded eastward in the examination of the coast; but unfavourable winds prevented him from doing this so completely as he wished, and some parts were passed unseen; and the impediments to his progress at length caused the examination to be quitted, in favour of prosecuting the main design of his voyage. The last land seen was Termination Island, in latitude 34° 32' and longitude 122° 8'. The coast to the north of this island appeared much broken; but, although in Nuyts' chart a considerable group of islands were laid down in about that situation, captain Vancouver rather supposed it to be a continued main land.[2]

So far as this examination extended, the general form of the coast was found to correspond with that of the old chart; nor was any material error found in Nuyts' latitude. A further, and more extended confirmation of the Dutch navigator's discovery, and of its having been well laid down, considering the period at which it was done, was obtained in the following year.

D'ENTRECASTEAUX. 1792.

The French rear-admiral BRUNY D'ENTRECASTEAUX, having been sent out with the ships La Recherche and L'Espérance in search of the unfortunate La Pérouse made the south coast of New Holland on Dec. 5, 1792, about twenty-eight leagues to the north-west of Cape Chatham.[3] The coast, from the South-west Cape to the longitude of Termination Island, was explored by the admiral, with all the minuteness that the state of the weather could permit; and he was, generally, able to keep the shore closer abord than captain Vancouver had done, and to supply the deficiencies in his chart. The broken land to the north of Termination Island was found to be conformable to what Nuyts had laid down: it made part of a very extensive group of islands, one of which afforded timely shelter to the French ships on Dec. 9, from a gale which had arisen at south-west.

They remained a week at this anchorage, whilst the naturalists explored the surrounding country, and the surveyors examined such of the islands as were visible from the ships. Seals, penguins, and some kangaroos were seen; but no fresh water, accessible to shipping, could any where be found; the country within their reach being sandy and sterile. From Dec. 17 to 24, the ships were occupied in coasting eastward, along the outskirt of the group of islands, and then found it to terminate at 2½° of longitude from its commencement. The main land at the back of the islands had been generally visible, but at too great a distance for the precise form of the coast to be ascertained, or to allow of fixing the positions of, or even seeing, many of the inner islands and reefs.

This group is the first of the two marked upon the chart of Nuyts; and admiral D'Entrecasteaux praises the general accuracy of the Dutch navigator, in that "the latitude of Point Leeuwin, and of the coast of Nuyts' Land, were laid down with an exactness, surprising for the remote period in which they had been discovered." This liberal acknowledgment renders it the more extraordinary, that in the appellation which it was judged proper to give to this extensive group, the French admiral had not rather thought of doing honour to the original discoverer, or to the Gulde Zeepaard, than to his own ship; more especially, as his examination was far from being complete. This would have been more conformable to his general practice; but ARCHIPEL DE LA RECHERCHE was the name adopted.

Beyond the archipelago, the South Coast was found to trend east-north-eastward; without any island lying off it, or presenting any place of shelter. The shore was either a steep calcareous cliff, of an equal height, or low and sandy, with a few naked hillocks behind; and above these, no hill., nor any thing of the interior country, could be discerned. "It is not surprising," says D'Entrecasteaux., "that Nuyts has given no details of this barren coast; for its aspect is so uniform, that the most fruitful imagination could find nothing to say of it."

1793.

Frustrated in his expectation of procuring fresh water, and having no more than sufficient, at a short allowance, to reach Van Diemen's Land, the admiral abandoned the investigation of the South Coast, on Jan. 3; being then in latitude 31° 49' south, and longitude 131° 38½' east of Greenwich.

In the otherwise excellent charts constructed by M. BEAUTEMPS-BEAUPRÉ, geographical engineer on board La Recherche, there is an extraordinary omission, arising either from the geographer, or the conductor of the voyage. In the first 12° of longitude no soundings are marked along the coast; whilst, in the last 50, they are marked with tolerable regularity: the cause of this difference is not explained.

In comparing the French chart with that of Nuyts, it appeared that the rear-admiral had not proceeded so far along this coast as the Dutch navigator had done; for he did not see the islands of St. Francis and St. Peter, nor the reef marked about thirty leagues to the west of them. The point, however, where D'Entrecasteaux's examination terminated, was, in all probability, within a few leagues of that reef; and the end of Nuyts' discovery would be between 133° and 134° to the east of Greenwich.

Conclusive Remarks

The South Coast was not known, in 1801, to have been visited by any other than the three navigators, Nuyts, Vancouver, and D'Entrecasteaux.[4] The coast line, from Cape Leeuwin to near the longitude of 132°, was generally so well ascertained, and the charts of Vancouver and D'Entrecasteaux appeared to be so good, that little remained in this space for future visitors to discover. At two places, the country and productions near the sea-side had also been examined; though no communication had any where been obtained with the inhabitants. It was known also from Nuyts, that at 133° or 134° of east longitude, commenced a second archipelago; and that the coast began there to assume an irregular form; but in what direction it trended, whether to the south-eastward for Bass' Strait, or northward for the Gulph of Carpentaria, was altogether uncertain.

The great point, then, which required to be ascertained, was the form of the land from longitude 133° to 146° east, and from south latitude 32° to 38½°; comprising a space of two hundred and fifty leagues in a straight line. What rendered a knowledge of this part more particularly interesting, was the circumstance of no considerable river having been found on any of the coasts of Terra Australis previously explored: but it was scarcely credible that, if this vast country were one connected mass of land, it should not contain some large rivers; and if any, this unknown part was one of two remaining places, where they were expected to discharge themselves into the sea.

The apparent want of rivers had induced some persons to think, that Terra Australis might be composed of two or more islands, as had formerly been suspected by the Dutch, and by Dampier; whilst others, believing in the continuity of the shores, thought this want might arise from the interior being principally occupied by a mediterranean sea; but it was generally agreed, that one end of the separating channels, or otherwise the entrance, if such existed, into the supposed sea, would most likely be found in this unexplored part of the South Coast.

Besides the solution of this important geographical problem, something remained to be done upon the parts already seen. The main land behind the first archipelago, as also the inner islands, were yet to be examined for harbours, where refreshment for ships might be obtained; a comparison of the persons and usages of the inhabitants, with those in other parts of this vast country, was desirable; and, although little utility could be drawn from the known productions at the two points visited, it might reasonably be hoped, that an investigation of a coast so extensive, would not fail to produce much useful information.

Many circumstances, indeed, united to render the south coast of Terra Australis one of the most interesting parts of the globe, to which discovery could be directed at the beginning of the nineteenth century. Its investigation had formed a part of the instructions to the unfortunate French navigator La Pérouse, and afterwards of those to his countryman D'Entrecasteaux; and it was, not without some reason, attributed to England as a reproach, that an imaginary line of more than two hundred and fifty leagues extent, in the vicinity of of one of her colonies, should have been so long suffered to remain traced upon the charts, under the title Of UNKNOWN COAST. This comported ill with her reputation as the first of maritime powers; and to do it away was, accordingly, a leading point in the instructions given to the Investigator.

Notes

[1] *Hist. des Nav. aux Terres Australes. Tome I. page 429.*
[2] *For captain Vancouver's account of his proceedings and observations on the South Coast, see his Voyage round the World, Vol. I. page 28-57.*
[3] *When the Investigator sailed, the journal of M. Labillardière, naturalist in D'Entrecasteaux's expedition, was the sole account of the voyage made public: but M. DE ROSSEI one of the principal officers, has since published the voyage from the journals of the rear-admiral and it is from this last that what follows is extracted.*
[4] *It afterwards appeared, that lieutenant James Grant had discovered a part of it in 1800, in his way to Port Jackson with His Majesty's brig Lady Nelson.*

Section IV - East Coast, With Van Diemen's Land - Part I.

Preliminary Observations

Van Diemen's Land would more properly have been arranged under the head of the South Coast; but the later discoveries here have so intimate a connexion with those on the East, as to render it impossible to separate them without making repetitions, and losing perspicuity in the narrative.

The anxiety of the Dutch government at Batavia, to know how far the SOUTH LANDS might extend towards the antarctic circle, was the cause of Tasman being sent with two vessels, to ascertain this point; and the discovery of Van Diemen's Land was one of the results. It was not, however, the policy of the Dutch government to make discoveries for the benefit of general knowledge; and accordingly this voyage "was never," says Dr. Campbell, "published intire; and it is probable, that the East-India Company never intended it should be published at all. However, Dirk Rembrantz, moved by the excellency and accuracy of the work, published in Low Dutch an extract of captain Tasman's journal, which has ever since been considered as a great curiosity; and as such, has been translated into many languages."[1]

If a judgment may be formed from the translations, Rembrantz must have omitted great part of the nautical details concerning Van Diemen's Land, a defect which is remedied in the following account. It is taken from a journal containing, besides the daily transactions and observations throughout the whole voyage, a series of thirty-eight manuscript charts, views, and figures. The expression by me, which often occurs in it, and followed by the signature Abel Jansz Tasman, shows that if this were not his original journal, it is a copy from it: probably one made on board for the governor and council of Batavia. With this interesting document, and a translation made in 1776, by Mr. C. G. Woide, chaplain of His Majesty's Dutch chapel at St. James's, I was favoured by the Right Hon. SIR JOSEPH BANKS.[2]

TASMAN. 1642.

CAPTAIN ABEL JANSZ TASMAN sailed from Batavia on Aug. 14, 1642, with the yacht Heemskerk and fly-boat Zeehaan; and, after touching at Mauritius, steered south and eastward upon discovery. Nov. 24, at four p.m., high land was seen in the E. by N., supposed to be distant forty miles. The ships steered towards it till the evening; when there were high mountains visible in the E. S. E., and two smaller ones in the N. E. They sounded in 100 fathoms, and then stood off from the land, with the wind at south-east.

In the morning of Nov. 25., it was calm; but on a breeze springing up from the southward, Tasman steered for the land; and at five p.m., when it was twelve miles distant, sounded in 60 fathoms, coral bottom: at four miles off, the bottom was fine white sand. The latitude was then 42° 30' south; the mean of all their longitudes 163° 50' east (of Teneriffe apparently); and the compass had no variation. The coast here lies S. by E. and N. by W. It is of an even height; and was named ANTONY VAN DIEMEN's LAND, in honour of the governor-general, "our master, who sent us out to make discoveries. The islands round about, as many of them as were known to us, we called in honour of the Council of India."

The ships stood off again for the night, with a light breeze at S. S. E. On the 26th, the wind was from the eastward, and weather rainy, so that no land could be seen; but its distance was supposed to be twelve or thirteen leagues. At noon, the latitude from dead reckoning was 43° 36', and longitude 163° 2'; the course having been S. S. W. 72 miles.[3] In the evening the wind shifted to the north-east, and their course was directed E. S. E.: the variation was then half a degree west.

Nov. 27, the land was again seen. At noon, a course of S. E. by E. 52 miles, gave the latitude by estimation 44° 4' south, and longitude 164° 2' east. The weather was thick and rainy, and the wind still from the north-eastward; and at the fourth hour of the night, the vessels lay to, not venturing to run in the dark. In the morning of the 28th, it was foggy, with rain. They made sail to the east; but on seeing the land from N. E. to N. N. E., hauled up for it. From what could be perceived of the coast, it extended S. E. by E. and N. W. by W., and seemed to decrease in height to the eastward. At noon, the latitude by estimation was 44° 1', longitude 165° 2'; and the course steered, E. by S. 44 miles. The wind was then at north-west; and in the evening, they came near three small islands, one of which was shaped like a lion's head, and lies twelve miles from the continent (this was the Mewstone, of Furneaux). The wind was from the eastward in the night, and the ships lay to.

Nov. 29, they were still near the cliffy, lion-head-shaped island. The wind was light and fair, and they steered parallel to the coast, which lies here east and west. At noon, having made a course of E. N. E. 48 miles, the latitude was judged to be 43° 53', longitude 166° 3'. They had, a little before, passed two cliffy islets lying to seaward; of which the westernmost (Swilly of Furneaux) is like Pedra Blanca near the coast of China: the easternmost (Eddystone of Cook) resembles an awkward tower, and is about sixteen miles from the main land. Continuing to coast along the shore, they came, at five in the evening, to a bay, into which it was resolved in council to enter; but when almost in it, a high wind rose, and obliged them to shorten sail and stand out to sea. At daylight of the 30th, they found themselves driven so far off by the storm (whence the name of STORM BAY, applied in the chart), that the land was scarcely visible. At noon, the general course had been E. by N. 80 miles; the latitude was found to be 43° 41', and longitude by estimation (corrected) 168° 3': the needle pointed here, true North. The land was in sight to the north-west, and the wind strong, but variable, from the northward. The ships steered westward for a short time; but the weather being too stormy to admit of approaching the land, they went upon the other tack; and kept as much to the northward., under easy sail, as the wind would permit.

Dec. 1, the wind was more moderate; and on its veering to W. S. W., the ships steered towards the shore. At noon, their course made good was N. N. W. 39 miles; the latitude was 43° 10' and longitude 167° 55'. It then fell calm, and a council of officers from the two vessels was called, in which it was resolved, if wind and weather permitted, "to get a knowledge of the land, and some refreshments." An eastern breeze sprung up soon afterward; and they got to anchor, an hour after sunset, "in a good port, in 22 fathoms, whitish good-holding sand; wherefore we ought to cc praise GOD ALMIGHTY." This port is called FREDERIK HENDRIK'S BAY, in the chart.

Next morning early, two armed boats were sent to an inlet (the inner bay), situate four or five miles to the northwestward of the ships, in order to search for fresh water, wood, and refreshments. They returned in the afternoon, and the officers gave the following account.

They rowed four or five miles round the point of the inlet, along a high and level shore. Wild greens were plentiful; some resembled those at the Cape of Good Hope, "and may be used in place of wormwood;" others were long and saltish, and like sea parsley. They found many dry gullies, and one watering place in which the water was good, but obtained with difficulty, and in very small quantities. Some human voices were heard, and a sound like that of a trumpet, or little gong, which was not far off; but they could see no person. Amongst the trees, two were remarked whose thickness was two, or two and a half fathoms, and the first branches from sixty to sixty-five feet above the ground. The bark had been taken off with a flint stone, and steps were cut, full five feet one from the other; whence the natives were presumed to be very tall, or able to get up these trees by some artifice. They supposed the steps to be made for the purpose of getting at the nests of birds; and that some of them had not been cut above four days before. They observed traces on the ground, as if made by the claws of a tiger; and saw the excrements, as was thought, of quadrupeds. Some well-looking gums, which dropped from the trees and somewhat resembled gum-lac, were brought on board.

Off the east point of the (inner) bay, they found thirteen to fourteen feet water; and that the tide flowed about three feet. They there saw a number of men, of wild ducks, and geese; but inland none were seen, though their noise was heard. Muscles were found sticking to bushes, in different places. The country was covered with trees; but so thinly scattered, that one might see everywhere to a great distance amongst them, and distinguish men and animals. Several of the trees were "much burnt about the foot; and the ground was here and there like little squares (vuysterchen), and become as hard as stone, by fire."

A short time before the boats returned, a thick smoke had been observed upon the continent, to the west of where the ships lay at anchor; and from the people staying so much longer than they had been ordered, it was thought to have been made by them, as a signal. But on inquiry, they answered in the negative; and said that they, also, had seen smoke in several places; and bushes--(here seems to be a line omitted.) "So that without doubt, here must be exceedingly tall people."

Dec. 3. A boat was sent to the south-east part of the (outer) bay, and found fresh water; but it broke through the low shore to the sea, and was brackish; and the soil was too rocky to dig wells. In the afternoon, commodore Tasman went, with several officers from both vessels in two boats, to the south-east extremity of the bay; taking with them the PRINCE'S flag, and a post upon which was cut a compass, to be erected on shore. One of the boats was obliged to return, from the bad weather; but the shallop went to a little cove W. S. W. of the ships. The surf being there too high to admit of landing, the first carpenter, Pieter Jacobsz, swam on shore with the post and Prince's flag; and set it up near the last of four remarkable trees, which stood in the form of a crescent, in the middle of the cove. "When the first carpenter had done this, in the sight of me ABEL J. TASMAN, of the master Gerrit Jansz, and under-merchant Abraham Coomans, we went with the shallop as near as possible to the shore, and the said carpenter swam back, through the surf. We then returned on board; and left this as a memorial to the posterity of the inhabitants of this country. They did not show themselves; but we suspected some to be not far from thence, watching carefully our doings."

The wind was from the northward all this day; and at sunset, it blew a storm. The variation at anchor was observed to be 3° east; the latitude was 43° south, and longitude 167½° east from Teneriffe.

Dec. 4. The wind was more moderate, and came from the westward, off the land. The anchors were then weighed, but the flukes of one were broken. On quitting Frederik Hendrik's Bay, the ships steered northward as much as possible, to look for a watering place. At noon, the course had been N. E. 32 miles; the latitude was 42° 40', and longitude 168°. In the evening, they saw a round mountain, about eleven leagues to the N. N. W.; and during the whole day, several smokes were visible along the coast. "Here," says Tasman, "I should give a description of the extent of the coast, and the islands near it, but I hope to be excused, and refer, for brevity's sake, to the chart made of it, and herewith joined." The ships kept close to the wind all night, as they did in the morning of Dec. 5, when it was N. W. by W. The high round mountain was then seen bearing west, eight leagues, and this was the furthest land visible, nor did the wind allow them to come in with it again. At noon, the latitude was judged to be 41° 34', and longitude 169°; the course for the last day having been N. E. by N. 80 miles. Tasman then steered "precisely eastward, to make further discoveries," agreeably to a resolution of the council, taken in the morning.

The copy of Tasman's charts, given in the Atlas, PLATE III. of D'Entrecasteaux's Voyage, and taken from Valentyn, is conformable to the manuscript charts in the Dutch journal. There is, however, an error of one degree too much east, in the scale of longitude; and Pedra Blanca is erroneously written against the Eddystone, in the general chart. In the plan of Frederik Hendrik's Bay, the name is placed within the inner bay, instead of being written, as in the original, on the point of land between the inner and outer bays: I conceive the name was intended to comprise both.[4]

COOK. 1770.

More than a century had elapsed after this celebrated voyage of Tasman, and the eastern limit of Terra Australis remained still unknown. But the British nation was then taking the lead in discovery; and the new and liberal principles upon which His Majesty, GEORGE III, ordered it to be prosecuted, was a sure indication that so considerable a part of the globe would not long escape attention. Captain JAMES COOK, accompanied by Mr. Green, was sent in the Endeavour to observe, at Taheity, the transit of Venus over the sun's disk; and after accomplishing that object, and making a survey of New Zealand, he continued his course westward, in order to explore the east side of the Terra Australis Incognita.

In the morning of April 19,1770, the land was seen bearing from north-east to west; the furthest part, in the latter direction, being judged to lie in 38° south, and 148° 53' east. But captain Cook could not determine whether it did, or did not, join to Tasman's Van Diemen's Land.

It would be superfluous, here, to follow our great navigator in his discoveries along the coast, northward to Botany Bay and from thence to Cape York. Such an abstract as suits the plan of this Introduction would be little satisfactory to the reader; when, by an easy reference to the original narrative, so much interesting information upon this new country, its productions, and inhabitants, may be obtained.[5]

This voyage of captain Cook, whether considered in the extent of his discoveries and the accuracy with which they were traced, or in the labours of his scientific associates, far surpassed all that had gone before. The general plan of the voyage did not, however, permit captain Cook to enter minutely into the details of every part; and had it been otherwise, the very extent of his discoveries would have rendered it impossible. Thus, some portions of the east coast of Terra Australis were passed in the night, many openings were seen and left unexamined., and the islands and reefs lying at a distance from the shore could, generally, be no more than indicated: he reaped the harvest of discovery, but the gleanings of the field remained to be gathered.

MARION. 1772.

The first visitor to Van Diemen's Land, after Tasman, its discoverer, was captain MARION. He commanded the Mascarin and Marquis de Castries, from the Isle Mauritius; and one of the objects of his expedition, was the discovery of the supposed SOUTHERN CONTINENT. This voyage possesses a considerable degree of interest, and was published at Paris in 1783; but not being generally known in England, the parts which relate to Van Diemen's Land, are here given in abridgment.

March 3, 1772, M. Marion made the west side, in latitude 42° 56', half a degree south of Tasman's first land fall; and behind a point in 43° 15', he saw an opening leading to the northward, but of which no particular mention is made. Steering eastward, round all the rocks and islets lying off the south coast, he arrived, on the evening of the 4th, in Frederik Hendrik's Bay; and anchored in 22 fathoms, sandy bottom. The great sandy cove of the outer bay bore from thence, S. 25° W. one league and a half; the extreme of Maria's Island, N. E. by N.; and the northernmost part of the main land, N. 5° W. six leagues: (these bearings appear to be as taken by the compass). The latitude observed here, was 42° 50' south, and longitude 145° 20 east of Greenwich; the first being 10', and the longitude above 5° less, than given by Tasman.[6]

The fires and smokes, seen by day and night, bespoke the country to be well inhabited; and, on anchoring, there were about thirty men assembled upon the shore. On the boats being sent next morning, the natives went to them without distrust; and, having piled together some pieces of wood, presented a lighted stick to the new comers, and seemed to ask them to set fire to the pile. Not knowing what this ceremony meant, they complied; and the act seemed neither to excite surprise, nor to cause any alteration in the conduct of the natives: they continued to remain about the French party, with their wives and children, as before.

These people were of the common stature, of a black colour, and were all naked, both men and women; and some of the latter had children fastened to their backs, with ropes made of rushes. All the men were armed with pointed sticks (spears), and with stones which appeared to have been sharpened in the manner of axe heads. They had, in general, small eyes, and the white duller than in Europeans; the mouth very wide, the teeth white, and flat noses. Their hair, which resembled the wool of the Caffres, was separated into shreds, and powdered with red ochre. They were generally slender, tolerably well made, kept their shoulders back, and upon their prominent chests, several had marks raised in the skin. Their language, appeared harsh; the words seeming to be drawn from the bottom of the throat.

The French tried to win them by little presents, but they rejected with disdain every thing that was offered; even iron, looking-glasses, handkerchiefs, and cloth. They were shown ducks and fowls, which had been carried from the ships; and it was endeavoured to make them understand, that such would be gladly purchased of them; but they took these animals, with which they seemed to be unacquainted, and threw them away in anger.

The party had been about an hour with the savages when captain Marion went on shore. One of the natives stepped forward, and offered him a firebrand to be applied to a small heap of wood; and the captain, supposing it was a ceremony necessary to prove that he came with friendly intentions, set fire to the heap without hesitation. This was no sooner done, than they retired precipitately to a small hill, and threw a shower of stones, by which captain Marion, and the commander of the Castries were both wounded. Some shots were then fired; and the French, returning to their boats, coasted along the beach to an open place in the middle of the bay, where there was no hill or eminence from whence they could be annoyed. The savages sent their women and children into the woods, and followed the boats along shore; and on their putting in to land, one of the natives set up a hideous cry, and immediately a shower of spears was discharged. A black servant was hurt in the leg; and a firing then commenced, by which several of the natives were wounded, and one killed. They fled to the woods, making a frightful howling, but carried off such of the wounded as were unable to follow. Fifteen men, armed with muskets, pursued them; and on entering amongst the trees, they found a dying savage. This man was a little more than five feet seven inches high; his breast was marked like those of the Mozambique Caffres, and his skin appeared as black; but on washing off the soot and dirt, his natural colour appeared to be reddish. The spears, which it was feared might have been poisoned, were proved not to be so by the facility with which the wound of the black servant was healed.

After the flight of the savages, captain Marion sent two officers with detachments, to search for water, and for trees proper to make a foremast and bowsprit for the Castries; but after traversing two leagues of country without meeting a single inhabitant, they returned unsuccessful in both pursuits; nor could any fresh water be found during the six days which the ships remained in Frederik Hendrik's Bay.

The land here is quite sandy, but covered with brush-wood, and with small trees which the savages had mostly stripped of the bark for cooking their shell fish. The greater part of the trees were burnt at the foot; but amongst them there was a kind of pine, less than ours, which was perfectly preserved; apparently from the natives finding them to be of use in some way or other.[7]

There were marks of fire almost every where; and in many places the earth was covered with ashes. Where it was not burnt, there was plenty of grass, ferns like those of Europe, sorrel, and alléluia. From the few animals seen, it was thought that the fires made by the natives near the coast, drove them inland. The shooters met with a tiger cat, and saw many holes in the ground, like those of a warren. They killed crows, blackbirds, thrushes, doves, a white-bellied paroquet whose plumage resembled that of the same bird at the River Amazons, and several kinds of sea birds, principally pelicans, and the black-bodied red bill.

The climate was cold, although in the end of summer; and it excited surprise, that the savages could go naked; the more so, as the nearest approach to houses consisted of branches of trees, set up behind the fire places to break off the wind. The many heaps of shells seemed to bespeak, that the usual food of these people was muscles and other shell fish.

Many large rays were caught by the French, as also sea cats, old wives, and several other fish whose names were not known. They found also plenty of cray-fish, lobsters, very large crabs, and good oysters; and the curious picked up sea stars, sea eggs, and a variety of fine and rare shells.

Finding he was only losing time in searching for water in this wild country, captain Marion determined to make sail for New Zealand, where he hoped to succeed better, and also to obtain masts for the Castries. He accordingly left Van Diemen's Land on the 10th of March; and the account of it concludes with the observation that they had very bad weather on the west coast, but on the east side the sky was much clearer and winds more moderate.

The chart of Mons. Crozet, which accompanies the voyage, appears, though on a very small scale, to possess a considerable degree of exactness in the form of the land. The wide opening, called Storm Bay, is distinctly marked; as is another bay to the westward, with several small islands in it, the easternmost of which are the Boreel's Eylanden of Tasman.

FURNEAUX. 1773.

A year after Marion had quitted Frederik Hendrik's Bay, Van Diemen's Land was visited by captain TOBIAs FURNEAUX, in His Majesty's ship Adventure. He made the South-west Cape on March 9, and steered eastward, close to the islands and rocks called Maatsuyker's, by Tasman; and behind which lay a bold shore, which seemed to afford several anchoring places. Some of these rocks resembled, says captain Furneaux, "the Mewstone, particularly one which we so named, about four or five leagues E. S. E. ½ E. off the above cape, which Tasman has not mentioned, or laid down in his draughts."[8] This is nevertheless the lion-head-shaped island, particularly mentioned by Tasman, as lying twelve miles out from the coast: the mistake arose from the imperfection of the accounts. After passing Maatsuyker's Isles, captain Furneaux sent a boat to the main land, on the 10th, and the people found places where the natives had been., and where pearl scallop shells were scattered about. "The soil seemed to be very rich; the country well clothed with wood, particularly on the lee sides of the hills; plenty of water which falls from the rocks in beautiful cascades, for two or three hundred feet perpendicular, into the sea; but they did not see the least sign of any place to anchor in with safety."

On the return of the boat, captain Furneaux made sail, and came to "the westernmost point of a very deep bay, called by Tasman Stormy Bay. From the west to the east point of this bay there are several small islands, and black rocks which we called the Friars." From the Friars he followed the coast N. by E. four leagues, and the same evening anchored in ADVENTURE BAY. "We first took this bay," says the captain, "to be that which Tasman called Frederik Henry Bay; but afterwards found that his is laid down five leagues to the northward."

Captain Furneaux here mistook the Storm and Frederik Hendrik's Bays of Tasman; and he has been followed in this error by all the succeeding navigators of the same nation, which has created not a little confusion in the geography of this part of the world.

The bay supposed to have been Storm Bay, has no name in Tasman's chart; though the particular plan shows that he noticed it, as did Marion more distinctly. The rocks marked at the east point of this bay, and called the Friars, are the Boreel's Eylanden of Tasman; and the true Storm Bay is the deep inlet, of which Adventure Bay is a cove. Frederik

Hendrik's Bay is not within this inlet, but lies to the north-eastward, on the outer side of the land which captain Furneaux, in consequence of his first mistake, took to be Maria's Island, but which, in fact, is a part of the main land. All this is evident from a close comparison of the forms of the land in the two charts, and is corroborated by the differences of longitude from the Mewstone.

Adventure Bay proved to be a valuable discovery, being a good and well-sheltered anchorage, where wood and water were abundant, and procurable without much difficulty. The country was found to be pleasant; the soil black and rich, though not deep; the sides of the hills covered with large trees of the evergreen kind, growing to a great height before they spread out into branches. There were several species of land birds; and the aquatic fowl were ducks, teal, and the sheldrake. An opossum was seen, and the excrement of another quadruped, judged to be of the deer kind. Sea fish were caught, but not in plenty. The lagoons abounded with trout and several other sorts of fish. No natives came down to the ships; but their fires were seen at a distance, and several of their miserable huts were examined. Not the least mark of canoe or boat was seen, and it was generally thought they had none; "being altogether, from what we could judge, a very ignorant and wretched set of people; though natives of a country capable of producing every necessary of life, and a climate the finest in the world. We found not the least sign of any minerals or metals."

After remaining five days in Adventure Bay, captain Furneaux sailed along the coast to the northward, in order to discover whether Van Diemen's Land were joined to New South Wales. He passed the Maria's, Schouten's, and Vanderlin's Islands of Tasman, at some distance; and then, closing more in with the coast, he found the land to be low and even, and of an agreeable aspect, "but no signs of a harbour or bay, where a ship might anchor in safety." In latitude 40° 50', the coast, from running nearly north, turned to the westward., and, as captain Furneaux thought, formed a deep bay. From thence to 39° 50', is nothing but islands and shoals; the "land high, rocky, and barren." In the course northward, past these islands, he had regular soundings, from 15 to 30 fathoms, though no land was visible; it was, however, seen again (or thought to be so) in latitude 39°, and nearly due north from the islands. The bottom then becoming uneven, our navigator discontinued his course, and steered for New Zealand.

Whether Van Diemen's Land were, or were not, joined to New South Wales, was a question not yet resolved; but captain Furneaux gave it as his opinion, "that there is no strait between New Holland and Van Diemen's Land, but a very deep bay."

COOK. 1777.

The next visitor to Van Diemen's Land was captain JAMES COOK, with his Majesty's ships Resolution and Discovery. He made the South-west Cape on Jan. 24, 1777, and steered eastward along the shore, as captain Furneaux had done, but generally at a greater distance: on the 26th he anchored in Adventure Bay.

Captain Cook's account of this bay agrees nearly with that of Furneaux; but he there procured abundance of fish, and had frequent communication with the natives: his description of them coincides, generally, with what has been recited in Marion's voyage. The most striking differences betwixt these people and those captain Cook had seen on the east coast of New South Wales, were in their language, in having no canoes, and in the different texture of the hair: in those it was "naturally long and black, though it be universally cropped short;" whilst in Adventure Bay, "it was as woolly, as that of any native of Guinea."[9] In these particulars, as in some others, they agreed with Dampier's description of the people on the North-west Coast, who were without canoes, and had woolly hair.

The following articles, to the conclusion of PART I. of this Section, are placed somewhat out of their chronological order, for the convenience of classing together all the discoveries which had no connection with the British settlement in New South Wales. Those made in vessels from that settlement, or which may be considered as a consequence of its establishment, will compose PART II. in uninterrupted order.

BLIGH. 1788.

Captain William Bligh put into Adventure Bay with his Majesty's ship Bounty in 1788, and with the Providence and Assistant in 1792; for the purpose of obtaining wood and water. These were procured with facility, as also plenty of fish; and many useful seeds and trees were planted.

No discoveries being made here, beyond those of Furneaux and Cook, the reader is referred to captain Bligh's Voyage to the South Seas, P. 45 to 54, for his observations on the country and inhabitants. There is, however, one remarkable circumstance recorded of these people, which is, that when presents wrapped up in paper were thrown to them, "they took the articles out, and placed them on their heads;" a ceremony which is similar to that recorded by Witsen, of the inhabitants on the east side of the Gulph of Carpentaria.

COX. 1789.

The brig Mercury, commanded by JOHN HENRY COX, Esq., anchored at the entrance of a deep bay on the south side of Van Diemen's Land, on July 3, 1789. This bay was then first discovered, and lies N. by W. ten miles from the Mew-stone.[10] The country was found to be agreeably interspersed with hills and vallies, and some of the hills were luxuriantly clothed with trees to their very summits. About four miles from the vessel, there was a stream of fresh water; and close to it stood a hut, or rather hovel, neatly constructed of branches of trees and dried leaves. "Around it were scattered a great quantity of pearl, escalop, oyster, and other shells, which had been lately roasted." The faeces of some large animal were met with in every direction; but neither the animal itself nor any of the natives could be found.

July 5. A heavy swell from the southward obliged Mr. Cox to get under way; and he worked along shore to the eastward. His intention was to put into Adventure Bay; but being set to the northward of his reckoning, on the 8th, he discovered, and came to an anchor in OYSTER BAY, on the inner side of Maria's Island, the shelter there being found secure, and wood and water plentiful. This bay lies in 42° 42' south, and 148° 25' east, and not more than three or four leagues to the northward of Tasman's Frederik Hendrik's Bay; though Mr. Cox, following in the error of captain Furneaux, seems to have had no idea of this proximity.

Some communication was obtained with the inhabitants of the island; but as nothing in this, or in other respects, was found materially different to what was observed by Mons. Marion and captain Cook in the neighbouring bays, it is unnecessary to enter into the details.

D'ENTRECASTEAUX. 1792.

The French rear-admiral, BRUNY D'ENTRECASTEAUX, made the coast of Van Diemen's Land with the intention of procuring wood and water at Adventure Bay; "but deceived by the forms of the coast, which resemble each other, he entered Storm Bay," April 20, 1792.[11] This is not, however, the Storm Bay of Tasman; but that which was taken for such by captain Furneaux.

The error was soon detected; but finding shelter and good anchoring ground, the admiral determined to remain where he was, and to examine the inlet. The result most amply repaid his labour, by opening to him the most important discovery which had been made in this country from the time of Tasman. Instead of an open bay, this inlet was found to be the entrance into a fine navigable channel, running more than ten leagues to the northward, and there communicating with the true Storm Bay. It contains a series of good harbours, or is itself, rather, one continued harbour, from beginning to end.

This new passage obtained the name of CANAL DE D'ENTRECASTEAUX; and, after passing through it with his ships, the admiral steered across Storm Bay, passing to the southward of the land which Furneaux and Cook had taken for Maria's Islands. At the head of Storm Bay other openings were seen; but the wind from the north and the pressure of time, did not allow him to examine them at that period.

1793.

On Jan. 21, of the following year, admiral D'Entrecasteaux anchored again in one of the ports on the west side of the entrance to his newly discovered channel; and after completing the wood and water of his two ships, La Recherche and L'Espérance, pursued his former course up the passage, sending boats to complete the surveys of the different harbours on each side. A boat was also sent to explore the two openings in the head of Storm Bay. The westernmost proved to be a river, up which the boat ascended twenty miles to the northward; and so far it was navigable for ships. It was not pursued further; so that the distance, to which this Rivière du Nord might penetrate into the country, was uncertain. The eastern opening led northward into a wide, open bay; and this into another large expanse of water to the eastward, but which was not examined. It was thought, however, that this eastern bay communicated with that of Frederik Hendrik; and on this supposition (which has not proved correct), the land which Furneaux and Cook had erroneously thought to be Maria's Island, was named Ile d' Abel Tasman.

The charts of the bays, ports, and arms of the sea at the south-east end of Van Diemen's Land, constructed in this expedition by Mons. BEAUTEMPS-BEAUPRÉ and assistants, appear to combine scientific accuracy and minuteness of detail, with an uncommon degree of neatness in the execution: they contain some of the finest specimens of marine surveying, perhaps ever made in a new country.

Admiral D'Entrecasteaux gives a very favourable account of the disposition of the native inhabitants on the shores of the channel; and he had frequent communications with them. In person and manner of living, they agree with those described by Marion and Cook; but the vocabulary of their language is somewhat different; and bark canoes, which preceding navigators had thought them not to possess, were found in the channel. The description of the country is, generally, favourable; though somewhat less so than that of captain Cook at Adventure Bay. The climate was thought good, though moist; and the supplies of wood, water, and fish, for ships, were abundant; but the preference, in these respects, was given to Adventure Bay, even by the French admiral.

Mons. Labillardière, in his previously published account of D'Entrecasteaux's voyage, says, that he found a small vein of coal near the South Cape; and that limestone rocks exist on the west-side of Adventure Bay. These circumstances are omitted by M. de Rossel; as is also the remark, that although the natives had their teeth perfect, in general, yet in some near the bay, one, and sometimes two of the upper front teeth were wanting. The same thing was observed by Dampier, of the inhabitants on the north-west coast of Terra Australis; and this coincidence, together with their similarity of person, particularly in the woolly hair, is sufficiently remarkable to induce a belief, that these people, placed at the two extremities of this vast country, have yet one common origin; although the intermediate inhabitants of the East Coast differ in some essential particulars.

HAYES. 1794.

Captain JOHN HAYES, of the Bombay marine, visited Storm Bay and D'Entrecasteaux's Channel, with the private ships Duke and Dutchess from India, in 1794. He went much further up the Rivière du Nord, than the boat from the French ships had done, and gave it the name of the DERWENT RIVER. This name is likely to efface the first appellation, and with some degree of propriety; both from the superior extent of captain Hayes' examination, and from North River being an equivocal term for a stream at the south end of Van Diemen's Land.

That captain Hayes had some intimation of the French discovery is evident, but not knowing the distinctive appellations given, he took upon himself to impose names every where. Succeeding visitors have gone with his sketch in their hands, whilst the charts of D'Entrecasteaux were unknown in that part of the world; from whence, and still more from those names having now become familiar to the settlement established in the Derwent River, it will be difficult, if not impossible in many cases, for the original discoverer to be reinstated in his rights.

The head of the Derwent is the sole part where captain Hayes' sketch conveys information, not to be found much more accurately delineated in the charts of D'Entrecasteaux.

Notes

[1] *Complete Collection of Voyages and Travels, originally published by John Harris, D. D. and F. R. S. London, 1744. Vol. I. page 325.*

[2] *I am proud to take this opportunity of publicly expressing my obligations to the Right Hon. President of the Royal Society; and of thus adding my voice to the many who, in the pursuit of science, have found in him a friend and patron. Such he proved in the commencement of my voyage, and in the whole course of its duration; in the distresses which tyranny heaped upon those of accident; and after they were overcome. His extensive and valuable library has been laid open; and has furnished much that no time or expense, within my reach, could otherwise have procured.*

[3] *This and the following courses and distances run from one noon to another, do not always agree with the latitudes and longitudes; but the differences are not great: They probably arose from the distances being marked to the nearest Dutch mile on the log board; whereas the latitude and longitude are taken to minutes of a degree.*

[4] *In Vol. III. just published, of captain Burney's History of Discoveries in the South Sea, a copy is given of Tasman's charts, as they stand in the original.*

[5] *Hawkesworth's Voyages, Vol. III. page 77, et seq.*

[6] *According to captain Cook, the longitude should be 148° 10'.*

[7] *It is more probable, that these trees are able to resist the fire better than the others.*

[8] *Cook's Second Voyage, Vol. I. p. 109.]*

[9] *See Cook's Third Voyage, Vol. I. p. 93-117.*

[10] *Observations, etc., made during a voyage in the brig Mercury; by Lieut. G. Mortimer of the Marines. London, 1791.*

[11] *Voyage de D'Entrecasteaux, rédigé par M. de Rossel: À Paris 1808. Tome I. p. 48.*

Section IV - East Coast, With Van Diemen's Land - Part II

Preliminary Information

The year 1788 will ever be a memorable epoch in the history of Terra Australis. On Jan. 18, Captain (now vice-admiral) ARTHUR PHILLIP arrived in Botany Bay, with His Majesty's brig Supply; and was followed by the Syrius, captain John Hunter, six sail of transports, and three store ships. The purpose of this armament was to establish a colony in New South Wales, over which extensive country Captain Phillip was appointed Governor and Captain-general. Botany Bay proved to be an unfavourable situation for the new colony; it was, therefore, abandoned in favour of PORT JACKSON, which lies three leagues to the northward, and was found to be one of the finest harbours in the world.

A history of this establishment at the extremity of the globe, in a country where the astonished settler sees nothing, not even the grass under his feet, which is not different to whatever had before met his eye, could not but present objects of great interest to the European reader; and the public curiosity has been gratified by the perusal of various respectable publications, wherein the proceedings of the colonists, the country round Port Jackson, its productions, and native inhabitants, are delineated with accuracy, and often with minuteness. The subject to be here treated is the progress of maritime geographical discovery, which resulted from the new establishment; and as the different expeditions made for this purpose are in many cases imperfectly, and in some altogether unknown, it has been judged that a circumstantial account of them would be useful to seamen, and not without interest to the general reader. These expeditions are, moreover, intimately connected with the Investigator's voyage, of which they were, in fact, the leading cause.

The first advantage to maritime geography which arose from the new settlement, was a survey of Botany and Broken Bays and Port Jackson, with most of the rivers falling into them. Botany Bay had, indeed, been examined by captain Cook; but of the other two harbours, the entrances alone had been seen. This survey, including the intermediate parts of the coast, was made by captain John Hunter, and was published soon after its transmission to England by governor Phillip. In the beginning of 1795, captain (now vice-admiral) Hunter sailed a second time for New South Wales, to succeed captain Phillip in the government of the new colony. He took with him His Majesty's armed vessels Reliance and Supply; and the author of this account, who was then a midshipman and had not long before returned from a voyage to the South Seas, was led by his passion for exploring new countries, to embrace the opportunity of going out upon a station which, of all others, presented the most ample field for his favourite pursuit.

On arriving at Port Jackson, in September of the same year, it appeared that the investigation of the coast had not been greatly extended beyond the three harbours; and even in these, some of the rivers were not altogether explored. Jervis Bay, indicated but not named by captain Cook, had been entered by lieutenant Richard Bowen; and to the north, Port Stephens had lately been examined by Mr C. Grimes, land surveyor of the colony, and by captain W. R. Broughton of H. M. ship Providence; but the intermediate portions of coast, both to the north and south, were little further known than from captain Cook's general chart; and none of the more distant openings, marked but not explored by that celebrated navigator, had been seen.

In Mr George Bass, surgeon of the Reliance, I had the happiness to find a man whose ardour for discovery was not to be repressed by any obstacles, nor deterred by danger; and with this friend a determination was formed of completing the examination of the east coast of New South Wales, by all such opportunities as the duty of the ship and procurable means could admit.

BASS and FLINDERS. 1795.

Projects of this nature, when originating in the minds of young men, are usually termed romantic; and so far from any good being anticipated, even prudence and friendship join in discouraging, if not in opposing them. Thus it was in the present case; so that a little boat of eight feet long, called Tom Thumb, with a crew composed of ourselves and a boy, was the best equipment to be procured for the first outset. In the month following the arrival of the ships, we proceeded round in this boat, to Botany Bay; and ascending George's River, one of two which falls into the bay, explored its winding course about twenty miles beyond where Governor Hunter's survey had been carried.

The sketch made of this river and presented to the governor, with the favourable report of the land on its borders, induced His Excellency to examine them himself shortly afterward; and was followed by establishing there a new branch of the colony, under the name of Bank's Town.

1796.

A voyage to Norfolk Island interrupted our further proceedings, until March 1796. Mr Bass and myself then went again in Tom Thumb, to explore a large river, said to fall into the sea some miles to the south of Botany Bay, and of which there was no indication in captain Cook's chart.

We sailed out of Port Jackson early in the morning of March 25, and stood a little off to sea to be ready for the sea breeze. On coming in with the land in the evening, instead of being near Cape Solander, we found ourselves under the cliffs near Hat Hill, six or seven leagues to the southward, whither the boat had been drifted by a strong current. Not being able to land, and the sea breeze coming in early next morning from the northward, we steered for two small islets, six or seven miles further on, in order to get shelter; but being in want of water, and seeing a place on the way where, though the boat could not land, a cask might be obtained by swimming, the attempt was made, and Mr Bass went on shore. Whilst getting off the cask, a surf arose further out than usual, carried the boat before it to the beach, and left us there with our arms, ammunition, clothes and provisions thoroughly drenched and partly spoiled. The boat was emptied and launched again immediately; but it was late in the afternoon before every thing was rafted off, and we proceeded to the islets. It was not possible to land there; and we went on to two larger isles lying near a projecting point of the main, which has four hillocks upon it presenting the form of a double saddle, and proved to be captain Cook's Red Point. The isles were inaccessible as the others; and it being dark, we were constrained to pass a second night in Tom Thumb, and dropped our stone anchor in 7 fathoms, under the lee of the point.

The sea breeze, on the 27th, still opposed our return; and learning from two Indians that no water could be procured at Red Point, we accepted their offer of piloting us to a river which, they said, lay a few miles further southward, and where not only fresh water was abundant, but also fish and wild ducks. These men were natives of Botany Bay, whence it was that we understood a little of their language, whilst that of some others was altogether unintelligible. Their river proved to be nothing more than a small stream, which descended from a lagoon under Hat Hill, and forced a passage for itself through the beach; so that we entered it with difficulty even in Tom Thumb. Our two conductors then quitted the boat to walk along the sandy shore abreast, with eight or ten strange natives in company.

After rowing a mile up the stream, and finding it to become more shallow, we began to entertain doubts of securing a retreat from these people, should they be hostilely inclined; and they had the reputation at Port Jackson of being exceedingly ferocious, if not cannibals. Our muskets were not yet freed from rust and sand, and there was a pressing necessity to procure fresh water before attempting to return northward. Under these embarrassments, we agreed upon a plan of action, and went on shore directly to the natives. Mr Bass employed some of them to assist in repairing an oar which had been broken in our disaster, whilst I spread the wet powder out in the sun. This met with no opposition, for they knew not what the powder was; but when we proceeded to clean the muskets, it excited so much alarm that it was necessary to desist. On inquiring of the two friendly natives for water, they pointed upwards to the lagoon; but after many evasions our barica[1] was filled at a hole not many yards distant.

The number of people had increased to near twenty, and others were still coming, so that it was necessary to use all possible expedition in getting out of their reach. But a new employment arose upon our hands: we had clipped the hair and beards of the two Botany Bay natives at Red Point; and they were showing themselves to the others, and persuading them to follow their example. Whilst, therefore, the powder was drying, I began with a large pair of scissors to execute my new office upon the eldest of four or five chins presented to me; and as great nicety was not required, the shearing of a dozen of them did not occupy me long. Some of the more timid were alarmed at a formidable instrument coming so near to their noses, and would scarcely be persuaded by their shaven friends, to allow the operation to be finished. But when their chins were held up a second time, their fear of the instrument--the wild stare of their eyes--and the smile which they forced, formed a compound upon the rough savage countenance, not unworthy the pencil of a Hogarth. I was almost tempted to try what effect a little snip would produce; but our situation was too critical to admit of such experiments.

Everything being prepared for a retreat, the natives became vociferous for the boat to go up to the lagoon; and it was not without stratagem that we succeeded in getting down to the entrance of the stream, where the depth of water placed us out of their reach.

Our examination of the country was confined, by circumstances, to a general view. This part is called Alowrie, by the natives, and is very low and sandy near the sides of the rivulet. About four miles up it, to the north-west, is the lagoon; and behind, stands a semicircular range of hills, of which the highest is Hat Hill. The water in the lagoon was distinctly seen, and appeared to be several miles in circumference. The land round it is probably fertile, and the slopes of the back hills had certainly that appearance. The natives were in nothing, except language, different from those at Port Jackson; but their dogs, which are of the same species, seemed to be more numerous and familiar.

Soon after dark the sea breeze was succeeded by a calm; and at ten o'clock we rowed out of the rivulet, repassed Red Point, and at one in the morning came to an anchor in 5 fathoms, close to the northernmost of the two first rocky islets.[2] In the afternoon of the 28th, we got on shore under the high land to the north of Hat Hill and were able to cook provisions and take some repose without disturbance. The sandy beach was our bed; and after much fatigue, and passing three nights of cramp in Tom Thumb, it was to us a bed of down.

The shore in this part is mostly high and cliffy; and under the cliffs were lying black lumps, apparently of slaty stone, rounded by attrition. These were not particularly noticed, but Mr. Clarke, in his disastrous journey along the coast, afterwards made fires of them; and on a subsequent examination, Mr. Bass found a stratum of coal to run through the whole of these cliffs.

March 29. By rowing hard we got four leagues nearer home; and at night dropped our stone under another range of cliffs, more regular but less high than those near Hat Hill. At ten o'clock, the wind, which had been unsettled and driving electric clouds in all directions, burst out in a gale at south, and obliged us to get up the anchor immediately, and run before it. In a few minutes the waves began to break; and the extreme danger to which this exposed our little bark, was increased by the darkness of the night, and the uncertainty of finding any place of shelter. The shade of the cliffs over our heads, and the noise of the surfs breaking at their feet, were the directions by which our course was steered parallel to the coast.

Mr Bass kept the sheet of the sail in his hand, drawing in a few inches occasionally, when he saw a particularly heavy sea following. I was steering with an oar, and it required the utmost exertion and care to prevent broaching to; a single wrong movement, or a moment's inattention, would have sent us to the bottom. The task of the boy was to bale out the water which, in spite of every care, the sea threw in upon us.

After running near an hour in this critical manner, some high breakers were distinguished ahead; and behind them there appeared no shade of cliffs. It was necessary to determine, on the instant, what was to be done, for our bark could not live ten minutes longer. On coming to what appeared to be the extremity of the breakers, the boat's head was brought to the wind in a favourable moment, the mast and sail taken down, and the oars got out. Pulling then towards the reef during the intervals of the heaviest seas, we found it to terminate in a point; and in three minutes were in smooth water under its lee. A white appearance, further back, kept us a short time in suspense; but a nearer approach showed it to be the beach of a well-sheltered cove, in which we anchored for the rest of the night. So sudden a change, from extreme danger to comparatively perfect safety, excited reflections which kept us some time awake: we thought Providential Cove a well-adapted name for this place; but by the natives, as we afterwards learned, it is called Watta-Mowlee.

On landing next morning, March 30, water was found at the back of the beach. The country round the cove is, in general, sandy and barren. No natives were seen, but their traces were recent. The extremity of the reef, which afforded us such signal shelter, bore S.E. by E. from the centre of the beach, the north head of the cove E.N.E.; and except at the intermediate five points of the compass, Watta-Mowlee affords shelter for large boats, with anchorage on a fine sandy bottom.

Between three and four miles to the northward of this cove, we found the river, or rather port, which was the original place of our destination; and it having been a pilot named Hacking, from whom the first information of it had been received, it was named after him: by the natives it is called Deeban.

April 1st, was employed in the examination of the port. It is something more than one mile wide in the entrance; but soon contracts to half that space, and becomes shallow. Neither have the three arms, into which it afterwards branches out, any deep channel into them; although, within the second branch, there are from 3 to 8 fathoms. Finding there was no part accessible to a ship, beyond two miles from the entrance, nor any prospect of increasing our small stock of provisions, Port Hacking was quitted early in the morning of April 2.

The shores of the port are mostly rocky, particularly on the north side; but there is no want of grass or wood; and without doubt there are many culturable spots on the sides of the streams which descend, apparently from the inland mountains, into the uppermost branch. Two natives came down to us in a friendly manner, and seemed not to be unacquainted with Europeans. Their language differed somewhat from the Port Jackson dialect; but with the assistance of signs, we were able to make ourselves understood.

After sounding the entrance of Port Hacking in going out, and finding 3½ fathoms water, we steered N.E. by E for Cape Solander; and the same evening Tom Thumb was secured alongside the Reliance in Port Jackson.

In this little expedition, I had no other means of ascertaining the situations of places than by pocket-compass bearings and computed distances; which was done as noted adjacently.

After this expedition, the duties of the ship, and a voyage to the Cape of Good Hope by the way of Cape Horn, suspended our projects for some time. On the return of the Reliance to New South Wales, we found there the supracargo of the Sydney Cove, a ship from India commanded by Mr. G. A. Hamilton, which, having started a butt end, had been run on shore at Furneaux's Islands and wrecked. Mr. Clarke had left the ship, with the chief mate and others, in the long boat, designing for Port Jackson, in order to procure means for transporting the officers and people, and such part of the cargo as had been saved, to the same place; but being overtaken by a heavy south-east gale, their boat had been thrown on shore near Cape Howe, three-hundred miles from the colony, and stove to pieces.

There was no other prospect of safety for Mr. Clarke and his companions, than to reach Port Jackson on foot; and they commenced their march along the sea shore, scantily furnished with ammunition, and with less provisions. Various tribes of natives were passed, some of whom were friendly; but the hostility of others, and excessive fatigue, daily lessened the number of these unfortunate people; and when the provisions and ammunition failed, the diminution became dreadfully rapid. Their last loss was of the chief mate and carpenter, who were killed by Dilba, and other savages near Hat Hill;[3] and Mr. Clarke, with a sailor and one lascar, alone remained when they reached Watta-Mowlee. They were so exhausted, as to have scarcely strength enough to make themselves observed by a boat which was fishing off the cove; but were at length conveyed into her, and brought to Port Jackson.

Mr. Clarke gave the first information of the coal cliffs, near Hat Hill; and from him it was ascertained, that, besides the known bays, many small streams and inlets had interrupted his march along the shore, from Cape Howe to Watta-Mowlee; but that there were none which he had not been able to pass, either at the sea side, or by going a few miles round, into the country. A journal of his route was published in the Calcutta newspapers, some time in 1798.

The colonial schooner Francis had made one voyage to Furneaux's Islands, and brought from thence captain Hamilton, and part of his people and cargo. The same vessel was about to proceed thither a second time, and I was anxious to embrace that opportunity of exploring those extensive and little known lands; but the great repairs required by the Reliance would not allow of my absence. My friend Bass, less confined by his duty, made several excursions, principally into the interior parts behind Port Jackson; with a view to pass over the back mountains, and ascertain the nature of the country beyond them. His success was not commensurate to the perseverance and labour employed: the mountains were impassable; but the course of the river Grose, laid down in Plate VIII, resulted from one of these excursions.

SHORTLAND. 1797.

In September, a small colonial vessel having been carried off by convicts, lieutenant JOHN SHORTLAND, first of the Reliance,[4] went after them to the northward, in an armed boat. The expedition was fruitless, as to the proposed object; but in returning along the shore from Port Stephens, Mr. Shortland discovered a port in latitude 33°, capable of receiving small ships; and what materially added to the importance of the discovery, was a stratum of coal, found to run through the south head of the port, and also pervaded a cliffy island in the entrance. These coals were not only accessible to shipping, but of a superior quality to those in the cliffs near Hat Hill. The port was named after His Excellency governor HUNTER; and a settlement, called New Castle, has lately been there established. The entrance is narrow, and the deepest water (about three fathoms) close to the north-west side of the Coal Island; but no vessel of more than three hundred tons should attempt it.

BASS. 1797.

In December, Mr. GEORGE BASS obtained leave to make an expedition to the southward; and he was furnished with a fine whale boat and six weeks provisions by the governor, and a crew of six seamen from the ships. He sailed Dec. 3., in the evening; but foul and strong winds forced him into Port Hacking and Watta-Mowlee. On the 5th, in latitude 34° 38', he was obliged to stop in a small bight of the coast, a little south of Alowrie. The points of land there are basaltic; and on looking round amongst the burnt rocks scattered over a hollowed circular space behind the shore, Mr. Bass found a hole of twenty-five or thirty feet in diameter; into which the sea washed up by a subterraneous passage.

Dec. 6., he passed a long sloping projection which I have called Point Bass, lying about three leagues south of Alowrie. Beyond this point, the coast forms a sandy bay of four or five leagues in length, containing two small inlets; and the southernmost being accessible to the boat, Mr. Bass went in and stopped three days. This little place was found to deserve no better name than Shoals Haven. The entrance is mostly choaked up by sand, and the inner part with banks of sand and mud; there is, however, a small channel sufficiently deep for boats. The latitude was made to be 34° 52' south; the sloping Point Bass, to the northward, bore N. 12° E., and a steep head at the southern extremity of the bay, S. 35° E. The tide was found to rise seven or eight feet, and the time of high water to be about eight hours and a half after the moon passed over the meridian.

The great chain of high land, called the Blue Mountains, by which the colony at Port Jackson is prevented from extending itself to the west, appeared to Mr. Bass to terminate here, near the sea coast. The base of this southern extremity of the chain, he judged to extend twenty-five or thirty miles, in a south-western direction from Point Bass; after which it turns north-westward. In the direction of west from Shoals Haven, and in all the space to the south of that line, was an extensive, flat country, where a party desirous of penetrating into the interior might reasonably hope to avoid those impediments which, at the back of Port Jackson., have constantly proved insurmountable.

In an excursion from the boat towards the southern end of the mountains, Mr. Bass fell in with a considerable stream, which he traced down to the shore, about three miles north of Shoals' Haven: this is the first inlet of the long bay, which had been observed from the sea, with a bar running across the entrance. The soil on the southern bank of this stream he compared, for richness, to the banks of the Hawkesbury; and attributes this unusual fertility to the same cause: repeated inundations. In fact, the stream has since been found to descend from the mountains at twelve or fifteen miles from the coast, and to run along their southern extremity to the sea; so that it performs the same office here that the Hawkesbury does further north--that of being a channel for the waters which descend from the high back land; but as, in the heavy rains, it is also unequal to the task, the banks are overflowed, and the low country to the south and west is inundated and fertilized. There are, however, at the back of Shoals Haven, many thousand acres of open ground, whose soil is a rich vegetable mould, and now beyond the reach of the floods.

Dec. 10. The boat left Shoals Haven and entered Jervis Bay, a large open place of very unpromising appearance. On the north side of the entrance, between Point Perpendicular and Long Nose, there is a small cove, where a ship's boat might lie at half tide; and with a hose fill water from the back of the beach, at two pits which appeared to be always full. The best anchorage for ships seemed to be on the east side of the bay, between Long Nose and the northern beach, though they would not, even there, be entirely land-locked. Bowen's Island lies a quarter of a mile from the south side of the entrance, but the passage between does not admit any thing larger than boats. There is a small beach at the back of the island, off which ships might anchor in 8 fathoms sandy bottom, and be sheltered as far round as south-east; but with the wind nearer to east they would be exposed.

The east shore of Jervis Bay runs, for twelve or fifteen miles, so near to north from the entrance, that it is not, at the head, more than four hundred yards across to the shore of the long outer bay. The piece of land, which is thus made a narrow peninsula, is rather high, with a face of steep cliffs toward the sea. The rocks on the inner side bear strong marks of volcanic fire; and being disposed in parallel layers, their inclination to the west is very evident: quantities of pumice stone were scattered along the shores.

The country round the bay is mostly barren. On the eastern side it is rocky, with heath and brush-wood; the west is low, swampy, and sandy, with some partial exceptions; but on the south side there are grassy spaces amongst the brush-wood which might afford pasturage for cattle.

Jervis Bay was quitted Dec. 13., and at noon the Pigeon House bore W. by N. In the evening Mr. Bass stopped in a cove, which Point Upright shelters from northern winds; and he employed the next day in looking round the country. The vallies and slopes of the hills were found to be generally fertile; but there being nothing of particular interest in this place, it was quitted on the 15th. Some small islands lying close under the shore (in Bateman Bay), bore west at noon; and the night was passed at anchor under a point, in latitude 36° 00', where, the wind being foul on the 16th, Mr. Bass laid the boat on shore, and proceeded to examine the surrounding country.

At eight or nine miles from the coast is a ridge of hummocky hills, extending to the southward; but the space between these hills and the sea is low and in great part occupied by salt swamps. The sea was found to have an entrance at the back of the point, and to form a considerable lagoon, which communicated with the swamps by means of several branching arms. The soil, as may be supposed, was generally bad, the sloping sides of some of the hills being alone capable of any utility. In a round of twelve or fourteen miles Mr. Bass could not find a drop of fresh water, or see a native. There were, however, many huts, and he traced the paths from them down to holes dug in the lowest grounds; but these were then all dried up, and the country in general seemed to be suffering from drought.

Dec. 17. The wind having veered to N. N. W., the boat was launched, and proceeded to the southward. Mount Dromedary was passed at eleven; and an island of about two miles in circuit was seen lying off it, a few miles to the eastward: the latitude at noon was 36° 23'. At four, the fair breeze died away, and a strong wind, which burst forth from the south, obliged Mr. Bass to run for a gap in the land, which had just before been noticed. Here, on a little beach at the mouth of an inlet, across which the sea was breaking, the boat was hauled up for the night. Next morning, the inlet being free of breakers, he entered the prettiest little model of a harbour he had ever seen. Unfortunately it is but a model; for although the shelter within be complete for small craft, yet the depth over the bar is too small, even for boats, except at high water, when there is eight or nine feet. This little place was named Barmouth Creek, and lies, according to Mr. Bass' computation, in 36° 47' south. The country round, so far as was examined, is rocky and barren near the sea; and towards the head of the creek, it is low and penetrated by the salt swamps.

Dec. 19. At day light Mr. Bass continued his course to the southward., with a fair breeze. At seven he discovered TWO-FOLD BAY; but unwilling to lose a fair wind, reserved the examination of it for his return. At five in the evening the wind came at S. S. W.; and he anchored under the lee of a point, but could not land. A sea breeze from E. N. E. next day, enabled him to continue onward; and at eleven, he bore away west, round Cape Howe, whose latitude was observed to be 37° 30'. In the evening he landed at the entrance of a lagoon, one mile north of the Ram Head, in order to take in as much fresh water as possible; for it was to be feared that a want of this necessary article might oblige him to discontinue his pursuit, at a time when, from the coast being unexplored, it would become more than ever interesting.

Dec. 21. A gale set in at W. S. W., and continued for nine days without intermission. This time was employed in examining the country, which, though hilly in external appearance, was found to be mostly low, sandy, and wet. The hills have a slight covering of green upon them, but consist of little else than sand; and from what could be seen of the back country, the soil there is scarcely better. The vallies are overgrown with long grass, ferns, brush-wood, and climbing plants, so as to be almost impenetrable; yet even there the soil is good for nothing.

At every landing place, from Jervis Bay to Barmouth Creek, the fresh water had been observed to diminish both in quantity and quality; and upon this coast of sand the difficulty of procuring it was expected to be very great. It was, on the contrary, plentiful; there being many little runs which drained out from the sand hills, and either trickled over the rocky spots at their feet, or sank through the beaches into the sea.

The western gale being at length succeeded by a breeze at E. N. E., Mr. Bass left the Ram Head early on the 31st. His course was W. by S., close to a low, sandy coast; the beach being interrupted by small, rocky points, not oftener than once in ten or fifteen miles. The back land consisted of short ridges of irregular hills, lying at no great distance from the sea. At noon, the latitude was 37° 42'; and the distance run from the Ram Head, by computation, was thirty or thirty-five miles.

The furthest land seen by captain Cook, is marked at fifteen leagues from the Ram Head, and called Point Hicks; but at dusk Mr. Bass had run much more than that distance close along the shore, and could perceive no point or projection which would be distinguishable from a ship: the coast continued to be straight, low, and sandy, similar to what had been passed in the morning. There arose many large smokes from behind the beach; probably from the sides of lagoons, with which, there was reason to think, the back country abounded.

1798.

The breeze continuing to be fresh and favourable, Mr. Bass ventured to steer onward in the night, and kept the shore close a-bord. At two in the morning, the increased hollowness of the waves made him suspect the water was becoming shallow; and he hauled off for an hour, until there was sufficient daylight to distinguish the land. It was still low, level, and sandy, and trended S. W. by W., nearly as the boat was steering. At seven o'clock, high land appeared at a considerable distance in the south-west; and the beach then trended in the same direction. It, however, changed soon afterward, to run nearly west; and Mr. Bass quitted it to keep on his course for the high land. The latitude at noon was 38° 41'; and the difference made from the noon before, upon the average course of S. W. by W., makes the distance run 107 miles; which, added to the preceding thirty or thirty-five, gives the length of the beach from the Ram Head, to be about 140 miles.[5]

The high land extended from the bearing of S. W. by S. to W. N. W., and was distant in the latter direction two or three leagues. North of it there was a deep bight; and further eastward, two or three places in the Long Beach which had the appearance of inlets. To the south there were several rocky islets; and great numbers of petrels, and other seabirds, were flying about the boat.

From the latitude of the high land, Mr. Bass considered it to be that seen by captain Furneaux (or supposed to have been seen), in 39°; and consequently, that he had traced the unknown space between Point Hicks and Furneaux's Land. His course was now steered to pass round this land; but on coming abreast of the rocky islets, a hummock appeared above the horizon in the S. E. by S., and presently, a larger one at S. ½ W.; and being unable to fetch the first, he steered for the latter, which proved to be an island; and at six in the evening, he anchored under its lee. Vast numbers of gulls and other birds were roosting upon it, and on the rocks were many seals; but the surf would not admit of landing. This island was judged to be thirty miles, S. by W., from the situation at noon.

Jan. 2. The wind was strong at E. N. E.; and Mr. Bass being apprehensive that the boat could not fetch the high main land, determined to steer southward for the islands, in the hope of procuring some rice from the wreck of the ship Sydney Cove, to eke out his provisions. The wind, however, became unfavourable to him, veering to E. S. E; so that with the sea which drove the boat to leeward, the course to noon was scarcely so good as S. S. W. The latitude observed was then 39° 51'; and no land being in sight, the prospect of reaching Furneaux's Islands became very faint. At four o'clock an accident caused it to be totally given up: water was observed to rush in fast through the boat's side, and made it absolutely necessary to go upon the other tack. The latitude to which Mr. Bass supposed himself arrived, was something to the south of 40°; and the weather was clear enough for land of moderate height to have been seen five leagues further, had there been any within that distance.

The boat was then kept north-eastward, towards Furneaux's Land. At nine in the evening, the wind blew hard at S. E. by E., accompanied by a hollow, irregular sea, which put our enterprising discoverer and his boat's crew into the greatest danger; but the good qualities of his little bark, with careful steerage, carried him through this perilous night. On the 3rd, at six o'clock the land was seen; and in the afternoon, whilst standing in to look for a place of shelter, a smoke and several people were observed upon a small island not far from the main coast. On rowing up, they proved to be, not natives, to Mr. Bass' great surprise, but Europeans. They were convicts who, with others, had run away with a boat from Port Jackson, in the intention of plundering the wreck of the Sydney Cove; and not being able to find it, their companions, thinking their number too great, had treacherously left them upon this island, whilst asleep. These people were seven in number; and during the five weeks they had been on this desert spot, had subsisted on petrels, to which a seal was occasionally added. Mr. Bass promised to call at the island, on his return; and in the mean time, proceeded to the west side of the high main land, where he anchored, but could not get on shore.

Jan. 4. The wind being at north-east, he continued his course onward, steering W. N. W. round an open bay; and afterwards N. W. by W., as the coast generally trended. The shore consisted of long, shallow bights, in which the land was low and sandy; but the intermediate rocky points were generally steep, with a ridge of hills extending from them, into the interior, as far as could be distinguished. In the evening an inlet was discovered, with many shoals at the entrance; and the deep channel being not found till a strong tide made it unattainable, Mr. Bass waited for high water; he then entered a spacious harbour which, from its relative position to the hitherto known parts of the coast, was named WESTERN PORT. It lies, according to the boat's run, about sixty miles N. W. by W. ½ W. from Furneauxs Land; and its latitude is somewhere about 38° 25' south.[6] The time of high water is near half an hour after the moon's passage over the meridian, and the rise of tide from ten to fourteen feet.

The examination of this new and important discovery, the repairs of the boat, and the continuance of strong winds, kept Mr. Bass thirteen days in Western Port. His sketch of it has since been superseded by the more regular examination of ensign Barralier, copied into the chart, where its form, situation, and extent will be best seen. The land upon its borders is, generally, low and level; but the hills rise as they recede into the country, and afford an agreeable prospect from the port. Wherever Mr. Bass landed, he found the soil to be a light, brown mould, which becomes peaty in the lowest grounds. Grass and ferns grow luxuriantly, and yet the country is but thinly timbered. Patches of brush wood are frequent, particularly on the eastern shore, where they are some miles in extent; and there the soil is a rich, vegetable mould. The island (since called Phillip Island) which shelters the port, is mostly barren, but is covered with shrubs and some diminutive trees.

Mr. Bass had great difficulty in procuring good water, arising, as he judged, from unusual dryness in the season; and the head of the winding creek on the east side of the port, was the sole place where it had not a brackish taste. The mud banks at the entrance of the creek may be passed at half tide by the largest boats; and within it, there is at all times a sufficient depth of water.

No more than four natives were seen, and their shyness prevented communication; the borders of the port, however, bore marks of having been much frequented, but the want of water seemed to have occasioned a migration to the higher lands. Kangaroos did not appear to be numerous; but black swans went by hundreds in a flight, and ducks, a small, but excellent kind, by thousands; and the usual wild fowl were in abundance.

The seventh week of absence from Port Jackson had expired, by the time Mr. Bass was ready to sail from Western Port; and the reduced state of his provisions forced him, very reluctantly, to turn the boat's head homeward.

Jan. 18. At daylight, he sailed with a fresh wind at west, which increased to a gale in the afternoon, with a heavy swell from the south-west; and he sought shelter behind a cape since named Cape Liptrap. Next morning, he ran over to the islands on the west side of Furneaux's Land; but was obliged to return to his former place of shelter, where a succession of gales kept him until the 26th. A quantity of petrels had been taken on the islands, and this week of detention was mostly employed in salting them for the homeward bound voyage.

At length, Mr. Bass was able to execute the project he had formed for the seven convicts. It was impossible to take them all into the boat; therefore to five, whom he set upon the main land, he gave a musket, half his ammunition, some hooks and lines, a light cooking kettle, and directions how to proceed in their course toward Port Jackson. The remaining two, one of whom was old and the other diseased, he took into the boat with the consent of the crew, who readily agreed to divide the daily bannock into nine with them. He then bore away, with a fresh wind at west, round Furneaux's Land.[7]

From Jan.26 to Feb. 1, Mr. Bass was detained by eastern gales from proceeding on his return. The boat lay in Sealers Cove, whilst he occupied the time in examining Wilson's Promontory. The height of this vast cape, though not such as would be considered extraordinary by seamen, is yet strikingly so from being contrasted with the low, sandy land behind it; and the firmness and durability of its structure make it worthy of being, what there was reason to believe it, the boundary point of a large strait, and a corner stone to the new continent. It is a lofty mass of hard granite, of about twenty miles long, by from six to fourteen in breadth. The soil upon it is shallow and barren; though the brush wood, dwarf gum trees, and some smaller vegetation, which mostly cover the rocks, give it a deceitful appearance to the eye of a distant observer.

Looking from the top of the promontory to the northward, there is seen a single ridge of mountains, which comes down, out of the interior country, in a southern direction for the promontory; but sloping off gradually to a termination, it leaves a space of twelve or sixteen miles of low, sandy land between them. This low land is nearly intersected by a considerable lagoon on the west, and a large shoal bay, named Corner Inlet, on the east side; and it seemed prob-able, that this insulated mass of granite has been entirely surrounded by the sea at no very distant period of time. There were no inhabitants on Wilson's Promontory; but, upon the sandy neck, some were seen near the borders of the inlets. The few birds were thought to have a sweeter note than those of Port Jackson.

Four small, barren islands lie seven or eight miles to the northeast, from Sealers Cove. The northernmost of them was visited, and found to be about one mile and a half in circuit, ascending gradually from the shore, to a hill of moderate elevation in the centre. There was neither tree nor shrub upon it; but the surface was mostly covered with tufts of coarse grass, amongst which the seals had every where made paths and the petrels their burrows. Mr. Bass was of opinion, that upon these islands, and those lying scattered round the promontory, which are all more or less fre-quented by seals, a commercial speculation on a small scale might be made with advantage. The place of shelter for the vessel would be Sealers Cove, on the main land; which, though small, and apparently exposed to east winds, would be found convenient and tolerably secure: fresh water is there abundant, and a sufficiency of wood at hand to boil down any quantity of blubber likely to be procured.

The observed latitude of the cove was 38° 50';[8] and the rise of tide found to be ten or eleven feet, ten hours and a quarter after the moon passed over the meridian. The flood, after sweeping south-westward along the great eastern beach, strikes off for the Seal Islands and the promontory, and then runs westward, past it, at the rate of two or three miles an hour: the ebb tide sets to the eastward. "Whenever it shall be decided," says Mr. Bass in his journal, "that the opening between this and Van Diemen's Land is a strait, this rapidity of tide, and the long south-west swell that seems to be continually rolling in upon the coast to the westward, will then be accounted for."

Feb. 2., Mr. Bass sailed to Corner Inlet; and next day fell in with the five convicts, whom he put across to the long beach.[9] but was himself unable to proceed until the 9th, in consequence of foul winds. Corner Inlet is little else than a large flat, the greater part of it being dry at low water. There is a long shoal on the outside of the entrance, which is to be avoided by keeping close to the shore of the promontory; but when the tide is out the depth, except in holes, no where exceeds 2½ fathoms. A vessel drawing twelve or thirteen feet may lie safely under the high land, from which there are some large runs of most excellent water. The tide rises a foot less here than in Sealers Cove, and flows an hour later; arising, probably, from the flood leaving it in an eddy, by setting past, and not into the inlet.

Feb. 9, Corner Inlet was quitted with a strong south-west wind, and Mr. Bass steered E. by N. along the shore. At the distance of five miles, he passed the mouth of a shallow opening in the low sandy beach, from which a half-moon shoal stretches three miles to the south-eastward. Four or five miles further, a lesser opening of the same kind was passed; and by noon, when the latitude was 38° 34' (probably 38° 46'), he had arrived at the point of the long beach, which in going out, had been quitted to steer for the promontory. His general course from thence was N. E. by E. along the shore, until nine o'clock, when judging the coast must begin to trend more eastwardly, he again steered E. b. N.; the wind blowing a fresh gale at W. S. W., with a following sea. At daylight, Feb. 10, the beach was distant two miles, and trending parallel to the boat's course.

The western gale died away in the morning, and was succeeded by one from the eastward. The boat was in no condi-tion to struggle against a foul wind; and Mr. Bass, being unwilling to return to Corner Inlet, ventured through a heavy surf and took refuge upon the beach; having first observed the latitude to be 37° 47' south.

The country at the back of the beach consisted of dried-up swamps and barren sand hills. Some natives came down with very little hesitation, and conducted themselves amicably: they appeared never to have seen or heard of white people before.

Feb. 11. the foul wind had ceased to blow, and the clouds threatened another gale from the south-west. So soon as there was sufficient daylight, the boat was launched, and at four the same afternoon anchored under the Rain Head. Mr. Bass was kept there till the 14th in the evening; when a strong breeze sprung up suddenly at south-west, and he sailed immediately, passing Cape Howe at ten o'clock. By noon of the 15th, he had reached Two-fold Bay, where the latitude was observed to be 36° 53' south;[10] and having ascertained that Snug Cove, on its north-west side, afford-ed shelter for shipping, he steered northward, and passed Mount Dromedary soon after midnight. At noon, Feb. 16, Mr. Bass landed upon a small island lying under the shore to the south-east of the Pigeon House, to examine a pole which he had before observed, and supposed might have been set up as a signal by shipwrecked people; but it proved to be nothing more than the dead stump of a tree, much taller and more straight than the others. He sailed next morn-ing; but the wind hung so much in the north and east quarters that he was forced successively into Jervis Bay, Shoals Haven, and Port Hacking; and it was not until the 24th at night, that our adventurous discoverer terminated his dan-gerous and fatiguing voyage, by entering within the heads of Port Jackson.

It should be remembered, that Mr. Bass sailed with only six weeks provisions; but with the assistance of occasional supplies of petrels, fish, seal's flesh, and a few geese and black swans, and by abstinence, he had been enabled to pro-long his voyage beyond eleven weeks. His ardour and perseverance were crowned, in despite of the foul winds which so much opposed him, with a degree of success not to have been anticipated from such feeble means. In three hundred miles of coast, from Port Jackson to the Ram Head, he added a number of particulars which had escaped captain Cook; and will always escape any navigator in a first discovery, unless he have the time and means of joining a close examination by boats, to what may be seen from the ship.

Our previous knowledge of the coast scarcely extended beyond the Ram Head; and there began the harvest in which Mr. Bass was ambitious to place the first reaping hook. The new coast was traced three hundred miles; and instead of trending southward to join itself to Van Diemen's Land, as captain Furneaux had supposed, he found it, beyond a certain point, to take a direction nearly opposite, and to assume the appearance of being exposed to the buffetings of an open sea. Mr. Bass, himself, entertained no doubt of the existence of a wide strait, separating Van Diemen's Land from New South Wales; and he yielded with the greatest reluctance to the necessity of returning, before it was so fully ascertained as to admit of no doubt in the minds of others. But he had the satisfaction of placing at the end of his new coast, an extensive and useful harbour, surrounded with a country superior to any other known in the southern parts of New South Wales.

A voyage expressly undertaken for discovery in an open boat, and in which six hundred miles of coast, mostly in a boisterous climate, was explored, has not, perhaps, its equal in the annals of maritime history. The public will award to its high spirited and able conductor, alas! now no more, an honourable place in the list of those whose ardour stands most conspicuous for the promotion of useful knowledge.

FLINDERS. 1798.

During the time that Mr. Bass was absent on his expedition in the whale boat, the Francis schooner was again sent with captain Hamilton to the wreck of his ship the Sydney Cove; to bring up what remained of the cargo at Preservation Island, and the few people who were left in charge. On this occasion I was happy enough to obtain governor Hunter's permission to embark in the schooner; in order to make such observations serviceable to geography and navigation, as circumstances might afford; and Mr. Reed, the master, was directed to forward these views as far as was consistent with the main objects of his voyage.

Feb. 1, we sailed out of Port Jackson with a fair wind; and on the following noon, the observed latitude was 35° 42', being 14' south of account. I prevailed on Mr. Reed to stand in for the land, which was then visible through the haze; and at sunset, we reached into Bateman Bay.[11] When the two rocky islets in the middle of the bay bore S. by W. ¼ W., a short mile, we had 8 fathoms water, and 6 fathoms a mile further in. The north head is steep with a rock lying off it; but Bateman Bay falls back too little from the line of the coast to afford shelter against winds from the eastward. The margin of the bay is mostly a beach, behind which lie sandy, rocky hills of moderate elevation.

In the morning of the 3rd, we steered S. by W. along the shore; and saw, in latitude about 35* 58', and eight or nine miles from the south point of Bateman Bay, a small opening like a river running south-westward. It was here that Mr. Bass found a lagoon, with extensive salt swamps behind it, and observed the latitude 36° 00'. At noon, the east point of the opening bore N. ¼ W. seven miles, and the top of Mount Dromedary was visible above the haze; but no observation could be taken for the latitude.

Soon after noon, land was in sight to the S. S. E., supposed to be the Point Dromedary of captain Cook's chart; but, to my surprise, it proved to be an island not laid down, though lying near two leagues from the coast. The whole length of this island is about one mile and a quarter, north and south; the two ends are a little elevated, and produce small trees; but the sea appeared to break occasionally over the middle part. It is probably frequented by seals, since many were seen in the water whilst passing at the distance of two miles. This little island, I was afterwards informed, had been seen in the ship Surprise, and honoured with the name of Montague.

When captain Cook passed this part of the coast his distance from it was five leagues, and too great for its form to be accurately distinguished. There is little doubt that Montague Island was then seen, and mistaken for a point running out from under Mount Dromedary; for its distance from the mount, and bearing of about N. 75° E., will place it in 36° 17', or within one minute of the latitude assigned to the point in captain Cook's chart.

At six in the evening, Mount Dromedary was set at N. 40° W. five leagues. We steered S. S. W. until two in the morning, when the land was so near as made it necessary to alter the course; and at daybreak of the 4th, the shore was not more than three miles distant; it was moderately high and rocky, and at the back were many hummocky hills. Having been much upon deck in the night, I then retired to rest; and in the mean time, the schooner passed Mr. Bass's Twofold Bay without its being noticed. At nine we came abreast of a smooth, sloping point which, from its appearance, and being unnoticed in captain Cook's chart, I named GREEN CAPE. The shore, for about seven miles to the northward, lies N. 16° W., and is rocky and nearly straight, and well covered with wood: the Cape itself is grassy. On the south side, the coast trends west, three or four miles, into a sandy bight, and then southward to Cape Howe.

The latitude at noon was 37° 25', giving a current of twenty miles to the south, in two days; Green Cape bore N. by E. four leagues, and Cape Howe S. by W. five or six miles. Captain Cook lays down the last in 37° 26', in his chart; but the above observation places it in 37° 30½', which I afterwards found to agree with an observation of Mr. Bass, taken on the west side of the cape. The shore abreast of the schooner was between one and two miles distant; it was mostly beach, lying at the feet of sandy hillocks which extend from behind Green Cape to the pitch of Cape Howe. There were several fires upon the shore; and near one of them, upon an eminence, stood seven natives, silently contemplating the schooner as she passed.

On coming abreast of Cape Howe, the wind chopped round to the south-west, and the dark clouds which settled over the land concealed it from our view; we observed, however, that it trended to the west, but sought in vain for the small island mentioned by captain Cook as lying close off the Cape.[12]

Our latitude was 38° 30' next day, or 38' south of account, although the wind had been. and was still from that direction. Mr. Reed then steered W. by N., to get in again with the coast; and on the following noon, we were in 38° 16' and, by account, 22' of longitude to the west of Point Hicks. The schooner was kept more northward in the afternoon; at four o'clock a moderately high, sloping hill was visible in the N. by W., and at seven a small rocky point on the beach bore N. 50° W. three or four leagues. The shore extended E. N. E. and W. S. W., and was low and sandy in front; but at some miles distance inland, there was a range of hills with wood upon them, though scarcely sufficient to hide their sandy surface.

At five in the morning of the 7th, the rocky point bore N. E. ½ N. six or seven miles, and the furthest visible part of the beach W. ½ S. The southern wind had died away in the night; and a breeze springing up at N. E. by E., we steered before it along the same low, sandy shore as seen in the evening. The hills which arose at three or four leagues behind the beach, appeared to retire further back as we advanced westward; they would, however, be visible to a ship in fine weather, long before the front land could be seen.

The observed latitude at noon was 38° 17' south, and by two sets of distances of the sun east of the moon, reduced up from the morning, the longitude was 147° 37' east.[13] The beach was six or seven miles distant, but after obtaining the noon's observation, we closed more in; and at two or three miles off, found a sandy bottom with 11 fathoms fathoms of line. Our course along the shore from two to four o'clock, was S. W. ¾ S., with a current in our favour. The beach then trended more to the west; but the breeze having veered to E. by N. and become strong, with much sea, it was considered too dangerous to follow it any longer. At five, the western and most considerable of two shallow-looking openings bore north-west, seven or eight miles; and at sunset, some high and remarkable land was perceived bearing S. W. by W., which proved to be the same discovered by Mr. Bass, and now bearing the name of Wilson's Promontory. It appeared, from a partial view given by a break in the clouds, as if cut in two, and the parts had been removed to some distance from each other: the gap was probably Sealers Cove.

The state of the weather, and the land to leeward, made it necessary to haul up south-eastward, close upon a wind. At day-break of the 8th, neither Wilson's Promontory nor any other land to the northward could be seen; but between the bearings of N. 84° and S. 63° E., six or eight miles distant, there was land rather high and irregular, with a cliffy shore; and a separate cluster of rocky islets bore south to S. 16° W., from three to five miles. We passed close to these last, at six o'clock, and perceived that the tide, which before had set to leeward, was then turned to the east: the moon had just before passed the meridian.

This small cluster consists of a steep island, near one mile in length, of two smaller round islets, and two or three rocks; one of which obtained the name of Judgment Rock, from its resemblance to an elevated seat. The higher and more considerable land to the eastward was seen, as we advanced, to divide itself also into several parts. This group is principally composed of three islands; and between the largest on the east and two others on the west, there appeared to be a deep channel. The other parts are rocks, which lie scattered mostly off the north-western island. These two clusters were called KENT'S GROUPS, in honour of my friend captain William Kent, then commander of the Supply.

Our latitude at noon was 39° 38'; the steep island of the small group bore N. 50° W., and the passage through the larger islands N. 12° E., six or eight miles. This observation places the centre of the passage and of the large group, in about 39° 29' south; and from the lunar observations of the preceding day, brought on by log, (for unfortunately I had no time keeper,) it should lie in longitude 147° 25' east. It is, however, to be observed, that a fortuitous compensation of errors can alone render a dead reckoning correct in the way of such tides as we had experienced during the last twenty-four hours.[14]

By keeping the wind to the southward, we came up with a pyramidal-shaped rock through which there is a chasm: it bore W. 8° S. one mile, at four o'clock, when the eastern island of Kents large group was set at N. 17° E., five or six leagues. At six, the pyramid bore N. 38° W. five miles, and high land came in sight to the eastward: one piece extended from N. 75° to S. 87° E., apparently about five leagues distant, and the bluff, southern end of another range of hills bore S. 51° E., something further. Captain Hamilton supposed these to be parts of the land he had seen to the north-west of Preservation Island, where the wreck of his ship was lying; but whether they might belong to Furneaux's Islands or to the main, was unknown to him. He had always gone to, and returned from his island by the east side of this land; and the wind having veered northward, the schooner was kept as much to the north-east as possible, in order to pursue the same track.

We came up with a low point or island at eleven at night, when the wind died away. At six in the morning of Feb. 9., the northern land extended from N. 49° E. three leagues, to S. 47° E. four or five miles; the southern land bore S. 24° to 2° E. five or six leagues, and seemed to form a hilly, separate island; although, as low land was seen between them, the two may probably be connected: there was also a cliffy island bearing north, seven or eight miles. On a breeze springing up from south-west, our course was steered to pass close round the northern land; but finding much rippling water between it and two islands called the Sisters by captain Furneaux, we passed round them also, and then hauled to the southward along the eastern shore.

This northern land, or island as it proved to be, has some ridges of sandy-looking hills extending north and south between the two shores; and they are sufficiently high to be visible ten leagues from a ship's deck in clear weather. On the west side of the north point, the hills come nearly down to the water; but on the east side, there is two or three miles of flat land between their feet and the shore. The small trees and brush wood which partly covered the hills, seemed to shoot out from sand and rock; and if the vallies and low land within be not better than what appeared from the sea, the northern part of this great island is sterile indeed. The Sisters are not so high as some of the hills on the great island, and are less sandy: the small, cliffy island, which lies eight or nine miles, nearly west, from the inner Sister, had no appearance of sand.

Whilst passing round the north end of Furneaux's Islands, I experienced how little dependence was to be put in compass bearings, in such, at least, as were taken with my best instrument, the steering compass of the schooner. The south extreme of the inner Sister shut on with the north-west point of the great island at E. ¾ S., magnetic bearing; but after passing round, they shut, on the other side, at W. by N. ¼ N.; so that, to produce an agreement, it was necessary to allow half a point more east variation on the first, when the schooner's head was N. by W., than on the last, when it was S. S. E. In a second instance, the north end of the outer Sister opened from the inner one at N. E. ½ N.; but they came on again at S. W. ½ W., making a difference of a whole point, when the head was N. by W. and E. S. E. These bearings were probably not correct within two or three degrees; but they showed that a change in the course steered produced an alteration in the compass.

The observed latitude at noon was 39° 50 1/3', the centre of the outer Sister bore N. 34° W., nearly five leagues, and our distance from the sandy, eastern shore of the great island was about six miles. At two, o'clock, we came up with an island of three miles in length, and nearly the same space distant from a sandy projection of the great island. The passage between them is much contracted by shoal spits of sand which run out from each side; and it seemed doubtful, whether the water were deep enough in any part of the channel to admit a ship. The form of the land here is somewhat remarkable: upon the low projection of the great island there are three pyramidal hills, which obtained the name of the Patriarchs, and stand apart from the more western high land; and upon the south-west end of the island opposite there is also a pyramid, which, with other hills near it, presents some resemblance to the Lion's Head and Rump at the Cape of Good Hope. This island and two rocky islets lying off its south-east end were afterwards called the Babel Isles. The largest is covered with tufted grass and brush wood; and the whole appeared to be much frequented by shags, sooty petrels, and other sea birds.

We had scarcely passed the Babel Isles, when the wind, which had been at W. by S., chopped round to the southward, with squally weather, and drove the schooner off to the north-east. In the night, it became less unfavourable; and at noon of the 10th, our latitude was 40° 3½'; the isles bore N. 78° W., three or four leagues, and the high land of Cape Barren S. 13° to 34° W. Having a fair wind in the afternoon, we passed along the outskirts of the Bay of Shoals, without perceiving any breakers; but in the space between the great island and the land of Cape Barren there were many rocks, and a low island of three or four miles long, with a hill in the middle, lay at the entrance of the opening.

The high part of Cape-Barren Island, but particularly the peak, may be seen eleven, and perhaps more leagues from a ship's deck. The extremity of the cape is a low point, which runs out two miles east from the high land; and off this point lies a flat, rocky islet and a peaked rock. The shore is sandy on each side of the Cape point: it trends N. 40° W., for about five miles, on one side, and S. 49° W., past two sandy bights on the other, to a rocky projection on which are two whitish cones, shaped like rhinoceros' horns.

We steered south-westward, in the evening, round the Cape point, and were sufficiently close to hear the bellowing of the seals upon the islet. Arrived off Cone Point, the schooner was hauled offshore; and the wind becoming strong and unfavourable in the night, it was not until the evening of the 12th, that we got to anchor in Hamilton's Road, at the east end of Preservation Island. This road is sheltered from all winds, except between south and S. S. E.; and these do not throw in much sea: the bottom is good-holding sand, in from 4 to 3 fathoms, at a quarter of a mile from the beach. The ship Sydney Cove had been run on shore between Preservation and Rum Islands, and part of her hull was still lying there; but the sea thrown in by western gales had, in great measure, broken her up, and scattered the beams, timbers, and parts of the cargo, upon all the neighbouring shores.

My purpose of making an expedition amongst the islands was delayed by the schooner's boat being out of repair; but in the mean time, a base line was measured round the sandy north-east end of Preservation Island, and angles taken from all the conspicuous points.

Feb. 16. The boat was fitted, and I made an excursion of five days, through the channel which separates the land of Cape Barren from the more southern islands. It is called ARMSTRONG'S CHANNEL, from the master of the Supply, who had gone to afford assistance in saving the cargo of the Sydney Cove, and was the first to pass through it on his return towards Port Jackson; but he never arrived there, having, in all probability, perished at sea with his sloop and crew. The stations whence angles were taken for a survey of the channel and surrounding lands, were--1st. Point Womat, a rocky projection of Cape-Barren Island, where a number of the new animals, called womat, were seen, and some killed. 2nd. Battery Island; so named from four rocks upon it, resembling mounted guns; sooty petrels, and large hair seals were found there. 3rd. The sandy north-east point of Clarke's Island; which, with the opposite Sloping Point, forms the narrowest part of the channel. Its width was found to be three-quarters of a mile, but is somewhat contracted by rocks lying on the south side. These rocks were also frequented by hair seals, and some of them (the old males) were of an enormous size, and of extraordinary power. I levelled my gun at one, which was sitting on the top of a rock with his nose extended up towards the sun, and struck him with three musket balls. He rolled over, and plunged into the water; but in less than half an hour had taken his former station and attitude. On firing again, a stream of blood spouted forth from his breast to some yards distance, and he fell back, senseless. On examination, the six balls were found lodged in his breast; and one, which occasioned his death, had pierced the heart: his weight was equal to that of a common ox.

The 4th station was on Sloping Point, where an aculeated ant-eater was caught, and some quartz crystals were picked up from the shore. 5th, At the east side of Kent's Bay, under the peak of Cape Barren. This peak I wished to ascend, in order to obtain a view of the surrounding lands, particularly of an extensive piece to the southward, which, from the smokes continually seen there, was supposed to be a part of Van Diemen's Land; but the almost impenetrable brush wood, with which the sides of the peak and surrounding hills were covered, defeated my purpose.

The 6th station was at Passage Point. The 7th, on Cone Point, where the number of seals exceeded every thing we had, any of us, before witnessed; and they were smaller, and of a different species from those which frequented Armstrong's Channel. Instead of the bull-dog nose, and thinly-set, sandy hair, these had sharp-pointed noses, and the general colour of the hair approached to a black; but the tips were of a silver grey, and underneath was a fine, whitish, thick fur. The commotion excited by our presence, in this assemblage of several thousand timid animals, was very interesting to me, who knew little of their manners. The young cubs huddled together in the holes of the rocks, and moaned piteously; those more advanced scampered and rolled down to the water, with their mothers; whilst some of the old males stood up in defence of their families, until the terror of the sailors bludgeons became too strong to be resisted. Those who have seen a farm yard, well stocked with pigs, calves, sheep, oxen, and with two or three litters of puppies, with their mothers, in it, and have heard them all in tumult together, may form a good idea of the confused noise of the seals at Cone Point. The sailors killed as many of these harmless, and not unamiable creatures, as they were able to skin during the time necessary for me to take the requisite angles; and we then left the poor affrighted multitude to recover from the effect of our inauspicious visit.

My 8th station was taken, in returning to the schooner, upon the south end of the eastern Passage Isle; 9th, the south-west end of the western Passage Isle; and 10th, the south-east point of Clarke's Island. The 11th and last station was at Look-out Head, the bearings from which included some parts of the southern land, between the extremes of S. 20° 20' E. and S. 59° 35' W. At these different stations, the needle of the theodolite was sometimes found to vary one or two degrees from itself, as it had done at Preservation Island; an effect which I attribute to the attraction of the rocks, having since experienced the same, and even greater, differences in most places where the rocks, as here, are granitic. In the wider parts of Armstrong's Channel there are many shoals of sand on each side, but a passage of sufficient width and depth is swept out by the tides, for ships to go through in safety. The bottom is either rocky or sandy: rocky in the deep and narrow parts, where the tides run three or four miles in an hour; and sandy in the bights and shoaler places. The sand of the beaches is mostly granitic, but it sometimes consists of black metallic particles, such as are found in the stone of the islands.

It was not until Feb. 25 that the remains of the Sydney-Cove's cargo were all on board, and that a favourable change in the wind permitted us to sail for Port Jackson. These four days of detention enabled me to continue the survey along the south side of Preservation Island, and as far as the Bay of Rocks upon that of Cape Barren. A meridian altitude from the south horizon, observed under more favourable circumstances than two others before taken, gave 40° 28' for the latitude of Hamilton's Road. The longitude is 19' 20" west of Cape Barren; and therefore should be 148° 6' east of Greenwich. It is high water in the road, according to Mr. Hamilton's report, half an hour before the moon passes over the meridian; but from what I observed, without paying particular attention to it, the tide did not appear to flow so late by an hour: the medium rise was about seven feet, as at Port Jackson.

Well tasted fresh water is collected, at certain seasons, in small pools near the east end of Preservation Island; but that which drains from the rocks was first used by the Sydney-Cove's crew, until several of them died. Small runs or pools of water are to be found almost every where under the high parts of Cape-Barren Island, and it is probable there may be some upon Clarke's Island; but at the Passage Isles we found it difficult to obtain wherewithal to satisfy our thirst.

The stone of which the southern, and probably the whole of Furneaux's Islands are composed, is mostly a whitish granite, but sometimes inclining to red; and is full of small, black specks. Quartz seems to have a more than usual share in its composition, and we occasionally found crystals of that substance upon the shores. The black specks were thought to be grains of tin, and to have communicated a deleterious quality to the water used by the shipwrecked people. The exceptions to the general prevalence of granite were few: they consisted of some black, and some grey slate, in thin strata, placed nearly perpendicular to the horizon; but even here, the granite had pervaded the fissures of the strata; and, in two instances, a substance which, from its appearance, I supposed to be a toad stone, had insinuated itself.

Some of the trees on Preservation Island had partly undergone a peculiar transformation. The largest of them were not thicker than a man's leg, and the whole were decayed; but whilst the upper branches continued to be of wood, the roots at the surface, and the trunks up to a certain height, were of a stony substance resembling chalk. On breaking these chalky trunks, which was easily done, rings of the brown wood sometimes appeared in them, as if imperfectly converted; but in the greater number, nothing more than circular traces remained. The situation in which these trees were principally found, is a sandy valley near the middle of the island, which was likewise remarkable for the quantity of bones of birds and small quadrupeds, with which it was strewed. The petrefactions were afterwards more particularly examined by Mr. Bass, who adopted the opinion that they had been caused by water.

Upon Cape-Barren Island the hills rise to a considerable height, that of the peak, which does not much exceed some others, being near twelve hundred feet; but on the smaller islands there is no elevation of importance. The upper parts of all are generally crowned with huge lumps of granite; and upon many of these, particularly on Rum Island, is a smaller, unconnected, round lump, which rests in a hollow at the top, as a cup in its saucer; and I observed with a glass, that there was a stone of this kind at the summit of the peak of Cape Barren. The lower parts of the islands are commonly sandy; and, in several places under the hills, swamps and pools are formed. The water in these is generally tinged red; and in one, situate between Passage and Cone Points, it had so much the appearance of blood, that I went to taste it; but, except being a little brackish, found nothing remarkable. Whether the water become thus tinged, in its course down the hills, by earthy or metallic substances, or acquire its colour from the roots and leaves of vegetables, I am unable to decide; but think the former most probable.

All the islands are over-run with brush wood, amongst which, in the more sheltered and less barren parts, are mixed a few stunted trees, which seem to shed their bark annually, and to be of the heavy kind called gum tree at Port Jackson. The brush wood overspreads even the rocks where it can get the least hold; it is commonly impenetrable, and on the south and west sides of the islands assumes a depressed, creeping form, strongly indicative of the strength and generality of the winds from those quarters. Many of the sandy parts are covered with the hassocks of wiry grass, which constitute the favourite retreat of the sooty petrel; and at the back of the shores, there is frequently some extent of ground where the creeping, salt plants grow, and to which the penguins principally resort. To this general account of the scanty vegetable productions of Furneaux's Islands, may be added several low shrubs, and a grass which grows on the moist grounds near the borders of the pools and fresh swamps, and which, though coarse, might serve as food for cattle.

Of the animal productions of the islands, the list is somewhat more extensive. Those for which they are indebted to the sea, are seals of two kinds, sooty petrels, and penguins. The hair seal appears to frequent the sheltered beaches, points, and rocks; whilst the rocks and rocky points exposed to the buffettings of the waves are preferred by the handsomer and superior species, which never condescends to the effeminacy of a beach. A point or island will not be greatly resorted to by these animals, unless it slope gradually to the water, and the shore be, as we term it, steep to. This is the case with the islet lying off Cape Barren, and with Cone Point; with parts of the Passage Isles, and the south end of Clarke's Island; and at these places only, did I see fur seals in any number.

The sooty petrel, better known at sea under the name of sheerwater, frequents the tufted, grassy parts of all the islands in astonishing numbers. It is known that these birds make burrows in the ground, like rabbits; that they lay one or two enormous eggs in these holes, and bring up their young there. In the evening, they come in from sea, having their stomachs filled with a gelatinous substance gathered from the waves; and this they eject into the throats of their offspring, or retain for their own nourishment, according to circumstances. A little after sunset, the air at Preservation Island used to be darkened with their numbers; and it was generally an hour before their squabblings ceased, and every one had found its own retreat. The people of the Sydney Cove had a strong example of perseverance in these birds. The tents were pitched close to a piece of ground full of their burrows, many of which were necessarily filled up from walking constantly over them; yet, notwithstanding this interruption, and the thousands of birds destroyed, for they constituted a great part of their food during more than six months, the returning flights continued to be as numerous as before; and there was scarcely a burrow less, except in the spaces actually covered by the tents. These birds are about the size of a pigeon, and when skinned and dried in smoke we thought them passable food. Any quantity could be procured, by sending people on shore in the evening. The sole process was to thrust in the arm up to the shoulder, and seize them briskly; but there was some danger of grasping a snake at the bottom of the burrow, instead of a petrel.

The penguin of these islands is of the kind denominated little; the back and upper parts are of a lead-coloured blue; the fore and under parts, white. They were generally found sitting on the rocks, in the day time, or in caverns near the water side. They burrow in the same manner as the sooty petrel; but, except in the time of rearing their young, do not seem, like it, to return to their holes every night. The places preferred for breeding are those at the back of the shore, where the sand is overspread with salt plants; and they were never found intermixed with the petrels, nor far from the salt water. Their flesh is so strong and fishy, that had not the skins served to make caps, rather handsome, and impenetrable to rain, the penguins would have escaped molestation.

No other quadrupeds than the kangaroo, womat, and duck-billed aculeated ant-eater were found upon the islands. The kangaroo, is of a reddish brown, and resembles the smaller species which frequents the brush woods at Port Jackson: when full grown, it weighs from forty to fifty pounds. There were no traces of it upon the Passage Isles; but, upon Cape-Barren and Clarke's Islands, the kangaroo, was tolerably abundant, though difficult to be procured, owing to the thickness of its retreats. There were also numbers on Preservation Island, when the Sydney Cove was first run on shore; but having been much harassed and destroyed, a few only were shot during the time of our stay.

Clarke's Island afforded the first specimen of the new animal, called womat; but I found it more numerous upon that of Cape Barren: Preservation and the Passage Isles do not possess it. This little bear-like quadruped is known in New South Wales, and called by the natives womat, wombat, or womback, according to the different dialects, or perhaps to the different rendering of the wood rangers who brought the information. It burrows like the badger, and on the Continent does not quit its retreat till dark; but it feeds at all times on the uninhabited islands, and was commonly seen foraging amongst the sea refuse on the shore, though the coarse grass seemed to be its usual nourishment. It is easily caught when at a distance from its burrow; its flesh resembles lean mutton in taste, and to us was acceptable food. Another species of this animal has been discovered in New South Wales, which lives in the tops of the trees and, in manners, bears much resemblance to the sloth.

The aculeated ant-eater was not found on any other of the islands than that of Cape Barren: it is exceedingly fat, the flesh has a somewhat aromatic taste, and was thought delicious.

Of the birds which frequent Furneaux's Islands, the most valuable are the goose and black swan; but this last is rarely seen here, even in the freshwater pools, and except to breed, seems never to go on shore. The goose approaches nearest to the description of the species called bernacle; it feeds upon grass, and seldom takes to the water. I found this bird in considerable numbers on the smaller isles, but principally upon Preservation Island; its usual weight was from seven to ten pounds, and it formed our best repasts, but had become shy. Gannets, shags, gulls, and red-bills were occasionally seen; as also crows, hawks, paroquets, and a few smaller birds. Fish were not plentiful, but some were taken with hook and line from the rocks.

Speckled yellow snakes, of three or four feet in length, were found upon Preservation Island, and exist, no doubt, upon the larger isles. They sometimes get into the burrows of the sooty petrel, and probably destroy the young. I saw one dragged out by a sailor who expected to have taken a bird; but, being quick in his movements, he was not bitten. These snakes possess the venomous fangs; but no person experienced the degree of virulence in their poison.

The schooner was ready to sail on Feb. 25; and the wind from the westward being fresh and favourable, we left Hamilton's Road to return to Port Jackson. It was still a matter of doubt whether the land to the south of the islands were, or were not, a part of Van Diemen's Land; and I therefore requested of Mr. Reed to make a stretch that way. At noon our latitude was 40° 44 2/3', and the peak of Cape Barren bore N. 13° E.; an island which had been visited by the Sydney-Cove's people, and was represented to be a breeding place for swans, bore from N. 68° W. to west, five or six miles, and there were some smaller islets behind it. The land lying two or three miles more to the south is sandy and low in front, but ascends in gently rising hills as it retreats into the country. Its general appearance was very different from that of Furneaux's Islands, the lower hills being covered with green grass, interspersed with clumps of wood, and the back land well clothed with timber trees.

We stretched on until the land was seen beyond 40° 50'; and then veered to the northward. In this latitude, captain Furneaux says, "the land trenches away to the westward;"[15] and as he traced the coast from the south end of the country to this part, there could no longer be a doubt that it was joined to the land discovered by Tasman in 1642. The smokes which had constantly been seen rising from it showed that there were inhabitants; and this, combined with the circumstance of there being none upon the islands, seemed to argue a junction of Van Diemen's Land with

New South Wales; for it was difficult to suppose, that men should have reached the more distant land, and not have attained the islands intermediately situated; nor was it admissible that, having reached them, they had perished for want of food. On the other hand, the great strength of the tides setting westward, past the islands, could only be caused by some exceedingly deep inlet, or by a passage through to the southern Indian Ocean. These contradictory circumstances were very embarrassing; and the schooner not being placed at my disposal, I was obliged, to my great regret, to leave this important geographical question undecided.

At the time we veered to the northward, the coast of Van Diemen's Land was about three miles distant, and the furthest extreme, a low point, bore S. 15° E. two or three leagues. On repassing Cape-Barren Point at four o'clock. I obtained two sets of distances of the sun west of the moon, to pair with others of the sun on the east side, taken on the 10th, also within sight of the Cape. The mean result, freed from the errors of the tables, gave its longitude 148° 20' E; being 14' more than is assigned to it by captain Furneaux, but 5½' less than what appears to be its real situation. Nothing worthy of notice occurred in our passage back to Port Jackson: we made Hat Hill on March 7, and on the 9th, anchored in Sydney Cove.

Mr. Bass had been returned a fortnight from his expedition in the whale boat; and he communicated all his notes and observations to be added to my chart. There seemed to want no other proof of the existence of a passage between New South Wales and Van Diemen's Land, than that of sailing positively through it; but however anxious I was to obtain this proof, the gratification of my desire was required to be suspended by a voyage to Norfolk Island in the Reliance.

FLINDERS and BASS. 1798.

In September following, His Excellency Governor Hunter had the goodness to give me the Norfolk, a colonial sloop of twenty-five tons, with authority to penetrate behind Furneaux's Islands; and should a strait be found, to pass through it and return by the south end of Van Diemen's Land; making such examinations and surveys on the way as circumstances might permit. Twelve weeks were allowed for the performance of this service, and provisions for that time were put on board; the rest of the equipment was completed by the friendly care of Captain Waterhouse of the Reliance.

I had the happiness to associate my friend Bass in this new expedition, and to form an excellent crew of eight volunteers from the king's ships; but a time keeper, that essential instrument to accuracy in nautical surveys, it was still impossible to obtain.

My report of the seals at Furneaux's Islands had induced Messrs. Bishop and Simpson, the commander and supracargo of the snow Nautilus, to prepare their vessel for a sealing speculation to that quarter; and on Oct. 7, we sailed out of Port Jackson together.[16]

The wind being fair, we passed Hat Hill at four in the afternoon, and next morning, made Mount Dromedary. I took this opportunity of passing between Montague Isle and the main; but the depth of water being uncertain, the Nautilus was desired by signal not to follow. There was no bottom with 13, and afterwards with 20 fathoms, at a mile distance from the island; and the passage seemed perfectly free from danger, and is five or six miles wide. Mount Dromedary, from which the island lies E by N ½ N., is the highest land upon this part of the coast; its elevation being, I think, not less than 3000 feet. The top is about three miles long, and the south end is somewhat the most elevated part; it is covered with wood, even there, but still more so down the sides; the shore under it is mostly a white, sandy beach. At noon the centre of the mountain bore N.N.W. four leagues; but the haziness of the weather prevented an observation being taken for the latitude, as it had before done when passing in the Francis[17]. We then hauled further off the coast, with the Nautilus in company, and being near the latitude of Cape Howe, at ten o'clock, lay to until daylight, for the purpose of obtaining a good departure; but on the 9th, the wind had veered to south-west, and the weather having a bad appearance, we bore up for Two-fold Bay. The course after passing Green Cape, was N. 16° W. seven miles to Haycock Point, and N. 44° W. three or four miles from thence to the south point of entrance to the bay; the shore being all along bold, and for the most part rocky. From the south point, which may be known by its reddish appearance and having a steep rock lying off it, we steered for Snug Cove, on the north-west side of the bay; and there anchored in 3½ fathoms, sandy bottom, at something more than a cable's length from the small beach, and the same distance from the two points which bound the cove. In this situation, the outer red point was hidden by Snug-cove Head; and further out, in 5 fathoms, where the Nautilus anchored, the head and point were in a line.

In order to make some profit of this foul wind, Mr Bass landed early next morning to examine the country, whilst I went with Mr Simpson to commence a survey of Two-fold Bay. In the way from Snug Cove, through the wood, to the long northern beach, where I proposed to measure a base line, our attention was suddenly called by the screams of three women, who took up their children and ran off in great consternation. Soon afterward a man made his appearance. He was of a middle age, unarmed, except with a whaddie, or wooden scimitar, and came up to us seemingly with careless confidence. We made much of him, and gave him some biscuit; and he in return presented us with a piece of gristly fat, probably of whale. This I tasted; but watching an opportunity to spit it out when he should not be looking, I perceived him doing precisely the same thing with our biscuit, whose taste was probably no more agreeable to him, than his whale was to me. Walking onward with us to the long beach, our new acquaintance picked up from the grass a long wooden spear, pointed with bone; but this he hid a little further on, making signs that he should take it on his return. The commencement of our trigonometrical operations was seen by him with indifference, if not contempt; and he quitted us, apparently satisfied that, from people who could thus occupy themselves seriously, there was nothing to be apprehended.

We measured 116 chains along the north beach, and having taken the necessary angles, returned to Snug Cove for the purpose of observing the latitude; but the thick squalls, which were continually passing over from the south-west, prevented a sight of the sun. The survey was continued in the afternoon; and on the following morning, 11 October, the wind being still unfavourable, the west side of the bay was nearly completed.

I was preparing the artificial horizon for observing the latitude, when a party of seven or eight natives broke out in exclamation upon the bank above us, holding up their open hands to show they were unarmed. We were three in number, and, besides a pocket pistol, had two muskets. These they made no objection to our bringing, and we sat down in the midst of the party. It consisted entirely of young men, who were better made, and cleaner in their persons than the natives of Port Jackson usually are; and their countenances bespoke both good will and curiosity, though mixed with some degree of apprehension. Their curiosity was mostly directed to our persons and dress, and constantly drew off their attention from our little presents, which seemed to give but a momentary pleasure. The approach of the sun to the meridian calling me down to the beach, our visitors returned into the woods, seemingly well satisfied with what they had seen. We could perceive no arms of any kind amongst them; but I knew these people too well not to be assured that their spears were lying ready, and that it was prudent to keep a good lookout upon the woods, to prevent surprise whilst taking the observation.

Oct. 12. We sailed in the afternoon, with a breeze from the eastward; but a return of the wind to south-west, with threatening weather, induced me to bear up again in the evening; and we anchored on the south side of the bay. This part is not so well sheltered as Snug Cove, for the Nautilus was not quite land-locked in 3 fathoms water. The weather became very bad in the night; and, being no better on the 13th, the two vessels were completed with wood, and the country further explored; a few more bearings were also added to our materials for laying down a plan of the bay, and thus terminated our examination.

The latitude of Snug Cove on the north-west side of Two-fold Bay, and by much the best anchorage in it, is 37° 4' south. The longitude, from two sets of distances of the sun west of the moon, deducting 16½' for the errors of the tables, was 150° 3' east of Greenwich. The variation of the azimuth compass observed on the beach, was 9° 29' and of the surveying theodolite 11° 8½' east. My haste to complete the survey did not allow of much attention being paid to the tides; but it was high water about nipte??? hours after the moon passed over the meridian, and the general rise from six to eight feet.

Two-fold Bay is not, of itself, worthy of particular interest; but as nothing larger than boats can find shelter in any other part of this coast, from Jervis Bay, in latitude 35° 6', round to Corner Inlet, or to Furneaux's Isles in 40½°, it thereby becomes of importance to whalers, and to other ships passing along the coast.

Besides its latitude, Two-fold Bay may be known by Mount Dromedary, which will be seen, in moderately fine weather, at the distance of fifteen or sixteen leagues to the northward; and also by the land behind the bay lying more in hummocks than elsewhere. One of these hummocks is round, and much higher than the rest; and when it bears S. 60° W. (S. W. ½ W. nearly, by compass,) a course for it will bring a ship to the middle of the bay. On approaching near, she should look for two rocks, rather pointed, of which one lies off the outer north, and the other off the outer south point. Snug Cove is difficult to be distinguished by a stranger; but on coming near the rocky head, at the south-west end of the long northern beach, it will be seen on the south side of that head; and the anchor must be then ready to be let go. If the wind be from the southward, it should be dropped a little before the head shuts on with the south point of the bay, in 5 or 6 fathoms water; and in veering away, the lead should be kept out astern of the vessel. There is room for two or three small ships in Snug Cove, but not for more.

Wood, in abundance, can be procured on every side of the bay; but there are only two places where fresh water was found, and that not very good. One of these was a swampy pond upon the low neck behind Snug Cove, where casks might be filled without much difficulty; the other is near the inferior anchorage on the south side of the bay; and both are indicated in the particular plan.

The ponds and lagoons, which are to be found at the back of most of the beaches, are frequented by ducks, teal, herons, red-bills, and some small flights of the curlew and plover. The bay seemed to be well stocked with fish; and our success with hook and line made us regret having no seine, for the hauling of which many of the beaches are particularly well adapted. It is not improbable that Two-fold Bay, like some of the open bays on the east coast of Africa, may be frequented by whales at certain seasons: of this I have no decisive proof; but the reef of rocks, called Whale Spit, received its name from the remains of one found there. The natives had taken their share; and the dogs, crows, and gulls were carrying away the rest.

Oct. 14. In the morning, we left Two-fold Bay with a breeze at north-east; and at sun-set, having run eleven leagues from the south point, our departure was taken from Cape Howe. I then steered S. W. by S., judging it to be the course best calculated to bring us within sight of the land supposed, by captain Furneaux, to lie in 39° south. On the 15th, at noon, our latitude was 38° 34'; the weather was fine., but no land visible to the southward. In the opposite direction there was a range of hills whose centre bore N. by W. ½ W.; at sunset it was seen as far as N. 37° W., from the sloop's deck, and from the mast head of the Nautilus, the land was distinguished, or thought to be so, as far as N. 60° W. These bearings, but particularly the last, seemed to show a strong current to the westward, for neither Mr. Bass nor myself could believe, that the hills at the back of the Long Beach were sufficiently elevated to be seen beyond fifteen leagues; I therefore took four sets of distances, of stars east and west of the moon, which placed us, an hour and a half after sunset, in longitude 149° 13' east, agreeing nearly with the dead reckoning. The land, if it really were such, was consequently twenty-five or more leagues off; and if the bearing of N. 60° W. were not a mistake, it must have been thirty leagues distant in that direction. This supposed land was visible all the afternoon; but it might possibly have been the dense clouds hanging over the hills at the back of the Long Beach, and not the land itself.

Our course to the south-westward was continued all night; but the wind having veered to W. S. W. at daybreak of the 16th, the sloop was then put on the northern tack. No land was visible in any direction; nor was there any at noon, when the observed latitude was 38° 42'. The wind veered round by the south until it fixed itself at east; and when the day broke, on the 17th, the signal was made to the Nautilus, and we bore away S.W. by W. until noon. The latitude was then 39° 11' south, and we judged ourselves to be nearly in the meridian of the Sisters; the weather was tolerably fine, and had been so all the morning, yet no land was any where to be seen; and I therefore concluded, that none could lie in or near the meridian of these islands, and be in the latitude of 39°.

The course steered at noon was west; but in half an hour it was altered for high irregular land which came in sight to the south-westward, and proved to be the largest of the two clusters which I had discovered when in the Francis, and named Kent's Groups. We sounded in 30 fathoms, but lost the lead, the sole deep-sea line with which we had been furnished, proving to be totally rotten. After running twenty miles, assisted by a flood tide, we came up with the group at four o'clock, and steered through the channel by which the principal islands are separated. It is about three miles long, and a full mile in width; is free from danger, and so deep, that our hand line could not reach the bottom. There are two sandy coves on the east, and one on the west side of the channel, where small vessels might find shelter, if there were any inducement to visit these steep, barren, granitic masses of rock. Above the cliffs we could occasionally perceive a brown-looking vegetation of brush wood, and here and there a few starved gum trees; but there was neither bird nor quadruped to enliven the dreary scene.[18] The principal island of the small, western group, opened at S. 68° W., on clearing the channel; and we then hauled the wind to the southward, for Furneaux's Islands, that the Nautilus might no longer be detained from her sealing business.

The wind blew fresh from the eastward all night, with hazy weather. At daylight, Oct. 18, a large piece of hilly land bore N. 48° to 64° E., four leagues; and soon afterward, Mount Chappell, a smooth round hill which had been seen from Preservation Island, was set at S. 78° E., distant seven or eight leagues, and was as conspicuous on this side as when seen from the eastward. Our latitude at noon was 40° 22', and Mount Chappell bore N. 71° E. seven or eight miles, which would place it to the north of its position before determined. Between us and the mount were two small, low islands, and to the northward the hilly land first seen was visible under the sun.

Finding the wind hang obstinately in the eastern quarter, we had tacked to the north in order to keep under the lee of the islands. This course brought us, in the evening, within two miles of the hilly northern land, the same which had been discovered in the Francis, and of whose connection with the great island of Furneaux I was doubtful; nor could it yet be determined. The shores of the south-western part are rocky; and the land rises, by a steep ascent, to hills of an elevation equal to that of Mount Chappell. These hills are slightly covered with grass and small brush wood, but the general appearance was that of great sterility.

About four miles to the south of this land we had passed a rocky islet, and observed a circular reef which seemed to connect the two together. The stormy appearance of the night induced me to stretch in, under this reef; and finding there was shelter from the east winds, we came to an anchor in 5 fathoms, coarse sand: the Nautilus followed; but not liking the place, captain Bishop preferred keeping the sea. On sounding round the sloop, I found the bottom every where foul, and that there were no means of escape in case of a shift of wind; therefore, after killing a few seals upon the granitic rocks, we weighed the anchor, ran two leagues to the southward, and then hauled the wind under storm sails for the night.

Oct. 19, the wind was at north-east; and we bore away to pass between Mount Chappell and the low islands lying to the westward. The passage is about two miles wide, and the water much discoloured; but 10 fathoms of line did not reach the bottom. A similar appearance in the water had been observed several leagues to the westward of the low islands, where there was 23 to 25 fathoms, on a bottom of sand and broken shells.

This small group, to which the name of Chappell Isles is affixed in the chart, consists of three, or perhaps four islands, for the mount seemed to stand detached from the land on the east side of the passage. The basis of the whole is probably of granite, and they seemed nothing superior in fertility to the worst of Furneaux's Islands; but in a distant view, a slight covering of small herbage upon their sloping, even surfaces, gave them a prepossessing appearance. Mount Chappell is five or six hundred feet above the water, a very conspicuous object until, by the clearing away of the haze the high mountains of the great island behind it became visible: their white, towering peaks, bathed in the late showers, reflected the gleaming sunshine with great splendour, and presented a spectacle so magnificent, that the circular, gently sloping Mount Chappell no longer attracted attention.

We joined the Nautilus off the south side of the islands and, after passing several rocks in our course eastward, anchored at the east end of Preservation Island about noon. Mr Hamilton had left his house standing, with some fowls and pigeons in it, when we had quitted the island nine months before. The house remained in nearly the same state but its tenants were not to be found, having probably fallen a prey to the hawks.

Oct 20, the wind was at north-west, and blew a gale, accompanied with rain, which continued for several days. This weather very much impeded our progress with the Nautilus in Armstrong's Channel, but Captain Bishop at length moored in Kent's Bay, the most secure place to be found within reach of the sealing points. The greater part of Kent's Bay is occupied by shoals; but along the shore of Sloping Point there is a deep channel running northward, which leads into the western head of the bay; and there, behind a reef of dry rocks, several ships may lie in 4 or 5 fathoms, sheltered from all winds. The Nautilus's tents were pitched upon the borders of a run of fresh water, about one mile north of the anchorage; and a garden, which Captain Bishop made there, produced some tolerable vegetables.

We had no prospect of advancing along the north coast of Van Diemen's Land whilst the strong western winds continued to blow; and therefore, whilst Mr Bass explored some of the islands, I occupied myself in sounding different parts of Armstrong's Channel, and in making some other additions to my former survey. At length, on Oct. 31., the gale moderated to a light breeze, and we stretched over, with the flood tide, towards the Swan Isles. At noon, our situation was as under.

	° '
Latitude observed,	40 39 S.
Peak of Cape Barren,	N. 16 E.
Van Diemens Land, eastern extr. about	S. by E.
Largest Swan Isle, the centre,	S. 53 W.

Soon after three o'clock, we anchored in a small sandy bay, at the south-east end of the largest Swan Isle, in 4 fathoms; being well sheltered from north and western winds, but entirely open to any that might arise from the opposite quarters. The furthest extreme of the opposite coast then bore S. 36° E. three leagues; but the nearest part, in the direction of S. by W., was little more than three miles distant.

I landed with Mr Bass; and leaving him to pursue his researches, went round to the north side of the island, to take angles. From a small, elevated projection there,

	° '
The peak of Cape Barren was set at	N. 28 40 E.
Mount Chappell,	N. 21 20 W.;

from which, and several intermediate bearings, this station became firmly connected with the survey of Furneaux's Islands. Mr. Bass thought the stone to contain a rather large quantity of iron, and the bearings seemed to confirm it, for they did not agree in any common intersection with the allowance of 9° east, which I considered to be the true variation; but with 6° 30', they not only coincided, but placed this station in latitude 40° 43' south, the same as deduced from three meridional observations taken within sight of the island.

One mile from the north-west end, lies a low, rocky islet, and several rocks both above and under water. All these are comprehended under the general name of the Swan Isles; a name which, on examination, they appeared very little to deserve, for we did not see a single bird of that species, or any of their nests; but there were several of the bernacle geese, and two of them were shot by Mr Bass.

The length of the largest Swan Isle is two and a quarter miles, by a medium breadth of one mile. The stony parts are over-run with thick brush wood, and the sandy are mostly covered with hassocks of wiry grass, to which the sooty petrels resort. In external appearance, this island bears a resemblance to that of Preservation; but its sterility is greater, and it is destitute of the kangaroo. We did not see any fresh water in the valleys, a seal upon the shores, nor any marks of the island having been ever visited by the natives of the opposite coast.

Nov 1. Having an unfavourable wind, I waited the flood tide, and then proceeded westward, along that part of Van Diemen's land to which the name of CAPE PORTLAND was given, in honour of His Grace the then secretary of state for the colonies. From the eastern extremity, the coast trends about N. 62° W. six leagues, and terminates in a point, off which lie some small rocky islets. The shore consists of long, sandy beaches, separated by low and stony points, which project very little beyond the coastline. The country for two or three miles behind the shore is low and sandy; but it then ascends in gradations of gently rising hills, and being covered with verdure, interspersed with clumps of wood and single trees of a fair growth, it had a very pleasing appearance. At the back of these hills, the bare and rugged tops of a ridge of distant mountains appeared here and there, and formed a striking contrast with the verdure of the front scene.

Our soundings along the south side of the largest Swan Isle were generally 8 fathoms, on a sandy bottom; nor was there much decrease until noon, when the low shore of Cape Portland was at something less, and the outer rocky islets something more than a mile distant, and we came rather suddenly into 3 fathoms. The latitude observed was 40° 43 2/3' south, and the island last quitted bore N. 85° to S. 84° E., distant six miles.

There being little wind at this time, the sloop, in passing round the rocky islets of Cape Portland, was carried by the tide over a ledge where there was scarcely 2 fathoms; and was then driven westward on a curved line of rippling water, which extended northward from the islets as far as the eye could reach. We passed over the rippling in 9 fathoms; and the wind being entirely gone, were then carried to the south-west.

Soon after four o'clock, the ebb appeared to be making; and the anchor was dropped in 11 fathoms, sandy bottom, about one mile west of Cape Portland. The shore on this side of the cape trends south, in rocky heads and beaches, and afterwards curves westward, forming an extensive bay, which terminates in a point. To this the name of Point Waterhouse was given, in honour of the commander of the Reliance, and an island, whose top is level and moderately high, lying off the point, was named ISLE WATERHOUSE.

The bottom of the large bay is sandy, and the hills of Cape Portland there retiring further back, permitted a view of the inland mountains, of which there was a high and extensive ridge. Mountains like these are usually the parents of rivers; and the direction of the ebb tide, which came from between S.W. by S. and S.W. by W. at the rate of two-and-a-half miles an hour, gave hopes of finding some considerable inlet in the bay, and increased our anxiety for a fair breeze.

A set of distances of the sun east of the moon, a meridian altitude of the planet Mars, and a western amplitude of the sun were taken at this anchorage, the results of which, with the bearings of the land, were as under:

	° '
Latitude observed,	40 44 S.
Longitude from lunar distances corrected,	147 56 E.
Variation of the compass (the sloop's head being S.W.)	12 30 E.
C. Barren peak, over the outer islets of C. Portland,	N. 47 E.
Mount Chappell,	North.
Isle Waterhouse, centre, dist. 5 or 6 leagues,	S. 71 W.
Point Waterhouse.	S. 61 W.
Ridge of inland mountains,	South to S. 42 W.
Highest part of ditto, a round top,	S. 19 W.

The flood tide ceased to run at three quarters past three in the morning, or about nine hours after the moon passed over the meridian.

Nov. 2. A light breeze having sprung up from the eastward we steered for the bottom of the bay, and at noon the nearest part of the beach was distant only two miles.

	° '
Observed latitude,	40 49¾ S.
C. Portland, with the outer islets behind,	N. 27 E.
Isle Waterhouse, extremes,	N. 78° to 89 W.
Point Waterhouse,	S. 88½ W.

We stood on another mile, and then bore away westward, following the round of the shore, but no inlet could be perceived. At three o'clock, we had passed Point Waterhouse, and seeing a fair channel of about two miles wide between it and the island, steered through, S.W. by W.

Isle Waterhouse is near four miles in length. Its southern shore consists of beaches and rocky points; but it rises abruptly to a moderate elevation. The level top is mostly covered with wood; and although its appearance did not bespeak fertility, it was superior to any we had seen of Furneaux's Islands. The land at the back of Point Waterhouse is higher than that of the island, and is composed of grassy, woody hills, rising over each other by gentle ascents. Upon the point there is a sandy hillock, and a reef of rocks extends out from it a quarter of a mile. We had 8 fathoms, whilst rounding this reef; and in steering through the passage, the soundings were 8, 7, 6, 5, 4, 5, 6 fathoms; the sandy bottom being visible under the sloop. At the further end of the channel, a rocky islet and a small reef were passed, leaving them on the starbord hand. The islet was almost covered with sea birds and hair seals; from which circumstance we judged, that the natives of Van Diemen's Land were not able to get across here, any more than to the Swan Isles; and that, consequently, they had no canoes upon this part of the coast.

From Point Waterhouse, the shore trends S. 67° W., five or six miles, and is mostly rocky. It then takes a direction of S. S. W., in a long sandy beach, and afterwards curves westward to a projecting point, near which we had no ground with 13 fathoms a little before sunset. Another island had been for some time visible, and was then distant six miles: It was called

Ninth Island, and bore	N. 32° W.
Isle Waterhouse, about the centre,	N. 50° E.
South side of the passage,	N. 62° E.
Projecting point, dist. one-third of a mile, South.	

The projecting point is over-topped with hillocks of almost bare sand, as is a second, which lies W. 6° S., two or three miles from, and much resembles, the first: these two projections received the joint name of Double Sandy Point. The back country was manifestly worse than any before seen on this coast. The pleasant looking hills of Point Waterhouse no longer approached the shore; but retiring far inland, left a low space between the back hills and the sea, which had every appearance of being sandy and barren.

In passing the western part of Double Sandy Point, we had 5, and then 4 fathoms; and saw a reef extending from it some distance to the westward. It was then nearly dark, and we hauled off upon a wind, for the night; the furthest visible extreme, a remarkable stony head, bearing S. 70° W. about eight miles.

The wind blew a moderate breeze all night, at north-east. At five in the morning, Nov. 3, the Ninth Island was distant two miles, and bore E. 2° N., in a line with Point Waterhouse. The top of the island appeared green and level; but I did not see any seals upon the rocks. Resuming our former course along shore, we passed close to Stony Head at ten o'clock, when two sets of distances of the sun east of the moon, gave its corrected longitude 147° 10' east. The wind having then veered more to the north, we hauled further off, and passed a rocky islet (the tenth), upon which a few overgrown hair seals were sunning themselves. At noon, our situation was as follows.

Latitude observed,	40° 55½' S.
Tenth I., distant four miles,	S. 87 E.
Stony Head, dist. six or seven miles,	S. 62 E.
A low head, distant ten miles,	S. 35 W.
Western extreme of the land,	S. 53 W.

Stony Head is the extremity of a ridge of hills which branches out from the inland mountains, and stretches across the low, sandy land in front, to the sea. On each side of the ridge there were several smokes, which induced me to suppose the flat lands might contain lakes of fresh water. The low head, bearing S. 35° W. seemed to be the termination of another branch from the inland mountains; round it there was some appearance of an opening, and at two o'clock, this excited so much hope that I ventured to bear away before the wind. We advanced rapidly with the flood, and at four, had passed LOW HEAD and were steering S. E. by S., up an inlet of more than a mile wide. Some shoals, not quite covered, we left on the starbord hand; keeping a straight course for the entrance of a basin or bay, at which the inlet seemed to terminate. This course took us over some strong ripplings of tide, on none of which, however, there was less than 5 fathoms; and so soon as they were passed, 13 fathoms did not reach the bottom. After advancing three miles, we approached a low, green island, lying nearly in mid-channel; and being uncertain which was the deepest side, I took the most direct, which lay to the west. From 8 fathoms, the next cast of the lead was 3½, and immediately the sloop was aground. Fortunately, the bottom was soft, and the strong flood dragged her over the bank without injury. The water deepened again as quick; and when the channel on the east side of Green Island was open, there was no bottom at 13 fathoms.

We could not but remark the contrast between the shores of this inlet, covered with grass and wood down to the water's edge, and the rocky sterile banks observed in sailing up Port Jackson: it spoke favourably for the country, and added to the satisfaction we felt in having made the discovery. There was, however, little time for meditation: the tide drove the sloop rapidly onward to the basin; and the evening coming on, I pushed between some dry rocks and a point on the western side, and anchored in 2 fathoms, on a bottom of sand and mud.

There appeared to be three arms, or rivers, discharging themselves into this extensive basin. That which came from the westward., had its embouchure close to the sloop; and Mr. Bass went off in the boat to look up it. His attention was, however, soon called to another pursuit: a number of black swans were swimming before him, and judging from former experience in Western Port, that several of them were unable to fly, he gave chase with the boat. On his return at dusk, he rejoiced us with the sight of four, and with a promise that we should not be in want of fresh provisions in this port.

Nov. 4. I landed Mr. Bass with two men, to examine the country, and then commenced a survey of the port by an examination of the Western Arm. It is narrow, and has not more in the entrance than 3 fathoms, although, about one mile up, there be 7 near the starbord shore. This arm is not accessible to ships beyond three miles; and even in that distance there is much more shoal than deep water.

The rocks lying at the entrance of the basin are covered at the top of the flood, but at other times are much frequented by shags. After observing the latitude and taking bearings there, I went down to Green Island; and the tide being then out, perceived the shoals in Sea Reach to be so numerous and extensive, that it was surprising how the sloop could have reached thus far without striking upon some of them. In the channel to the east of Green Island I found from 7 to 25 fathoms, and both the sides of it steep to; a rock lies in the middle of the passage, but at twenty yards from it there was 3 fathoms all round. Green Island is covered with long, coarse grass and bushes, with a few small trees intermixed. The large, noisy gulls frequent it for the purpose of breeding, as do the swans, several of whose deserted nests were found with the broken egg-shells in them. These were corroborating proofs, that the natives of this part of Van Diemen's Land have not the means of transporting themselves across the water; for Green Island is scarcely two cables length from the shore.

In returning to the sloop, I took off Mr. Bass and his party, together with a kangaroo weighing between eighty and ninety pounds, which he had shot out of a considerable flock. Our fresh provisions were still further increased by an addition of six swans, caught this evening with the boat.

Nov. 5 was employed in the survey of the Western Arm, and searching, but in vain, for the means of conveniently replenishing our water casks. Next morning we steered across the basin., and sought to anchor under an island which, from its situation at the entrance of the eastern arm, was called Middle Island; but there not being a sufficient depth of water behind it, the course was continued up the eastern arm, in 10 or more fathoms water, for two or three miles; when we anchored upon a five-fathom bank, near a small cove on the northern shore. On landing, a little stream was found descending from the hills into the south-east corner of the cove, and in the middle was a gully with several deep holes in it full of excellent water: this last, though not accessible till half flood, was the most convenient for our purpose.

There were many recent traces of natives on the shore; and after returning to the sloop, we saw, on the opposite side of the arm a man who employed or amused himself by setting fire to the grass in different places. He did not stay to receive us, and we rowed down to Middle Island where a smoke was rising. The natives shunned us there also; for soon after landing, I saw three of them walk up from the shoal which joins Middle Island to the opposite low, sandy point. The party appeared to consist of a man, a woman, and a boy; and the two first had something wrapped round them which resembled cloaks of skins.

The gently-sloping hills of Middle Island afford about forty acres of pasture land, well covered with grass, and thinly wooded. No fresh water was seen, but it might probably be obtained by digging. This island is little frequented by aquatic birds, from the circumstance of its being accessible, at low water, to the inhabitants of the main.

Nov. 7. Mr. Bass and myself landed on the south shore upon our respective pursuits. The sandy point at the back of Middle Island was particularly favourable to the survey; and a base of sixty-six chains measured round it, with the concomitant angles, enabled me to connect the eastern arm with the basin. The sloop had been completed with water in the morning, and was ready to proceed in continuation of the voyage; but the width of the arm, the depth of water in it, and strength of the tides, were too strong indications of a river of extensive course for me to be able to quit it without some further examination.

A rainy gale from the eastward did not allow of moving until Nov. 9th; we then got under way with the flood tide, and beat up the first, or Long Reach, against a south-east wind. Abreast of Point Rapid (see the chart), where the river turned sharp round to the south-west, I went away in the boat to examine the upper end of Long Reach; but the haste required in following after the sloop, which the tide assisted in driving fast upward, allowed me to do it but very cursorily. In Crooked Reach, I stopped at two places, and measured a short base near Glen Bight. The sloop was then lost to view, although the wind had died away; and on reaching Brush Island, it was not easy to know which way she had taken, Round-head Bay having as much the appearance of being a continuation of the river, as had Whirlpool Reach. This reach stretches south-eastward, and its width is much less than in any of the lower parts of the river, being no more than a short quarter of a mile; but, as might be expected, the depth in it, from 10 to 22 fathoms, is greater, and its borders are steep and rocky. At the end of Whirlpool Reach, the banks of the river opened out so considerably that, from our little boat, it appeared like a sea, the land at the further end being scarcely distinguishable. Fortunately, we got sight of the sloop in Anchor Bight before it was dark, and carried with us another black swan.

Nov. 10, being under the necessity of going down to Brush Island, to bring the survey up from thence to the position of the sloop, we did not get under way till near noon. The wind was from the westward, and I went forward in the boat to Egg Island, so named from the number of eggs, mostly of the gull and red bill, which were there found. It is small and stony; but covered with grass, and had not been visited by the natives. My next station was on the opposite side of the river, upon a low sandy point which is lengthened by a dry shoal. These project out from the general line of the southern shore, and contract the river to less than half a mile; whereas its width above and below, is one mile and a half. On the east, or lee side of this point and shoal was a flock of swans, in number not less than from three to five hundred; and their cast quills were so intermixed with the sand, as to form a component part of the beach. This countless number of quills gave me an insight into the cause why so many of the swans, though not young birds, were unable to fly: they moult their wing feathers, probably at stated periods, though not, I should think, every year. This sandy projection was named Swan Point.

On steering southward from thence, I found that the bight in which this great number of birds had assembled, was full of shoals producing the long aquatic grass which forms the principal part, if it be not their sole food. We sailed through the flock, and might have procured a good number, had not the progress of the sloop obliged us to hasten onward to Shoal Point: one incautious bird was caught by his long neck as we sailed past him.

The change in the direction of the river, from south-east to south, made the extension of a new base necessary. From the end of Shoal Point, I ran thirty-two chains westward, across a small stream of fresh water; and having taken the necessary angles, returned to the sloop, which had then anchored at half a mile from the point, in 4 fathoms. The shoal was dry in the evening, within two cables length of the vessel, and rendered the fresh stream inaccessible to a boat.

The time of our absence from Port Jackson being restricted to the beginning of January, I did not think it advisable to take the sloop any further up the river; but determined, after devoting one day more to an excursion in the boat, to return and proceed along the north coast of Van Diemen's Land, in prosecution of the main object of the voyage.

Nov. 11, Mr. Bass landed near Shoal Point, to go as far back into the country as the limited time would permit. I steered from thence over to a red bank on the east side of the river, measured a base of seventy nine chains, and took angles from a variety of stations. At the Crescent Shore, the river was contracted to a quarter of a mile in width, the water was half fresh, and the depth across as follows: 1½, 3, 5½, 8, 8½, 12½, 11, 6, 4 fathoms at half flood.

The direction of the river, from where the sloop was lying to this part, is nearly S. S. W.; but it then winds round the Crescent Shore, and runs E. S. E. My uppermost station was upon a hill near the water side, at the commencement of this new reach; and from thence the river appeared, at the distance of a mile and a half, to reopen out its banks, and to turn more southward. In an eastern direction, across the wide part, there were three ridges of hills, and beyond them some blue peaks and caps of distant mountains, which I judged to be the same we had seen from Cape Portland; and amongst which the source, or some of the sources of this river most probably arose. The distance of these mountains concurred with the strength of the tides and the depth of water to indicate, that, at the Crescent Shore, the larger half of the river still remained to be explored.

The morning of Nov. 12 was foggy and calm. We rowed the sloop down with the assistance of the ebb tide, to Roundhead Bay, and anchored in 3½ fathoms. At high water, the anchor was again weighed; and at dusk, having had a breeze, we reached the five-fathom bank in Long Reach, near Watering Cove. From the upper end of Whirlpool Reach to Point Rapid, I went ahead in the boat and examined all the creeks and gullies on the western shore, for watering places. There were drains of fresh water down some of these, but in none, not even in Glen Bight, was there any accessible to boats.

Nov. 13, we beat down with the ebb tide to Middle Island, and then steered across the basin for the Middle Arm, which was yet totally unexplored; but after many ineffectual attempts to find a passage over the shoals, we came to, in 5 fathoms, near the Shag Rocks, and I went to examine the arm with the boat. From Inspection Head I discovered a narrow channel leading into it, where there was more than sufficient depth for ships; but this arm is altogether of little consequence.

In the evening, it blew a gale of wind from the north-westward, with hail and rain; and the same weather continuing next day, I employed the time in examining Sea Reach. On the 15th, somewhat finer weather enabled us to get down to Outer Cove, a place opposite to Green Island, where there is room for a larger vessel than the Norfolk to ride at single anchor, in 8 fathoms. The head of the cove is shoal, and the stream that falls into it is salt to a greater distance than a boat can go; nor could any accessible fresh water be found in the neighbourhood. Middle Rock, so named from its situation in the deep channel between the cove and Green Island, is hidden at half flood. Fine muscles were gathered from it, many of them containing small, discoloured pearls, such as are found in those of Adventure Bay.

From this time to the 20th, the western winds continued to blow strong; and finding, after an ineffectual attempt, that it was impossible to make any progress in the voyage, we remained in port, taking astronomical observations, completing the survey, and examining the country, until a favourable change should take place. At the back of the longest beach near Low Head, and on the same side, I found a deep pool of tolerably good water, at which our casks were again replenished; and when the boat was not employed in this, or other services, the people were sent swan hunting, and never without success.

Nov. 20. The wind having become moderate at north-west, we beat out of the port with the ebb tide; and at one p.m., took a departure from Low Head. The breeze had then veered to E. N. E.; and when we had run nine leagues, a head on the west side of the port bore S. 53° E., and the furthest visible part of the coast was at west: being then dusk, the wind was hauled off shore.

We had rainy weather in the night, and the wind shifted back to W. N. W., and blew a fresh gale. This soon raised a high sea, and reduced us to a close-reefed main sail and jib; nor were we without apprehensions of the shore for the following night, so much did the sloop drive to leeward. On the 22nd at noon the gale was more moderate, the wind at W. by S., and the weather permitted an observation to be taken for the latitude; it was 40° 13', and we had land bearing E. N. E. about three leagues distant. So soon as I had satisfied myself that this could be no other than the hilly land lying five leagues to the northward of the Chappell Isles, we bore away before the sea; and by carrying all sail, secured an anchorage in Hamilton's Road before dark.

It was not safe to move on the 23rd, and there being a lunar eclipse announced in the ephemeris to take place in the following night, I landed to observe it with the telescope of the sextant. The times at which the beginning and end happened by the watch, being corrected from altitudes of the stars Rigel and Sirius observed in an artificial horizon, gave 148° 37½' for the uncorrected longitude of Preservation Island; which is 37' more than was deduced from the lunar distances in the Francis. The penumbra attending the earth's shadow is usually supposed to render this observation uncertain to two or three minutes of time, or more than half a degree of longitude.

Nov. 24. The gale had subsided to a moderate breeze, and we tried to beat back to the westward; but finding too much sea, bore away into Armstrong's Channel to speak the commander of the Nautilus; that, through him, governor Hunter might be informed of our discoveries thus far, and of the delays experienced from the western winds. I was happy to find captain Bishop proceeding successfully in his sealing business, though slower than he might have done, had the anchorage been nearer to the eastern points.[19]

In the evening it fell calm, and the tide being favourable, we rowed back for Hamilton's Road; but a fair breeze springing up when abreast of it, instead of anchoring we made all sail to the west-south-west for Van Diemen's Land.

On the 25th at day-light, the Ninth Island bore south, five miles; the wind had then shifted to N. by W., and blew strong, with rainy weather; and at eight o'clock, it was at N. W. by W., and obliged us to tack offshore. This gale cleared away on the 26th, and at noon our situation was in

Latitude	40° 34½' S.
Mount Chappell bore	N. E.
Peak of Cape Barren,	N. 78° E.
Land taken for Isle Waterhouse,	S. 7° E.

We were then steering south-westward again with a fair breeze; but had scarcely passed Stony Head, next morning, when another gale sprung up from the north-west. It was a happy circumstance that we were able to reach our new discovered port, and take refuge at the former secure anchorage near the Shag Rocks; for this gale was more violent and of longer continuance than any of the preceding. This long succession of adverse winds caused us almost to despair of accomplishing the principal object of the voyage; for of the twelve weeks, to which our absence from Port Packson was limited, nearly eight were already expired.

Dec. 2. The gale moderated, and we made an attempt to continue the voyage, but were driven back. On the 3rd, the attempt was repeated; and the wind being light, we anchored at the entrance of the port, to prevent losing by the flood what had been gained by the ebb tide. In the evening a fair wind sprung up; and at length, to our great satisfaction, we were enabled to proceed in the discovery of the strait.

The harbour, which we entered with so much pleasure on Nov. 3, and finally quitted with still more on Dec. 3, was named PORT DALRYMPLE, by His Excellency governor Hunter, as a mark of respect to Alexander Dalrymple, Esq., the late hydrographer to the Admiralty. The following is a summary of the observations taken there, for fixing the position of Low Head, on the east side of the entrance:

Latitude from six meridian altitudes, of which three were taken in port, and three at sea within sight of Low Head	41° 3' 30" S.
Longitude from two sets of distances of the sun east, and two west of the moon, with Troughton's nine inch sextant No. 251, corrected for the errors of the lunar and solar tables	146° 43' 45" E.
From two do. do. with a five-inch sextant of Adams	146° 52' 46"

Mean from sun and moon	146° 48' 15" E.
	===============

From one set of a star east, and one west of the moon, with No. 251	146° 52' 34"
From two ditto, ditto, with the five-inch	146° 56' 50"

Mean from stars and moon	146° 54' 42"

Mean of all	146° 51' 28" E.[20]
	===============

Variation of the theodolite., observed on the shore of Outer Cove	7 28 east
Do. of the azimuth compass, observed in the same place,	8 30
Do. of the same, taken at anchor off the port, the sloop's head being N. by E. (magnetic),	7 44

The time of high water in Port Dalrymple, is one quarter of an hour before the moon passes over the meridian; and the rise of tide is from six to eight, or it is said to ten, feet. The ebb sets out seven hours; and both ebb and flood run with much rapidity in the narrow parts, but the particular rate was not ascertained.

Port Dalrymple and the River Tamar[21] occupy the bottom of a valley betwixt two irregular chains of hills, which shoot off north-westward, from the great body of inland mountains. In some places, these hills stand wide apart, and the river then opens its banks to a considerable extent; in others, they nearly meet, and contract its bed to narrow limits. The Tamar has, indeed, more the appearance of a chain of lakes, than of a regularly-formed river; and such it probably was, until, by long undermining, assisted perhaps by some unusual weight of water, a communicating channel was formed, and a passage forced out to sea. From the shoals in Sea Reach, and more particularly from those at Green Island which turn the whole force of the tides, one is led to suppose, that the period when the passage to sea was forced has not been very remote.

Of the two chains of hills which bound the valley, the eastern one terminates at Low Head; the other comes down to the sea, five or six miles from it, on the west side of the port. The ends of these chains, when seen from directly off the entrance, appear as two clusters of hills having some resemblance to each other; and in fine weather, the distant blue heads of the back mountains will be seen over the tops of both clusters. These appearances, joined to the latitude and longitude, are the best distant marks for finding Port Dalrymple. If a ship come along shore from the eastward, the Ninth Island, and afterward Stony Head with the Tenth Islet lying three or four miles to the north-west, will announce the vicinity of the port; and Low Head will be perceived in the bight to the S. S. W., but it is not a conspicuous object. Three or four leagues to the westward of the port, the back land is uncommonly high, and the top of the ridge is intersected into uncouth shapes. From the brilliancy of some of these mountains, on the appearance of the sun after rain, I judged them to be of granite, like those of Furneaux's Islands. These mountains, with the direction of the coast and what has been said of the clusters of hills, may serve as marks for Port Dalrymple to ships coming along shore from the westward.

Reefs and banks extend out to a considerable distance on the west side of the entrance; so that strangers should avoid that side, and endeavour to come in with Low Head. The greater part of these shoals, as also of those in Sea Reach, are covered at half tide; therefore the first of the flood, or even a little before, is the best time to enter Port Dalrymple, as almost the whole of the dangers are then visible. A signal post, with pilots, was fixed at Low Head on the settlement of the new colony in 1804, and beacons have since been placed on the most dangerous rocks and shoals; it has therefore become unnecessary to give particular instructions for sailing up the port, especially as they may be found in my Observations on the coasts of Van Diemen's Land, etc.; a little memoir published by Mr. Arrowsmith, in 1801.[22]

We found Port Dalrymple to be an excellent place for refreshment. Out of the flocks of black swans, from one-fifth to one-tenth of them were unable to fly; and since the same thing has been found to obtain in the months of January and May, as well as in October. it is probably so at all times of the year. These birds are endowed with a considerable portion of sagacity: they cannot dive, but have a method of immersing themselves so deep in the water, as to render their bodies nearly invisible, and thus frequently to avoid detection. In chase, their plan was to gain the wind upon our little boat; and they usually succeeded when the breeze was strong, and sometimes escaped from our shot also.

Kangaroos appeared to be rather numerous in this part of Van Diemen's Land; but as they were shy, and we had little time or necessity to go after them, one only was procured; it was of the large, forest kind, and the flesh was thought superior to that of the same animal at Port Jackson.

Ducks and teal went by flocks in Port Dalrymple; but they were shy, and we took no trouble after them. The white-bellied shag, and the black and pied red bills were common in the lower parts of the port, and some pelicans were seen upon the shoals. The large black shag, usually found in rivers, was seen in different parts of the Tamar; and upon another occasion, we found these birds to be tolerable food.

Neither our wants nor leisure were sufficient to induce any attempt to catch fish. Muscles were abundant upon those rocks which are overflowed by the tide; and the natives appeared to get oysters by diving, the shells having been found near their fire places.

The country round Port Dalrymple has, in general, a pleasing and fertile appearance; nor did examination prove it to be deceitful. But this subject, and what concerns the natives, came more particularly within the department of Mr. Bass; and his observations upon them having been published, I proceed to the continuation of the voyage.

Dec. 3, in the evening, the Norfolk was lying at anchor off the entrance of the port, when a breeze sprung up from the north-eastward, and enabled us to proceed along the coast. At dusk, Low Head bore S. 77° E. six miles, and we then hauled off for the night. The shore on the west side of Port Dalrymple falls back to the southward and forms a bight under the high land, where it is possible there may be some small opening; for the haziness of the weather did not allow the coast line to be distinctly traced. Upon the back mountains are many variously-shaped tops, of which the easternmost bore S. 5° E., and a flat one towards the other end of the ridge, S. 38° W. The furthest land which could be seen was a round hill, making like an island, and bore very nearly west from the mast head.

Dec. 4. We resumed our course westward, but the wind being at N. N. E., did not dare to approach very near the shore. At noon, the observed latitude was 40° 58', and the hills on the west side of Port Dalrymple bore S. 65° E. five or six leagues. From thence to S. 38° W., where another chain of hills came down to the sea, the country is well wooded, and lies in hills and vallies. The Round Hill bore S. 65° W. five or six leagues, and in the evening, when three leagues distant, the low land connecting it with the main was visible.

During the night, and next day, Dec. 5, the winds were light and variable, so that we made little progress. At noon, the furthest land seen to the westward appeared like a small flat-topped island, but being found to be connected with the main land, received the descriptive name of Circular Head; a nearer projection, of a jagged appearance, was called Rocky Cape, and a steep cliffy head still nearer, Table Cape, from its flat top. Our situation was then as under;

Latitude observed,	40° 56' S.
Round Hill, distant three leagues,	S. 22 E.
Table Cape, north extreme,	N. 88 W.
Rocky Cape, highest knob,	N. 77 W.
Circular Head	N. 71 W.
A flat-topped peak, inland,	S. 14 W.

The sandy shore abreast was seven or eight miles distant, and behind it the land was low, but tolerably well covered with wood. The sole remarkable object inland, was the flat-topped peak, which had very much the appearance of an extinguished volcano. From after bearings, it was found to lie S. 1° E. eleven leagues from Table Cape; and in that direction its top assumes the form of a pointed cone.

In the morning of Dec. 6, our situation was N. 8° E. four miles from the cliffy, north-east end of Table Cape, and the Round Hill bore S. 41° E. Having a favourable breeze, we passed, at eight o'clock, within half a mile of the reef which surrounds Rocky Cape, and steered onward for Circular Head, which as yet was the furthest visible land.

Table Cape, Rocky Cape, and Circular Head lie nearly in a line of N. 62° W., and are about ten miles apart from each other. Between these, the coast forms two shallow bights; the shore of the first is mostly rocky, and an islet lies in the middle; the western bight is sandy, and promises better anchorage, particularly near Circular Head, where a vessel may be sheltered against all winds from the western half of the compass. The land at the back of the shore, from Table Cape westward, is of a different description to that before passed: instead of having an extensive view over a var-iegated, and well wooded country, the sight was there confined by a ridge of stony hills, of which Rocky Cape is no more than a projecting part.

Circular Head is a cliffy, round lump, in form much resembling a Christmas cake; and is joined to the main by a low, sandy isthmus. The land at the back is somewhat lower than the head, and is formed into very gentle slopes. A slight covering of withered grass gave it a smooth appearance; and some green bushes scattered over it much resembled, at a distance, a herd of seals basking upon a rock.

We passed Circular Head at ten, and three hummocks of land then came in sight to the north-westward, the south-ernmost and highest having something of a sugar-loaf form. Between these hills and the smooth land to the west of Circular Head, there was a large bight, in which some patches of land were indistinctly visible through the haze; but as the wind was then blowing directly into the bight, the fear of getting embayed prevented its examination. Our posi-tion at noon was as follows:

Latitude observed,	40° 39¾' S.
Circular Head, distant seven miles,	S. 17 E.
West extreme of the smooth land behind it,	S. 6 W.
Sugar-loaf hummock,	N. 55 W.
Northernmost hummock,	N. 49 W.

From the time of leaving Port Dalrymple no tide had been observed, until this morning. It ran with us, and continued until three o'clock; at which time low land was seen beyond the three hummocks. This trending of the coast so far to the north made me apprehend, that it might be found to join the land near Western Port, and thus disappoint our hopes of discovering an open passage to the westward; the water was also discoloured, as if we were approaching the head of a bay, rather than the issue of a strait; and on sounding, we had 17, and afterwards 15 fathoms on a sandy bottom.

The wind having become light and the tide turned to the eastward, our situation at dusk was little altered from what it had been at three o'clock; but from the clearing away of the haze, the lands in the great bight had become more dis-tinguishable, and the following bearings were taken:

Table Cape, distant 11 or 12 leagues,	S. 43½° E.
Circular Head,	S. 26 E.
Sugar-loaf hummock,	N. 75 W.
Extreme of the three-hummock land,	N. 48 W.
Low point in the great bight, with a cliffy head at a further distance behind it,	S. 70 W.

The cliffs visible behind the low point had every appearance of being the north head of an opening, but of what kind, our distance was too great to determine.[23]

During the night and next day, Dec. 7, the wind was variable, with alternate calms. The latitude at noon was 40° 28', and the sugarloaf hill bore W. by S. ten miles. On the 8th a breeze sprung up from the south-westward, and threat-ened a gale from that boisterous quarter. We were in 40° 23' at noon, and trying to work up to the land of the three hummocks, to prevent losing ground; and at six in the evening, got to an anchor in a quarter less 4 fathoms, in a small sandy bight under the northern hummock, being sheltered from N. 2° E., round by the west to S. 30° E. Circular Head was still visible, bearing S. 35° E.; and the difference of longitude made from Port Dalrymple was calculated at 1¾°, subject to future revision.

Mr. Bass and myself landed immediately to examine the country and the coast, and to see what food could be pro-cured; for the long detention by foul winds had obliged me to make a reduction in the provisions, lest the object of our voyage and return to Port Jackson should not be accomplished in the twelve weeks for which we were victualled. At dusk, we returned on board, having had little success as to any of the objects proposed; but with the knowledge of a fact, from which an interesting deduction was drawn: the tide had been running from the eastward all the after-noon, and contrary to expectation, we found it to be near low water by the shore; the flood, therefore, came from the west, and not from the eastward, as at Furneaux's Isles. This we considered to be a strong proof, not only of the real existence of a passage betwixt this land and New South Wales, but also that the entrance into the Southern Indian Ocean could not be far distant.

The little time there was for examining the coast, confined my observations to what were necessary for giving it the formation it has in the chart. The country is hilly, and Mr. Bass found it impenetrable from the closeness of the tall brush wood, although it had been partially burnt not long before. There was very little soil spread over the rock and sand, and the general aspect was that of sterility. Several deserted fire places, strewed round with the shells of the sea ear, were found upon the shore.

The south-west wind died away in the night; and at six next morning, Dec. 9, we got under way with a light air at south-east. After rounding the northeast point of the three-hummock land, our course westward was pursued along its north side.

A large flock of gannets was observed at daylight, to issue out of the great bight to the southward; and they were followed by such a number of the sooty petrels as we had never seen equalled. There was a stream of from fifty to eighty yards in depth, and of three hundred yards, or more, in breadth; the birds were not scattered, but flying as compactly as a free movement of their wings seemed to allow; and during a full hour and a half, this stream of petrels continued to pass without interruption, at a rate little inferior to the swiftness of the pigeon. On the lowest computation, I think the number could not have been less than a hundred millions; and we were thence led to believe, that there must be, in the large bight, one or more uninhabited islands of considerable size.[24]

From the north-east point of the three-hummock land, the shore trended W. 1° N. three miles; then S. 39° W. four miles, to a rocky point, forming the south-west extremity of what was then ascertained to be THREE-HUMMOCK IS-LAND. The channel which separates it from the land to the west, is, at least, two miles in width, and is deep; so that it was difficult to conjecture how the Indians were able to get over to the island. It was almost certain that they had no canoes at Port Dalrymple, nor any means of reaching islands lying not more than two cables length from the shore; and it therefore seemed improbable that they should possess canoes here. The small size of Three-hummock Island rendered the idea of fixed inhabitants inadmissible; and whichever way it was considered, the presence of men there was a problem difficult to be resolved.[25]

The coast on the west side of the channel lies nearly south, and rises in height as it advances towards the cliffy head, set on the 6th p.m. The north end of this land is a sloping, rocky point; and the first projection which opened round it, was at S. 32° W., five or six miles. Beyond this there was nothing like main land to be seen; indeed, this western land itself had very little the appearance of being such, either in its form, or in its poor, starved vegetation. So soon as we had passed the north sloping point, a long swell was perceived to come from the south-west, such as we had not been accustomed to for some time. It broke heavily upon a small reef, lying a mile and a half from the point, and upon all the western shores; but, although it was likely to prove troublesome, and perhaps dangerous, Mr. Bass and myself hailed it with joy and mutual congratulation, as announcing the completion of our long-wished-for discovery of a passage into the Southern Indian Ocean.

We had a fine breeze at east; and our course was directed for a small, rocky island which lies W. ½ N. 6 miles from the north point of the barren land. This island appeared to be almost white with birds; and so much excited our curiosity and hope of procuring a supply of food, that Mr. Bass went on shore in the boat whilst I stood off and on, waiting his return. No land could be seen to the northward, and the furthest clearly distinguishable in the opposite direction was a steep island at the distance of four leagues. The observations taken at noon were,

Latitude,	40° 23½' S.
The bird island, distant two miles,	S. 16 to 64 E.
Three-hummock Island, the sugar loaf,	S. 64 E.
Steep-head Island	S. 9 E.

Mr. Bass returned at half past two, with a boat load of seals and albatrosses. He had been obliged to fight his way up the cliffs of the island with the seals, and when arrived at the top, to make a road with his clubs amongst the albatrosses. These birds were sitting upon their nests, and almost covered the surface of the ground, nor did they any otherwise derange themselves for the new visitors, than to peck at their legs as they passed by. This species of albatross is white on the neck and breast, partly brown on the back and wings, and its size is less than many others met with at sea, particularly in the high southern latitudes. The seals were of the usual size, and bore a reddish fur, much inferior in quality to that of the seals at Furneaux's Islands.

Albatross Island, for so it was named, is near two miles in length, and sufficiently high to be seen five or six leagues from a ship's deck: its shores are mostly steep cliffs. The latitude is 40° 25', and longitude made by the running survey, 2° 7' west of Port Dalrymple; but it afterwards appeared from the Investigator's time keepers, to lie in 144° 41' east of Greenwich.

The tide (apparently the ebb) had set so strong to the south-westward, that notwithstanding our efforts to keep up with the island, it was distant five miles when Mr. Bass returned and the boat was hoisted in. A black lump of rock was then seen three or four leagues to the south-westward, and the following bearings were taken just before making sail.

Albatross Island,	N. 75° to 86° E.
Steep-head Island,	S. 31 E.
Black. pyramidal rock,	S. 59 W.

We kept close to the wind at north-east, in order to fetch Steep-head Island; but were carried so far to leeward by the tide, that soon after four o'clock our situation was as follows:

Albatross Island,	N. 18° E.
Sugar-loaf hummock,	N. 71 E.
Western part of the barren land,	N. 61 E.
Steep-head Island, centre,	S. 71 E.
Black, pyramidal rock,	N. 77 W.
High black rock, dist. 2 miles,	
having breakers to the south-westward,	S. 18 E.

Besides these islands and rocks, we passed another cliffy island four or five miles to the south of Steep-head, and to which I gave the name of Trefoil Island, its form appearing to be nearly that of a clover leaf; there were, also, several others of less importance, mostly lying near the barren land. The steep south end of this land was set over the north end of Trefoil at N. 65° E.; and being almost assured of its separation from Van Diemen's Land, I added it, under the name of Barren Island, to the rest of this cluster; and in honour of His Excellency, the governor of New South Wales, I gave to the whole the title of HUNTER'S ISLES.

The north-west cape of Van Diemen's Land, or island, as it might now be termed, is a steep, black head, which, from its appearance, I call CAPE GRIM. It lies nearly due south, four miles, from the centre of Trefoil, in latitude 40° 44'; the longitude will be 144° 43° east, according to the position of Albatross Island made in the Investigator. There are two rocks close to Cape Grim, of the same description with itself. On the north side of the cape, the shore is a low, sandy beach, and trends north-eastward, three or four miles; but whether there be a sufficient depth for ships to pass between it and Barren Island, has not, I believe, been yet ascertained. To the south of the cape, the black cliffs extend seven or eight miles, when the shore falls back, eastward, to a sandy bay, of which little could be perceived.

Our situation at dusk, was three miles from the cliffs, with Cape Grim bearing N. 18° E. The furthest land, beyond the sandy bay, bore S. 4° E. four or five leagues, and proved to be near the westernmost point of Van Diemen's Land. The wind being strong at E. N. E. and the night dark and tempestuous, we kept as much under the land as possible; but found ourselves in the morning, Dec. l0, to be driven far to the south-westward. At eight o'clock, the wind having moderated, we made sail, S. E. ½ E; and at noon, were in the following situation.

Latitude observed,	41° 13¾' S.
Sandy west Pt. of V. D. Land, dist. 10 m. N. 10 W.	
Furthest extreme, a low point,	S. 22 E.
An inland mount,	S. 53 E.

The nearest part of the coast was between two and three miles distant, and consisted of sandy beaches, separated by points which had many straggling rocks lying off them. At the back of the shore, the land was low for two or three miles, and then rose gently to a ridge of barren, low hills. The inland mount, set at S. 53° E., appeared to be the north end of a second chain, much higher, and better wooded, than the front ridge: it lies eight miles back from the shore, and is named Mount Norfolk, after my little vessel.

After obtaining the noon's observation and bearings, we steered southward along the shore; and at six o'clock, had passed five leagues of the same kind of coast as before described; but the wind then flew round to W. N. W., and made it necessary to haul further off. At 6° 30',

Mount Norfolk bore	N. 56° E.
Low, rocky projection, distant four miles,	N. 35 E.
Distant mount, at the southern end of the back ridge,	
and the furthest land in sight,	S. 42 E.

Dec. 11. Before five o'clock, we came in with the land a few miles from where it had been quitted in the evening.

Mount Norfolk then bore	N. 27° E.

Low, rocky projection, dist. three leagues,	N. 12 W.
Two conic rocks, at the southern extreme,	S. 42 E.

The wind was moderate at north-west, and we bore away along the shore, which was distant four miles, and much similar to that of the preceding day; but it had no scattered rocks lying in front. Behind some low cliffs, passed at seven o'clock, was perceived a small opening like a river, whose course seemed to run northward, between the front and back ridges of hills: a smoke, which arose from the inner side of the opening, was the first seen upon this west coast. I steered a short time for the entrance; but seeing rocks in it, and the wind coming more on shore, hauled off south, to increase our distance.

Two miles from the opening are the conic, and several low rocks, which were passed at the distance of one mile and a half. At ten, we kept two points more away, having gained an offing of seven miles; and at noon had,

Latitude observed,	42° 2¼' S.
Furthest extreme of the coast,	S. S. E.
Mount at the southern end of the back ridge,	N. 42 E.
A peaked hill, four miles E. S. E. from it,	N. 60 E.

The two last appear to have been the smaller mountains seen by TASMAN to the north-east, on his discovering this land Nov. 24, 1642; and I have therefore named the first Mount Heemskerk, and the latter Mount Meehan, after his two ships. The back ridge of woody hills does not terminate here; but it retreats further inland, and as far as could be perceived through the haze, rises in height to the southward. The extreme of the coast, which bore S. S. E., forms the southern point of a sandy, and rather deep bight, where I thought it probable there might be some small opening; but as the wind blew strong directly into it, there was too much danger in bearing away for its examination.

At three o'clock, we passed the southern point of the bight, at the distance of four miles; and the coast then again trended S. S. E., waving in rocky bights and projections. The land here rises by a gentle ascent for two or three miles from the shore; its appearance was smooth and uniform; but it was destitute of wood, and almost of other vegetation: the back mountains were obscured by the haze.

The heavy south-west swell, which had met us at the entrance of the Indian Ocean, still continued to roll in, and set dead upon this coast; and the wind blew fresh at W. N. W. Under these circumstances, we looked out for some little beach where in case of necessity, the sloop might be run on shore with a prospect of safety to our lives; for should the wind come three or four points further forward, there was no probability of clearing the land on either tack. No such beach could, however, be discovered; and we therefore carried all possible sail to get past this dreary coast. A remarkable pyramid came in sight in the evening; at eight o'clock it was distant five miles to the east, and seen to be a rock on the north side of a point, which projects two or three miles from the coast line. This point, named Point Hibbs after the colonial master of the Norfolk, is higher than the neck by which it is joined to the back land; and from thence, it appears to have been taken for an island by Tasman; for I consider Point Ebbs and the pyramid to be the two islands laid down by him, in 42° 35': their latitude, by our run from noon, is 42° 39'.

We hauled off, upon a wind, at eight o'clock; and at four next morning, Dec. 12, came in again with the same land. At five, when our course was resumed along shore, Point Hibbs was distant two or three miles, and the pyramid, which bore N. 31° E. over its extremity, then appeared like the crown of a hat. The coast to the southward is more irregular in its trending, is of somewhat greater elevation, and not so destitute of wood as on the north side of the point. At the distance of three leagues we passed a cliffy head, with high rocks lying a mile from it; and two leagues further, there were some patches of breakers two miles off the shore: the general trending was between S. by E. and S. S. E.

At ten o'clock, a projection which merited the name of Rocky Point bore S. 74° E., five miles; and here the direction of the coast was changed to east, for near seven miles, when it formed a bight by again trending south-eastward. The shore round the bight is high, and at the back were several bare peaks which, from their whiteness, might have been thought to be covered with snow; but their greatest elevation of perhaps 1200 feet, combined with the height of the thermometer at 62°, did not admit the supposition. These peaks are probably what Tasman named De Witt's Isles, from his distance having been too far off to distinguish the connecting land, and I therefore called the highest of them, lying in 43° 9½' south, Mount De Witt.

This morning, two sets of distances of the sun west of the moon were observed, and our situation at noon was as follows:

Latitude,	43° 7' S.
Longitude from the lunar observations,	145 16 E.
Rocky Point, distant six or seven miles,	N. 3 W.

Mount De Witt,	S. 77 E.
Highest of two smaller hills, at the S. extreme,	S. 59 E.

It afterwards appeared, that these smaller hills stood upon the extremity of a point; and in honour of the noble admiral with whose victory we had become acquainted, it was named POINT ST. VINCENT.

The western breeze died away in the evening, and the sloop was drifted in by the swell, and perhaps by a tide, towards an opening round Point St. Vincent. This opening is indicated in the small chart which accompanies the voyage of M. Marion, but does not appear to have been seen by any other navigator. Our bearings of the land, at sunset, deduced from the sun's amplitude and sextant angles, were as follow:

Mount De Witt,	N. 18° E.
Point St. Vincent, distant five miles,	N. 57 E.
Steep head on the east side of the opening, dist. 8 m.	N. 86 E.
Pyramidal rock, lying off a cliffy head,	S. 46 E.

At a further distance, and in the same bearing with the pyramidal rock, was a steep, jagged point, which proved to be the south-west cape of Van Diemen's Land. Our latitude at this time was 43° 18½', the passage of the moon having allowed me to get an observation at four o'clock; from whence to eight, our position had changed only one-and-half mile to the east.

It remained nearly calm all night; and on the 13th, at daybreak, I was much surprised to find our situation near ten miles to the southward, instead of being in the same place. This circumstance, and a breeze which arose at north, precluded me from examining the opening as I had intended; for a width of three or four miles at the entrance, and the form of the mountains behind, made it probable that a considerable river discharged itself there; and the offset during the night strengthened the supposition. At six o'clock,

Mount De Witt bore	North.
Point St. Vincent,	N. 7° E.
Steep head on the east side of the opening,	W. 27 E.
Pyramidal rock, off the cliffy head,	N. 33 E.
South-west Cape, the extreme.	S. 82 E.

We were then steering for the South-west Cape, and at nine I set Mount De Witt over it at N. 22° W., our distance from the cape being then about three miles.

Seven islands and rocks were counted to the eastward, lying at different distances from the coast; and the wind having veered to west, permitted us to pass within them. At noon, the shore to the north being too near for the sun's altitude to be observed, its supplement was taken to the south, and gave the latitude 43° 27½'. A steep head which lies N. 79° E. four or five miles from the south-west Cape, then bore S. 74° W, three miles;[26] whence the latitude of the Cape should be 43° 29', which is 10 less than given by captain Furneaux, and 8' by captain Cook. This difference naturally excited some suspicion of an error in the observation, and I measured the supplement in the same manner on the following noon, when it gave 2' 40" less than the latitude determined by D'Entrecasteaux in Storm Bay. The South-west Cape is therefore placed 2' 40" further south than my observation gave it; that is, in latitude 43° 32'.[27] The longitude of the Cape, from the observations taken off Rocky Point and brought forward by the survey, would be 145° 47'; but its situation in 146° 7', by captain Cook, appears to be preferable: D'Entrecasteaux places it in 146° 0'. The nearest land, at noon, was a steep head bearing N. 66° E., one mile and a half; and between this, and the head which bore S. 74° W., the shore forms a sandy bay four miles deep, where it is probable there may be good anchorage, if two clumps of rock, which lie in the entrance, will admit of a passage in. After taking bearings of Maatsuyker's Isles and the different headlands, we bore away eastward, and passed another deep, sandy bight, probably the same in which Mr. Cox anchored in 1789. At two o'clock, the

South-west Cape, distant 15 or 16 miles, bore	W. 2° S.
A steep head at the furthest extreme,	
which proved to be the South Cape,	S . 72° E. [28]

At this time we were one mile within, or north of the largest of the islands; and saw with some surprise, for it is three miles from the main, that its grassy vegetation had been burnt. From hence we steered for the easternmost isle, lying off a wide open bight in the coast, and afterwards hauled up for the South Cape. The wind died away at six o'clock, when the Cape was one mile distant; but thick clouds were gathering in the south and west, and strong gusts with heavy rain presently succeeded. Fortunately, the squalls came from the westward, so that we were enabled to get further from those stupendous cliffs; had they come from the south, the consequences might have been fatal to the Norfolk.

The first steep head, to the eastward of the South Cape, opened round it at E. 7° N., (allowing 4° east variation,) and a second from the first, at E. 16° N., their distances asunder being each about five miles. It is the middlemost of these three heads which is called South Cape by captain Cook, as appears from the relative situations of his Peaked Hill and of Swilly rock; but he had not the opportunity of seeing the heads opening one from the other, as we had in the Norfolk. I make the latitude of the Cape (adding the 2' 40") to be 43° 37', nearly as captain Furneaux did; and as captain Cook would have done, had his latitude at noon been taken 43° 42½', according to the Astronomical Observations, instead Of 42° 47', as in the voyage.

Pedro Blame, or Swilly rock, became visible at half past seven, when the squalls had mostly blown over; and the following bearings where then taken:

South Cape, distant five miles,	W. by N.
East extreme of the next steep head, dist. 2½ miles,	N. 14° E.
Pedro Blanca,	S. 33 E.
Distant land through the haze,	N. 60 E.

At nine o'clock we hauled up for D'Entrecasteauxs Channel, of which I had the sketch of Mr. Hayes, and stood off and on, in the entrance, during the night; the wind blowing hard at west, with dark rainy weather.

Dec. 14, at four in the morning, our situation was far to leeward; and having no prospect of fetching into the channel, we bore away for Boreel's Isles, which were seen bearing N. 65° E. two leagues. Three of these produce some vegetation, and that of the largest had been partially burnt not long before. The two easternmost, called the Friars by captain Furneaux, are bare pyramidal rocks, and, except where they had been made white by the gannets, are of a black, weather-beaten colour: a patch of breakers lies one mile to the north-east from them.

Fluted Cape opened round Tasman's Head at N. 18° E. We passed these steep projections at a mile distance; and not being able to fetch into Adventure Bay, did the same by Cape Frederick Henry.[29] At noon, this cape bore S. 13° W. eight miles, and Fluted Cape was behind it in the same bearing. I proposed to enter the Derwent River; but on making a stretch toward Betsey's Island,[30] it appeared that the Henshaw's Bay of Hayes, instead of being a shallow bight, was a deep opening; and as the north-west wind blew out of the Derwent, we stretched on, seven miles above the island, and came to an anchor in 10 fathoms, sandy ground. This opening is the North Bay of D'Entrecasteaux; but I was totally ignorant, at that time, of its having ever been entered.

Dec. 15, the wind being at north-west, we passed a sloping island (Isle St. Aignan of D'Extrecasteaux), and steered north-eastward, to explore the inlet. After running three-and-half miles, with soundings from 13 no bottom, to 5 fathoms, we anchored under a small island, which lies S. 75° W., one mile and a half, from Point Renard, the uppermost station of the French boats. This small spot received the descriptive name of Isle of Caves, and lies in the passage from North Bay to a large extent of water which appeared to the eastward, and which the French boats did not explore.

From the Isle of Caves we ran six miles, E. S. E. up the new bay, for Smooth Island. The width of the entrance, from Point Renard to Green Head, is two miles, the soundings are from 6 to 16 fathoms, and there are no dangers. Smooth Island, behind which we anchored in 4 fathoms, and where I again landed to take bearings, is three quarters of a mile long, and covered with grass and a few small trees. It had been visited by the natives, as had the Isle of Caves; but from the eggs of gulls found upon both, I judge they do not go often.

Dec. 16, we anchored two miles to the south-east of Smooth Island, in 6 fathoms, near a point of the main where a round hill afforded me a good view of this extensive bay. The country there is stony and barren, though covered with wood and much frequented by kangaroos. In the evening, the appearance of a southern gale induced me to shift our berth to the north side of the point; between which, and an islet lying half a mile from it, the depth was 5 to 7 fathoms.

On the 17th, we landed upon the islet, and killed some out of the many gulls by which it is frequented. A small arm of the bay extending north-eastward, where we hoped to obtain fresh water, was the object of our examination in the afternoon. There was a little stream falling in at the head, but rocks prevented it from being accessible to boats, or to a raft; and a walk of perhaps a mile to the eastward, afforded nothing but the sight of a stony country, and of a few miserable huts. Our greyhound started a kangaroo, but it was lost in the wood; and there were no birds to shoot.

Dec. 18, the wind still blowing fresh from the westward, we worked up to Smooth Island; and then stretched over to the south side of the bay. The soundings were generally 9 fathoms, on mud and sand, to within a mile of the shore; and at half a mile, where the anchor was dropped, the depth was 4 fathoms.

We landed at a steep, but not high point near the sloop, where I took some bearings, and observed the meridian altitude of the moon in an artificial horizon, which gave the latitude 43° 1½'; Mr. Bass, in the mean time, walked a little distance inland, but saw nothing of particular interest. Some further bearings were taken next morning, from a head lying to the west; after which the anchor was weighed, and we steered northward along the west side of the bay, with soundings from 8 to 4 fathoms. In the evening, we had worked back into North Bay, and come to an anchor under the north-east end of Sloping Island.

The great eastern bay now quitted had never been entered till this time; and as it is proved not to be Frederik Hendrik's, I have named it NORFOLK BAY. It is about eight miles long, north and south, and three to five miles broad from east to west. The largest fleet may find shelter here, with anchorage on a good bottom of 4 to 9 fathoms deep. We saw but one small stream of fresh water, and that was of difficult access; but it is scarcely probable that, amongst the many coves all around the bay, water convenient for ships should not be found. The country near the shore is rocky; but as the kangaroo seemed to be abundant, there are probably many grassy plains further inland. Wood abounds every where, except at Green Head, which is mostly covered with grass. Of the four islands in the bay, Smooth and Gull Islands were found superior in fertility to the main land: the first contains about forty acres of tolerable pasturage.

In North Bay, the upper part seemed to be circumscribed by a sandy beach, and to offer nothing of particular interest; we therefore steered downward, on Dec. 20, for the Derwent River; but rainy squalls coming on from the south, ran for a small beach on the western shore, and anchored off it in 2½ fathoms. A narrow inlet there, from which the tide issued with some strength, excited the hope of finding a short cut into the Derwent; but it proved, on examination, to terminate in a shoal lagoon. The country on its borders affords good pasturage, with some spots fit for cultivation; there is, also, fresh water on the north side, but only for domestic purposes. The lagoon is frequented by ducks, black shags, pelicans, and gannets.

Dec. 21, we proceeded round for the Derwent. On clearing North Bay, I went off in the boat to Betsey's Island, leaving Mr. Bass to conduct the sloop. This island is high, and accessible only towards its north end; its length is one mile, and mean breadth about half that quantity; the soil is fertile, and nourishes a luxuriant vegetation of grass and wood; and though the natives visit it occasionally, none of their traces were recent. On rejoining the sloop, I found she had passed between the island and two flat rocks near the main, with from 5 to 9 fathoms water; in which depths the gigantic sea-weed grows up to the surface. At eight clock we anchored in 9 fathoms, off Cape Direction, at the entrance of the river.

Dec. 22, a base was measured and bearings taken for a survey of the entrance, which proved to be near three miles wide. On the 23rd, the wind being fair, we ran upwards between shores which were sometimes steep, but generally of a gradual ascent, and well clothed with grass and wood. At nine miles from the entrance lies Sullivan Cove, on the west side, where a settlement has since been established by colonel Collins;[31] and here the width of the river is suddenly contracted, from one mile and a half to less than three-quarters of a mile, but the depth is not diminished. Four miles higher up we found Risdon Cove, and anchored there in 4 fathoms, with the intention of filling our empty water casks at the Risdon River of Mr. Hayes; but finding it to be a little creek which even our boat could not enter, I determined to seek a more convenient watering place higher up the Derwent.

Dec. 24, the wind being adverse to proceeding upward, an extensive set of angles was taken from the top of Mount Direction; and next day, I carried the survey up the river, whilst Mr. Bass ascended the great Mount Table, on the western side. At the northern foot of this mount lie King George's Plains, a name given by Mr. Hayes to about three hundred acres of pasture land; and in the front of the plains is his Prince of Wales' Bay, a small shallow cove. Such names as these led us, at first, into some errors with respect to the importance of the places sought; but after the above examples, we were no longer deceived by them.

In the afternoon of the 25th, we got the sloop, with much difficulty, five or six miles further up the river, to an inlet which I called Herdsman's Cove, from the pastoral appearance of the surrounding country. Two streams fall into it; and up the principal one, in the north-east corner, I went two miles with the boat. The water was there found to be fresh, and the depth sufficient to allow of its being reached by the sloop; but the banks being steep and channel narrow, I was deterred from watering in this place, by the fear of detention from foul winds.

The width of the Derwent abreast of Herdsman's Cove is half a mile; but except a very narrow channel close to the eastern shore, it is too shallow even for boats. The intention of proceeding further with the sloop was therefore abandoned; but so soon as the rainy, blowing weather permitted, which was not until the 28th, I accompanied Mr. Bass in a boat excursion up the river. Three miles above Herdsman's Cove the banks open out to a mile in width; the river, from running north-westward, turns to the south-west; and the deep channel makes a short cut across to the convex bank, leaving the mud to collect in the opposite elbow. A great deal of long, aquatic grass growing upon these mud flats, seemed to have attracted the black swans, for the number collected there was not estimated at less than five hundred.

The width of the Derwent is contracted in the south-west reach to little more than a quarter of a mile, and we had not rowed far up it before the water became perfectly fresh. The land on both sides rises to hills of moderate elevation, and the rather steep acclivities being well clothed with verdure, they had an agreeable appearance. Our attention was suddenly called from contemplating the country, by the sound of a human voice coming from the hills. There were three people; and as they would not comply with our signs to come down, we landed and went up to them, taking with us a black swan. Two women ran off, but a man, who had two or three spears in his hand, stayed to receive us, and accepted the swan with rapture. He seemed entirely ignorant of muskets, nor did any thing excite his attention or desire except the swan and the red kerchiefs about our necks; he knew, however, that we came from the sloop, and where it was lying. A little knowledge of the Port Jackson, and of the South-Sea-Island languages was of no use in making ourselves understood by this man; but the quickness with which he comprehended our signs spoke in favour of his intelligence. His appearance much resembled that of the inhabitants of New South Wales; he had also marks raised upon the skin, and his face was blackened and hair ruddled as is sometimes practised by them. The hair was either close cropped, or naturally short; but it had not the appearance of being woolly. He acceded to our proposition of going to his hut; but finding from his devious route and frequent stoppages, that he sought to tire our patience, we left him delighted with the certain possession of his swan, and returned to the boat. This was the sole opportunity we had of communicating with any of the natives of Van Diemen's Land.

At one o'clock, when advanced five miles above the elbow, the ebb tide made; and the wind being unfavourable, we landed to dine. The general course of the river had been nearly south-west; but it there turned west-by-north. The width, found by extending a base line, was two hundred and thirty yards, and the depth, as it had generally been in the channel from Herdsman's Cove, was 3 fathoms; but in some parts there may not be more than 2, at low water. We arrived on board the sloop in the evening, with fourteen swans, in time to get a short distance down the river, before the ebb tide had done running; and no place more convenient than Risdon Cove having offered itself, we anchored there next day, and proceeded to complete our water, and refit the sloop for returning to Port Jackson. The late rains had so much increased the stream at the head of the cove, that our labour was much abridged; and in the evening of Dec. 30, everything was completed.

This cove is the highest part of the Derwent to which a ship can advance. There is no danger in proceeding thus far, except off Shoal Point, about two miles below, on the western shore; and on the opposite side, near the echoing cliffs, there are 12 to 17 fathoms. Above Risdon Cove the mud flats commence, and will stop any vessel which draws more than ten or twelve feet; although there be, in some places higher up, from 5 to 8 fathoms. Mount Direction, on the north side of Risdon Cove, forms two round heads which are distinguishable from the entrance of the river, bearing N. 16° W. from Cape Direction. The latitude observed under the mount, from the moon's meridian altitude, was 42° 48' 12" south; variation of the azimuth compass on the south side of the cove, 8° 28', and of the surveying theodolite 9° 15' east; but I found it alter one or two degrees in different places, both in Norfolk Bay and in the Derwent, owing to partial attractions in the land.[32]

In Risdon Cove the tide rises between four and five feet, which is more, by at least a foot, than it appeared to be at the entrance of the river. The time of high water is about eight hours after the moon's passage over the meridian, or one hour later than in Adventure Bay.[33] In the narrow parts, above Sullivan Cove, the tides run with tolerable regularity, and with some degree of strength; but towards the entrance of the river, the water at the surface sometimes ran down twelve hours together, and at other times as much upwards, whilst the rise and fall by the shore were at the usual periods. These anomalies were probably occasioned by the wind, and seemed not to extend far below the surface; for I found a counter current at the bottom.

The banks of the Derwent are not remarkably high, but the country in general may be termed mountainous. Mount Table, at the back of Sullivan Cove, is supposed to be three-quarters of a mile in height; nor do I think, from having seen it beyond the distance of thirty miles from the sloop's deck, that it can be much less. The publication of Mr. Bass' remarks upon the soil and productions of this part of Van Diemen's Land dispenses me from entering upon those subjects; it is sufficient to say, that the reports of them were so favourable as to induce the establishment of a colony on the banks of the Derwent, four years afterward; and that the discoveries which have since been made are marked in the chart.

1799.

The last day of December and the first of January were occupied in beating down to the entrance of the river.
Jan. 2. The wind blew strong from the south-east, with heavy rain; and finding no advantage could be made by beating in Storm Bay, we ran into D'Entrecasteaux's Channel, passed the large North-west Port, and anchored in Pruen

Cove, in 4 fathoms. We landed, so soon as the rain cleared away, and found a small creek in which the water was fresh at a few hundred yards above where it falls into the cove. A tree had been felled on the bank, probably in 1793 or 4 by Mr. Hayes, who called this stream Amelia's River; but it would be very difficult to fill casks here, except when long continued rains should bring the fresh water to the entrance of the creek. The valley through which it comes from the westward, seemed to be of a rich, though damp soil.

On Jan. 3, having a breeze at north-west, we got under way at daylight; and after repassing the northern entrance of D'Entrecasteaux's Channel, steered across Storm Bay. At two clock I had the following bearings:

Tasman's Head.	S. 37° W.
Cape Frederik Henry,	S. 71 W.
Quoin Island, distant six miles,	N. 28 W.
Low point, distant 1¼ miles,	N. 6 E.
Cape Raoul,[34] distant 3 miles,	S. 71 E.

Cape Pillar opened round Cape Raoul at E. 5° N., and the distance run from one to the other was nine miles. These two high, columnar capes are the extreme points of the land which captain Furneaux took to be Maria's Island. Between them, the shore falls back about four miles, and forms a small bay at the head, where there appeared to be shelter against all winds except those from the southward; and perhaps from those also, for the water seemed to reach behind the inner western point. At five clock we passed Tasman's small, cliffy Island and Cape Pillar, and Maria's Island came in sight at N. 6° E. We then hauled up to keep close in with the shore to the northward; but the wind came in such violent puffs down those steep cliffs, that the necessity of steering further off frustrated my intention: the outer Hippolite Rock bore N. 56° W. three miles, at dusk.

Jan. 4. At daylight, Maria's Island appeared to be divided into two, Schouten's Island was visible, and the principal bearings taken were as follow:

Tasman's small Island,	S. 24° W.
A deep bight in the coast,	S. 56 W.
South head of Frederik Hendrik's Bay,	S. 72 W.
Maria's Island, south part,	N. 64° to 43 W.
north part,	N. 39 to 19 W.
Schouten's Island,	North to N. 5 E.

The wind shifted to north at ten o'clock, and we tacked towards Maria's Island. At noon, the north-east extreme, a cock's-comb-like head, was distant four or five miles; but the islet lying off it, in Mr. Cox's chart, was not visible, nor yet the isthmus which connects the two parts of the island.

Observed latitude,	42° 41½' S.
South head of Frederik Hendrik's Bay,	S. 40 W.
Maria's Island, south part, Clouded.	
--------------- north part,	S. 82° to N. 64 W.
Schouten's Island, dist. 4 leagues,	N. 3 W. to 8 E.

We had squally weather in the afternoon, with the wind at north-west; and being unable to get near Maria's Island before the evening, bore away northward, having then a fresh breeze at W. S. W. Schouten's Island was passed within two miles at ten o'clock, and at eleven, a piece of land called Vanderlin's Island by Tasman, but which has since been found to be the southern extremity of a peninsula. We then steered north, to keep in with the coast; but the wind drawing forward in the morning of the 5th, the sloop was drifted off, by noon, to four or five leagues. The land then abreast rose in ranges of irregular, well-wooded hills; and behind them were two peaks and a flat-topped piece of land, seemingly not many leagues from the shore. The southernmost of the two peaks is the most elevated, and appears to be the high round mountain seen by Tasman on Dec 4 and 5, 1642; I have, therefore, called it Tasman's Peak. It is the northernmost part seen by him on this side of Van Diemen's Land, as Mount Heemskerk was on the west coast: the flat-topped mountain is that which colonel Paterson afterwards named Benlomen. To the southward, the land was visible at a great distance; and if Schouten's Island and the cape of the peninsula near it can possibly be seen so far as twenty leagues from the deck, it must have been them. My observation and bearings at this time were as follow:

Latitude observed,	41° 27½' S.
South extreme of the coast,	S. 18 W.
Another piece of land, like an island,	S. 23 W.
Tasman's Peak,	S. 63 W.
Northern extremity of the land,	N. 32 W.

It was to me a subject of regret, that the wind did not allow of keeping close in with this east coast, since captain Furneauxs examination was made at too great a distance to be exact; but my limited time of absence being expired, and provisions nearly out, nothing more could be attempted than what might be done in the way to Port Jackson.

Jan. 6, in latitude 40° 45½' no land was in sight; but on the 7th, when in 40° 24¾', the high land of Cape Barren was visible through a thick haze, bearing S. 76° W. five or six miles. The wind being then nearly at east, we steered to pass between Cape Barren and the great northern island, intending to explore the west side of the latter in our way. At five o'clock breakers were seen two miles to the north, though no bottom could be found at 17 fathoms; at six, however, we fell suddenly into 3 fathoms; but hoping to find a sufficient depth for the sloop round the island which lies in the opening, stood on till the soundings diminished to nine feet, and breakers were seen all round ahead, from beam to beam. It was then near sun-set, and the breeze right aft; but whilst I was considering what could be done for our safety, the wind shifted suddenly, as if by an act of Providence, to the opposite quarter, and enabled us to steer back, out of this dangerous place, with all sail. At nine o'clock the wind returned to the south-eastward, having just lasted long enough to take us out of danger; at eleven we had 20 fathoms; and in two hours more steered N. by W., for the Babel Isles, with a fresh and fair wind.

Jan 8, at six o'clock, Mr. Bass went on shore to the small, south~ eastern islet; whence he brought a boat load of seals and gannets. Besides these, the islet is inhabited by geese, shags, penguins, gulls, and sooty petrels; each occupying its separate district, and using its own language. It was the confusion of noises amongst these various animals which induced me to give the name of Babel Isles to this small cluster.

After taking on board our seals and gannets, we steered north-westward; and at one o'clock took a departure from the Sisters. I wished to make another effort to find the supposed Furneaux's Land, represented to lie north of these islands and in latitude 39°; but the wind being strong from the south-eastward, the course steered was N. by E. At eight o'clock we had passed the 39th degree; and no land being visible, the course was then altered to north-east, for Cape Howe.

Jan. 9, the wind blew strong at S. S. E., with thick, hazy weather. At eight in the morning, high land was distinguished two points on the weather bow, and sand hills from thence to abaft the lee beam, not more than six or seven miles distant. We immediately hauled the wind to the eastward, and carried every sail the sloop could bear in such a sea as was then running. The land to windward was judged to be near the Ram Head; although our reckoning was 20' short in latitude, and we supposed ourselves to the eastward.

To make certain of clearing Cape Howe, the eastern course was prolonged until day-light of the 10th; we then bore away, and at noon were in latitude 37° 5'. On the 11th, the observation gave 34° 30'; and the gale still continuing, we anchored within the heads of Port Jackson at ten o'clock the same evening, having exceeded, by no more than eleven days, the time which had been fixed for our return.

To the strait which had been the great object of research, and whose discovery was now completed, governor Hunter gave, at my recommendation, the name of BASS' STRAIT. This was no more than a just tribute to my worthy friend and companion, for the extreme dangers and fatigues he had undergone in first entering it in the whale boat, and to the correct judgment he had formed from various indications, of the existence of a wide opening between Van Diemen's Land and New South Wales.

FLINDERS. 1799.

The success of this expedition favoured my views of further discovery; and the Reliance not being immediately wanted for service, His Excellency accepted a proposition to explore Glass-house and Hervey's Bays, two large openings to the northward, of which the entrances only were known. I had some hope of finding a considerable river discharging itself at one of these openings, and of being able by its means to penetrate further into the interior of the country than had hitherto been effected.

The sloop Norfolk was again allotted to me, with nearly the same volunteer crew as before; and I was accompanied by Mr. S. W. Flinders, a midshipman of the Reliance, and by Bongaree, a native, whose good disposition and manly conduct had attracted my esteem. Of the assistance of my able friend Bass I was, however, deprived, he having quitted the station soon after our last voyage, to return to England. The time of my absence was limited by the governor to six weeks, some arrivals being then expected which might call the Reliance into active service.

We sailed out of Port Jackson on July 8; and next morning came in with a part of the coast, north of Port Stephens, which captain Cook had passed in the night.[35] Off a projection which I called Sugar-loaf Point, in latitude 32° 29', lie two rocks to the south-eastward, at the distances of two and four miles. We passed between these rocks and the point, and kept close in with the shore as far to the north as the hills called Three Brothers by captain Cook, of which the northernmost and highest lies in latitude 31° 43' south.

July 10, the observed latitude of 31° 38' showed a set of 33' to the south; whereas it had the day before been 8' the contrary way. Our distance from the shore had then become six leagues, owing to a foul wind; but we got in with it again in the evening, and steered northward with a fair breeze. On the 11th we sailed amongst the Solitary Isles, of which five were added to the number before seen; and the space from thence to twelve leagues northward having been passed by captain Cook in the night, I continued to keep close in with the coast.

In latitude 29° 43', we discovered a small opening like a river, with an islet lying in the entrance; and at sunset, entered a larger, to which I gave the name of SHOAL BAY, an appellation which it but too well merited. On the south side of the entrance, which is the deepest, there is ten feet at low water; and within side, the depth is from 2 to 4 fathoms in a channel near the south shore: the rest of the bay is mostly occupied by shoals, over which boats can scarcely pass when the tide is out. High water appeared to take place about seven hours after the moon's passage; at which time, a ship drawing not more than fourteen feet might venture in, if severely pressed. Shoal Bay is difficult to be found, except by its latitude, which is 29° 26½'; but there is on the low land about four leagues to the southward, a small hill somewhat peaked, which may serve as a mark to vessels coming from that direction.

July 12. The morning was employed in examining the bay, and in looking round the country. The sloop had sprung a bad leak, and I wished to have laid her on shore; but not finding a convenient place, nor any thing of particular interest to detain me longer, we sailed at one o'clock, when the tide began to rise. Cape Byron, in latitude 28° 38', and the coast for twelve miles to the north and south, were passed on the 13th: but no particular addition or correction could be made to captain Cook's chart. At Moreton Bay, further on, that navigator had left it in doubt whether there were any opening; and therefore we closed in again with the land at Point Look-out, on the 14th. At noon, the point bore S. 42° E., three or four miles, and a small flat islet E. 3° N. three miles; the opening in Moreton Bay was then evident, and bore W. N. W. It is small, and formed by two sandy points, beyond which a large extent of water was visible. Our latitude at this time, was 27° 24', giving that of Point Look-out to be 27° 27' south. Captain Cook says it is "in latitude 27° 6';"[36] a difference which probably arose from his having allowed for a strong northern current during the run of four or five hours from the preceding noon, whereas, in reality, none existed; for his course and distance by log, from the noon's observation, would give the point in its true latitude.

We stood on to within two miles of the opening in Moreton Bay; but seeing it blocked up by many shoals of sand, and the depth having diminished from 12 to 4 fathoms, the course was altered for Cape Moreton, which was visible seven or eight leagues to the northward. At eight in the evening, the anchor was dropped in 7 fathoms at the entrance of Glass-house Bay, Cape Moreton bearing E. S. E. two or three miles.

But little progress was made up the bay on the 15th, owing to the many shoals in it, and to a foul wind. At noon, the latitude of Cape Moreton was ascertained to be 27° 0½' south, and the longitude from distances of stars east and west of the moon, corrected by the observations at Greeenwich, was 153° 25' east; being 4½' south, and 7' west of its position by captain Cook. In the evening, when the lunar distances were observed, the sloop was at anchor in 11 fathoms on the west side of the entrance, within two miles of a low projection which an unfortunate occurrence afterwards caused to be named Point Skirmish.

On the 16th, whilst beating up amongst the shoals, an opening was perceived round the point; and being much in want of a place to lay the sloop on shore, on account of the leak, I tried to enter it; but not finding it accessible from the south, was obliged to make the examination with the boat, whilst the sloop lay at anchor five miles off. There was a party of natives on the point, and our communication was at first friendly; but after receiving presents they made an attack, and one of them was wounded by our fire. Proceeding up the opening, I found it to be more than a mile in width; and from the quantities of pumice stone on the borders, it was named Pumice-stone River. It led towards the remarkable peaks called the Glass Houses, which were now suspected to be volcanic, and excited my curiosity.

On board the sloop, the leak had, in the mean time, been found to arise from a plank having started from the timbers, at three or four streaks above the keel; and the open space being filled up with oakum from the inside, very little water came in; I therefore left the river and the Glass Houses for a future examination, and proceeded up the bay with the afternoon's flood. On the 18th at noon, we had passed two low islands surrounded with shoals, and were at anchor in 6 fathoms, abreast of a third. The south point of the opening from Moreton Bay then bore N. 77° E., ten miles; and the observed latitude being 27° 27¼', confirmed the observation taken without side on the 14th. Next day, we beat up against a southern wind to a sixth island; but the shoals then became more numerous, and the channels between them so narrow, that it was very difficult to proceed further.

The latitude observed upon the sixth island was 27° 35', being thirty-four miles south of Cape Moreton at the entrance of the bay. Above this island, the east and west shores, from being nine or ten miles apart, approach each other within two miles, and the space between them takes the form of a river; but the entrance was too full of shoals to leave a hope of penetrating by it far into the interior, or that it could be of importance to navigation. Under this discouragement and that of a foul wind, all further research at the head of Glass-house Bay was given up; and I returned on board to seek in Pumice-stone River for a place to stop the leak, and the means of visiting the Glass Houses. On the 22nd, we got into the river after many difficulties, arising principally from shoals in the entrance, which could only be passed at high water. The place chosen for laying the sloop on shore was on the east side, five miles above Point Skirmish, at a small beach, close to which the depth was 7 fathoms.

July 25. The leaky plank being secured, and the sloop restowed and completed with water, we proceeded two miles further up the river, amongst mangrove islets and muddy flats. Next morning I landed on the west side, as far above the sloop as the boat could advance; and with my friend Bongaree and two sailors, steered north-westward for the Glasshouse peaks. After nine miles of laborious walking, mostly through swamps or over a rocky country, we reached the top of a stony mount, from whence the highest peak was four miles distant to the north-west. Three or four leagues beyond it was a ridge of mountain, from which various small streams descend into Pumice-stone River; the principal place of their junction seeming to be at a considerable extent of water which bore N. 80° E., and was about six miles above the sloop. Early on the 27th, we reached the foot of the nearest Glass House, a flat-topped peak, one mile and a half north of the stony mount. It was impossible to ascend this almost perpendicular rock; and finding no marks of volcanic eruption, we returned to the boat, and to the sloop the same evening.

July 28, we proceeded down the river; but owing to strong winds and squalls from the south-east, did not clear it before the 31st. Some communications with the natives had been obtained whilst the sloop was lying on shore; and this detention afforded opportunities of repeating them. I am happy to say they were all friendly, which is attributable to their opinion of us having undergone a salutary change from the effect of our fire arms at Point Skirmish.

These people were evidently of the same race as those at Port Jackson, though speaking a language which Bongaree could not understand. They fish almost wholly with cast and setting nets, live more in society than the natives to the southward, and are much better lodged. Their spears are of solid wood, and used without the throwing stick. Two or three bark canoes were seen; but from the number of black swans in the river, of which eighteen were caught in our little boat, it should seem that these people are not dextrous in the management either of the canoe or spear.

The entrance of Glass-house Bay, from Point Skirmish to the inner part of Cape Moreton, is eight miles wide; but it contains so many shoals that a ship would have much difficulty in finding a passage. These shoals are of sand, and in the channels between them are various depths from 5 to 13 fathoms upon similar ground; but towards the head of the bay, both on the shoals and in the deeper parts, the bottom is almost universally of mud. The land on the borders of Pumice-stone River is low; and is either sandy or rocky, with a slight superficies of vegetable soil; yet not ill clothed with grass and wood. On the west side of Glass-house Bay, the appearance of the land was much similar, but with a diminution of sand in the upper part. The long slip on the east side, which I have called Moreton Island, as supposing it would have received that name from captain Cook, had he known of its insularity, is little else than a ridge of rocky hills, with a sandy surface; but the peninsula further south had some appearance of fertility. I judged favourably of the country on the borders of what seemed to be a river falling into the head of the bay, both from its thick covering of wood, and from the good soil of the sixth island, which lies at the entrance. The other islands in the bay are very low, and so surrounded with forests of large mangrove, that it must be difficult to land upon them. It was high water in Pumice-stone River, nine hours and a half after the moon's passage over the meridian; and the rise of tide was from three to six feet, the night tide being much the highest.

July 31, we sailed out of Pumice-stone River; and by keeping near the shore of Point Skirmish had generally 6 fathoms; but two narrow shoals were passed upon which the depth was only twelve feet. At noon, when the east extreme of the point bore S. 40° W. one mile and a half, the observed latitude was 27° 4', and depth 10 fathoms; but before one o'clock, it suddenly diminished to 3; and during five miles run to the N. N. E., varied from that to 6 fathoms. It then deepened to 9, and the outer edge of the shoals, a well-defined line of discoloured water, was seen stretching S. 60° E. for Cape Moreton. At five o'clock, the top of the highest Glass House, appearing like a small peak upon the mountainous ridge behind, bore S. 62° W., and Cape Moreton S. 11° E. twenty-two miles. The cape was then disappearing from the deck; whence its elevation should be between three and four hundred feet above the sea.

August 2 at noon, the eastern extremity of Sandy Cape bore N. 51° W., six miles, and its latitude was found to be 24° 42', being three minutes north of its situation by captain Cook. In running northward, within two or three miles of the edge of Break-sea Spit, we had 12 fathoms; and at five o'clock, passed over the end of the spit in 3½; Sandy Cape then bearing S. 9° E. six leagues. The water deepened almost immediately to more than 17 fathoms; and in keeping close to a south-east wind, up Hervey's Bay, the depth was from 20 to 14, during the night.

On the 3rd, the wind veered to S. S. W; and at noon the anchor was dropped in 17 fathoms, with the extreme of Sandy Cape bearing N. 66° E. seven or eight miles. The observed latitude was 24° 45 1/3', and a tide of one mile per hour came from the southward. A fair wind sprung up in the afternoon, and we ran five leagues by log in a S. by W. direction, anchoring at dusk in 11 fathoms, sandy bottom.

Aug. 4 was employed in beating up along the eastern shore, against a south-west wind. At three leagues above the anchorage, our progress was stopped by a mass of shoals which seemed to preclude all further access towards the head of the bay on that side. In the night, we stretched north-westward, to get round them; and in the evening of the 5th, anchored in 5 fathoms, three or four miles from the western shore.

Aug. 6. The wind being off the land, we followed the line of the coast upwards, as close as the shoals would allow; and before noon entered an opening formed by the western shore on one side, and an island of moderate height, three or four miles long, on the other. The opening was not more than two miles wide, and was still further contracted by a low islet in the middle, surrounded with shallow banks. There was a large expanse of water above; but we had not advanced two miles before shoal water obliged us to tack; and after having tried for a channel in every direction, without success, I anchored in 3 fathoms, half a mile north-west from the low islet, and landed.

This rocky, sandy spot lies in latitude 25° 17'. It is much frequented by aquatic birds, particularly by that species whence it obtained the name of Curlew Islet; and since a small shield and three wooden spears were found there, it must also be visited occasionally by men. The larger island, lying to the east, is richly covered with grass and wood. Its position is nearly in the middle of the entrance to what may be called the upper bay; and as no deep channel past the island could be found on the west, I determined to try on the east side; having much difficulty in believing, that a piece of water six or seven miles in extent every way, should not have a channel into it sufficiently deep for the Norfolk.

The anchor was weighed soon after four o'clock, and several attempts made to get round the larger island; but being constantly repulsed by shoals, I was at length forced to relinquish the hope of penetrating further up Hervey's Bay. We then steered north-westward, to complete the examination of the west side down to the coast seen by captain Cook.

Aug. 7. At daylight, a sloping hummock, in latitude 24° 50', bore W. 16° N., our distance off the shore under it being one mile and a half, and the depth 7 fathoms. At nine, the water shoaled suddenly, and obliged us to haul off north-eastward. The coast was then seen extending to the W. N. W., and having been laid down by captain Cook, the north-eastern course was continued for Break-sea Spit, and the examination of Hervey's Bay concluded.

This inlet is about fifteen leagues across, from the sloping hummock to the eastern extremity of Sandy Cape, and nearly as much in depth. The east side is formed by a great sandy peninsula, of which the cape is the northern extremity; but about half way up, there are several white cliffs, and others in the upper bay, which had the appearance of chalk. The shores at the head and on the west side are more rocky than sandy. The back land is low for some miles, and not ill covered with grass and wood; it then rises to hills of considerable elevation, amongst which Double Mount was most remarkable. The smokes in different places bespoke the country to be inhabited in the scanty numbers usual on other parts of the east coast; but none of the people were seen.

Aug. 7, at ten in the evening, we passed the end of Break-sea Spit in 13 fathoms, and hauled up south-east; but the winds were so unfavourable, that on the 14th our latitude was no more than 29° 19'. I kept the land barely within sight, in order to obtain the greatest advantage from the southwardly current; for, contrary to captain Cook's observation, it was found to be strongest at the distance of six, and from thence to twenty leagues. Close in with the shore, more especially in the bights which fall within the general line of the coast, an eddy had been found setting to the northward.

Light northern winds favoured us for two days; but returning to the south-west, and sometimes blowing strong, it was the 20th in the evening before the sloop was secured in Port Jackson, although the current had set us 210 miles on the way.

I must acknowledge myself to have been disappointed in not being able to penetrate into the interior of New South Wales, by either of the openings examined in this expedition; but, however mortifying the conviction might be, it was then an ascertained fact, that no river of importance intersected the East Coast between the 24th and 39th degrees of south latitude.

Conclusive Remarks

The account of the discoveries which resulted from the establishment of the colony in New South Wales, closes with this expedition; and it remains only to point out what was wanted to be done in these parts of Terra Australis.
In Van Diemen's Land, the opening round Point St. Vincent and the space between Maria's Island and Cape Portland required to be further explored. The north side also, from the want of a time keeper in the Norfolk, required to have the longitude of its points better ascertained; and that the bight between Circular Head and Cape Grim should be ex-

amined. In Bass' Strait, some of the islands were known, but the middle of the strait and its western entrance were in want of much investigation, before it could be deemed a safe passage for ships; and the greater part of the coast on the north side, remained as laid down by Mr. Bass, with all the uncertainty attending the navigation of an open boat. On the east coast of New South Wales, from Bass' Strait to Bustard Bay in latitude 24°, the shore might be said to be well explored; but from thence northward to Cape York, there were several portions which had either been passed by captain Cook in the night, or at such a distance in the day time, as to render their formation doubtful: The coast from 15° 30' to 14° 30' was totally unknown.

The following openings or bights had been seen and named by captain Cook, but were yet unexamined: Keppel and Shoal-water Bays; Broad Sound; Repulse, Edgecumbe, Cleveland, Halifax, Rockingham, and Weary Bays. To the northward of these were Weymouth, Temple, Shelburne, and Newcastle Bays; and perhaps many others which distance did not permit our great navigator to notice. There was also a numerous list of islands, of which a few only had been examined; and several were merely indicated from a distant view.

From 16° northward to Cape York, an extensive chain of reefs had been found to lie at a considerable distance from the coast, without side of the islands; and two vessels from Port Jackson had met with others further south, extending nearly from 21° to 23°. It was of importance to ascertain the limits of these vast bodies of coral, were it only on account of the ships employed in the whale fishery; but in the view to future settlements within the tropic, it was necessary to be known whether these reefs might form such a barrier to the coast, as to render it inaccessible from the eastward: if not, then the open parts were to be ascertained.

Of the persons, manners, and customs of the inhabitants, little new information could be expected. The skirts of their country had been examined in the southern parts, and extensive collections in natural history made there; but to the north of Endeavour River, the country had been seen only at a distance. The vast interior of this new continent was wrapped in total obscurity; and excited, perhaps on that very account, full as much curiosity as did the forms of the shores. This part of the subject, however, will scarcely be thought to belong to a naval expedition; except in so much as rivers and other inlets might conduce to obtaining the desired information.

On a general review of the various objects in Terra Australis, to which investigation might be usefully directed at the commencement of the nineteenth century, and in which natural history, geography, navigation, and commerce were so much interested, the question, Why it should have been thought necessary to send out another expedition? will no longer be asked. But rather it will be allowed that, instead of one, there was ample room for two or three ships; each to be employed for years, and to be conducted with a zeal and perseverance not inferior to the examples given by the best navigators.

On the arrival of His Majesty's ship Reliance in England, at the latter end of 1800, the charts of the new discoveries were published, and a plan was proposed to the Right Hon. SIR JOSEPH BANKS for completing the investigation of the coasts of Terra Australis. The plan was approved by that distinguished patron of science and useful enterprise; it was laid before EARL SPENCER, then first Lord Commissioner of the Admiralty; and finally received the sanction of HIS MAJESTY, who was graciously pleased to direct that the voyage should be undertaken; and I had the honour of being appointed to the command.

Notes

[1] *A small cask, containing six or eight gallons.*

[2] *These islets seem to be what are marked as rocks under water in captain Cook's chart. In it, also, there are three islets laid down to the south of Red Point, which must be meant for the double islet lying directly off it, for there are no others. The cause of the point being named red, escaped our notice.*

[3] *This Dilba was one of the two Botany-Bay natives, who had been most strenuous for Tom Thumb to go up into the lagoon, which lies under the hill.*

[4] *Afterwards captain of the Junon. He was mortally wounded, whilst bravely defending his Majesty's frigate against a vastly superior force; and died at Guadaloupe.*

[5] *But the latitude observed appears to be 8' or 10' too little; and if so, the length of the beach would be something more than 150 miles. It is no matter of surprise if observations taken from an open boat, in a high sea, should differ ten miles from the truth; but I judge that Mr. Bass' quadrant must have received some injury during the night of the 31st, for a similar error appears to pervade all the future observations, even those taken under favourable circumstances.*

[6] *The true latitude of the east entrance into Western Port, is about 38° 33' south.*

[7] *I have continued to make use of the term Furneaux's Land conformably to Mr. Bass' journal; but the position of this land is so different from that supposed to have been seen by captain Furneaux, that it cannot be the same, as Mr. Bass was afterwards convinced. At our recommendation governor Hunter called it WILSON'S PROMONTORY, in compliment to my friend Thomas Wilson, Esq. of London.*

[8] *This appears to be from 10' to 15' too little: an error which probably arose from the same cause as others before noticed.*

[9] Nothing more had been beard of these five men., so late as 1803.

[10] The true latitude of the mouth of Two-fold Bay is 37° 5', showing an error of 12' to the north, nearly similar to what has been specified in the observations near Wilson's Promontory.

[11] The bearings in the following account are corrected, as usual, for the variation; but I am sorry to say that the steering compasses of the schooner proved to be bad, and there was no azimuth compass on board.

[12] Hawkesworth, Vol. III. p. 80. Mr. Bass sailed close round the cape in his whale boat, but did not ace any island lying there.]

[13] It was 147° 10'; but as I afterwards found that observations of the sun to the east gave 27' less, by this small five inch sextant, and those to the west 27' greater than the mean of both, that correction is here applied; but not any which might be required from errors in the solar or lunar tables.

[14] The longitude of the large group, as given by my time keepers in a future voyage, is 147° 17'.

[15] Cook's Second Voyage, Vol. I. page 114.

[16] Mr. Bass' Journal of observations upon the lands, etc. discovered or seen in this voyage, has been published by colonel Collins, in his Account of the English Colony in New South Wales, Vol. II. page 143 et seq.; his observations will, therefore, be generally omitted in this account.

[17] The highest part of Mount Dromedary appears to lie in 36° 19' south, and longitude 150° 11' east; or about 2' south and 11' east of its position in captain Cook's chart.

[18] Kent's large group is not, however, so barren and deserted as appearances bespoke. It has since been ascertained that, in the central parts of the larger islands, there are vallies in which trees of a fair growth make part of a tolerably vigorous vegetation, and where kangaroos of a small kind were rather numerous; some seals, also, were found upon the rocks, and fresh water was not difficult to be procured in certain seasons.

[19] Nine thousand skins of the first quality, with several tons of oil, were procured by the Nautilus, and Furneaux's Islands have since been frequented by small vessels from Port Jackson upon the same errand. Unfortunately, this species of fishery is soon exhausted in any one place; or it would have been the means of raising up an useful body of seamen, and thus proved of advantage, both to the colony and to the mother country.

[20] The longitude of Low-Head, deduced from the Investigator's time keepers, combined with my surveys in the Francis and Norfolk, is 146° 47½ east; as the observations with the large sextant, No. 251, taken alone, would give it very nearly.

[21] So named by the late lieut. colonel Paterson, who was sent from Port Jackson to settle a new colony there, in 1804. The sources of the river were then explored, and the new names applied which are given in the chart. The first town established was Yorktown at the head of the Western Arm, but this proving inconvenient as a sea port, it was proposed to be removed lower down, near Green Island. Launceston, which is intended to be the capital of the new colony, is fixed at the junction of the North and South Esks, up to which the Tamar is navigable for vessels of 150 tons. The tide reaches nine or ten miles up the North Esk, and the produce of the farms within that distance may be sent down the river by boats, but the South Esk descends from the mountains by a cataract, directly into the Tamar, and, consequently, is not accessible to navigation of any kind.

[22] In Mr. Horsburgh's Sailing Directions, etc. Part II., are given, upon my friend captain Kent's authority, notices of the beacons laid down, and directions respecting them; to which I add, from the information of lieut. Oxley, that a rock, on which H. M. ship Porpoise struck, lies W. ½ N. by compass, one cable's length from Point Roundabout. There is no more than four feet upon it at low water, but it way be safely passed on either side.

[23] In 1804, Mr. Charles Robbins, acting lieutenant of His Majesty's ship Buffalo, was sent from Port Jackson to examine this great bight; and from his sketch it is, that the unshaded coast and soundings written at right angles are laid down in the chart.

[24] Taking the stream to have been fifty yards deep by three hundred in width, and that it moved at the rate of thirty miles an hour, and allowing nine cubic yards of space to each bird, the number would amount to 151,500,000. The burrows required to lodge this quantity of birds would be 75,750,000; and allowing a square yard to each burrow, they would cover something more than 181 geographic square miles of ground.

[25] Future visitants to these islands have seen the Indians passing over in bodies, by swimming, similar to those whom Dampier saw on the north-west coast of New Holland. Why the natives of Port Dalrymple should not have had recourse to the same expedient, where the distance to be traversed is so much less, seems incomprehensible.

[26] This head opened round the Cape at E. 14° N.. magnetic, the sloop's head being E. by N.; and shut at W. 20° S., when the head was north. In the first case I allow 3½° east variation, and in the last, 8°; which makes them agree as nearly as can be expected from bearings taken under sail.

[27] Captain Furneaux says (in Cook's second Voyage, Vol. I. page 109), that on March 9, 1773, at noon, the South-west Cape bore north, four leagues; and by referring to the Astronomical Observations, p. 193, I find that his latitude was 43° 45 2/3', which would place the Cape in 43° 33 2/3'; nevertheless the captain says it is in 43° 39', and it is so laid down in his chart. The observation by which captain Cook appears to have fixed the South-west Cape, is that of Jan. 24, 1777, at noon; when he says, "our latitude was 43° 47' south" (Third Voyage, Vol. I. p. 93.) But the Astronomical Observations of that voyage show (p. 101), that the observed latitude on board the Resolution was 43° 42½'; which would make the Cape in 43° 32½' south. I consulted captain King's journal at the Admiralty, but found no observed latitude marked by him on that day.

[28] The magnetic bearing of the South-west Cape was W. 5° S., and that of the South Cape E. 15° S. The true variation I believe to have been 8° E.; but as the sloop's head was at east, no more than 3° are allowed, from a system which will be hereafter explained. It seemed necessary to say this, because the formation of the south end of Van Diemen's Land in my chart, differs from

that given by captain Cook, and from those of most others. In Bayly's Astronomical Observations, page 192, it appears that six sets of variations were observed on board the Resolution, Mar. 24, 1777, off the South Cape; the mean result of which was 4° 43' east. Next morning six other sets were taken near the same place, and the mean variation came out 10°8' east. In captain King's journal, I found the same observations entered, and that the ship's head was E. by N. ½ N. in the first case, and N. W. by W. in the second. This, with the example in the Francis, page cxxvi, and that in the Norfolk on the preceding page, may serve to show, for the present, that corrections are required to the variation, according to the direction of the vessel's head.

[29] This name, given by Captain Furneaux, is altered in D'Entrecasteaux's voyage to that of >Cape Trobriand. The captain was undoubtedly mistaken in his idea concerning Frederik Hendrick's Bay; but this does not appear to be a sufficient reason for changing the established name of the cape, unless Tasman had applied it to some other land, which is not the case.

[30] This is the Isle Willaumez, of D'Entrecasteaux; but it was known to me from the sketch of captain Hayes, and is still to the colonists, under the name of Betsey's Island.

[31] The first settlement was made in Risdon Cove, in 1803, by captain John Bowen of the navy, who was sent from Port Jackson for that purpose, by his Excellency governor King; but on the arrival of colonel Collins in 1804, it was removed to Sullivan Cove.

[32] Upon the top of Mount Table, the compass has since been found to vary as much as 20°, from one part of the mountain to another.

[33] See Bligh's Voyage to the South Seas; page 53.

[34] This is the cape which, from its appearance, I had called by the descriptive name of Cape Basaltes; not knowing that D'Entrecasteaux, or any other navigator, had previously affixed an appellation. I give it up the more readily, because it is said these columns are not strictly basaltes.]

[35] The journal of this expedition, delivered to governor Hunter on my return, having been published in great part by colonel Collins, the account here given will be brief, and almost wholly confined to nautical subjects. The reader who desires more information upon the lands visited, and upon their productions and inhabitants, is referred to the Account of the English Colony in New South Wales, Vol II. page 225 to 263.

[36] Hawkesworth's Voyages, Vol III. page 119.

A Voyage to Terra Australis - Book I - Transactions From The Beginning of the Voyage to the Departure From Port Jackson.

Chapter One

1801, January

In England. Sheerness.

On the 19th of January 1801, a commission was signed at the Admiralty appointing me lieutenant of His Majesty's Sloop INVESTIGATOR, to which the name of the ship, heretofore known as the Xenophon, was changed by this commission; and captain John Henry Martin having received orders to consider himself to be superseded, I took the command at Sheerness on the 25th of the same month.

The Investigator was a north-country-built ship, of three-hundred and thirty-four tons; and, in form, nearly resembled the description of vessel recommended by captain Cook as best calculated for voyages of discovery. She had been purchased some years before into His Majesty's service; and having been newly coppered and repaired, was considered to be the best vessel which could, at that time, be spared for the projected voyage to Terra Australis.

The ship was in a state of re-equipment; but, on obtaining permission from the Navy Board to fit her out in such manner as I should judge necessary, without reference to the supplies usually allotted to vessels of the same class, all the stores were returned, and others of the best quality demanded, upon a more extensive scale. Such of the officers and crew as were aged, or did not volunteer for this particular service, were discharged; and able young men were received in lieu from His Majesty's ship Zealand, on board of which the flag of vice-admiral Graeme was flying at the Nore. Upon one occasion, where eleven volunteers were to be received from the Zealand, a strong instance was given of the spirit of enterprise prevalent amongst British seamen. About three hundred disposable men were called up, and placed on one side of the deck; and after the nature of the voyage, with the number of men wanted, had been explained to them, those who volunteered were desired to go over to the opposite side. The candidates were not less than two-hundred and fifty, most of whom sought with eagerness to be received; and the eleven who were chosen, proved, with one single exception, to be worthy of the preference they obtained.

In making the various alterations required in the ship, and in performing the duties incident to an equipment of this nature, I received the most ready concurrence and assistance from Isaac Coffin, Esq., (now vice-admiral Sir Isaac Coffin, Bart.) the resident naval commissioner at Sheerness. At his suggestion I had the ship coppered two streaks higher than before, and took on board a spare rudder, which, after being fitted, was stowed away in pieces, ready against those accidents to which ships employed in examining new, or little known coasts, are more peculiarly liable. To Mr. Whidbey, the master attendant, who had served in the expedition of captain Vancouver. I was also much indebted, for his valuable advice and assistance in the selection of the proper stores. Both these officers constantly took pleasure in promoting whatever could be useful to the voyage, or add to our comfort and convenience; and in some cases, our wants, and even wishes, were anticipated.

February. March.

February 16, I was promoted to the rank of commander. On the 14th of the following month, the guns, twelve six-pounders, with their ammunition and a chest of fire works were received; and the provisions and stores being all on board on the 27th, and the ship ready for sea, we dropped out to the Nore. I was anxious to arrive upon the coasts of Terra Australis in time to have the whole of the southern summer before me; but various circumstances retarded our departure, and amongst others, a passport from the French government, to prevent molestation to the voyage, had not arrived. I took advantage of this delay to remedy an inconvenience, under which we were otherwise likely to suffer. The quantity of provisions necessary to be carried out did not leave room in the holds for more water than fifty tons; but by removing ten of the long guns, and substituting a few light carronades which could be carried on the upper deck, ten tons more of water might be received, without reducing our efficient strength; for the ship was too deep to admit of the guns below being used in bad weather, whereas the carronades would be always serviceable. My application to have this exchange made, was complied with; and on May 20 it was effected.

May.

On the 22nd, a set of astronomical and surveying instruments, for the use of myself and officers, was sent down by direction of the Navy Board; as also various articles for presents to, and barter with, the native inhabitants of the countries to be visited, and many for our own use and convenience. Amongst the latter were most of the books of voyages to the South Seas, which, with our own individual collections, and the Encyclopedia Britannica, presented by the Right Hon. Sir Joseph Banks, formed a library in my cabin for the use of all the officers. Every chart at the Admiralty, which related to Terra Australis and the neighbouring islands, was copied for us under the direction of the late hydrographer, Alexander Dalrymple, Esq.; who also enriched our stock of information by communicating all such parts of his works as were appropriate to the voyage.

The expense to officers of an outfit for several years, was much alleviated by the liberality of the Hon. East-India Company. The sum of £600. was ordered by the Court of Directors, to be paid as an allowance to the men of science, to the officers of the ship, and myself, for our tables; and the same sum to be given at the conclusion of the voyage. This allowance the directors were pleased to make, from the voyage being within the limits of the Company's charter, from the expectation of our examinations and discoveries proving advantageous to their commerce and the eastern navigation, and partly, as they said, for my former services.

On the 26th, I received orders to proceed round to Spithead; but the winds being generally from the westward, we did not arrive there before the 2nd of June. A circumstance occurred during the passage, which, amongst many others, showed the necessity there was for a regulation since adopted, to furnish His Majesty's ships with correct charts. No master had been appointed to the Investigator; nor was any officer on board intimately acquainted with the navigation of the Channel; and having been most of my life engaged in foreign voyages, I was under the necessity, after leaving the pilot in the Downs, to trust almost wholly to my chart, which was that of Mr. J. H. Moore. In working up under Dungeness, on the evening of May 28, we made a trip in shore, towards the town of Hythe, as I supposed from the chart. A little after six, the officer of the watch had reported our distance from the land to be near two leagues; and there being from 10 to 14 fathoms marked within two or three miles of it, and no mention of any shoal lying in the way, I intended to stand on half an hour longer; but in ten minutes, felt the ship lifting upon a bank. The sails were immediately thrown aback; and the weather being fine and water smooth, the ship was got off without having received any apparent injury.

This sand is laid down in the Admiralty charts, under the name of the Roar; and extends from Dungeness towards Folkstone, at the distance of from two and a half, to four miles from the land. The leadsman, having found no bottom with 15 fathoms at ten minutes before six, had very culpably quitted the chains when his watch was out, without taking another cast of the lead; and the ship, in going at the rate of two knots and three-quarters, was upon the bank at twenty minutes after six; so that it appears to be steep on the east side.

The bearings given by the azimuth compass, whilst the ship was aground, were as under:

Dungeness light house,	S. W.
Lidd church	W. by S. ½ S.
Town of Dim, but taken to be Hythe,	N. W. by N.
Cheriton church, then supposed to be Folkstone,	E. N. E.
Cliffy eastern extreme of the land, near Dover,	E. ½ N.

The distance from the town of Hythe (Dim,) was guessed to be not less than two-and-half, nor more than four miles.

In England. Portsmouth.

June.

In consequence of this accident, we went into Portsmouth Harbour and into dock on June 10; and it being ascertained that the ship had received no injury, we returned to Spithead next day, and moored as before, waiting for orders. On the 18th, commissioner Sir Charles Saxton paid the ship's company their wages up to the end of May, with an advance of two months; and the officers were permitted to draw bills for three months pay in advance.

July.

On July 17, I received the following instructions for the execution of the voyage.

By the Commissioners for executing the office of Lord High Admiral of the United Kingdom of Great Britain and Ireland, etc.

Whereas the sloop you command has been fitted and stored for a voyage to remote parts; And whereas it is our intention that you should proceed in her to the coast of New Holland for the purpose of making a complete examination and survey of the said coast, on the eastern side of which His Majesty's colony of New South Wales is situated; You are hereby required and directed to put to sea the first favourable opportunity of wind and weather, and proceed with as little delay as possible in execution of the service above-mentioned, repairing in the first place to Madeira and the Cape of Good Hope in order to take on board such supplies of water and live stock as you may be in want of.

Having so done you are to make the best of your way to the coast of New Holland, running down the said coast from 130 degrees of east longitude to Bass's Strait; (putting if you shall find it necessary, into King George the third's Harbour for refreshments and water previous to your commencing the survey;) and on your arrival on the coast, use your best endeavours to discover such harbours as may be in those parts; and in case you should discover any creek or opening likely to lead to an inland sea or strait, you are at liberty either to examine it, or not, as you shall judge it most expedient, until a more favourable opportunity shall enable you so to do.

When it shall appear to you necessary, you are to repair to Sydney Cove for the purpose of refreshing your people, refitting the sloop under your command, and consulting with the governor of New South Wales upon the best means of carrying on the survey of the coast; and having received from him such information as he may be able to communicate, and taken under your command the Lady Nelson tender, which you may expect to find at Sydney Cove, you are to recommence your survey, by first diligently examining the coast from Bass's Strait to King George the third's Harbour; which you may do either by proceeding along shore to the westward, or, in case you should think it more expedient., by proceeding first to King George's Sound, and carrying on your survey from thence to the eastward.

You are to repair from time to time, when the season will no longer admit of your carrying on the survey, to Sydney Cove; from whence your are to return in the execution of these instructions, so soon as circumstances will enable you so to do.

You are to be very diligent in your examination of the said coast, and to take particular care to insert in your journal every circumstance that may be useful to a full and complete knowledge thereof, noting the winds and weather which usually prevail there at different seasons of the year, the productions and comparative fertility of the soil, and the manners and customs of the inhabitants of such parts as you may be able to explore; fixing in all cases, when in your power, the true positions both in latitude and longitude of remarkable head lands, bays, and harbours, by astronomical observations, and noting the variation of the needle, and the right direction and course of the tides and currents, as well as the perpendicular height of the tides; and in case, during your survey, any river should be discovered, you are either to proceed yourself in the tender, or to direct her commander to enter it, and proceed as far up as circumstances will permit; carefully laying down the course and the banks thereof, and noting the soundings, going on shore as often as it shall appear probable that any considerable variation has taken place either in the productions of the soil or the customs of the inhabitants; examining the country as far inland as shall be thought prudent to venture with the small number of persons who can be spared from the charge of the vessel, wherever there appears to be a probability of discovering any thing useful to the commerce or manufactures of the United Kingdom.

When you shall have completely examined the whole of the coast from Bass's Strait to King George the third's Harbour, you are, at such times as may be most suitable for the purpose, (which may be seen on a reference to Mr. Dalrymple's memoir, an extract of which accompanies this,) to proceed to and explore the north-west coast of New Holland, where, from the extreme height of the tides observed by Dampier, it is probable that valuable harbours may be discovered.

Having performed this service, you are carefully to examine the Gulf of Carpentaria, and the parts to the westward thereof, between the 130th and 139th degrees of east longitude; taking care to seize the earliest opportunity to do so, when the seasons and prevalent winds may be favourable for visiting those seas.

When you shall have explored the Gulf of Carpentaria and the parts to the westward thereof, you are to proceed to a careful investigation and accurate survey of Torres' Strait, and when that shall have been completed, you are to examine and survey the whole of the remainder of the north, the west, and the north-west coasts of New Holland, and especially those parts of the coast most likely to be fallen in with by East-India ships in their outward-bound passages. And you are to examine as particularly as circumstances will allow, the bank which extends itself from the Trial Rocks towards Timor, in the hope that by ascertaining the depth and nature of the soundings thereon, great advantage may arise to the East-India Company's ships, in case that passage should hereafter be frequented by them.

So soon as you shall have completed the whole of these surveys and examinations as above directed, you are to proceed to, and examine very carefully the east coast of New Holland, seen by captain Cook, from Cape Flattery to the Bay of Inlets; and in or-

der to refresh your people, and give the advantage of variety to the painters, you are at liberty to touch at the Fejees, or some other of the islands in the South Seas.

During the course of the survey, you are to use the tender under your command as much as possible; moving the Investigator onward from one harbour to another as they shall be discovered, in order that the naturalists may have time to range about and collect the produce of the earth, and the painters allowed time to finish as many of their works as they possibly can on the spot where they may have been begun: And when you shall have completed the whole of the surveys and examinations as abovementioned, you are to lose no time in returning with the sloop under your command to England for farther orders, touching on your way, if necessary, at the Cape of Good Hope, and repairing with as little delay as possible to Spithead, and transmit to our secretary an account of your arrival.

During your continuance on the service above-mentioned, you are, by all proper opportunities, to send to our secretary for our information, accounts of your proceedings and copies of the surveys and drawings which you shall have made, and such papers as the Naturalist and the Painters employed on board may think proper to send home; and upon your arrival in England you are immediately to repair to this office in order to lay before us a full account of your proceedings in the whole course of your voyage; taking care before you leave the sloop to demand from the officers and petty officers the log books and journals which they may have kept and such drawings and charts as they may have taken, and to seal them up for our inspection.

And whereas you have been furnished with a plant cabin for the purpose of depositing therein such plants, trees, shrubs, etc., as may be collected during the survey above-mentioned, you are, when you arrive at Sydney Cove, to cause the said plant cabin to be fitted up by the carpenter on the quarter deck of the sloop you command, according to the intention of its construction; and you are to cause boxes for containing earth to be made and placed therein, in the same manner as was done in the plant cabin carried out by the Porpoise store ship, which plant cabin you will find at Sydney Cove.

You are, to place the said plant cabin, with the boxes of earth contained in it, under the charge and care of the naturalist and gardener, and to cause to be planted therein during the survey, such plants, trees, shrubs, etc., as they may think suitable for the Royal Gardens at Kew; and you are, as often as you return to Sydney Cove, to cause the said plants to be deposited in the governor's garden and under his charge, there to remain until you sail for Europe: And so soon as you shall be preparing to return home, you are to cause the small plant cabin to be removed from the sloop's quarter deck, and the one brought out by the Porpoise (which is something larger), to be placed there in its stead. In this last mentioned cabin the naturalist and gardener are to place the plants, trees, shrubs, etc., which may have been collected during the survey, in order to their being brought home for His Majesty; and you are, so soon as the sloop shall arrive at any port in England, to give notice of her arrival to His Majesty's botanic gardener at Kew, and to transmit to him a list and state of the said plants etc., which the gardener employed under your orders is to furnish you with for that purpose.

Given under our hands the 22nd of June, 1801.

(Signed),

ST. VINCENT.
T. TRUBRIDGE.
J. MARKHAM.

To **MATTHEW FLINDERS, Esq.**
Commander of His Majesty's sloop
Investigator, at Spithead.

By command of their Lordships,
(Signed,)
EVAN NEPEAN.

The instructions were accompanied with the extract of a memoir from Mr. Dalrymple, respecting the winds and weather to be expected, principally upon the south coast of Terra Australis. Also with the following PASSPORT from the French government.

LE PREMIER CONSUL DE LA RÉPUBLIQUE FRANÇAISE, sur le compte qui lui a été rendu de la demande faite par le LORD HAWKESBURY au Citoyen Otto, commissaire du gouvernement Français à Londres, d'un Passeport pour la corvette Investigator, dont le signalement est ci-après, expédiée par be gouvernement Anglais, sous le commandement du capitaine Matthew Flinders, pour un voyage de découvertes dans la Mer Pacifique, ayant décidé que ce passeport seroit accordé, et que cette expédition, dont l'objet est d'étendre les connoissances humaines, et d'assurer davantage les progrès de la science nautique et de la géographie, trouveroit de la part du gouvernement Français la sureté et la protection nécessaires.

LE MINISTRE DE LA MARINE ET DES COLONIES ordonne en conséquence à tous les commandants des bâtiments de guerre de la République, à ses agens dans toutes les colonies Françaises, aux commandants des bâtiments porteurs do lettres de marque, et à tous a autres qu'il appartiendra, de laisser passer librement et sans empêchement, ladite corvette Investigator, ses officiers, équipage, et effets, pendant la durée de leur voyage; de leur permettre d'aborder dans les différents ports de la

République, tant in Europe que dans les autres parties du monde, soit qu'ils soient forcés par le mauvais tems d'y chercher un refuge, soit qu'ils viennent y reclamer les secours et les moyens de reparation nécessaires pour continuer leur voyage. Il est bien entendu, cependant, qu'ils ne trouveront ainsi protection et assistance, que dans le cas ou ils ne se seront pas volontairement détournés de la route qu'ils doivent suivre, qu'ils n'auront commis, ou qu'ils n'annonceront l'intention de commettre aucune hostilité contre la République Française et ses alliés, qu'ils n'auront procuré, ou cherché à procurer aucun secours à ses ennemis, et qu'ils ne s'occuperont d'aucune espéce de commerce, ni de contrebande.

Fait à Paris le quatre Prairial an neuf de la République Française.
Le Ministre de la Marine et des Colonies
(signed)
FORFAIT.

Par le Ministre de la Marine et des Colonies
(Signed)
Ches. M. JURIEN.

Signalement de la corvette.

La corvette l'Investigator est du port de 334 tonneaux. Son équipage est composé de 83 hommes, outre cinq hommes de lettres. Son artillerie est de 6 carronades de 12.

> *2 ditto   de 18.*
> *2 canons   de 6.*
> *2 pierriers.*

Le soussigné, commissaire du gouvernement Français à Londres, certifie le signalement ci-dessus conforme à la note qui lui a été communiquée par le ministre de Sa Majesté Britannique.

Londres le 4 Messidor an 9.

(Signed)
OTTO.

In consequence of this passport, I received directions from the Admiralty "to act in all respects towards French ships as if the two countries were not at war; and," it was added, "with respect to the ships and vessels of other powers with which this country is at war, you are to avoid, if possible, having any communication with them; and not to take letters or packets other than such as you may receive from this office, or the office of His Majesty's secretary of state." From His Grace the duke of Portland, I carried an order to the governor of New South Wales to place the brig Lady Nelson under my command, on arriving at Port Jackson; and also one from the Admiralty, directing the governor, in his quality of senior naval officer, not to take the Investigator from the purposes of the voyage; but to assist me with all the means in his power to put them into execution.

So soon as my sailing orders were received, demands were sent on shore for provisions to replace what had been consumed at Spithead; and they came on board next morning, when the ship was unmoored. We were able to stow a proportion of provisions for twelve months, bread excepted, of which only seven months could be taken, including a part in flour. Of salt meat I took for eighteen months, knowing that little reliance could be had upon the colony in New South Wales for that article; and further to guard against any detriment to the voyage from a want of provisions, I left an application to the Admiralty for a general supply, for twelve months; to be sent after me, and lodged in the store houses at Port Jackson for our sole use.

Of the various extra provisions usually furnished as preservatives of health to the crews of His Majesty's ships going upon similar service, our supply was abundant; and the surgeon was as liberally furnished with antiscorbutic medicines.

The complement of the Xenophon had been seventy-five men; but on the name and destination of the ship being changed, the following establishment was ordered. The names of the officers are added to the list, and also of the men of science who took part in the expedition.

Astronomer,	1 John Crosley.
Naturalist,	1 Robert Brown.
Natural-history painter,	1 Ferdinand Bauer.
Landscape painter,	1 William Westall.
Their servants,	4

Gardener,	1 Peter Good.
Miner,	1 John Allen.
	-
Supernumeraries	10
Commander,	1 Matthew Flinders.
Lieutenants,	2 Robert Fowler.
	Samuel W. Flinders.
Master,	1 John Thistle.
Surgeon,	1 Hugh Bell.
Surgeon's assistant,	1 Robert Purdie.
Master's mates and	
midshipmen	6 Thomas Evans.
	William Taylor.
	John Franklin.
	Thomas Bell.
	Nathaniel Bell.
	Kennet Sinclair.
	Sherrard P. Lound.
	James Wolsey.
Boatswain,	1 Charles Douglas.
Gunner,	1 Robert Colpits.
Carpenter,	1 Russel Mart.
Clerk,	1 John Olive.
Cook and mate,	2
Sailmaker and mate,	2
Armourer,	1
Master at arms,	1
Boatswain's mates,	2
Gunner's mate,	1
Carpenter's mates,	2
D. crew,	2
Quarter masters,	4
Able and ordinary seamen	
and landsmen,	35
Marines.	
Serjeant,	1
Corporal,	1
Drummer,	1
Privates,	12
	--
Complement	83
Deficiency.	
Sailmaker,	1
Master at arms,	1
Quarter masters,	2
Cook's mate,	1
Carpenter's crew,	1
Seaman,	1
	--
Deficient of complement	7
	--

The deficiency of seven, and the two young gentlemen more than allowed, left the whole number of persons on board to be eighty-eight, at the time of sailing.

Mr. Crosley, the astronomer, brought with him an assortment of instruments from the Board of Longitude; part for use at sea, and the larger instruments for making observations on shore, at such ports and bays as we might anchor in during the voyage. His time keepers were the numbers 543 and 520, and watch 465 of Earnshaw; and the numbers

176 and 82 of Arnold. Amongst the instruments supplied to me by the Navy Board, which were unconnected with the above and mostly intended for surveying, was Arnold's watch number 1786, sent for the purpose of being taken up rivers in the tender, or in boats. Its error from mean Greenwich time, at noon July 17, was 2' 38.71" slow, and its rate of losing per day 4.41". This error and rate were given me by Mr. Bayly, mathematical master of the naval academy at Portsmouth, who had the kindness to take charge of the watch during our stay at Spithead.

Chapter Two

1801, July

Towards Madeira.

On July 18 we sailed from Spithead; and in the afternoon of the 20th, having a light breeze from the eastward, with fine weather, our departure was taken from the Start, bearing N. 18° W. five or six leagues. On the following day we fell in with vice-admiral Sir Andrew Mitchell, with a detachment of four three-decked ships from the grand fleet cruising before Brest. It was gratifying to learn from the admiral, that although he had not dropped an anchor for seventeen weeks, there was not a scorbutic man on board; nor any in the sick list, except from slight hurts.
The variation of the compass off St. Alban's Head, had been observed by Mr. Thistle, the master, to be 28° 43' west, from amplitude; off the Start it was 29° 34' from a western azimuth, and 29° 30' from amplitude; but on the following afternoon, where the variation should have been nearly the same, azimuths gave 24° 12' and an amplitude 23° 43' west; the mean 5° 35' less than off the Start. The same compass was always used, and the ship's head was at west (magnetic), or within one point of it, in all the cases; but in the first observations the compass was placed on the binnacle, and in the last, was upon the booms. In order to ascertain clearly what effect this change of place did really produce, I took observations a few days afterward [MONDAY 27] with every compass on board, and Mr. Thistle did the same upon the booms, ten or twelve feet before the main mast, where the compasses were as far removed from any quantity of iron, as they could be placed in any part of the ship. The head was south-west by the steering compass, our latitude was 38° 1' north, longitude 14° 18' west, and the results were as under.

	Binnacle.	Booms.
	° '	° '
Variation from an azimuth compass by Walker, marked No 1: mean of both sides of the vane.	25 47	22 17 W.
From a ditto marked No. 2,	25 35	19 15
ditto marked No. 3,	24 41	21 27
Walker's meridional compass,	25 46	- -
Ditto used as a common azimuth,	25 51	20 35
Compass made by Adams,	25 44	21 9
Means,	25 34	20 57 W.

Thus a change of place from the binnacle to a little before the centre of the ship, produced an alteration of 4° 37' in the mean variation, the same way as, but a less quantity than Mr. Thistle had found it off the Start, when the ship's head was west. The true variation I judge to have been 23°, and that the observations on the booms showed 2° too little, and those on the binnacle 2½° too much. The error in excess, upon the binnacle, appeared to continue so long as the ship was in the northern hemisphere and the head to the westward; but it diminished gradually as we approached the equator, and the observations on the binnacle and booms then nearly coincided. This example is sufficient to show the impropriety of allowing a variation upon the ship's course, from observations taken elsewhere than at the binnacle.

Thursday 30 July 1801.

We continued our course for Madeira, with fair winds. Our latitude on the 30th, was 30° 5' north, longitude 15° 31' west; and in the afternoon Porto Santo was seen, bearing west-north-west; the wind then became light and variable, and soon afterwards died away. The variation observed on the binnacle by the master, when the head was south-west-by-south, was 22° 45', but on the booms 19° 51'; the true variation being as I believe, 20° 51' west.

Friday 31 July 1801.

It was calm on the 31st, and I had a boat lowered down and went round the ship with the carpenter, to inspect the seams near the water line, for we had the mortification to find the ship beginning to leak so soon as the channel was cleared, and in the three last days she had admitted three inches of water per hour. The seams appeared sufficiently bad, especially under the counter and at the butt ends, for the leak to be attributable to them; and as less water came in when the ship was upright than when heeling to a beam wind, I hoped the cause need not be sought lower down. Before hoisting up the boat, a small hawke's-bill turtle was picked up; and between this time and that of anchoring in Funchal Road, several others were seen, and a second, weighing about thirty pounds, was caught.

Saturday August 1 1801.

Aug. 1, at noon, Porto Santo bore N. 11° W., and the rocky islands called Dezertas, from N. 65° to S. 85° W. distant three leagues. The south end of these islands lies, by our observations, in latitude 32° 24' 20" north, which differs less than one mile from its position in Mr. Johnston's chart of the Madeiras. There being little wind next morning [SUNDAY AUGUST 2], I went off in one of the cutters, accompanied by Messieurs Brown and Bauer, the naturalist and natural-history painter, to the southernmost island, called Bujio, which was not far distant. On the way, I shot several birds of the puffin kind, one of which had a fathom of small brass wire attached to its wing. The distance of the land proved to be more considerable than was expected; and there being a current setting southward we did not reach the shore until near three in the afternoon, when it was necessary to think of returning.

At Madeira--Funchal Road.

A small ledge of rocks, which projected a little from under the cliffs at the south-west part of Bujio, afforded a landing place; but it was impossible to ascend the top of the island. We saw no other animated beings than a few birds something like green linnets, but which were said, at Madeira, to have been canary birds; and the other productions were scarcely sufficient to afford amusement even to a naturalist. The cliffs over head showed marks of irregular stratification, and in some of the lines there was a red tinge, apparently of iron. The base underneath was black and honeycombed, as if it had been in the fire, resembling in this respect the common stone at Funchal.
We left Bujio well satisfied that, so far as we could judge of the islands, the name Dezertas, or Desert Islands, was well chosen; and soon after dusk, reached the ship. There was then a good breeze from the north-eastward, with which we steered for Madeira. tacking occasionally during the night, to take advantage of the different flaws of wind. At the following noon [MONDAY 3 AUGUST], the ship was under Brazen Head, which forms the east side of Funchal Road; and being there becalmed, we towed in with the boats, and came to an anchor at four o'clock, in 22 fathoms, steadying with a kedge to the north-west. In this situation, which seems to be as good as any in the road, the bearings by compass were as follow:

Brazen Head,	S. 71° E.
Punta de Cruz, on the west side,	N. 85 W.
Loo Fort, distant one-third of a mile,	N. 12 W.

The north-east winds usually prevail at Madeira in the summer season, and sometimes blow very strong. To reach Funchal Read, ships are accustomed to sail between the east end of Madeira and the Dezertas, before the wind. They are not very desirous of passing close to Brazen Head, where they would be becalmed, but keep off a mile or two, in the skirt of the north-east wind, until they are off the town, or even off Punta de Cruz, where they generally find a breeze from the south-west, which takes them to the anchorage. This south-west wind is the sea breeze of Funchal; and during the time we lay in the road, it usually set in at eight or nine o'clock in the morning, and prevailed as far as three or four miles in the offing, till sunset. A variable breeze comes off the land in the night; at which time it is recommended to ships to pass close to Brazen Head and tow into the road.
We found his Majesty's ship Argo lying here; and I waited upon captain James Bowen, immediately that the ship was secured. Lieutenant Flinders was sent, at the same time, to present my respects to the Portuguese governor, and to ask his Excellency's permission to purchase the necessaries of which we stood in need; as also for the scientific gentlemen to make such an examination of the natural productions of the island, as our short stay would allow. The first request was granted by the governor in polite terms, and accompanied with offers of assistance; but an answer to the second was deferred until he should see me.

This evening the ship was heeled three streaks, when it was found that she admitted more than three inches of water per hour; whereas, when upright, it scarcely amounted to one inch. Next morning [TUESDAY 4 AUGUST], therefore, the carpenters began caulking two seams above the copper, all round, whilst the seamen were employed in shifting the top masts and examining the rigging.

By the assistance of Joseph Pringle, Esq., the British consul, I procured boats from the shore to be sent for our empty water casks; and an ox was killed for our use, and wine prepared for embarkation. His Excellency, the governor, had appointed noon of this day to receive my visit; and I waited upon him in form, accompanied by the consul, who interpreted between us. The governor repeated his offers of assistance; and on being made to understand the nature of the excursions which our gentlemen desired to make into the country, he granted his permission with the utmost readiness. After I had answered some questions relative to the settlement of political affairs in the north of Europe, we took our leave; and were attended out by the officers in waiting, and saluted by the guard.

Thursday 6 August 1801.

On the 6th in the evening, our supply of provisions was received, and the caulking of the ship completed. The scientific gentlemen returned from an expedition towards the Pico Ruivo; which is the highest of a ridge of mountains occupying the central parts of the island, and is said to be 5067 feet, or nearly an English mile, above the level of the sea. The ascent was found to be very difficult; and this, with the heat of the weather and limitation of their time to this evening, disabled them from reaching the summit. It was late when they arrived at the shore; and in embarking abreast of the town, they had the misfortune to be swamped, and to lose the greater part of their collections and sketches, although the boat was managed by Portuguese watermen, accustomed to the place.

The best landing is behind the Loo Rock; but the stony beach in front of the town is usually safe in the summer time. It was so on our first arrival, until the strong eastern winds in the offing raised so much swell as to make it dangerous, even for people experienced in the management of a boat in the surf.

The town of Funchal is placed at the foot of a mountain, which projects from the great central ridge; and the houses being mostly white, they form a strong, but agreeable contrast with the back land. At different elevations up the side of the mountain, are scattered the country houses of the richer inhabitants, placed amongst groups of trees and surrounded with vines. These, with a convent dedicated to Our Lady of the Mountain, which, like the houses, is white, but partly hidden by foliage, give to the whole a picturesque and pleasing appearance from the ships in the road. The town is larger, and there was more trade and activity in it than I was prepared to expect in a small colony, where the students of the college and ecclesiastics of different orders form no inconsiderable part of the superior class of inhabitants. Several British merchants reside at Madeira; their houses of business are at Funchal, but their favourite residences are upon the side of the mountain. I accompanied captain Bowen to one of these, the hospitable seat of Mr. Murdoch, and thought it one of the prettiest places I had seen. The house of Mr. Pringle, the consul, was my home when on shore; indeed the politeness of our countrymen prevented me from experiencing the accommodation afforded to strangers at a house in the town, dignified with the name of hotel. Some of our gentlemen complained of its being miserable enough, even without the swarms of fleas and other vermin by which they were molested.

His Majesty's ships Argo, Carysfort, Falcon, and transports, under the command of captain James Bowen, had arrived in Funchal Road about nine days before us; having on board the 85th regiment under colonel Clinton. After making their dispositions, the two commanders sent to inform the Portuguese governor, that His Britannic Majesty, considering the probability of an attack from the French upon the island, had sent troops to assist in its defence; and they demanded permission for the forces to land. A council was called by the governor; and it being agreed that even were they inclined yet no effectual resistance could be made, the permission was given, and a place assigned for the encampment of the troops to the west of the town. A part of the 85th was afterwards quartered in the Loo Fort and in that of St. Diego, which command both the town and the road; and the men were employed in putting these fortifications into a state of defence.

These arrangements caused no change in the administration of the government, nor in the trade of the island; but the governor was said to be not satisfied that his conduct would be approved. On the day of our arrival, he received intelligence of peace being concluded between Portugal and Spain, but that the war with France was continued; and before we sailed, His Majesty's sloop Voltigeur brought despatches from the Court of Lisbon, which directed the governor to receive the British troops; and it was supposed that every thing connected with the defence of the island would be committed to them. This was the state of things when I took leave of captain Bowen and of colonel Clinton. Water, wine, and fresh beef, were the supplies procured at Madeira. Wine for the ship's company was charged at the enormous price of 5s. 8d. per gallon, and the beef at 10d. per pound; I therefore took only small quantities of each. For good Madeira, we paid as much as £42. the pipe. Fruit and onions were in abundance, and probably were not of less advantage to the health of the people than the more expensive articles.

The latitude observed in Funchal Road was 32° 37' 44" north. The longitude, as given in the Requisite Tables, is 17° 6' 15" west; but in the Connoissance des Temps for 1792, it is laid down by a member of the Academy of Sciences, probably the Chevalier de Borda, at 16° 56' from Greenwich. Arnold's watch No. 1736, in my care, gave 16° 22' 42", and the greatest longitude shown by any of the six time keepers was 16° 54' 26". This was given by Earnshaw's watch No. 465, which had kept an uniform rate during fifteen months previously to its being brought on board. We made use of this watch to reduce some lunar observations taken a few days before arriving, and others after sailing, to the place of anchorage; and the result was as follows:

Ten sets of distances, east and west of the moon,
taken by Mr. Crosley in Funchal Bay and afterwards,
with a Troughton's sextant,   16° 59' 21" W.
Eight sets,[1] east and west, taken by me with a
Troughton's circle and two sextants, before and afterwards,   16 51 28

West longitude of Funchal by lunar observations,   16 55 24

We were therefore induced to prefer the 16° 56', in the Connoissance des Temps, as being nearer the true longitude of Funchal from Greenwich, than the 17° 6' 15" of the Requisite Tables.
Every person had returned on board on Friday morning; and a young man, a native of Ireland, who had been sent here sick in a French cartel, applying to go the voyage, I ordered him to be entered, on the surgeon reporting him to be a fit man for His Majesty's service.

FROM MADEIRA--TOWARDS THE CAPE

On quitting Funchal Road, we were taken aback, at two o'clock, by the east-north-east wind, about two miles off Brazen Head. It blew so strong as to make it necessary to clew down all the sails; and until next morning [SATURDAY AUGUST 8], nothing above close-reefed top sails could be carried with safety. At noon, the log gave 162 miles from Funchal; but the cloudy weather did not admit of taking observations.

Sunday 9 August 1801

At daybreak of the 9th the island Palma was in sight, bearing S. 72° E. ten or twelve leagues. Albacores and bonitas now began to make their appearance, and the officers and men were furnished with hooks and lines, and our harpoons and fizgigs were prepared. This day I ordered lime juice and sugar to be mixed with the grog; and they continued to be given daily to every person on board, until within a short time of our arrival at the Cape of Good Hope.

Saturday 15 August 1801

We carried fair, and generally fresh winds, until the 15th in the morning, when St. Antonio, the north-westernmost of the Cape-Verde Islands was in sight. At eight o'clock, the extremes bore N. 69° E. and S. 13° W., and the nearest part was distant four miles; in which situation no bottom could be found at 75 fathoms. A boat was observed near the shore, and our colours were hoisted; but no notice appeared to be taken of the ship.
The north-west side of St. Antonio is four or five leagues in length; and rises abruptly from the sea, to hills which are high enough to be seen fifteen, or more leagues from a ship's deck. These barren hills are intersected by gullies, which bore marks of much water having passed down them. By the side of one of these gullies, which was near the place where we lost sight of the boat, there was a path leading up into the interior of the island. The south-west and south points are low; they lie N. 14° W. and S. 14° E. and are five or six miles asunder. Between them, the land hollows back so as to form somewhat of a bay, which, if it afford good anchorage, as it is said to do, would shelter a ship from all winds between north and east-south-east. We did not observe any beach at the head of the bay, perhaps from having passed at too great a distance.
No observations could be taken for fixing the situation of this island; but in 1795, Mr. Crosley and myself made the high land near the south-west point to lie in 17° 00' north, and by uncorrected lunar observations, in 25° 12' west; which agrees well with the position of the north-west point, as given by captain Vancouver.[2] The variation from azimuth on the evening of the 14th, before making the land, was 13° 51' west, and 13° 3' this evening, when four leagues to the west of it; the compass being placed on the binnacle, and the ship's head south-south-west (magnetic)

in both cases. The true variation here, at this time, I judge to have been 12° 24' west. Captain Vancouver observed 12° 32', in 1791; but it does not appear how the ship's head was directed.

Some distant land opened from the south point of St. Antonio, at S. 75° E.; which I took to be a part of the island St. Lucia.

During the three days before making St. Antonio, the wind varied from the regular north-east trade, to east-north-east, and as far as south-east-by-east; and about the time of seeing the land, it dwindled to a calm. For three days afterwards it was light, and variable between north and south-east; after which it sometimes blew from the north-west and south-west, and sometimes from the eastward. These variable winds, with every kind of weather, but most frequently with rain, continued until the 23rd [SUNDAY], in latitude 11° north and longitude 23° west; when a steady breeze set in from the south-westward, and the weather became more settled and pleasant. The clouds were sufficiently dense to keep off the intense heat of the vertical sun, but did not often prevent us from obtaining daily observations for the latitude and longitude. At the same time with the south-west wind came a swell from the southward, which made the ship plunge considerably; and so far opened her leaks, that she again made two inches of water in the hour.

Thursday 27 August 1801

On the 27th, in latitude 6° north and longitude 17½° west, a noddy was caught, and next day a swallow was found dead in my sleeping cabin. This poor little bird had been our companion for three or four days before, and had become a favourite. It was generally seen darting past the lee scuttles and ports, apparently after the flies which were carried out by the streams of air; sometimes it alighted upon the boats which hung on the ship's quarters, and more than once rested itself in the cabin where, at length, it was found dead.

Wednesday 2 September 1801

The south-western winds continued to blow without intermission, and drove us, much against my inclination, far to the eastward, towards the coast of Africa. One or two attempts were made to go upon the western tack; but this could not be done with any advantage until the 2nd of September, when we were in latitude 3° 50' north, and longitude 11¼° west. The wind had veered gradually round, from south-west to south, as we approached the African coast, to the direction of which it kept at nearly a right angle. I had not fully adverted to the probability, that the winds blowing upon this coast would prevail to a greater extent at this season than at any other time of the year; otherwise, as I wished to avoid Africa, I should have passed some degrees to the westward of the Cape-Verde Islands, and probably have carried the north-east trade to the 12th, or perhaps to the 10th degree of north latitude; and in 8°, or at furthest in 6°, the south-east trade might have been expected.

Captain Cook, in his second voyage, experienced the same south-western winds, and was carried so far eastward, that he crossed the equator in longitude 8° west. Monsieur de la Pérouse also experienced them, and both were here at the same season with ourselves; that is, in the months of August and September, when the African continent had received its greatest degree of heat.

Although I preferred to avoid Africa, it is by no means certain that a good passage to the Cape of Good Hope may not be made, especially at this season, by steering round the Bight of Benin with the south-west and south winds. It is probable, that on approaching the meridian of Greenwich the wind would be found to return to the south-west, and perhaps more westward, and enable a ship to reach the 10th degree of south latitude before meeting the south-east trade; in which case, the circuit to be made before attaining the western winds beyond the southern tropic, would be much shortened. The East-India-Company's ships bound to St. Helena, do, I believe, now generally follow that route. The leakiness of the ship increased with the continuance of the south-west winds; and at the end of a week, amounted to five inches of water an hour. It seemed, however, that the leaks were mostly above the water's edge, for on tacking to the westward they were diminished to two inches. This working of the oakum out of the seams indicated a degree of weakness which, in a ship destined to encounter every hazard, could not be contemplated without uneasiness. The very large ports, formerly cut in the sides to receive thirty-two-pound carronades, joined to what I had been able to collect from the dock yard officers, had given me an unfavourable opinion of her strength; and this was now but too much confirmed. Should it be asked, why representations were not made, and a stronger vessel procured? I answer, that the exigencies of the navy were such at that time, that I was given to understand no better ship could be spared from the service; and my anxiety to complete the investigation of the coasts of Terra Australis did not admit of refusing the one offered.

Thursday 3 September 1801

The wind was at south when we tacked to the westward; but it shortly veered to south-by-east, and as far as south-east-by-south, which enabled me to look up for the small Isle Sable, or St. Paul, said to lie in 0° 25' south, and about 18½° west. I was desirous of ascertaining the true position of this, and of some other small islands, laid down in the neighbourhood of the equator. They are placed so much in the tracks, both of outward and homeward bound ships, that it was not improbable some one of the vessels missed at different times, might have suffered shipwreck upon them; and the hope that we might be the happy means of restoring to their country and friends some unfortunate fellow creatures, perhaps countrymen, was an additional incitement to look after them.

Monday 7 September 1801

On the 7th, our latitude was 0° 43' north, and we expected to cross the equator some time in the following night. It was a part of my plan for preserving the health of the people, to promote active amusements amongst them, so long as it did not interfere with the duties of the ship; and therefore the ancient ceremonies used on this occasion, were allowed to be performed this evening; and the ship being previously put under snug sail, the seamen were furnished with the means, and the permission, to conclude the day with merriment. At noon next day, the latitude was 0° 17' south, and longitude 17° 7' west; so that the line had been crossed in nearly 17°, about seven in the morning [TUESDAY 8 SEPTEMBER].

From the longitude of 11°, we had been constantly attended by that species of the pelican called man-of-war bird by our seamen, and frègate by the French; but not one of them was to be seen at this time, although we were drawing near to the supposed situation of St. Paul. At four in the afternoon, our latitude was judged to be 0° 29' south; and the course then steered was west, by compass, for a current of ten miles to the north had fully counteracted the western variation on the two preceding days. On the 9th [WEDNESDAY], the latitude was 0° 43' south, and longitude 18° 35'. We ran northward four hours, finding the current had not prevailed as before; and then steered in the parallel of the island. Next day at noon [THURSDAY 10 SEPTEMBER], our situation was in 0° 22' south and 20° 5' west; and seeing no land, nor any signs of being in its neighbourhood, I gave up the search after the island, and hauled south-westward on our way to the Cape of Good Hope.

In the morning, I had observed the variation with Walker's meridional compass, when the ship's head was W. by N. (magnetic); upon the binnacle it gave 14° 30', and on the booms 13' 0' west. Thus the difference, arising from a change of place in the compass, appeared to diminish sensibly as we approached the magnetic equator. The true variation I judge to have been 13° 11' west.

During the two nights of our search for St. Paul's, the quantity of sail was so reduced that not more than ten or twelve leagues should be passed between dusk and daylight; by which means the view astern, in the morning, nearly reached to the horizon of the preceding evening, and any thing, a little elevated above the surface of the water, could scarcely escape being seen from the mast head, more especially as we were fortunate in having distinct views towards each setting and rising sun. The look-out, also, was particularly attended to; for at this time was commenced the system which, in all similar cases, I intended to pursue throughout the voyage. A part of this plan was an order to the three warrant officers to take charge of the look-out betwixt dark and daylight, and to be answerable for the vigilance with which it should be executed, both in their own persons, and in those who were placed upon the same duty under them. The leisure usually enjoyed by this class of officers, particularly by the gunner and carpenter, I conceived to admit of this abridgment, without injury to their ordinary sea duties.

I had twice before crossed the equator, at the respective distances of twenty-six and seventy-three miles to the west of where our search for the Isle of St. Paul ceased; and Mr. Thistle, the master, had crossed the parallel of 25' south, in longitude 22° 12', a few months before; indeed if the Isle had existed between the longitudes of 20° and 25°, it must have been repeatedly seen. I therefore think it may be asserted, that there is no land between 17° and 25° west, either in, or about the latitude of 25' south. The track of Mons. de la Pérouse cuts that parallel in longitude 16°; and he saw no other marks of the vicinity of land than the man-of-war birds which had followed him for several days. If the presence of these birds be any indication of land, I should suppose that there was some lying between the 11th and 16th degrees of west longitude; and if such an island as St. Paul exist, it will probably be found within those limits. Having lost all hope of finding this island, I could have wished to recross the equator and run in the latitude of 55' north; in which parallel the isle Pennedo de St. Pedro, sometimes also called St. Paul, is said to be situate. In Arrowsmith's general chart, it is marked in 24° west longitude, whilst another authority places it to the west of 27°,[3] but I considered that the search might carry me as far as 29°, and perhaps further; and my orders being silent with respect to these islands, I did not think myself authorized to thus occupy so much time; and we therefore hauled to the south-westward on the afternoon of the 10th, as before mentioned. On the following day [FRIDAY SEPTEMBER

11], a gannet was seen, which seemed to imply that our situation of 1 ¾° south, and 21½° west, was not far removed from some island or rock; for I do not recollect to have seen this bird at a greater distance from land than thirty leagues.

The trade wind varied from south-south-east to east-south-east, and commonly blew fresh, with frequent squalls. The swell from the southward, with which these winds were for some days accompanied, caused the ship to work so much, that she soon let in as great a quantity of water on this tack, as she before had done on the other; I therefore judged it advisable to alter the plan of keeping within seven points of the wind, and to go with it upon the beam; and also to put in practice every means of lightening the upper works, for they seemed to be very inadequate to support the weight with which they had been unavoidably loaded. Two eighteen-pound carronades, stern chacers, were taken off the upper deck and struck into the hold; the spare rudder, and a variety of other things which a want of room had obliged us to stow in the main and mizen channels, were taken within board; and every exterior weight concentrated as much as possible. After this was done, the tremulous motion caused by every blow of the sea, exciting a sensation as if the timbers of the ship were elastic, was considerably diminished; and the quantity of water admitted by the leaks was also somewhat reduced.

Sunday 13 September 1801

On the 13th, in latitude 4° 44' south and longitude 23° 17' west, a swallow, a gannet, and two sheerwaters were seen; and from six to eight in the evening, the officer of the watch and myself thought the water to be much smoother than before, or than it was afterward. Had it been in an unknown sea, I should have been persuaded that some island, or shoal, lay at no great distance to the south-eastward of our situation at that time.

Sunday 20 September 1801

The trade wind continued, with some little variety in its direction, to blow fresh until the 20th, when it became light, and sometimes calm. We were then approaching the small island Trinidad. Many gannets were seen at twenty-four leagues off, but none at a greater distance. On the 23rd [WEDNESDAY], the island was in sight; and at noon, when our latitude was 20° 1' south, and longitude 29° 13' west, a peaked hummock near the eastern extremity bore S. 25° W., nine or ten leagues. The western extremity bore S. 29° W., and at first appeared to be a bluff head; but it afterwards assumed the form of a conical rock, and was, in all probability, the Nine Pin of captain D'Auvergne's chart. One of the rocks called Martin Vas, was visible from the main top, and angled 49° 43' to the left of the peaked hummock; its bearing was consequently very near S. 25° E.

Mons. de la Pérouse, who sent a boat on shore to Trinidad, lays down the latitude of the south-east point at 20° 31' south, and longitude from lunar observations, 28° 37' west of Greenwich. The latitude appeared to agree with our observations; but in the longitude there is some difference. According to Earnshaw's two time keepers, No. 465 and 543, which kept better rates than the remaining four, the longitude of the Nine Pin is 29° 25½' west; which being reduced to the south-east point, will place it in 29° 23', or 46' west of the French navigator.[4] The longitude in captain D'Auvergne's plan of Trinidad, constructed 1782, is 29° 55', or 32' still further west. From two sets of distances of the star Altair to the west, and two of Aldebaran east of the moon, I made the longitude of the south-east point to be 29° 19' west; the difference from the time keepers, which I consider to have given the best longitude, being no more than 4'.

Thursday 24 September 1801

Azimuths taken upon the binnacle in the morning, with three compasses, and the ship's head at S. W. by S., gave variation 3° 54'; and in the evening, at S. W., 3° 50'; but next morning, when Trinidad was just disappearing from the deck in the N. 60° E., other azimuths then showed the variation to be 1° 35' west, the ship's head being S. S. W.; it therefore appears, that there is a difference off the north, and off the south-west sides of the island. From the first observations I deduce the true variation to be 4° 14' west, and from the last 1° 50' west. Captain D'Auvergne marks the variation 0° 45' west, in 1782; but under what circumstances it was ascertained, does not appear.

Tuesday 29 September 1801

The trade wind having again arisen from east-south-east, we were enabled to make between eighty and ninety miles a day. It afterwards veered gradually round, by the north-east and north, to the westward, and blew fresh; so that on the 29th, our latitude was 31° 2' and longitude 26° 0' west. This was 17' to the south, and about 6° west of the situation usually assigned to Saxemberg; an island which has been frequently sought by the East-India, and other ships, in the place which it still occupies in the charts; and not finding it there, they have run a few degrees to the eastward, in the same parallel, but always without success. The opportunity which presented itself of now adding 6° of longitude to the examined space, and on the opposite side, I should have thought myself culpable in neglecting; and therefore, having placed the ship in the supposed parallel of the island, we steered due east for it; adopting the same regulations for the look-out at night, as when searching for St. Paul's.

We had seen an unusual number of pintado and sooty petrels on the preceding afternoon, as also of a brown bird, apparently one of the sea-swallow tribe, having a white belly and the form and size of a woodcock; and this evening it was reported to me from the mast head, and confirmed by others on deck, that a turtle was seen lying upon the water. These indications of land gave me some hope that the long lost Saxemberg might be brought to light. On the following noon [WEDNESDAY 30 SEPTEMBER], the observed latitude was 30° 41' and longitude 22° 46'; and nothing further had transpired to betoken the vicinity of land. Next day [THURSDAY 1 OCTOBER], our observations gave 30° 34' south, and 20° 28' west; and I then steered east-south-east, a course which should have taken us almost directly over the supposed situation of Saxemberg, if the same current of 11' north had prevailed, as on the preceding day. But this not proving to be the case, our track lay a few miles to the south; though sufficiently near for us to be satisfied of the non-existence of the island in the place assigned to it, if that could any longer admit of a doubt.[5]

Sunday 4 October 1801

The fresh western winds continued, with short intervals of calm, as far as the latitude 33° 23', and longitude 13° 0' west; when they died away, and a breeze sprung up from the eastward. With this wind we could do little more than look up for the isles of Tristan d'Acunha, whose bearing was then S. 16° E., and distance seventy-seven leagues. From the description given by sir Erasmus Gower[6] of the anchorage, and the convenience with which water may be obtained, and his account of the animals which resort there, I should not have considered it to be lost time, had the wind made it advisable to put in at Tristan d'Acunha, for a few days; but it veered round to the north-west, on the [TUESDAY] 6th. and we resumed our former course to the Cape of Good Hope.

Wednesday 14 October 1801

In the morning of the 14th, the variation by mean of amplitude and azimuth, was 25° 10' west; the ship's head being E. by S., and our latitude 35° 4' south, and longitude 12° 50' east. It is worthy of being mentioned, that in the year 1797, and near the same place, I observed the variation to be 19° 40' west, on board His Majesty's ship Reliance; and as the compass was upon the binnacle in both cases, the sole cause to which I can attribute this great difference is, that the ship's head was west, instead of E. by S. The true variation could not be far from the mean of the two observations, since it was 26° at the Cape of Good Hope. In the English Channel, the compass on the binnacle had shown nearly 4° too much west variation, when the ship's head was at west; but here, it gives at least 2° too much, with the head in an opposite direction! This difference in the two hemispheres merits particular notice; it is part of a series of apparent anomalies in the compass which have hitherto remained unaccounted for; but which seem reducible to one general cause, as I have attempted to show in the Appendix No. II. to the second volume.

Friday 16 October 1801

At daybreak of the 16th, we expected to see the high land of the Cape; but the weather being hazy, it could not be distinguished until eight o'clock, when it bore north-east, eight leagues; being three leagues more than Earnshaw's pocket time keeper, in which we had most confidence, led us to expect, and four miles less than was given by my uncorrected lunar observations of the 14th p.m., brought forward by the time keeper.

At this time we had not a single person in the sick list, both officers and men being fully in as good health, as when we sailed from Spithead. I had begun very early to put in execution the beneficial plan, first practised and made known by the great captain Cook. It was in the standing orders of the ship, that on every fine day the deck below and the cockpits should be cleared, washed, aired with stoves, and sprinkled with vinegar. On wet and dull days they were cleaned and aired, without washing. Care was taken to prevent the people from sleeping upon deck, or lying down in their wet clothes; and once in every fortnight or three weeks, as circumstances permitted, their beds, and the contents of their chests and bags, were opened out and exposed to the sun and air. On the Sunday and Thursday mornings, the ship's company was mustered, and every man appeared clean shaved and dressed; and when the evenings were fine, the drum and fife announced the fore castle to be the scene of dancing; nor did I discourage other playful amusements which might occasionally be more to the taste of the sailors, and were not unseasonable.

Within the tropics, lime juice and sugar were made to suffice as antiscorbutics; on reaching a higher latitude, sour krout and vinegar were substituted; the essence of malt was reserved for the passage to New Holland, and for future occasions. On consulting with the surgeon, I had thought it expedient to make some slight changes in the issuing of the provisions. Oatmeal was boiled for breakfast four days in the week, instead of three; and when rice was issued, after the expenditure of the cheese, it was boiled on the other three days. Pease soup was prepared for dinner four days in the week, as usual; and at other times, two ounces of portable broth, in cakes, to each man, with such additions of onions, pepper, etc. as the different messes possessed, made a comfortable addition to their salt meat. And neither in this passage, nor, I may add, in any subsequent part of the voyage, were the officers or people restricted to any allowance of fresh water. They drank freely at the scuttled cask, and took away, under the inspection of the officer of the watch, all that was requisite for culinary purposes; and very frequently two casks of water in the week were given for washing their clothes.

With these regulations, joined to a due enforcement of discipline, I had the satisfaction to see my people orderly and full of zeal for the service in which we were engaged; and in such a state of health, that no delay at the Cape was required beyond the necessary refitment of the ship, and I still hoped to save a good part of the summer season upon the south coast of Terra Australis.

Cape of Good Hope. False Bay.

The usual time for His Majesty's ships to leave False Bay and go round to Table Bay, I found to be the latter end of September; but being then unacquainted with the precise time, and knowing of the loss of the Sceptre in Table Bay, on November 5, from a heavy gale at north-west, I determined to go into False Bay; unless we should get previous information that it had been quitted by the squadron. At noon, the extremes of the land bore N. by W. ½ W. and E. ½ N. The Cape Point bore north, three leagues; and our observed latitude being 34° 32', showed the Requisite Tables to be erroneous in the position of this point; but that 34° 23', as assigned to it by captain King, was correct.[7]

At one o'clock we hauled round the rocks which lie off the Cape Point, and steered into False Bay. Near these rocks were two whales; and one or more of what seamen call thrashers were engaged in a furious combat with them, at a less distance than half a mile from the ship. The sinewy strength of the thrasher must be very great; for besides raising his tail high out of the water to beat the adversary, he occasionally threw the whole of his vast body several feet above the surface, apparently to fall upon him with greater force. Their struggles covered the sea with foam for many fathoms round.

At three o'clock we got sight of the squadron lying in Simon's Bay. It consisted of His Majesty's ships Lancaster, Jupiter, Diomede, Imperieuse, Hindoostan, Rattlesnake, and Euphrosyne, under the command of vice-admiral sir Roger Curtis, Bart. The master of the Lancaster came on board to pilot the ship to a proper berth, and I went on shore to wait upon the vice-admiral. On showing my orders, and presenting an account of the supplies and the work requisite to put the Investigator in the same state as on leaving England, I found that the naval magazines could furnish only some part, and that many articles, especially biscuit, were not to be obtained; but with great consideration for the service on which I was sent out, the commander in chief ordered every request to be granted either in the articles specified, or by substitution; and a thorough caulking, both within and without side of the ship, being the work most essential to be done, a gang of caulkers, collected from the squadron, was sent on board on the following morning.

Saturday 17 October 1801

The water which is conducted in pipes to the wharf, for the convenience of shipping, was said not to keep well at sea; and the master of the Lancaster, from whom this information was obtained, recommended, as much superior, that which drains through the sand, from the hills on the north side of Simon's Bay. I went, accordingly, to make an examination; and found that by sinking a cask in the sand, with the head out and the upper hoops taken off, the water drained through the spaces between the staves, sufficiently fast for our purpose. This plan was therefore adopted; and the watering of the ship immediately commenced.

Having seen this, and some other duties set forward under the proper officers, I accompanied Mr. Crosley, the astronomer, in search of a place where the observatory and tents could be conveniently set up. The situation chosen was near a small rill on the south side of the bay, about three-hundred yards from the magazine; and the permission of the military commandant being obtained, two tents, the observatory, and astronomical instruments were landed in the afternoon, with a guard of marines. The whole was placed under the charge of Mr. Flinders, the second lieutenant, who was also to act as an assistant in making and calculating the observations, for which he was qualified. The situation of the tents was tolerably well sheltered from the south-eastern gales, which begin to prevail at this season of the year; but the quantity of sand put in motion by every breeze, was a great molestation, and proved injurious to the instruments. Besides this inconvenience, there was another attached to the situation which had not been foreseen. The road from Simon's Town to a place called the Company's garden, led close past the observatory; and this was the sole ride or walk in the neighbourhood, which the inhabitants and the gentlemen belonging to the ships in the bay could enjoy. From those of the first rank, who took their morning's ride, to the sailor who staggered past on a Sunday, and even the slave with his bundle of fire wood, all stopped at the observatory to see what was going on. Ramsden's universal theodolite, set up for the purpose of observing transits, excited its share of attention from the curious. Some wanted information, some amusement, and all would have liked to see how the sun appeared through the telescope. By the end of October, our provisions and stores were received; the sails had been examined and repaired on board the Lancaster, and were rebent; and the caulkers having completed their work, the ship was fresh painted. Being anxious to commence the investigation of the coasts of Terra Australis, the stripping of the masts and reparation of the rigging were deferred to King George's Sound, and no more was done at the ship than necessity required; for I preferred passing the time necessary to a complete re-equipment in a port where astronomical observations and surveys could be at the same time usefully carried on, and the naturalists employ themselves in a field almost unexplored, rather than in a bay already well known, and where the surrounding country had been so often traversed. Mr. Crosley had been frequently unwell during the passage from Madeira; and after trying the effect of a few days on shore, he decided to remain at the Cape of Good Hope, and relinquish the expedition. The instruments supplied by the Board of Longitude he agreed to leave in my care; after having consulted with the commander in chief upon the subject, and received his approbation. The loss of the astronomer was severely felt by me, both from being deprived in the surveys of his more accurate observations, and from being called upon to supply his place so far as was in my power. The duties of commander joined to the occupation of surveyor, left little time for other employment; but through an increase of effort, and with the assistance of my officers, I hoped to carry on the surveys and fulfil the most essential parts of the instructions from the Board of Longitude, at the same time. Of these instructions, Mr. Crosley permitted me to take a copy.

Sunday 1 November 1801

The rates of going with mean solar time of the four time keepers committed to my charge, were deduced by Mr. Crosley from three days observation of equal altitudes, with a sextant and quick-silver horizon, between the 21st and 27th of October. These rates, which he left with me, I extended to November 1, by equal altitudes taken on that day; and their respective errors were deduced by allowing 1h 13' 40.47" to be the longitude in time of Simon's Bay.[8]

Earnshaw's No. 543, slower than mean Greenwich time at noon there Nov. 1,	h ' "	"
	0 14 35.33 and losing	5.33
No. 520,	34 16.62	15.84
Arnold's No. 176,	50 59.29	8.96
No. 82	--------	-----
No. 1736, watch, faster	21 20.03	17.27

The watch was intended to be taken up rivers, and to such places as the ship did not go; and in order to gain some knowledge of its probable performance, I wore it five days in the pocket. Its rate of losing during that time, was from 11.59" to 8.79" per day; so that upon the average, it lost 7" less in the pocket than when in a fixed situation; for the above rate of 17.27" was what it kept in the box, during the last three days. Arnold's No. 89, altered its rate on the last day, from 2.98" to 1' 18.68", without any apparent cause; no rate could therefore be fixed for it, with any probability of its being kept. Of the excellent watch No. 465 of Earnshaw, being Mr. Crosley's private property, we were deprived at the same time with the astronomer; he also took with him the reflecting circle, No. 74 of Troughton, both of which I considered to be an addition to our loss.

So soon as the corresponding altitudes of Sunday afternoon were obtained, I took on board the time keepers and instruments, with the tents and observatory. The ship was then ready for sea; but the wind blew a gale from the southeastward, which continued until Tuesday [3 NOVEMBER 1801]. It then fell calm, and we unmoored; but before getting under way, the same wind again set in, and obliged us to drop a second anchor.

Through the kind attention of sir Roger Curtis, the commander in chief, the state of the ship and our provisions and stores were as complete as when leaving Spithead. The ship's company had been regularly served with fresh meat every day, beef and mutton alternately; vegetables were not to be purchased, but we several times received small quantities, with oranges and lemons, from the naval hospital in Cape Town; and a proportion of these for a week, with a few days fresh meat, were carried to sea. Two of my ship's company, whose dispositions required more severity in reducing to good order than I wished to exercise in a service of this nature, were exchanged by the vice-admiral; as also two others, who from want of sufficient strength, were not proper for so long a voyage. In lieu of these, I received four men of good character from the flag ship, who made pressing application to go upon a voyage of discovery. Mr. Nathaniel Bell, one of the young gentlemen of the quarter deck, having expressed a wish to return to England, he was discharged; and Mr. Denis Lacey, midshipman of the Lancaster, received in his place.

Simon's Bay is known to be a large and well-sheltered cove, in the north-western part of the sound, called False Bay. Since the loss of the Sceptre in Table Bay, it has been more frequented than formerly; and I found it to be a prevailing sentiment, that were it not for the advantages of Cape Town, Simon's Bay would, in every respect, be preferable for the royal dockyard, and the equipment of His Majesty's ships. It was remarked to me by an officer of discernment, captain of the flag ship, that instances of vessels being driven from their anchors by winds blowing into Simon's Bay, were exceedingly rare. He had observed that the strain upon the cables with these winds, was much less than with those of equal strength blowing off the land; and he accounted for it from the water thrown into the bay by sea winds, rebounding from the shore and forming what is called an under-tow, which tended to keep a ship up to her anchors. This takes place in Simon's Bay, with the south-east winds, but not in Table Bay with those from the north-west, which blow into it; owing, in part, to the distance at which ships there ride from the land, and apparently, also, from the under-tow passing out on the eastern side of the bay, clear of the anchoring ground.

The Cape of Good Hope cannot now be supposed to furnish much of novelty in the department of natural history, especially to transient visitors; but it still continues to afford much amusement and instruction to English botanists. It did so to our gentlemen, who were almost constantly on shore upon the search; and their collections, intended for examination on the next passage, were tolerably ample. They were sufficiently orthodox to walk many miles for the purpose of botanising upon the celebrated Table Mountain; for what disciple of Linnaeus could otherwise conscientiously quit the Cape of Good Hope? In taking so early a departure, though it were to proceed to the almost untrodden, and not less ample field of botany, New Holland, I had to engage with the counter wishes of my scientific associates; so much were they delighted to find the richest treasures of the English green house, profusely scattered over the sides and summits of these barren hills.

Notes

[1] *Four of these are uncorrected for the errors of the lunar and solar tables. They were taken Aug. 29, on which day no observation of the moon was made at Greenwich; and the errors observed on the 27th and 30th were so irregular, that no proportion can be made between them with any prospect of accuracy. Were the errors of the 30th applied, the longitude of Funchal would be 4' less.*

[2] *Voyage round the World, Vol. I. page 10.*

[3] *Voyage of La Pérouse, page 50 of the London translation. I am lately informed, that Pennedo de St. Pedro lies in latitude 0° 55' north, and longitude 27° 0' west; that it makes like four sail of ships, and is covered with birds, but affords no water.*

[4] *The error of No. 465 was found, at the Cape of Good Hope, to be 10' 57", 2 to the east, and of No. 543, to be 39' 21", 5 east, contracted in 96 days upon their English rates. To obtain the above longitude, a proportional part of these errors according to the number of days, has been applied to the keepers; and the difference between them is then no more than 2".*

[5] *At the Cape of Good Hope, in 1810, His Excellency the Earl of Caledon favoured me with the following extract from the log book of the sloop Columbus--Long, master; returning to the Cape from the coast of Brazil.*

"September 22, 1809, at five p.m., saw the island of Saxonburg, bearing E. S. E., first about 41 leagues distant: clear weather. Steered for the said island, and found it to be in the latitude of 30° 18' south, longitude 28° 20' west, or thereabout.

"The island of Saxonburg is about four leagues in length, N. W. and S. E., and about 2½ miles in breadth. The N. W. end is a high bluff of about 70 feet, perpendicular form, and runs along to the south-east about 8 miles. You will see trees at about a mile and a half distance, and a sandy beach."

The situation of Saxemberg in the common tables and charts, was 30° 45' south and 19° 40' west, almost 9° of longitude too little; and therefore it is not surprising that ships have missed it. At the time so many birds were seen, on the 28th, the Investigator was not more than eighty miles from the position of the island, as above given from Mr. Long.

[6] *Lord Macartney's Embassy to China, by sir G. Staunton, Vol. I. p. 198-201.*

[7] *See Cook's third Voyage, Vol. III. page 484.*

[8] *In 1763, Mr. Mason determined the longitude of his observatory in Cape Town, from the transit of Venus, to be 18° 23' 7" east; and the difference of longitude from thence to Simon's Bay, by the Dutch survey, is 2' 00" east.*

Chapter Three

Towards New Holland.

Wednesday 4 November 1801

At daybreak of November 4, a light breeze from the eastward enabled me to quit Simon's Bay, after a stoppage of eighteen days. The high land of Great Smit's Winkel afterwards becalmed the sails; and we were no further advanced, at noon, than to have the Cape Point bearing south-west, at the distance of two or three leagues. On receiving the breeze, which came from the south-south-west, we stretched towards Cape Agulhas, veering ship at eleven at night, on coming into 50 fathoms. This wind died away in the morning, and remained calm till noon; the Cape Point then bore N. W. ¾ N., Cape False N. ¾ E., and our latitude was 34° 36'. Near this situation, the bottom is a greenish mud, at the depth of 78 fathoms.

The report of the guns fired by the squadron in Simon's Bay, to commemorate the escape from gunpowder treason, was distinctly heard at one o'clock, when we were occupied in making sail to a fine breeze which had sprung up from the south-westward. At six in the evening, it blew fresh with cloudy weather; the extremes of the land bore from N. 20° W to W. 58° E., and we took our departure for New Holland.

Lieutenant Flinders observed azimuths this evening from the binnacle with two compasses; the ship's head was south (magnetic), and the variation found to be 26° 13' west; and in default of observations on shore, I consider this to have been the true variation at the Cape of Good Hope in 1801.

During our run across the Agulhas Bank, I did not find any current setting to the westward; but in the five days taken to reach the latitude 36° 30' and longitude 33° 38', [TUESDAY 10 NOVEMBER 1801] the ship was set 59' to the north of the reckoning. The swell which followed after the ship probably counteracted the effect of the usual westwardly current; and indeed it must have done something more, if our log were correct, since the longitude by time keepers was then 30' ahead of account.

I considered the parallel of 37° south, at this season of the year, to be sufficiently distant from the verge of the south-east trade to insure a continuance of western winds; and to be far enough to the north, to avoid the gales incident to high latitudes. Having made this passage three times before, I was satisfied of the impropriety of running in a high southern latitude, particularly when the sun is in the other hemisphere, and there is nothing else in view than to make a good passage; not only from the winds there being often stronger than desired, but because they will not blow so steadily from the westward. In the latitude of 42°, I have experienced heavy gales from the north, and from the south, and even from the eastward, in the months of June and July; allowances for lee way were also frequent in that passage, and light winds or calms not uncommon. The parallel of 42° seems to be a very proper one, when the sun is in his highest south declination, and from that time until the middle of February; but in the opposite months of the year, I should prefer to run down my easting two or three degrees even to the northward of what was now chosen for the Investigator.

It may not be improper to anticipate upon the voyage so far as to state what was the result of keeping in the parallel of 37°, in the month of November. From the Cape of Good Hope to the island Amsterdam, the winds were never so strong as to reduce the Investigator to close-reefed top sails; and on the other hand, the calms amounted to no more than seven hours in nineteen days. The average distance on the log board upon direct courses, for we had no foul winds, was a hundred and forty miles per day; and the Investigator was not a frigate, but a collier-built ship, and deeply laden. In the following twelve days run, from Amsterdam to the south-west cape of New Holland, the same winds attended us; and a hundred and fifty eight miles per day was the average distance, without lee way or calm.

Thursday 12 November 1801

On the 12th, I took the opportunity of light winds to send down a bucket, fitted with valves to bring up water from a depth; but having no thermometer of a proper size to go into the bucket, I could only immerse one after the water was brought up. In this imperfect way, the temperature at 150 fathoms depth was found to be 63°,1, differing very little from that of the water at the surface, which was 63°,8. In the air, the thermometer stood at 63°,6. The specific gravity of the water brought up was afterwards tried at King George's Sound, and proved, at the temperature of 69°, to be 1,026, taking that of the crystal-glass bulb, with which the experiment was made, at 3,150; and the specific gravity of the surface water, taken up at the same time, was exactly the same. The latitude of our situation was 36° 36' south, and longitude 38° 23' east. The mean inclination of the dipping needle, placed upon the cabin table, was 58° 4' of the south end; and the variation, by mean of azimuths on the preceding evening and amplitude this morning, taken on the binnacle when the ships head was S. E. by E., magnetic, was 31° 47'; but the true variation, or such as would have been obtained with the head at north, or south, I consider to have been 29° 22' west.

Throughout the passage to the island Amsterdam, we were accompanied by some, or all of the oceanic birds usually found in these latitudes; but not in the numbers I had been accustomed to see them further south. The spouting of a whale was occasionally perceived, and became more frequent on approaching the island; the number of small blue petrels was also increased, and a few Cape hens then made their appearance.

Tuesday 24 November 1801

At five in the evening of the 24th, the mean variation from three compasses on the binnacle, was observed to be 23° 7' west, with the ship's head E. S. E., or 20° 4' true. Our latitude was then 38° 20' south, longitude 76° 26' east; and at eleven at night, having nearly reached the longitude of Amsterdam, whose situation I wished to compare with the time keepers, we hove to, in a parallel between it and the island St. Paul. At five next morning [WEDNESDAY 25 NOVEMBER 1801], we steered southward to make Amsterdam; but having reached its latitude, and no land being visible, our eastwardly course was resumed. The weather was thick, so that objects could not be distinguished beyond five or six miles; and at noon the ship was found to have been set 23' of longitude to the east of what the log gave. From these joint causes it must have been that Amsterdam was not perceived, if its situation of 38° 43' south and 77° 40' east, as made in His Majesty's ship Providence, in 1792, were rightly ascertained.

In passages like this, when fortunately made, it is seldom that any circumstance occurs, of sufficient interest to be related. Our employments were to clean, dry, and air the ship below; and the seamen's clothes and bedding, with the sails, upon deck. These, with the exercise of the great guns and small arms, were our principal employments in fine weather; and when otherwise, we were wet and uncomfortable, and could do little. It was a great satisfaction that frequent pumping of the ship was not now required, the greatest quantity of water admitted during this passage being less than two inches an hour. The antiseptics issued were sour krout and vinegar, to the extent of the applications for them; and at half an hour before noon every day, a pint of strong wort, made by pouring boiling water upon the essence of malt, was given to each man. It was drunk upon deck; and with half a biscuit, made a luncheon for both officers and people. The allowance of grog was never issued until half an hour after the dinner time.

South Coast. Cape Leeuwin.

Sunday 6 December 1801

On the 6th of December, our latitude was 35° 10' and longitude 114° 19'; which placed us about S. W. ½ S. twenty-two leagues from the westernmost isles lying off the south-west cape of New Holland, according to their position by the French rear-admiral D'Entrecasteaux; a traced copy of whose general chart of this coast had been furnished to me from the hydrographical office at the Admiralty. There were no names applied in this copy; but in the charts of the French voyage, lately published, these islets are called Îles St. Alouarn.

Notwithstanding the nearness of the land there were no signs of such proximity: no discolouring in the water, no sea weed, no new birds, and but few of the species before seen. The current had, indeed, somewhat changed; for while, during the three preceding days, it had set N. 12° W. twenty-seven miles per day, on an average, it was found this day to have run N. 47° E. twenty-two miles. This change, however, could scarcely be thought a sign of land, since equal, or greater differences had occurred during the passage, and might arise, in part, from errors in the log.

At two in the afternoon, the wind being north-westward, we hauled up to make the south-western point of Leeuwin's Land, and bent the cables. At seven, land was seen right ahead, bearing N. 14° E., at the supposed distance of ten leagues; and on sounding there was 85 fathoms, coral sand. We stood for it until eleven at night, and then veered to the south-west, in 65 fathoms, same bottom.

The examination of Nuyts' and of Leeuwin's Lands was not prescribed in my instructions to be made at this time; but the difference of sailing along the coast at a distance, or in keeping near it and making a running survey, was likely to be so little that I judged it advisable to do all that circumstances would allow whilst the opportunity offered; and I had the pleasure to find this slight deviation approved at the Admiralty.

Monday 7 December 1801

At two in the morning we had 80 fathoms, and veered towards the land. It was seen from the mast head at five; and the highest part, the same which had been set in the evening, bore N. 12° W. This is the largest of the before-mentioned Isles of St. Alouarn; but at half past seven we saw hills extending from behind, and, to all appearance, joining it to the main land. This supposed isle is, therefore, what I denominate CAPE LEEUWIN, as being the south-western and most projecting part of Leeuwin's Land. The highest hill lies nearly in latitude 34° 19' south, and longitude 115° 6' east; it is a sloping piece of land of about six hundred feet in elevation, and appeared to be rocky, with a slight covering of trees and shrubs; but this cape will be best known from Mr. Westall's sketch. (Atlas Plate XVII. View I.). A piece of lower land was seen to the north-west, probably a continuation of the coast, and there are some rocky islets scattered on the south side of the cape. The largest of these islets, lying about four miles off, was passed before eight o'clock, at the distance of seven or eight miles, and seen to be surrounded with high and extensive breakers. On the east side of Cape Leeuwin the land falls back north-eastward three or four leagues, and afterwards curves to the south-east, forming a large bight which appeared to be wholly exposed to the southern winds. The coast-line round the upper part of this bight was not distinguishable; but the hills at the back showed more of bare sand than of vegetable covering. At ten o'clock a low, black projection, forming the eastern point of the bight, bore east three miles; and the depth was 15 fathoms upon a coarse sandy bottom. We then veered round to the south-eastward, following the direction of the coast, with the wind at west-south-west and weather somewhat squally; and at noon, our situation and principal bearings were as follow:

Latitude observed,	34° 32 2/3' S.
Longitude by time keepers,	115 30 E.
C. Leeuwin, furthest visible part,	N. 55 W.
The low, black point,	N. 4 W.
Furthest extreme of the coast ahead,	S. 53 E.

The shore abreast was seven or eight miles distant; and behind it ran a continuation of the same ridge of sandy hillocks which surrounds the bight, and it extended to the southern extreme. Over this ridge were perceived, here and there, the tops of some higher and less sandy hills, standing a few miles inland; but the general aspect of the country was that of great sterility; nor was there, as yet, any appearance of its being inhabited.
Soon after four we passed the noon's extreme at the distance of four miles. It is a steep, rocky cape, named in the French chart, Point D'Entrecasteaux; and is one of the most remarkable projections of this coast. I make its latitude, from the bearings, to be 34° 52' south, and longitude by time keepers 116° 1' east. A low rock lies two or three miles to the east-south-east, from the point, and a patch of breakers nearly the same distance from the south; and soon after passing the point, two other rocks, white and rather high, were seen lying from it five leagues to the south-east. At a quarter past seven, when the night closed in

The two white rocks bore	N. 20° E.
Furthest extrem of the land, like a steep head,	N. 71° E.

Tuesday 8 December 1801

The wind was then at south-west, and we stretched onward until one in the morning, before tacking to the north-west for the land. At daylight the ship was found to have been carried to the eastward, and neither Point D'Entrecasteaux nor the two white rocks were in sight; but in the N. 19° E., about eight miles, was a head not far from the extreme set in the evening. It afterwards proved to be a smooth, steep rock, lying one mile from the main; and is the land first made upon this coast by captain Vancouver, who called it Cape Chatham. Its latitude is very nearly 35° 3' south, longitude 116° 29' east, and it was sketched by Mr. Westall. (Atlas Plate XVII. View 2.)
Whilst stretching in for the shore, with the ship's head north-west-by-north (magnetic) I took azimuths with two compasses on the binnacle; after which they were immediately placed on a stand near the taffrel and other azimuths taken. The variation resulting from the observations on the binacle was 5° 59' west, and from those near the taffrel 8° 24' west; affording another instance of the effect produced by changing the place of the compass. In 1803, and at twenty leagues to the west of Cape Leeuwin, we had 10° 4' variation on the binnacle, with the head south-east; from which, and the above 5° 59', the true variation off the cape, or such as would be obtained with the ship's head at north or south, should be 7° 48' west.[1]
At seven o'clock we got sight of the two white rocks, which enabled me to take up the survey of the preceding evening; and we then bore away along the coast at the distance of four or five miles, with a pleasant breeze and fine weather.
Some parts of the shore between Point D'Entrecasteaux and Cape Chatham were not distinctly seen. That which is nearest to the cape lies in the line of N. 38° W. from its outer part, and presents an intermixture of steep cliffs and small sandy beaches, with a back land moderately high, and better covered with wood than that before described. On

the east side of Cape Chatham the shore falls back to the northward, and makes a bight in which is a small reef of rocks. It then projects in a cliffy head, which lies S. 75° E. seven miles from the cape, and is called Point Nuyts in the French chart; upon the supposition, probably, that this was the first land seen by Nuyts in 1627. Beyond this point the coast trends very nearly east; but forms several projections, some of which are steep and others low; and between them are sandy bights where small vessels might obtain shelter from all northern winds. The hills lying at the back of the shore seemed to be barren, though trees grew thickly on their eastern sides; they are not high, but it was rare to perceive any thing of the interior country above them.

At noon the nearest parts of the coast were a steep and a more eastern low point, both distant about four miles; and from the bight between them was rising the first smoke seen upon this coast. Our situation at this time, and the principal bearings taken, were as under;

Latitude, observed to the north and south,	85° 7' 5".
Longitude by time keepers,	116 50.
Point Nuyts, with Cape Chatham behind,	N. 75 W.
Steep point, near the smoke,	N. 15 W.
Furthest visible extreme ahead,	N. 84 E.

Soon after two o'clock we passed at the distance of five miles from a steep point which has a broad rock lying near it. This point, being unnamed and somewhat remarkable, I call Point Hillier; it lies in 35° 4' south and 117° 9' east. The coast extends from thence nearly east-by-south, without any considerable projection except at the furthest extreme then visible; and on coming up with it, at half-past five, it proved to be the Cape Howe of Vancouver. There is another Cape Howe upon this same coast, named by Captain Cook, which makes it necessary to distinguish this by a descriptive adjunct, and I shall therefore call it West Cape Howe. The situation of this projecting cliffy cape is in 35° 8½' south and 117° 40' east. Beyond it the land trends north-by-east, four miles, into a sandy bight, in which there is a small islet; and further along the shore, which then stretches eastward and again becomes cliffy, there are two others. When the cape bore N. 10° W. four miles, the highest of the Eclipse Isles was in sight, bearing E. 4° N.; but "the small detached islet," which Captain Vancouver says (Vol. I p. 32) "lies from Cape Howe S. 68° E., three leagues," could not be seen; though it should have lain nearly in our track.[2]

South Coast. King George's Sound.

The wind blew fresh at this time, and a current of more than one mile an hour ran with us, so that, by carrying all sail, I hoped to get sight of King George's Sound before dark. At seven we passed close on the south side of the Eclipse Isles; but Bald Head at the entrance of the sound had so different an appearance from what I had been led to expect, being a slope in this point of view, that the steep east end of Break-sea Island was at first taken for it. The error was fortunately perceived in time; and at eight o'clock we hauled up round the head, with the wind at west, and made a stretch into the sound. It was then dark; but the night being fine, I did not hesitate to work up by the guidance of captain Vancouver's chart; and having reached nearly into a line between Seal Island and the first beach round Bald Head, we anchored at eleven o'clock in 8 fathoms, sandy bottom.

Wednesday 9 December 1801

King George's Sound had been chosen as the proper place in which to prepare ourselves for the examination of the south coast of Terra Australis, and I sought to make the best use of the advantages it might furnish. The first essential requisite was a place of secure shelter, where the masts could be stripped, the rigging and sails put into order, and communication had with the shore without interruption from the elements; but this, from captain Vancouver's chart and description, I did not expect the outer sound to afford. The facility of quitting Princess-Royal Harbour, with such a wind as would be favourable for prosecuting the investigation of the coast, induced me so far to prefer it to Oyster Harbour as to make it the first object of examination; and in the morning, after we had sounded round the ship and found her so placed as to require no immediate movement, I went in a boat for the purpose, accompanied by the master and landscape painter; the naturalist and some other gentlemen landing at the same time, to botanise in the vicinity of Bald Head.

Seal Island, where we stopped in passing, is a mass of granite, which is accessible only at its western end, as represented in Mr. Westall's sketch. After killing a few seals upon the shore, we ascended the hill to search for the bottle and parchment left by captain Vancouver in 1791;[3] but could find no vestiges either of it or of the staff or pile of stones; and since there was no appearance of the natives having crossed over from the main, I was led to suspect that a second ship had been here before us.

At Point Possession, on the south side of the entrance to Princess-Royal Harbour, we had a good view of that extensive piece of water. Wood seemed not to be abundant near the shores; and therefore a projection two or three miles to the south-west, which was covered with trees, first attracted my notice. The depth of water in going to it was, however, too little for the ship; nor was there any fresh stream in the neighbourhood. Some person, but not captain Vancouver, had nevertheless been cutting wood there; for several trees had been felled with axe and saw. Not far from thence stood a number of bark sheds, like the huts of the natives who live in the forests behind Port Jackson, and forming what might be called a small village; but it had been long deserted. Going across from the woody point to the north side of the harbour, we there found 3 fathoms within less than half a mile of the shore; and an increasing depth from thence out to the entrance. The soundings in the entrance were from 5 to 7 fathoms; but the channel was too narrow to admit of getting in without a leading wind and much caution.

Thursday 10 December 1801

On Thursday morning the master was sent to examine the north side of the harbour for water and wood; and we got the ship under way to beat up to the entrance, the wind blowing still from the westward. At eleven o'clock the anchor was dropped in 6 fathoms half a mile from Point Possession; and as I was doubtful of the master's success, I went in a boat, accompanied by lieutenant Flinders, to examine Oyster Harbour. We carried 7 and 6 fathoms from the ship towards the entrance until Michaelmas and Break-sea Islands were closing on with each other; after which the depth diminished to 5, 4, 3, and 2¾ fathoms. On hauling westward we got into six feet; but steering the other way, it deepened to seventeen, the east side of the opening behind then in a line with the middle of some high, flat-topped land, at the back of the harbour. Keeping in that direction, we carried 3, 4, and 5 fathoms; and had 6 in the narrowest part of the entrance. Within side the deep water turned on the starboard hand, but in many parts there was not more than 3 fathoms.

As I proposed to make a new survey of King George's Sound, we landed to take a set of angles upon the small central island; the same which captain Vancouver describes (Vol. I. page 35), as covered with luxuriant grass and other vegetables, and where he planted vine cuttings, water-cresses, and the seeds of various fruits. There were no remains of these valuable gifts, although nothing indicated the island to have been visited since his time; and, to our disappointment, the vegetation upon it now consisted of tufts of wiry grass and a few stunted shrubs, supported by a thin layer of sandy soil, which was every where perforated with rat-holes.

From the island we rowed in various directions, sounding the harbour; but the boat could seldom approach the shore within a cable's length, or the eighth part of a mile. On the south-west side there were two small streams, in one of which the water was fresh, though high-coloured. Returning to the entrance, we landed on the east side, and found a spot of ground six or eight feet square, dug up and trimmed like a garden; and upon it was lying a piece of sheet copper, bearing this inscription: "August 27, 1800. Chr. Dixson--ship Elligood"; which solved the difficulty of the felled trees and the disappearance of captain Vancouver's bottle. On digging in this place I found that fresh water of a high colour, but well tasted, might be obtained; wood was abundant, and the depth of the entrance admitted of the ship being made fast to the shore; so that this was a situation adapted to our purpose of refitment, provided the ship could be got over the bar. This point I was desirous to ascertain in my way on board, but the strength of the wind prevented it.

The report of the master from Princess-Royal Harbour was, that water could be obtained at the north side by digging near the shore, at the foot of the highest hill; but that there was no wood at a convenient distance. I therefore sent him, next morning [FRIDAY 11 DECEMBER 1801], to land the naturalists at the entrance of Oyster Harbour, and then to sound the bar; and not being satisfied with his report, that there was not so much as fourteen feet, which the ship drew when captain Vancouver had marked seventeen, I went to the nearest head, with a theodolite and signal flags, to direct his movements. No more, however, than thirteen feet could now be found upon the shallowest part of the bar; and, consequently, the idea of refitting in Oyster Harbour was abandoned. The boat which brought off Mr. Brown and his party in the evening collected a good quantity of oysters, and of the large fan muscles, from the shoals.

Saturday 12 December 1801

The wind continuing foul for going into Princess-Royal Harbour, a wooding party was sent next morning to a bight round the north side of the entrance, where the wood was found to split better than at some other places. Another party went to the same place with the launch, to haul the seine, but the wind coming round to the eastward, the boat was recalled and a kedge anchor and hawser put into it. We then weighed and ran into the harbour under the top-sails; and at eleven anchored in seventeen feet upon muddy ground, at one-third of a mile from the shore under the highest hill. When the ship was moored Michaelmas Island was on with the north, and Break-sea Island with the south point of the entrance, and the highest hill bore N.E. by N. by compass. The least depth of water we had in passing the entrance was 4 fathoms; but to those who may wish to go in, the plan in Plate II of the Atlas, and a good look-out from the masthead, will be of more service than any written directions.

So soon as the ship was secured, I landed with the naturalists; and after fixing upon a place for our tents, ascended the highest hill to take angles. Amongst other objects I perceived in the bearing of N. 87° 20' W. two distant pieces of water, at the back of the bight near West Cape Howe; but whether they were lakes or an inlet of the sea could not be distinguished. Our tents, under the guard of a party of marines, were set up this evening; and in the morning [SUNDAY 13 DECEMBER 1801] the observatory and instruments were sent on shore, under the care of lieutenant Flinders, who had undertaken to assist me in performing the office of astronomer.

Marks of the country being inhabited were found every where, but as yet there was nothing to indicate the presence of the natives in our neighbourhood; I therefore allowed a part of the ship's company to divert themselves on shore this afternoon; and the same was done every Sunday during our stay in this harbour. On Monday [14 DECEMBER 1801] the topmasts were struck, and our various duties commenced; the naturalists ranged the country in all directions, being landed at such places as they desired; whilst my own time was divided betwixt the observatory and the survey of the Sound.

Some smokes being perceived at the head of the harbour, Mr. Brown and other gentlemen directed their excursion that way and met with several of the natives, who were shy but not afraid. One man with whom they had communication was admired for his manly behaviour, and they gave him a bird which had been shot, and a pocket-handkerchief; but, like the generality of people hitherto seen in this country, these men did not seem to be desirous of communication with strangers; and they very early made signs to our gentlemen to return from whence they came. Next morning [TUESDAY 15 DECEMBER 1801], however, we were agreeably surprised by the appearance of two Indians, and afterwards of others, upon the side of the hill behind our tents. They approached with much caution, one coming first with poised spear, and making many gestures, accompanied with much vociferous parleying, in which he sometimes seemed to threaten us if we did not be gone, and at others to admit of our stay. On Mr. Purdie, the assistant-surgeon, going up to him unarmed, a communication was brought about, and they received some articles of iron and toys, giving in exchange some of their implements; and after a short stay, left us, apparently on very good terms.

Monday 17 December 1801

On the 17th one of our former visitors brought two strangers with him; and after this time, they and others came almost every day, and frequently stopped a whole morning at the tents. We always made them presents of such things as seemed to be most agreeable, but they very rarely brought us anything in return; nor was it uncommon to find small mirrors and other things left about the shore, so that at length our presents were discontinued.

Wednesday 23 December 1801

I formed a party on the 23rd, consisting of the officers of the ship, the scientific gentlemen, and others, amounting to thirteen, well armed and provided for two days, in order to visit the lakes behind West Cape Howe. We walked along the shore to the north-western extremity of Princess-Royal Harbour, where several small runs of fresh water were found to drain in from peaty swamps. Striking from thence into the country in a western direction, we had not advanced far when a native was seen running before us; and soon afterward an old man, who had been several times at the tents, came up, unarmed as usual. He was very anxious that we should not go further; and acted with a good deal of resolution in first stopping one and then another of those who were foremost. He was not able to prevail; but we accommodated him so far as to make a circuit round the wood, where it seemed probable his family and female friends were placed. The old man followed us, hallooing frequently to give information of our movements; and when a paroquet was shot, he expressed neither fear nor surprise, but received the bird with gladness and attended with some curiosity to the reloading of the gun.

Our course for the lakes led us through swamps and thick brushwoods, in which our new acquaintance followed for some time; but at length, growing tired of people who persevered in keeping a bad road in opposition to his recommendation of a better, which, indeed, had nothing objectionable in it but that it led directly contrary to where our object lay, he fell behind and left us. We afterwards took to the skirts of the sea-coast hills and made better progress; but were obliged to recross the swamps and force our way through a thick brush before reaching the eastern lake.

This piece of water was found to be one mile and a half east and west, and one mile in breadth, and appeared to receive the drainings from the numerous swamps round about. In coasting round the north side, to reach the south-

View from the south side of King George's Sound

western lake, we were stopped by a serpentine stream, upon which were two black swans; but they took to flight before we could get near to shoot them. After following the windings of this riverlet some distance to the north-west, without being able to pass over, we struck inland towards the skirt of some rising hills, and crossed the stream early enough to walk a mile to the south-west before sunset, when the convenience of dry ground, with wood and water at hand, induced us to halt for the night.

Thursday 24 December 1801

On Thursday morning we reached the south-western lake, and found it to be larger than the first. Its water was brackish, which bespoke a communication with the sea; and as there was no certainty that this communication might not be too deep to be passed, it was thought prudent to give up the intention of proceeding to the sea side, and our steps were retraced across the rivulet and round the northern lake. We then struck southward and ascended the hills to the top of the cliffs facing the sea; from whence I had an opportunity of seeing the bight near Cape Howe, and the form of the lakes; but no water communication was visible between them.

Our course homeward was pursued along the sandy ridge at the back of the cliffs, where the want of water was as great as the superabundance had been in the low land going out. Towards sunset, when Princess-Royal Harbour was still some miles distant, the natural-history painter became unable to proceed further, being overcome with the labour of the walk, with the excessive heat, and with thirst. To have detained the whole party in a state of sufferance would have been imprudent; and Mr. Brown and two others having volunteered to stay, we left them the scanty remains of our provision, and pushed forward to the tents, which we reached at eight o'clock. At midnight we had the pleasure to see our friends arrive, and the preparation made for sending to their assistance, at daybreak, became unnecessary.

The country through which we passed in this excursion has but little to recommend it. The stony hills of the sea coast were, indeed, generally covered with shrubs; but there was rarely any depth of vegetable soil, and no wood. The land slopes down gradually behind these hills; and at the bottom water drains out and forms a chain of swamps extending from Princess-Royal Harbour to the lakes. Here the country is covered with grass and brushwood, and in the parts a little elevated there are forest trees; nevertheless the soil is shallow and unfit for cultivation.

Wednesday 30 December 1801

On the 30th, our wooding and the watering of the ship were completed, the rigging was refitted, the sails repaired and bent, and the ship unmoored. Our friends the natives continued to visit us; and the old man with several others being at the tents this morning, I ordered the party of marines on shore to be exercised in their presence. The red coats and white crossed belts were greatly admired, having some resemblance to their own manner of ornamenting themselves; and the drum, but particularly the fife, excited their astonishment; but when they saw these beautiful red-and-white men, with their bright muskets, drawn up in a line, they absolutely screamed with delight; nor were their wild gestures and vociferation to be silenced but by commencing the exercise, to which they paid the most earnest and silent attention. Several of them moved their hands involuntarily, according to the motions; and the old man placed himself at the end of the rank, with a short staff in his hand, which he shouldered, presented, grounded as did the marines their muskets, without, I believe, knowing what he did. Before firing, the Indians were made acquainted with what was going to take place; so that the vollies did not excite much terror.

Sunday 3 January 1802

The tents and observatory were already struck; and everything being sent on board, we took leave of the natives, and embarked with the intention of running into the Sound this evening; but a change in the wind, to south-by-east, prevented it. This wind veered to east and north-east, and for a short time blew strong; so that it was the 3rd of January in the afternoon before we steered out of Princess-Royal Harbour. It was not my intention to proceed immediately to sea; and I therefore took the opportunity of standing backward and forward in the Sound, with the dredge and trawl overboard; and a variety of small fish were brought up. These were of little use as food; but with the shells, sea weeds, and corals they furnished amusement and occupation to the naturalist and draughtsman, and a pretty kind of hippocampus, which was not scarce, was generally admired.

In the evening the anchor was dropped in 7 fathoms, abreast of the second sandy beach near a flat rock on the south side of the Sound, almost in the same spot where captain Vancouver had anchored in 1791. I think the Sound does not afford a more secure place, the sole points of exposition being between Bald Head and Break-sea Island, making an angle of no more than 10°; and as both wood and water are procurable here, though neither very good, a ship proposing to stay only a few days is under no necessity of having recourse to the harbours.

Monday 4 January 1802

On the 4th a fresh gale blew from the westward and prevented me from moving the ship. A bottle, containing a parchment to inform future visitors of our arrival and intention to sail on the morrow, was left upon the top of Seal Island; and the wind having moderated next day, and the weather become finer, though still squally, we then made sail out of King George's Sound to prosecute the further examination of the coast.

Tuesday 5 January 1802

The refreshments we had procured were fish and oysters. The seine was frequently hauled upon the different beaches; but although it was done in the evening, round fires which had been previously kindled, little success was obtained in this way. With hook and line we were more fortunate, both alongside and from boats stationed off the rocky points; and the whole ship's company had generally a fresh meal once in three or four days. Of oysters, as many were taken from the shoals in both harbours as we chose to spare time for gathering. Our fire wood was procured from the north point of entrance to Princess-Royal Harbour, at the inner end of the long middle beach; but the trees best calculated for sawing into planks were obtained at the easternmost of the two woody projections on the south side of the harbour. A good number of planks and logs were taken on board for making garden boxes to contain the most curious plants collected by the naturalist, and for a variety of other purposes. The fresh water, procured by digging near the tents, was a little discoloured, but good; and it was sufficiently abundant for every purpose: its specific gravity was 1.003 at the temperature of 69°.

Captain Vancouver has described the country in the neighbourhood of King George's Sound, and therefore a few observations upon it will suffice. The basis stone is granite, which frequently shows itself at the surface in the form of smooth, bare rock; but upon the seacoast hills, and the shores on the south sides of the Sound and Princess-Royal Harbour, the granite is generally covered with a crust of calcareous stone; as it is, also, upon Michaelmas Island. Captain Vancouver mentions (Vol. I. p. 49) having found upon the top of Bald Head, branches of coral protruding through the sand, exactly like those seen in the coral beds beneath the surface of the sea; a circumstance which should seem to bespeak this country to have emerged from the ocean at no very distant period of time. This curious fact I was desirous to verify; and his description was proved to be correct. I found, also, two broken columns of stone three or four feet high, formed like stumps of trees and of a thickness superior to the body of a man; but whether they were of coral or of wood now petrified, or whether they might not have been calcareous rocks worn into that particular form by the weather, I cannot determine. Their elevation above the present level of the sea could not have been less than four hundred feet.

But little calcareous matter was found elsewhere than on the southern shores. In Oyster Harbour a rather strongly impregnated ironstone prevails, but mixed with quartz and granite; and in some parts of both harbours a brown argillaceous earth was not uncommon.

The soil of the hills is very barren, though, except near the sea coast, generally covered with wood; and that of the plains at the head of Princess-Royal Harbour has been described as shallow, and incapable of cultivation. In the neighbourhood of Oyster Harbour the land was said to be better, especially near the rivulet which falls into the northern corner; and on the borders of a small lake, at the back of the long beach between the two harbours, the country was represented to be pleasing to the eye and tolerably fertile.

The timber trees of the woods consist principally of different species of that extensive class called gum tree by the colonists at Port Jackson, by botanists eucalyptus. They do not grow very large here, and the wood is heavy and seldom fit for other than common purposes. Amongst the plants collected by Mr. Brown and his associates was a small one of a novel kind which we commonly called the pitcher plant. Around the root leaves are several little vases lined with spiny hairs, and there were generally found to contain a sweetish water, and also a number of dead ants. It cannot be asserted that the ants were attracted by the water, and prevented by the spiny hairs from making their escape; but it seemed not improbable that this was a contrivance of nature to obtain the means necessary either to the nourishment or preservation of the plant.

Amongst the animal productions the kangaroo and cassowary hold the first ranks. The kangaroo appeared to be numerous, and of more than one species; but none were caught. Three of them seen by me bore a resemblance to the large kind which inhabits the forests of Port Jackson; and the cassowary showed nothing distinguishable at a distance from the same animal at that place: both were shy; as were the ducks, swans, and all the birds.

Near Point Possession were found two nests of extraordinary magnitude. They were built upon the ground, from which they rose about two feet; and were of vast circumference and great interior capacity, the branches of trees and other matter, of which each nest was composed, being enough to fill a small cart. Captain Cook (see Hawkesworth, Vol. III. p. 195) found one of these enormous nests upon Eagle Island, on the East Coast; and if the magnitude of the constructor be proportionate to the size of the nest, Terra Australis must be inhabited by a species of bird little inferior to the condor of the Andes.

Amongst the reptiles was a variety of lizards; one of which, of the larger size, was met with by Dampier on the West Coast, and is described by him "as a sort of guano, but differing from others in three remarkable particulars: for these had a larger and uglier head, and had no tail: and at the rump, instead of the tail there, they had a stump of a tail, which appeared like another head; but not really such, being without mouth or eyes. Yet this creature seemed, by this means, to have a head at each end; and, which may be reckoned a fourth difference, the legs, also, seemed all four of them to be fore legs, being all alike in shape and length, and seeming by the joints and bendings to be made as if they were to go indifferently either head or tail foremost. They were speckled black and yellow like toads, and had scales or knobs on their backs like those of crocodiles. They are very slow in motion and when a man comes nigh them they will stand and hiss, not endeavouring to get away. Their livers are also spotted black and yellow; and the body when opened hath a very unsavoury smell. The guano's I have observed to be very good meat, and I have often eaten of them with pleasure; but though I have eaten of snakes, crocodiles, and alligators, and many creatures that look frightfully enough, and there are but few I should have been afraid to eat of, if pressed by hunger, yet I think my stomach would scarce have served to venture upon these New Holland guano's, both the looks and the smell of them being so offensive." The animal is certainly of a singular form; but it is scarcely necessary to say that the merit of Dampier's description does not consist in being strictly accurate.

The fish caught with hook and line were principally small mullet, and an excellent kind of snapper, nearly the same as that called wollamai by the natives of Port Jackson; but these were larger, weighing sometimes as much as twenty pounds.

Our frequent and amicable communication with the natives of this country has been mentioned. The women were, however, kept out of sight with seeming jealousy; and the men appeared to suspect the same conduct in us, after they had satisfied themselves that the most beardless of those they saw at the tents were of the same sex with the rest. The belief that there must be women in the ship induced two of them to comply with our persuasion of getting into the boat, one morning, to go on board; but their courage failing, they desired to be relanded, and made signs that the ship must go on shore to them.

It was with some surprise that I saw the natives of the east coast of New South Wales so nearly portrayed in those of the south-western extremity of New Holland. These do not, indeed, extract one of the upper front teeth at the age of puberty, as is generally practised at Port Jackson, nor do they make use of the womerah, or throwing stick; but their colour, the texture of the hair, and personal appearance are the same; their songs run in the same cadence; the manner of painting themselves is similar; their belts and fillets of hair are made in the same way, and worn in the same manner. The short, skin cloak, which is of kangaroo, and worn over the shoulders, leaving the rest of the body naked, is more in the manner of the wood natives living at the back of Port Jackson than of those who inhabit the sea coast; and everything we saw confirmed the supposition of captain Vancouver, that they live more by hunting than fishing. None of the small islands had been visited, no canoes were seen, nor was any tree found in the woods from which the bark had been taken for making one. They were fearful of trusting themselves upon the water; and we could never succeed in making them understand the use of the fish hook, although they were intelligent in comprehending our signs upon other subjects.

The manners of these people are quick and vehement, and their conversation vociferous, like that of most uncivilised people. They seemed to have no idea of any superiority we possessed over them; on the contrary, they left us, after the first interview, with some appearance of contempt for our pusillanimity; which was probably inferred from the desire we showed to be friendly with them. This opinion, however, seemed to be corrected in their future visits.

Notwithstanding the similarity of person and manner to the inhabitants of Port Jackson, the language of these people is very different. We found their pronunciation difficult to be imitated; more so, indeed, than our language was to them. Several English words they pronounced perfectly; whilst of such where an f or an s entered they could make but little: Finger, was pronounced bing-gah, ship, yip; and of King George they make Ken Jag-ger. In the difficulty of pronouncing the f and s they resemble the Port Jackson natives; and the word used by them in calling to a distance, cau-wah! (come here) is nearly similar to cow-ee! The word also to express eye is nearly the same. But in the following table, which contains all the words that, with any certainty, I was able to collect, the most essential differences will be found both from the Port Jackson language and from that of the south end of Van Diemen's Land; and the words collected by Captain Cook at Endeavour River bear no resemblance to any of them.

English.	K.George's Sound,	Port Jackson [4]	Van Diemen's Land. [5]
Head	Kuāt	Ca-ber-ra	
Hair	Kaat-joū	De-war-ra	Péliloguéni
Nose	Mo-il	No-gro	Mugui (Muidge, Cook)
Cheek, or beard	Ny-a-nŭk	Yar-rin	Canguiné
Teeth	Yea-al	Da-ra	Pégui or Canan (Kamy, C.)
Ear	Du-ong	Go-ray	Vaigni (Koygee, Cook)
Lips	Ur-luk	Wil-ling	Mogudé lia
Throat	Wurt	Cad-le-an	
Nipple	Bpep	Na-bung	
Belly	Ko-būl	Bar-rong	Lomangui
Posteriors	Wa-la-kah	Boong	Nuné
Thigh	Dtou-al		
Knee	Wo-nat	Go-rook	Ronga
Leg	Maāt	Dar-ra	Lérai
Foot	Jaān	Ma-no-e	Peré
The sun	Djaāt	Co-ing	Panuberé

The following anatomical admeasurement of one of the best proportioned of our visitors was furnished by the surgeon, Mr. Hugh Bell:

	Ft.	in.	l.		Ft.	in.	l.
Full height	5	7	6	the great trochanter to its			
Circumference of the head	1	11	0	lower end	1	5	6
From the transverse nasal				Length of the tibia	1	4	6
suture, to the posterior				———— foot	0	10	0
ridge of the occiput	1	3	0	Length from the protuber-			
From the small rim of each				ance of the inner ancle, to			
ear across the forehead	1	0	0	the tip of the heel,	0	3	9
From the nasal suture, over				Ditto, to the end of the			
the nose, to the tip of				great toe	0	8	6
the chin,	0	5	2	Circumference of the neck	1	0	6
From ditto, to the tip of the				———— chest	2	8	9
nose,	0	1	0	———— pelvis	2	4	9
From the tip of the nose to				———— arm	0	10	6
the edge of the upper lip	0	1	0	———— elbow			
From the edge of the un-				joint	0	9	6
der lip, to the tip of the				————forearm	0	9	9
chin	0	1	5	———— wrist	0	6	0
Extent of the mouth	0	2	1	———— thigh	1	7	6
———— nostrils	0	1	6	Circumference just above			
———— lower jaw from				the knee joint	1	1	0
each angle	0	8	6	————of the knee joint	1	1	0
Length of the arm	1	1	6	———— leg,			
———— fore arm	1	0	0	immediately below the			
middle meta-				knee joint	0	11	0
carpal bone	0	4	0	————leg	1	0	0
———— middle finger	0	4	3	———— the small	0	7	6
femur, from				———— foot	0	10	6

Our operations at the observatory were not favoured by the weather; but a sufficient number of observations was obtained for all the purposes of navigation:

The Latitude of the tents in Princess-Royal Harbour, from three meridian zenith distances of the sun, observed with Ramsden's universal theodolite, was 35° 2' 5" south.

Longitude from thirty-one sets of distances of the sun east and west of the moon, of which the particulars are given in Table I of the Appendix to this volume, 117° 53' 10" east.

These being reduced by the survey to BALD HEAD, at the entrance of the sound, will place it in

Latitude	35° 6' 15" south.
Longitude	118° 0' 45" east.[6]

The mean rates of the time keepers, deduced from equal altitudes taken on and between Dec. 15 and Jan. 1, and their errors from mean time at Greenwich, at noon there on the last day of observation, were as under:

	h ' " "
Earnshaw's	No. 543, slow 0 21 46,69 and losing 6,46 per day.
	No. 520, 0 51 2,81 16,72
Arnold's	No. 176, 1 0 45,46 9,26
	No. 82 went too irregularly to be worth taking.

The longitude of the tents given by the time keepers on the first day of observation, with the Cape rates, was as follows:

Earnshaw's	No. 543, 118° 14' 49" east.
	520, 117 59 22
Arnold's	176, 118 1 14

The two first, which generally throughout the voyage showed themselves to be the best time keepers, were on a mean 13' 56" to the east of the lunar observations; but by using rates accelerating in arithmetic progression from those of the Cape of Good Hope to the new ones of King George's Sound, the mean of Earnshaw's two time keepers will then differ only 8' 19" to the east in forty-four days. In fixing the position of places from Cape Leeuwin to the Sound, these accelerating rates have been used; and the longitude has been further corrected by allowing an equal proportion of the error, 8' 19", according to the number of days after Nov. 1, when the last observations were made at the Cape of Good Hope. In the Appendix, the nature of these corrections is more particularly explained.

The height of the thermometer at the tents, as observed at noon, varied between 80° and 64°. On board the ship, it never exceeded 70½°, nor was below 60°. The range of the barometer was from 29,42 inches in a gale of wind from the westward, to 30,28 inches in a moderate breeze from south-west.

Mean Dip of the S. end of the needle, taken onshore,	64° 1'
On board, upon the cabin table,	64° 52'.

The increase being probably occasioned by the iron ballast in the bread room underneath.

The Variation given by three compasses at the observatory was 6° 22½' west, by Walker's meridional compass 5° 25', and by the surveying theodolite 8° 17'; but upon the eastern part of the flat granite rock, on the south side of the sound, two theodolites gave only 4° 1' west. On board the ship, at anchor off Point Possession, the variation from the three compasses on the binnacle., when the head was southeastward, was 9° 28'; or, corrected to the meridian, 7° 12' west. It seems not easy to say what ought to be considered as the true variation; but the mean of the observations at the tents being 6° 42', and on board the ship 7° 12', I conceive it will not be far wrong if taken at 7° 0' west.

This is what I allowed in tracing a base line upon the beach between the two harbours; and the back bearings from different stations did not vary more than a degree from it, except at the west end of Michaelmas Island, where the variation, in one spot, was greater by 3°.

The above different variations show that the needle was affected by the rocks; and there will be frequent occasion, in the course of the voyage, to point out similar anomalies in the observations on land; for they were found to take place upon almost all those parts of Terra Australis, where the basis stone is of granite, as here; and also in those where green-stone, porphyry, basaltes, or iron-stone prevail; whereas in the lime, or grit-stone countries, the needle did not appear to suffer any derangement. In the Appendix No. II. to the second volume, where the changes on ship board, which arose from altering the direction of the head, are explained, this subject of the differences on shore is mentioned; for they also were not without a certain degree of regularity.

No set of Tide was perceived on board, either whilst the ship was in the Sound or in Princess-Royal Harbour; nevertheless it was sometimes found to run with considerable strength in the narrow entrances of both harbours. According to lieutenant Flinders' observations on shore during sixteen days there was only one high water in twenty-four hours, which always took place between six and twelve at night; for after, by gradually becoming later, it had been high water at twelve, the next night it took place soon after six o'clock; and then happened later by three-quarters of an hour each night as before. The greatest rise observed was three feet two inches, and the least two feet eight inches. The accumulation was made in this manner: After low water it rose for several hours; then ceased, and became stationary, or perhaps fell back a little. In a few hours it began to rise again; and in about twelve from the first commencement was high water. It was observed by Captain Cook upon the east coast of this country[7], and since by many others, including myself, that the night tide rose considerably higher than that of the day; which is conformable to our observations in King George's Sound; but with this difference, that in the day we had scarcely any tide at all.

The base line for my survey of the Sound was of 2.46 geographic miles, measured round the curve of the long beach between the two harbours. The other stations whence bearings were taken with the theodolite were--in the Sound, four; at the entrance of and within Princess-Royal Harbour, three; and in Oyster Harbour, four; at each of which a point with a circle is marked in the plan. The soundings were either taken in the ship, with simultaneous cross bearings, or in boats, generally accompanied with notices of known objects in a line, or the angles between them taken with a sextant.

There are many small but no very essential differences between my plan and that of captain Vancouver. The most important to navigation is that in the soundings going into Oyster Harbour; I could find only thirteen feet over the bar, whereas he marked seventeen; a difference, however, which may not improbably have taken place between 1791 and 1801.

Notes

[1] *The mode by which these, and other observations made with the compass on the binnacle, are reduced to what is conceived to be the true variation, is explained in the Appendix No. II, to the second volume.*

[2] *This islet, seen by Captain Vancouver in the evening, must have been the highest of the Eclipse Isles; but from the apparent difference of its situation, was thought not to be the same on the following morning. The change in the variation of the compass, which had taken place on altering the direction of the ship's head, seems to have been the cause of this apparent difference.*

[3] *See his Voyage, Vol. I. Page 40.*

[4] *From Collins' Account of the English Colony in New South Wales, Vol. I. p. 610-611*

[5] *Voyage de D'Entrecasteaux, par M. de Rossel. Tome I. p. 552 et seq. These words are written after the French pronunciation of the letters.*

[6] *The situation of Bald Head, in captain Vancouver's chart, is 35° 6' 40" south, and 118° 16' 30" east from lunar observations which were not corrected for the errors of the astronomical tables. The situation assigned to Bald Head in the voyage of the French admiral D'Entrecasteaux, is 35° 10' south, and 118° 2' 40" east; but since the admiral passed it at six in the evening, and in blowing weather, an error of a few minutes may have entered into both latitude and longitude.*

[7] *See Hawkesworth's Voyages, Vol. III. p. 224.*

Chapter Four

South Coast. From King George's Sound.

January 1802

In running along that part of the South Coast which lies to the west of King George's Sound, I had endeavoured to keep so close in with the land that the breaking water on the shore should be visible from the ship's deck; by which means our supposed distance would be little subject to error, and no river or opening could escape being seen. This close proximity could not, however, be obtained in every part, especially where the coast retreated far back; but it was always attempted where practicable and unattended with much danger or loss of time; and when it could not be done, I was commonly at the mast head with a glass. All the bearings were laid down so soon as taken whilst the land was in sight, and before retiring to rest I made it a practice to finish up the rough chart for the day, as also my journals of astronomical observations, of bearings, and of remarks. When we hauled off from the coast at night, every precaution was taken to come in with the same point in the morning, as soon after daylight as practicable; and when the situation of the ship relatively to the land of the preceding evening was ascertained, our route along the coast was resumed. This plan, to see and lay down everything myself, required constant attention and much labour, but was absolutely necessary to obtaining that accuracy of which I was desirous; and now, on recommencing the survey from King George's Sound to the eastward, I persevered in the same system; and it was adhered to, although not particularly mentioned, in all the succeeding part of the voyage.

Tuesday 5 January 1802

On the 5th of January, in the morning, we got under way from the Sound, having a fresh wind from the westward and squally weather. I steered between Michaelmas Island and the main, in order to explore better that part of the Sound, and ascertain the extent of a shoal running off from the north-west end of the island. It was found to run out not further than half a mile, at which distance we passed in 5 fathoms water; and at noon, when the east end of Break-sea Island bore S. 30° W., we had 33 fathoms.

Mount Gardner is a high, conic-shaped hill, apparently of granite, very well delineated in captain Vancouver's atlas. It stands upon a projecting cape, round which the shore falls back to the northward, forming a sandy bight where there appeared to be shelter from western winds; indeed, as the coast-line was not distinctly seen round the south-west corner of the bight, it is possible there may be some small inlet in that part.

The south end of an island, called Ile Pelée (Bald Island) by D'Entrecasteaux, opened round the cape of Mount Gardner at N. 69° E. The French navigator having passed without side of this island, I steered within, through a passage of a short mile wide; and had 17 fathoms for the shoalest water, on a sandy bottom. Bald Island is of moderate elevation, and barren, as its name implies; it is about two-and-half miles in length, and the south end lies in 34° 55' south and 118° 29' east. It lies off a rocky projection of the mainland, at which terminates a ridge of mountain extending three leagues along the shore from the bight behind Mount Gardner. There are a number of small peaks upon the top of this ridge which induced me to give it the name Mount Manypeak.

After clearing the passage of Bald Island I found the shore to trend north-eastward, and to be low and sandy; but at the distance of eight leagues inland there was a chain of rugged mountains, of which the eastern and highest peak, called Mount Rugged, lies N. 11½° W. from the passage. At six we came up with a steep rock, one mile from the main, and then hauled to the wind, offshore, for the night. This lump, which appeared to be of granite, I called Haul-off Rock; it lies in 31° 43' south and 118° 39' east, and two leagues to the south-west of a cliffy point which bears the name of Cape Riche in the French chart.

Wednesday 6 January 1802

At one in the morning, being seven or eight leagues from the coast and in 45 fathoms, we tacked ship towards the land, having a fresh breeze at west-south-west, with fine weather. Haul-off Rock bore N. 77° W., three or four miles, at six, and we then bore away along the coast. Beyond Cape Riche the shore forms a sandy bight, in which is a small island; and on the north side of another cliffy projection, four leagues further, there is a similar falling back of the coast, where it is probable there is also good shelter for boats, if not a small inlet. At noon a projecting head two miles long, which, from the lumps of rock at the top, I called Cape Knob, was three miles distant; and our observations and bearings of the land were then as under;

Latitude, observed to the north and south	34° 35' 26"
Longitude by time keepers,	119 15
The cliffy projection past Cape Riche,	
with Mount Rugged behind it,	N. 75 W.
Two rocks, distant 7 or 8 miles,	N. 56 W.
Cape Knob, eastern extremity,	N. 11 E.
A cliffy projection further eastward,	N. 46 E.
One of the Doubtful Isles,	N. 54 E.

The coast is sandy on both sides of Cape Knob, but especially on the west side, where the hillocks at the back of the shore are little else than bare sand.

At four o'clock we had passed the Point Hood of Vancouver; and seeing a channel of nearly a mile in width between it and the two outer of his Doubtful Islands, steered through it with soundings from 20 to 24 fathoms. I then hauled up south-westward, along the inner island and point, and sent away the master to sound between them; it being my intention to anchor, if a sufficient depth should be found for the ship to escape in case the wind came to blow from the eastward: it was then light at south-east-by-south. Mr. Thistle found the opening to be very narrow, and no more than 2 fathoms in the shoalest part; we therefore stood out, repassing within a small black islet, upon which were some seals. At eight, tacked to the southward and weathered the Doubtful Islands.

On the north side of the isles and of Point Hood the shore falls back five or six miles to the west-south-west before it curves northward, and affords good shelter against all winds which do not blow strong from between north-east and east. At the time we stood out of the bay the ship was three miles within the outermost islands, and not more than a cable's length from the shore of Point Hood, and we had 7½ fathoms, sandy bottom. The point and islands are steep and rocky, but the western shores of this great bay are mostly sandy beaches. On the north-western and north sides there are some masses of tolerably high land which appeared to be granitic; and for distinction in the survey they are called West, Middle, and East Mount Barren.

Thursday 7 January 1802

The wind was variable between east and north-by-east during the night. At daybreak the three mounts were in sight, and the north end of the Doubtful Isles bore N. 74° W. three leagues. As the wind veered round to the west and southward, we steered more in for the north side of Doubtful Island Bay; and at noon, our situation and the bearings of the land were these:

Latitude, observed to the north and south	34° 16' 40"
Longitude by time keepers	119 47
Doubtful Isles, south extreme, dist. 11 miles,	S. 55 W.
West Mount Barren,	N. 77½ W.
Middle do.,	N. 25 W.
East do., the furthest visible land,	N. 28 E.

Our course was directed to the northward, with the wind at south-east-by-south; but seeing the appearance of an opening in the north-west corner of the bay, with smokes rising there, we steered north-west for it. In an hour the low land was seen from the mast head to extend across the supposed opening, and we then hauled up east-by-north, to the wind, at the distance of five or six miles from the high, rocky shore between the Middle and East Mount Barren. At seven in the evening the eastern mount bore N. 44° W., three leagues, and the coast, which from thence becomes sandy, was seen as far as N. 76° E. A small reef, one of two before laid down both by Vancouver and D'Entrecasteaux, was then observed three or four miles to seaward. It was important to get sight of this reef before dark, for we should otherwise have been at great uncertainty during the night, more especially as the surf upon it broke only at times. The wind being at south-by-east, we tacked and stood westward, nearly in our afternoon's track, until midnight; and the breeze having then veered to south-west, we were able to stretch off south-south-east to windward of the breakers. At half-past five in the morning [FRIDAY 8 JANUARY 1802], East Mount Barren was four leagues distant to the northward, and our course was resumed along the shore. The breakers were passed at the distance of two miles, and the mount was set over them, bearing N. 38° W. at seven o'clock. The second small reef lies nearly east-north-east from the first, and was left three miles to the northward.

On the preceding evening a small rocky island had been seen indistinctly from the mast head, and it now again came in sight to the eastward. The French ships had passed without side of this island, and I therefore steered to go between it and the mainland; but breaking water was seen to extend so far to the north that the uncertainty of finding a passage made the attempt too dangerous with the wind right aft. We accordingly hauled up to windward of the island, and had 38 fathoms between it and a small reef lying S. 72° W., between two and three miles from it. The island is low, smooth, and sterile, and is frequented by seals; its latitude is 34° 6' and longitude 120° 28', and it lies eight or nine miles from the mainland.

At noon the rocky island was near ten miles astern, and a cluster of four small islets appeared in the offing at the distance of four leagues. The nearest part of the main land, seven or eight miles distant, was low and sandy, as it had been all the way from East Mount Barren, and continued to be to the furthest extreme visible from the masthead; there were, however, a few scattered sandy hillocks on the shore, but nothing could be seen of the back country. Our situation, and the bearings taken at this time were as under:

Latitude, observed to the north and south,	34° 1' 48"
Longitude by time keepers,	119 38

East Mount Barren,	N. 80½ W.
The small island astern,	S. 65 W.
Four islets in the offing,	S. 77 E.
Mast-head extreme of the coast,	N. 59 E.

We passed at nearly an equal distance between the four rocky islets and the main land, that is to say, at six or eight miles from each; and at five o'clock were abreast of a projecting part of the coast where the sandy hills seemed to form white cliffs. This is called Cap des Basses (Shoal Cape) in the French chart; and we saw, in fact, an islet under the land, surrounded with much broken water, and the soundings decreased from 35 to 25 fathoms soon after passing it at the distance of five or six miles. There was an appearance of small inlets on each side of Shoal Cape, but as admiral D'Entrecasteaux passed within three miles and does not mark any, it was probably a deception, caused by the land being very low between the sand hills.

South Coast. Recherche's Archipelago.

Before sunset the westernmost isle of D'Entrecasteaux's Archipel de la Recherche was in sight to the eastward, and at half-past seven our distance from it was about six miles. The French admiral had mostly skirted round the archipelago, a sufficient reason for me to attempt passing through the middle, if the weather did not make the experiment too dangerous. It was fine at this time, and the breeze moderate at south-south-west; and I therefore took measures to be in with the western group as early on the following morning as possible, to have the whole day for getting through.

Saturday 9 January 1802

At a quarter-past five we bore away for the south end of the westernmost island, passed in within a mile and a half at seven, and steered eastward for the clusters rising ahead and on both bows. At noon the number of rocks above water, the patches of breakers, and the islands with which we were surrounded made it necessary to heave to, in order to take the angles of so many objects with some degree of accuracy. The situation of the ship, and the three most material bearings were these:

Latitude, observed to the north and south	35° 0' 25"
Longitude reduced up from eight o'clock	121 49 45
Observatory I. (Of D'Entrecasteaux) dist. 6 miles,	N. 37 W.
High Peak on Cape Le Grand,	N. 84½ E.
Small, high, peaked island, distant 7 or 8 miles,	S. 57 E.

This last peak had been visible from daybreak, and appears to be the top of the imperfectly formed Ile de Remarque of D'Entrecasteaux's chart. and from it I measured with a sextant the angles of most of the other objects. The long reef of rocks called La Chaussée (The Causeway) was four or five miles distant to the southward; and a sunken rock, upon which the sea broke at times, was three miles off to the north-east. The islands were more particularly numerous to the east-south-east, where our course lay; but as they were generally high, with bold rocky shores, and we had hitherto found deep water, I bore away for them so soon as all the bearings were obtained.

The chart alone can give any adequate idea of this labyrinth of islands and rocks, or of our track amongst them until half past five in the evening. We were then abreast of the Ile du Mondrain, and the view from the mast head was almost as crowded as before; but with this difference, that the islands were smaller, and the low rocks and patches of breakers more numerous. Seeing no probability of reaching a space of clear water in which to stand off and on during the night, and no prospect of shelter under any of the islands, I found myself under the necessity of adopting a hazardous measure; and with the concurrence of the master's opinion, we steered directly before the wind for the main coast, where the appearance of some beaches, behind other islands, gave a hope of finding anchorage. At seven in the evening we entered a small sandy bay; and finding it sheltered everywhere except to the south-westward, in which direction there were many islands and rocks in the offing to break off the sea, the anchor was dropped in 7 fathoms, sandy bottom. The master sounded round the ship, but nothing was found to injure the cables; and except the water being shallow in the north-west corner of the bay, there was no danger to be apprehended, unless from strong south-west winds. The critical circumstance under which this place was discovered induced me to give it the name of LUCKY BAY.

Sunday 10 January 1802

I had intended to pursue our route through the archipelago in the morning; but the scientific gentlemen having expressed a desire for the ship to remain two or three days, to give them an opportunity of examining the productions of the country, it was complied with; and they landed soon after daylight. I went on shore also, to make observations upon the rates of the time-keepers; and afterwards ascended a hill at the back of the bay to take angles with a theodolite. A party of the gentlemen were upon the top, eating a fruit not much unlike green walnuts in external appearance, and invited me to partake; but having breakfasted, and not much liking their flavour, I did but taste them. Mr. Thistle and some others who had eaten liberally were taken sick, and remained unwell all the day afterward. The plant which produced these nuts was a species of zamia (Zamia spiralis of Brown's Prodr. flor. Nov. Holl., I. 348); a class of plants nearly allied to the third kind of palm found by captain Cook on the East Coast, the fruit of which produced the same deleterious effects on board the Endeavour.[1]

The weather, unfortunately for my bearings, was so hazy that unless objects were eminently conspicuous they could not be distinguished beyond four or five leagues. My list, however, contained forty-five islands and clusters of rocks, independently of many patches of breakers where nothing above water appeared; yet most of those in the western part of the archipelago were invisible, either from their distance or from being hidden by other lands.

In turning from the view of these complicated dangers to that of the interior country the prospect was but little improved. Sand and stone, with the slightest covering of vegetation, every where presented themselves on the lower lands; and the many shining parts of the sides of the hills showed them to be still more bare. The vegetation, indeed, consisted of an abundant variety of shrubs and small plants, and yielded a delightful harvest to the botanists; but to the herdsmen and cultivator it promised nothing: not a blade of grass, nor a square yard of soil from which the seed delivered to it could be expected back, was perceivable by the eye in its course over these arid plains.

Upon a rock on the side of the hill I found a large nest, very similar to those seen in King George's Sound. There were in it several masses resembling those which contain the hair and bones of mice, and are disgorged by the owls in England after the flesh is digested. These masses were larger, and consisted of the hair of seals and of land animals, of the scaly feathers of penguins, and the bones of birds and small quadrupeds. Possibly the constructor of the nest might be an enormous owl, and if so, the cause of the bird being never seen, whilst the nests were not scarce, would be from its not going out until dark; but from the very open and exposed situations in which the nests were found, I should rather judge it to be of the eagle kind, and that its powers are such as to render it heedless of any attempts from the natives upon its young.

Monday 11 January 1802

On the following morning I sent the master to examine a small bay or cove lying two miles to the westward of Lucky Bay. He found it to be capable of receiving one ship, which might be placed in perfect security in the western corner, with anchors out on the off bow and quarter, and hawsers on the other side fast to the shore. She would thus lie in from 3 to 5 fathoms, almost near enough to lay a stage to the beach. There was wood for fuel; and at less than a hundred yards from the shore, a lake of fresh water, one mile in circumference, from which a small stream runs into the cove; but another stream, descending from the hills nearer into the western corner, would better suit the purposes of a ship. This account was from the master, after whom this little but useful discovery was named Thistle's Cove. It seems to be much superior to Lucky Bay, where neither wood nor water can be procured without much time and trouble, nor is the shelter so complete.

Tuesday 11 January 1802

Next day Mr. Thistle was sent to examine the coast and islands to the eastward, when he found the archipelago to be full as dangerous in that direction as to the west. He landed upon an island three leagues distant, and brought me from thence a list of other islands and rocks further on, whose bearings had been taken. Several seals were procured on this and the preceding day, and some fish were caught alongside the ship; but our success was much impeded by three monstrous sharks, in whose presence no other fish dared to appear. After some attempts we succeeded in taking one of them; but to get it on board required as much preparation as for hoisting in the launch. The length of it, however, was no more than twelve feet three inches, but the circumference of the body was eight feet. Amongst the vast quantity of substances contained in the stomach was a tolerably large seal, bitten in two, and swallowed with half of the spear sticking in it with which it had probably been killed by the natives. The stench of this ravenous monster was great even before it was dead; and when the stomach was opened it became intolerable.

Wednesday 13 January 1802

On the 13th the wind blew fresh from the eastward; and as we could not sail with the ship, lieutenant Fowler and Mr. Thistle went over to Mondrain Island, the largest we had yet seen in the archipelago. An observation of the latitude and a set of angles were there taken, and they brought back some seals of a reddish fur, and a few small kangaroos of a species different from any I had before seen. The island was covered with brush wood; but some of the party, either from accident or design, set it on fire, and the wind being fresh, there was a general blaze in the evening all over the island.

Very little other stone was seen about Lucky Bay than granite; and all the surrounding hills, as well as the islands visited, were composed of varieties of the same substance; and some specimens from Mondrain Island contained garnets. In many places the surface of the rocks was scaling off in layers, and in the steep parts great lumps had fallen off, and some caverns were formed in the cliffs. This propensity to decomposition was more remarkable in the high peak of Cape Le Grand, about five miles to the westward, to which Mr. Brown made an excursion. He found a perforation at the top forming an arch of great width and height, and above it, at the very summit of the peak, were loose pieces of granite of considerable size.

There did not appear to be any Indians at this time in the neighbourhood of Lucky Bay; but from their fire places, it was judged that they had not quitted it long since. Geese and ducks were found here, and not being very shy, some of them were killed by the shore parties. The goose was also found upon the islands; and is the same bird spoken of in the Introduction [2] as resembling the bernacle goose, and frequenting Furneaux's Islands in Bass Strait.[3]

The latitude, observed upon a point of the main land on the east side of Lucky Bay, from one supplement of the sun's altitude, was 33° 59' 45"; but as the supplement of the preceding day gave 39" less than the mean of both observations, I consider the true latitude to be more nearly 34° 0' 20" S.

The longitude from sixteen sets of distances of the sun east and west of the moon, of which the individual results are given in Table II of the Appendix to this volume, was 122° 15' 42"; but from the two best time keepers, in which, from the short period since leaving King George's Sound, I put most confidence, it will be more correctly 122° 14' 14" E.

Dip of the south end of the needle, taken on shore upon the granite rock, 66° 4' 0"

But I am inclined to think it was attracted by the granite; and that, had the needle been considerably elevated, it would not have shown more dip than at King George's Sound, where it was 64°.

The variation deduced from observations taken on shore, morning and evening, with three compasses placed on the same rock, was 2° 35' west; with Walker's meridional compass, 4° 55'; and with the surveying theodolite 0° 30' west.[4] An amplitude taken on board the ship, with the head east-south-east, gave 7° 25', which, reduced to what it should be with the head in the meridian, is 4° 26' west. The mean, and what I consider to be nearest the true variation in this neighbourhood, will be 3° 6' west.

This is what I allowed upon the bearings taken with the theodolite upon the top of the hill behind the bay, and it appeared to be the same upon two small islands, one to the east and the other west, where Mr. Thistle took angles; but at Mondrain Island there seemed to be considerable differences.

Before entering the archipelago, the variation was observed to be 9° 21' west, with the ship's head east-south-east; but at three leagues to the east of Termination Island, in the following year, and with the head at east-north-east, it was no more than 3° 50' west. From the first, I should deduce the true variation on the west side of the archipelago to be 6° 28', and off Termination Island, from the second, to be 0° 57' west; both of which coincide with the other observations in showing the islands of the archipelago to possess a considerable degree of magnetic attraction.

The rise of tide in Lucky Bay was so trifling, that under the circumstances of our stay no attention was paid to it.

Thursday 14 January 1802

In the morning of the 14th, the wind being then light from the northward, we got under way and steered for Mondrain Island. In our route eastward from thence, several low rocks and patches of breakers were left on each side, besides small islands whose bearings had been taken from the hill behind Lucky Bay; the depth of water, however, was between 20 and 30 fathoms. The wind was then moderate from the south-westward, but the weather so hazy that there was much difficulty, and some uncertainty, in recognizing the different islands.

At half-past ten we steered more towards the main land, that no opening in it might escape unseen; and at noon, hove to for the purpose of taking bearings. The latitude observed to the north was 34° 2', and longitude 122° 36'. A chain of islands and breakers lay about two miles to the northward; and amongst the cluster to the east were two islands with peaks upon them, which, from their similarity, were named the Twins: the southernmost and nearest bore E. 7° N., three leagues. The nearest part of the main land was a projection with hills upon it which had been set from Lucky Bay, whence it is nearly five leagues distant; the intermediate space being a large bight with a low, sandy coast at the back, and containing many small islands and breakers. To the eastward of the hilly projection the coast seemed again to be sandy; but although our distance from it was not more than six or seven miles, it was scarcely visible through the haze.

After the bearings were obtained we bore away along the south side of the chain of islands and rocks; and at half-past one steered north-east to look for a place of shelter, either amongst the cluster near the Twins or in the opposite main land. The water shoaled amongst the small islands, from 30 to 10 fathoms, and suddenly to 3, when the bottom was distinctly seen under the ship. The next cast was 7 fathoms, and we steered on eastward for two islets three-quarters of a mile asunder, between which the master was sent to sound. On his making the signal we followed through, having 20 fathoms, and afterwards hauled the wind to the south-east, seeing no hope of shelter either amongst the islands or near the main land. The coast stretched eastward with little sinuosity, and was sandy, but not so low as before.

At six o'clock we had some larger, flat islands to windward, and in the east-south-east was one much higher and of greater extent, which proved to be the I. du Milieu (Middle Island) of D'Entrecasteaux. Betwixt this island and his Cap Aride on the main there were many small isles and apparently passages; and we therefore bore away in the hope of finding anchorage against the approaching night. Many patches of breakers were passed; and seeing a small bay in the north side of Middle Island, we stood in for it under shortened sail, and came to an anchor in 7 fathoms, sandy bottom, off the first of three small beaches. The island sheltered us from east-north-east, round by the south to west-by-north; and to the northward there was, besides the main land, a number of reefs and small isles, of which the nearest and largest was a quarter of a mile distant, as Middle Island was on the other side. The master was immediately sent to examine the passage through to the eastward, that we might know whether there were a possibility of escape in case the anchor should not hold; for the wind blew fresh at west-south-west, and threw some swell into the bay; he found 3 fathoms in the shallow part of the opening.

Friday 15 January 1802

The botanists landed in the morning upon Middle Island; for I had determined to stop a day or two, as well for their accommodation as to improve my chart of the archipelago. I went to the northern island, which is one mile long and near half a mile in breadth, and found it to be covered with tufts of wiry grass intermixed with a few shrubs. Some of the little, blue penguins, like those of Bass Strait, harboured under the bushes; and amongst the grass and upon the shores were a number of the bernacle geese, of which we killed nine, mostly with sticks; and sixteen more were procured in the course of the day.

After taking bearings from the uppermost of the small elevations of GOOSE ISLAND, as it was now named, I ascended the high north-western hill of Middle Island, which afforded a more extensive view. The furthest visible part of the main land was a projecting cape, with a broad-topped hill upon it bearing N. 58° E., six or seven leagues. This projection not having been seen by D'Entrecasteaux, was named after the late admiral Sir Thomas Pasley, under whom I had the honour of entering the naval service. The shore betwixt Cape Pasley and Cape Arid is low and sandy, and falls back in a large bight, nearly similar to what is formed on the west side of Cape Arid. Behind that cape was a high bank of sand, which stretched from one bight nearly to the other, and had the appearance of having been the sea shore not very long since.

The mount upon which I stood is the highest part of a ridge of almost bare granite, extending along, or rather forming the west side of Middle Island. The other parts of the island are low, and thickly covered with brush wood and some trees, where a small species of kangaroo seemed to be numerous, though none were caught. In the north-eastern part was a small lake of a rose colour, the water of which, as I was informed by Mr. Thistle who visited it, was so saturated with salt that sufficient quantities were crystallised near the shores to load a ship. The specimen he brought on board was of a good quality, and required no other process than drying to be fit for use. This lake is at the back of the eastern-most of three small beaches on the north side of the island, and it might be concluded that the salt was formed by the evaporation of the water oozing through the bank which separates it from the sea; but as, in the small drainings from the hills, the water was too salt to be drinkable, this may admit of a doubt.

Saturday 16 January 1802

On Saturday morning a part of the people were employed cutting a boat load of fire wood, and the master was again sent to sound the passage out to the eastward, and amongst the rocks lying beyond it. The shallowest depth he found was 3 fathoms, after which the water deepened to 7 and 10, past the north-east point and out to sea. He landed upon some of the rocky islets, and brought from thence twenty-seven more geese, some of them alive. The botanical gentlemen employed the day in going round Middle Island, but they found very little to reward their labour. A piece of fir plank, with nails in it, which seemed to have been part of a ship's deck, was picked up on the shore; but no trace of the island having been visited, either by Europeans or the natives of the main land, was any where seen.

The basis stone of this, as it appears to be of all the islands as well as of the coast of the archipelago, is granitic; but at the south side of Middle Island there is a thick crust of calcareous rock over it, as there is at the south end of Goose Island. It was also on the south side of King George's Sound that the calcareous rock covered the granite; a coincidence which may perhaps afford some light to the geologist.

The latitude of Goose Island Bay, for so this anchorage was named, is 34° 5' 23" south, and longitude by the two best time keepers corrected 123° 9' 30",5 east; the observations being made on the middlemost of the three southern beaches.

The variation from azimuth, observed on the binnacle when the ship's head was west-south-west, was 0° 54' west, and in the following year similar observations taken at anchor one mile to the eastward, with the head east, gave 6° 10' west; whence I deduce the variation which would have been obtained with the head at north or south, to be 3° 25' west. From the bearings on shore, compared with the latitudes and longitudes, it appeared to be 5¼° on the centre of Goose Island; and 4° upon the granitic mount of Middle Island.

No run of tide was observed, notwithstanding the narrowness of the channel, where the ship lay.

Goose-Island Bay may be useful as a place of refreshment, but the geese were not found to be so numerous at a different season of the year: a few hair seals may be procured, probably at all times. The wood is a species of eucalyptus, neither abundant nor large; but two or three ships may be supplied with fuel. Fresh water was not to be obtained upon either of the islands; but upon the opposite Cape Arid, five miles to the north, I judged there might be small streams running down from the hills. The lake of salt will be the greatest inducement for vessels to stop in this bay; they must not, however, come to it in the winter season, as there will be occasion to show hereafter.

Sunday 17 January 1802

On the 17th in the morning, the anchor was weighed and we steered out eastward. The shallowest water was seventeen feet, between the south-east point of Goose Island and the opposite west point of the middle beach; after which it deepened; and abreast of the middle rock there was 7 fathoms. Having cleared the islets lying off the north-east point of Middle Island, we steered for Cape Pasley, leaving the South-East Isles of the archipelago far distant on the starbord hand. A low islet and some rocks lie three miles to the south of the Cape, and the soundings we had in passing between them were 28 and 34 fathoms.

The wind at this time was moderate at south-west, with fine weather. Middle Island and Cape Arid were still visible at noon, and the Eastern Group, which, according to D'Entrecasteaux, terminated the archipelago, was coming in sight. Our situation and most material bearings were then as under:

Latitude, observed to the north and south,	33° 54' 55"
Longitude reduced up from eight o'clock,	123 55
Middle Island, top of the mount,	S. 65 W.
Cape Pasley, the hill, dist. 6 miles,	S. 84 W.
Furthest extreme, a low point, dist. 3 leagues,	N. 38 E.
A ragged mount in the interior of the country,	N. 21 W.
Eastern Group, the northern hill upon the highest and southernmost isle, dist. 8 leagues,	N. 80 E.

At half-past one we passed within three miles of the point which had been the furthest extreme at noon; it is low and sandy, and a ledge of rocks extends from it to the north-east. I named it Point Malcolm, in honour of Captain Pultney Malcolm of the navy. The depth diminished from 20 to 10 fathoms, in passing near a sunken rock two miles to the south-east of the point, and upon which the sea breaks only at times. The coast from thence trended rapidly to the northward; and in following its direction at from three to five miles distance, we left eight islands of the Eastern Group on the starbord and two on the larbord hand. These, with the exception of the southernmost, which has a hill at each end and some vegetation, are little better than low sterile rocks.

At seven in the evening, the water being smotth, we anchored in 8 fathoms, sandy bottom, three or four miles from the shore; where our calculated situation and the bearings of the land were as follows:

Latitude,	33° 17' S.
Longitude,	124° 6' E.
Northern extreme of the coast,	N. 27 E.

| Southern extreme, | S. 36 W. |
| A point in the interior country, | S. 68 W. |

From Cape Pasley to the northern extreme the coast is sandy and low, presenting, with trifling exceptions, a continued beach. On the north side of Point Malcolm it stretches north, and then eastward, forming a bight five miles within the land; after which the general trending is north-north-east, with very little sinuosity. Four or five miles behind the shore, and running parallel with it, is a bank of moderately high and level land, over which the tops of some barren-looking mountains were occasionally seen. The most remarkable of these is Mount Ragged, lying N. 8° W. nine or ten leagues from Cape Pasley.

South Coast. Between the Archipelagos.

We had now altogether lost sight of the Archipelago of the Recherche. The chart which I have constructed of this extensive mass of dangers is much more full, and in many parts should be more accurate than that of D'Entrecasteaux; but I dare by no means assert that the very great number of islands, rocks, and reefs therein contained are the whole that exist; nor that every individual one is correctly placed, although the greatest care was taken to obtain correctness. All the islands seem to be more or less frequented by seals; but I think not in numbers sufficient to make a speculation from Europe advisable on their account; certainly not for the China market, the seals being mostly of the hair kind, and the fur of such others as were seen was red and coarse. There is, besides, a risk of being caught in the archipelago with strong south or western winds, in which case destruction would be almost inevitable, for I know of no place where a ship might take refuge in a gale. The shelter in Thistle's Cove is, indeed, complete, when a vessel is once placed; but the cove is too small to be entered except under favourable circumstances, and the shelter in the western corner could not be attained with winds blowing strong out of it. The archipelago should not, therefore, be entered without the assurance of carrying fine weather to the proposed anchorage.

During the night of the 17th there was no current or set of tide past the ship. Every thing was kept prepared for getting under way at a moment's notice; but the wind blew gently off the land, and the people of the watch occupied themselves successfully in catching dog-fish. At daybreak [MONDAY 18 JANUARY 1802] we made all sail to the north-eastward, along the same low and, if possible, more sandy coast. The wind was light, and at nine it fell calm. This was succeeded by a sea breeze at east-south-east, and we trimmed close to it, keeping on our former course until four in the afternoon; when the land being one mile and a half distant, we tacked in 12 fathoms, and stretched to the southward.

The shore curved round here, and took a more eastern direction; and the bank of level land, which continued to run along behind it, approached very near to the water side. Three leagues further on it formed cliffs upon the coast; and a projecting part of them, which I called Point Culver, bore N. 77° E. four leagues: this was the furthest land in sight. This afternoon we passed a number of pale red medusas, such as I had usually seen on the East Coast at the entrances of rivers, and which, on being touched, produced a sensation like the stinging of a nettle. There was also a red scum on the water, and some of it was taken up to be examined by Mr. Brown in a microscope. It consisted of minute particles not more than half a line in length, and each appeared to be composed of several cohering fibres which were jointed; the joints being of an uniform thickness, and nearly as broad as long. These fibres were generally of unequal length, and the extremities of the compound particle thence appeared somewhat torn. The particles exhibited no motion when in salt water; and the sole effect produced by immersing them in spirit of wine was the separation of each into its component fibres.

Until daybreak next morning the wind was unfavourable; but it then veered round to the south, and enabled us to pass Point Culver. Our situation at noon, and the bearings taken were these:

Latitude, observed to the north and south,	32° 52' 51"
Longitude reduced up from eight o'clock,	124 58
Point Culver, distant five leagues,	S. 78 W.
Small rock under the cliffs, dist. 5 miles,	North.
Furthest extreme of the coast, cliffs,	N. 39 E.

Our course along the shore was so favoured by the wind that at seven in the evening we had passed another projecting part of the cliffs, named POINT DOVER, distant from Point Culver fifty miles; and the extreme in sight ahead was twenty miles further, and still cliffy. The nearest part was two or three leagues distant; and the wind being still at south, we hauled up to it, and at nine o'clock stood back to the westward.

The elevation of these cliffs appeared to be about five hundred feet, and nothing of the back country was seen above them. In the upper part they are brown, in the lower part nearly white, and the two strata, as also the small layers of which each is composed, are nearly horizontal. They were judged to be calcareous, as was the white, grey, and brown sand which the lead brought up when the bottom was not of coral.

A surveyor finds almost no object here whose bearing can be set a second time. Each small projection presents the appearance of a steep cape as it opens out in sailing along; but before the ship arrives abreast of it, it is lost in the general uniformity of the coast, and the latitude, longitude, and distance of the nearest cliffs are all the documents that remain for the construction of a chart. Point Culver and Point Dover are exceptions to the general uniformity; but it requires a ship to be near the land before even these are distinguishable. The latter point was somewhat whiter than the cliffs on each side, which probably arose from the front having lately fallen off into the water.

Tuesday 19 January 1802

In the night of the 19th the wind shifted round to the eastward, and continued there for three days; and during this time we beat to windward without making much progress. Several observations were taken here for the variation of the compass: with the ship's head east-by-north, azimuths gave 7° 15' west, and at south, 4° 26'; five leagues further eastward they gave 6° 13' with the head north-east, and eight leagues further, an amplitude 4° 18' at south-by-east. These being corrected would be 4° 13', 4° 26', 4° 2', and 3° 42' west; so that the variation had now reassumed a tolerably regular course of diminution. The mean of the whole is 4° 6' west variation in the longitude of 125° 51' east.

Friday 22 January 1802

At the end of three days beating our latitude in the evening of the 22nd was 32° 22', and longitude 126° 23', the depth in that situation was 7 fathoms at two miles from the land, and the furthest extremes visible through the haze bore west-half-north and east, the latter being distant four or five miles. The bank which before formed the cliffs had retired to a little distance from the coast, and left a front screed of low, sandy shore. Several smokes arose from behind the bank, and were the first seen after quitting the archipelago.

The barometer had kept up nearly to 30 inches during the east and south-east winds, but it now fell to 29,65; and we stretched off for the night in the expectation of a change of wind, and probably of blowing weather. At ten the sails were taken aback by a breeze from the westward; but at daylight [SATURDAY 23 JANUARY 1802] it had veered to south-by-west, and the mercury was rising. We then bore away for the land; and having reached in with the low, sandy point which had borne east in the evening, steered along the coast at three or four miles distance in from 7 to 11 fathoms water. The latitude at noon from very indifferent observations was 32° 22½', and longitude 127° 2'; the coast, four miles distant to the northward, was low and sandy, but rose quickly to the level bank, upon which there were some shrubs and small trees. Nothing of the interior country could be seen above the bank; but this might possibly have been owing to the haze, which was so thick that no extremes of the land could be defined. The wind was fresh at south-south-west, and by seven in the evening our longitude was augmented 55'; the land was then distant six or seven miles, trending east-north-eastward; and we hauled to the wind, which had increased in strength though the barometer was fast rising.

Having stood to the south-east till midnight, we then tacked to the westward; and at five next morning [SUNDAY 24 JANUARY 1802] bore away north for the land, the wind being then at south-by-east, and the barometer announcing by its elevation a return of foul winds. At six we steered eastward, along the same kind of shore as seen on the preceding day; but the wind coming more unfavourable, and depth diminishing to 5 fathoms soon after eight o'clock, made it necessary to stretch off to sea. The coast in latitude 32° 1' and longitude 128° 12' was three miles distant to the north. A league further on it took a more northern direction, but without much changing its aspect; it continued to be the same sandy beach, with a bank behind it of level land topped with small trees and shrubs as before described.

Monday 25 January 1802

The rest of the day and the whole of the 25th were taken up in beating fruitlessly against an eastern wind. Azimuths observed when the ship's head was east-by-north gave variation 6° 4'; and ten miles to the south a little eastward they gave 3° 8' west, at south-by-east; corrected 3° 2' and 2° 32', and the mean 2° 47' for the true variation, showing a decrease since the last of 1° 19' for 2° 11' of longitude.

At ten in the evening our situation was less advanced than on the morning of the 24th, when we tacked off shore; but the mercury was again descending, and during the night the wind veered to north-east, to north, and at eight in the morning [TUESDAY 26 JANUARY 1802] to west-by-north, when we steered in for the land. At ten the shore was eight or nine miles distant, and our course was north-east, nearly as it trended. The latitude at noon, from observations to the north and south, was 31° 51' 34", and longitude by timekeepers 128° 41'; the beach was distant three or four miles in the north-north-west, and the bank behind it lay two or three miles inland and was somewhat higher, but had less wood upon it than further westward. The wind was fresh at south-west, and the mercury was rising; but the haziness of the weather was such that no extremes of the land could be set.

Our course from noon was nearly east at the distance of five or six miles from the shore; and we ran at the rate of between seven and eight knots, under double-reefed top-sails and foresail. Abreast of our situation at half-past two the level bank again closed in upon the shore, and formed cliffs very similar to those along which we had before run thirty leagues. Their elevation appeared to be from four to six hundred feet, the upper part was brown, and the lower two-thirds white; but as we advanced, the upper brown stratum was observed to augment in proportional quantity. We could not distinguish, as before, the smaller layers in the two strata; and from the number of excavations in the white part, apparently from pieces having fallen down (see Mr. Westall's sketch, Atlas, Plate XVII. View 6.), I was led to think the lower portion of these cliffs to be grit stone rather than calcareous rock. The bank was not covered with shrubs, as before it came to the water side, but was nearly destitute of vegetation, and almost as level as the horizon of the sea.

At dusk we hauled up south-east-by-south to the wind, at one in the morning [WEDNESDAY 27 JANUARY 1802] tacked to the westward, and at four bore away north for the land. Having reached within six miles of the cliffs, we steered eastward again, with a fair breeze; and at noon were in latitude 31° 40' 52' and longitude 130° 59'; the cliffs were then distant seven miles to the northward, and at N. 9° E. was their termination.

The length of these cliffs, from their second commencement, is thirty-three leagues; and that of the level bank, from near Cape Pasley where it was first seen from the sea, is no less than one hundred and forty-five leagues. The height of this extraordinary bank is nearly the same throughout, being no where less, by estimation, than four hundred, nor any where more than six hundred feet. In the first twenty leagues the ragged tops of some inland mountains were visible over it; but during the remainder of its long course the bank was the limit of our view.

This equality of elevation for so great an extent, and the evidently calcareous nature of the bank, at least in the upper two hundred feet, would bespeak it to have been the exterior line of a vast coral reef, which is always more elevated than the interior parts, and commonly level with high-water mark. From the gradual subsiding of the sea, or perhaps by a sudden convulsion of nature, this bank may have attained its present height above the surface; and however extraordinary such a change may appear, yet, when it is recollected that branches of coral still exist upon Bald Head, at the elevation of four hundred or more feet, this supposition assumes a great degree of probability; and it would further seem that the subsiding of the waters has not been at a period very remote, since these frail branches have yet neither been all beaten down nor mouldered away by the wind and weather.

If this supposition be well founded, it may, with the fact of no hill or other object having been perceived above the bank in the greater part of its course, assist in forming some conjecture of what may be within it; which cannot, as I judge in such case, be other than flat, sandy plains, or water. The bank may even be a narrow barrier between an interior and the exterior sea, and much do I regret the not having formed an idea of this probability at the time; for notwithstanding the great difficulty and risk, I should certainly have attempted a landing upon some part of the coast to ascertain a fact of so much importance.

At the termination of the bank and of the second range of cliffs the coast became sandy, and trended north-eastward about three leagues; after which it turned south-east-by-east, and formed the head of the Great Australian Bight, whose latitude I make to be 31° 29' south, and longitude 131° 10' east. In the chart of admiral D'Entrecasteaux the head of the Great Bight is placed in 31° 36' and 131° 27'; but I think there is an error at least in the latitude, for the admiral says, "At daybreak I steered to get in with the land; and the wind having returned to south-east, we hauled our starbord tacks on board, being then four or five leagues from the coast. At eleven o'clock the land was seen ahead and we veered ship in 32 fathoms, fine sand."[5] The latitude observed at noon, as appears by the route table, was 31° 38' 58"; and if we suppose the ship, lying up south-south-west, to have made 2' of southing in the hour, as marked in the chart, she must have been in 31° 37' at eleven o'clock; which is within one mile of the latitude assigned to the head of the bight, where the shore curves to the south-east-by-east. This does not accord with the land being only then seen ahead, since the weather appears to have admitted the sight of it at the distance of four or five leagues. If we suppose the admiral, when he veered, to have been eight, instead of one mile from the head of the Great Bight, and the account strongly favours the supposition, it will then agree with my latitude. I had only 27 fathoms in crossing the head, and although it is possible there may be 30 closer in, yet in such a place as this the probability is, that the ship having the greatest depth of water was the furthest from the land.

After steering east-north-east, east, and east-south-east, and having seen the beach all round the head of the Great Bight, we hauled up parallel to the new direction of the coast, at the distance of six miles; and at five o'clock were abreast of the furthest part seen by the French admiral when he quitted the examination. The coast is a sandy beach in front; but the land rises gradually from thence, and at three or four miles back is of moderate elevation, but still sandy and barren. According to the chart of Nuyts, an extensive reef lay a little beyond this part. (Atlas, Plate IV.) It was not seen by D'Entrecasteaux, but we were anxiously looking out for it when, at six o'clock, breakers were seen from the mast head bearing S. 43° E. some distance open from the land. We kept on our course for them, with the wind at south-south-west, until eight o'clock, and then tacked to the westward in 27 fathoms; and the ship's way being stopped by a head swell, we did not veer towards the land until three in the morning, at which time it fell calm.

Thursday 28 January 1802

On a light breeze springing up from the northward we steered in for the coast; and at noon were in the following situation:

Latitude, observed to the north,	32° 2½'
Longitude reduced up from eight o'clock,	131 51
Breakers, distant two or three miles,	N. 22 to 42 E.
A sandy projection of the coast, south part,	N. 37 E.
Extremes of the land from the deck,	N. 15 W. to 89 E.

The breakers lie five or six miles from the land, and did not appear to have any connection with it, nor with two other sets of small reefs which came in sight to the east and east-south-east, soon afterward. At two o'clock our situation was betwixt these last reefs. The southernmost patches are two or three miles in length, and there are large rocks upon them, standing above water; the northern patches extend eight miles along the coast, from which they are distant three miles, and on the eastern parts there are also some rocks above water, but there were none upon the western reef first seen. It may be doubted whether the western reef were known to Nuyts, but there can be no doubt concerning these last; and I call the whole NUYTS' REEFS.

The aspect of the shore to the northward was nearly the same as that seen the preceding afternoon, but behind the second reefs it began to assume a more rocky appearance. A high cliffy cape is formed a little further eastward; it has a pyramidal rock near it, and the coast there takes a direction somewhat on the north side of east. This remarkable projection, being within a few leagues of the furthest part of the main coast discovered by the Dutch, I have called CAPE NUYTS: its latitude is 32° 2' south, and longitude 132° 18' east.

After clearing Nuyts' Reefs we steered east-north-east, past the cape, to look for anchorage in two bights, but there were rocks in both, and they were open to the southward. Beyond them was a low, cliffy point, lying E. 3° N. seven or eight miles from Cape Nuyts; and seeing a bay behind it which promised shelter from south-west and south winds, we hauled round the point at half-past five. The water shoaled gradually from 11 to 3 fathoms, on which I hove the sails aback and sent the master ahead to sound; and as he did not make the signal for deeper water, as we were already in tolerable shelter, the anchor was dropped in 3¼ fathoms, sandy bottom. We had then the following bearings:

Low cliffy point, distant 2 or 3 miles	S. 35° E.
Head of the bay, distant 1 ½ miles,	S. 58 W.
Cliffs, appearing like an island, dist. 4 leagues,	N. 77 E.
Furthest land visible from the masthead	E. S. E.

Between the first and the last of these bearings we were exposed to the sea, but sheltered at all other points of the compass.

Being arrived at the extremity of that part of the south coast of Terra Australis which had been previously explored, it may be useful, before entering on the unknown part, to compare my examination of it with what was contained in former charts. It will thence appear that the employment of fifteen days in running along the coast, more than would probably have been required had I kept at a distance, was not without some advantage to geography and navigation. At Cape Leeuwin, the largest Ile St. Alouarn of D'Entrecasteaux was seen to be joined to the main, and to form the south-western extremity of Leeuwin's Land, and of Terra Australis. The coast from thence to King George's Sound was more accurately investigated than the French admiral had an opportunity of doing and his omission of soundings supplied. Captain Vancouver's chart is superior to that of the French from Cape Chatham to the Sound; but that officer's distance from some parts prevented him from seeing them correctly. In the Sound, no particular advantage will be derived from the new survey, the plan given by Vancouver being sufficiently correct for nautical purposes, with the exception of the bar to Oyster Harbour, over which he had marked seventeen feet, but where thirteen now appeared to be the greatest depth. From King George's Sound to Point Hood the coast had been very indistinctly, and sometimes not at all seen by Vancouver; but I found it, speaking generally, to be laid down by D'Entrecasteaux with accuracy, though the bights in the land are marked somewhat too deep, from his distance not allowing the low beaches to be always distinguished. These trifling inaccuracies were remedied, the passages between Bald and Doubtful Islands and the main land opposite to them ascertained to be safe, and the omission of soundings along the coast remedied.

In Doubtful Island Bay the French chart does not give the north-western part sufficiently deep; but the coast from thence to the Archipelago of the Recherche, as also the reefs and rocks, were well distinguished, better perhaps than by me; but the usual want of soundings, with the exception of some distant ones by Vancouver, still continued. D'Entrecasteaux's chart appeared to be excellent in the western part of the archipelago, and good in the positions of the islands on the outskirts; so that I have, in some cases, borrowed from it. With respect to the inner islands and the main coast, it was necessarily defective, from the French ships having sailed round the archipelago, and not through the middle of it as I did in the Investigator. Here, my survey, though far from complete in the details, will afford much new information and useful also, since it has brought to light a well-sheltered cove affording wood and water, and two other tolerable anchorages at which some refreshments may be procured, and at one, quantities of salt in the summer season.

From the archipelago eastward the examination of the coast was prosecuted by D'Entrecasteaux with much care, and with some trifling exceptions very closely; but as far as the 127th degree of longitude from Greenwich no soundings were given. These have been supplied, and a more minute description given of the coast. At the 129th degree the French ships seem to have been closer in with the land than was the Investigator; and it would appear by the track that they were also closer at the 30th, and at the head of the Great Bight, but these last are not corroborated by the soundings. From thence to the bay in which we anchored on the 28th, the Dutch chart of 1627 was the sole authority; and making allowances for the state of navigation at that time, it is as correct in form as could reasonably have been expected.

The latitudes and longitudes of the points and islands along the coast have been either verified or corrected, for there are commonly some differences between any longitudes and those of Vancouver and D'Entrecasteaux. The observations by which certain places, taken as fixed points, are settled in longitude, are mentioned at those places, as also are the corrections applied to the time-keepers for laying down the intermediate parts; and both are more particularly specified in the Appendix to this volume.

Monsieur Beautemps Beaupré, geographical engineer on board La Recherche, was the constructor of the French charts; and they must be allowed to do him great credit. Perhaps no chart of a coast so little known as this was will bear a comparison with its original better than those of M. Beaupré. That the Plates II and III in the accompanying Atlas, are offered as being more full and somewhat more correct, does neither arise from a wish to depreciate those of my predecessor in the investigation, nor from an assumption of superior merit; there is, indeed, very little due to any superiority they may be found to possess; but there would be room for reproach if, after having followed with an outline of his chart in my hand, improvements should not have been made in all or some of those parts where circumstances had not before admitted a close examination.

Notes

[1] *Hawkesworth, Vol. III. p. 220.,221.*
[2] *"Of the birds which frequent Furneaux's Islands, the most valuable are the goose and black swan; but this last is rarely seen here, even in the freshwater pools, and except to breed, seems never to go on shore. The goose approaches nearest to the description of the species called bernacle; it feeds upon grass, and seldom takes to the water. I found this bird in considerable numbers on the smaller isles, but principally upon Preservation Island; its usual weight was from seven to ten pounds, and it formed our best repasts, but had become shy. Gannets, shags, gulls, and red-bills were occasionally seen; as also crows, hawks, paroquets, and a few smaller birds. Fish were not plentiful, but some were taken with hook and line from the rocks."*
[3] *This goose is described by M. Labillardière, page 258 of the London translation, as a new species of swan.*
[4] *It is remarkable, that the difference between these three kinds of instruments is directly the reverse here of what it was in King George's Sound.*
[5] *Voyage de D'Entrecasteaux, par M. de Rossel, Tome I. page 220. The 32 fathoms are, I believe, of five French feet each, making very nearly 30 fathoms English measure.*

Chapter Five

Thursday 28 January 1802

The bay in which we anchored on the evening of January 28, at the extremity of the before known south coast of Terra Australis, was named FOWLER'S BAY, after my first lieutenant; and the low, cliffy point which shelters it from southern winds and, not improbably, is the furthest point (marked B) in the Dutch chart, was called POINT FOWLER. The botanical gentlemen landed early on the following morning [FRIDAY 29 JANUARY 1802] to examine the productions of the country, and I went on shore to take observations and bearings, and to search for fresh water.

The cliffs and rocks of Point Fowler are calcareous, and connected with the main land by a low, sandy isthmus of half a mile broad. Many traces of inhabitants were found, and amongst others, some decayed spears; but no huts were seen, nor anything to indicate that men had been here lately. Upon the beach were the foot marks of dogs, and some of the emu or cassowary. I found in a hole of the low cliffs one of those large nests which have before been mentioned, but it contained nothing, and had been long abandoned.

No fresh water was discovered round the shores of the bay, nor was there any wood large enough for fuel nearer than the brow of a hill two or three miles off. Two teal were shot on the beach, whence it seemed probable that some lake or pond of fresh water was not far distant; a sea-pie and a gull were also shot, and a few small fish caught alongside. These constituted everything like refreshment obtained here, and the botanists found the scantiness of plants equal to that of the other productions; so that there was no inducement to remain longer.

Fowler's Bay, however, may be useful to a ship in want of a place of shelter. It is open to the three points of the compass between south-east-by-south and east-south-east; and it was evident, from plants growing close to the water side, that a swell capable of injuring a vessel at anchor was seldom if ever thrown into it.

The latitude of the east extremity of Point Fowler is 32° 1' south.

Longitude of the point, deduced from twenty-two sets of distances (see Table III of the Appendix to this volume) is 132° 30'; but that given by time keepers with accelerated rates and supplemental correction, as explained at the end of Chap. VI, and in the Appendix, is preferred, and is 132° 27' east.

The variation observed upon the binnacle, with the ship's head east-south-east, was 3° 11' west by the surveying compass; and in the offing, with the head north-north-east, it was 1° 41' west. These, corrected, will be 0° 19' and 0° 30'; and therefore the variation allowed upon the bearings on shore was 0° 25' west.

The wind was at south-east-by-south at one in the afternoon, when the anchor was weighed to beat out of the bay. At half past five we were three miles from a cliffy head which had been taken for an island at the anchorage, and set at N 77° E. The shore forms a small bight on the east side of this head, and then stretches south-south-eastward in a sandy beach, with a ridge of barren land behind. At sunset we passed to windward of Point Fowler, and stood off to sea for the night.

South Coast. Nuyts' Archipelago.

Saturday 30 January 1802

Cape Nuyts bore north, two or three leagues, soon after daylight, and the wind was then at east; but as the day advanced it veered to the south-east, and permitted us to make a stretch toward the furthest land. At five in the evening we tacked near some low, whitish cliffs, which had been seen from the mast head when in Fowler's Bay; they were two or three miles off, and the furthest land visible from the deck bore S. 63° E. at no great distance. The coast here is broken into sandy beaches and small, cliffy points, and the same ridge of barren land runs behind it, but the elevation is not great.

Sunday 31 January 1802

At three in the afternoon of the 31st we reached in again with the coast, about four leagues beyond our situation on the preceding day. The depth at two miles off shore was 7 fathoms on a coral bottom; the northern extreme bore N. 58° W., and a low point on the other side, named Point Bell, S. 45° E., seven miles. To seaward, a flat rock bore W. 3° S., one mile and a half; it is the largest of four which were called Sinclair's Rocks, and lie scattered at the distance of two or three miles off the coast. We stood off at this time; but so little could be gained upon the south-east winds that when we came in next morning [MONDAY 1 FEBRUARY 1802] it was almost exactly in the same spot, and Point Bell was not passed until late in the afternoon; the weather, also, was adverse to the examination, being so hazy that the highest land could not be seen beyond three or four leagues.

At half-past six in the evening, when we tacked to stand off for the night, Point Bell bore N. 68° W. four miles. It lies in 32° 16½' south and 133° 5' east; and there is a broad, flat rock, surrounded with breakers, one mile to the westward. The main coast beyond the point forms some bights, and is divided betwixt sand and rock, as before described: its general trending is nearly east. A small island, somewhat elevated, lies six miles to the south-east of Point Bell, and has a ledge of rocks and islets extending from it a league to the north-eastward, and a separate islet one or two miles to the east: these obtained the name of Purdie's Isles. After we had tacked in 9 fathoms, a wave was perceived to break upon a sunken rock within less than half a mile of the ship; and I think it would be dangerous to pass between Point Bell and Purdie's Isles.

Tuesday 2 February 1802

At noon of the 2nd February no land was in sight. The weather was still hazy, and the wind at south-east; but in the afternoon it favoured us two points, and we got sight of a higher and larger island than any before seen on this part of the coast. At half-past four, being then near a smaller isle and several rocks, we tacked towards the large island which was six or seven miles to the southward; and soon after eight in the evening got to an anchor in a little sandy bay on its north side. The depth was 6 fathoms in passing the north-west point of the bay, but 10 within side, on a fine sandy bottom, where the anchor was dropped. At daylight [WEDNESDAY 3 FEBRUARY 1802] we found ourselves hall a mile from the shore, and the extremes bearing from N. 32° W., round by the west and south, to S. 77° E.; and at the distance of two miles we were sheltered by four small islands, extending from N. 41° to 88° E. The master was sent to sound in the bay; but the bottom was everywhere good, and nothing found to injure the cables. The scientific gentlemen landed upon their respective pursuits; and I followed them to take angles for my survey, and see what could be procured for the ship's company.

The island is nearly three miles long, north-west and south-east, and is moderately high and cliffy at the ends; the middle part is a sandy isthmus, not more than half a mile broad, but the breadth of the higher ends is from one-and-half to two miles. This island is the central one of a group; for besides the four small isles to the north-east, there are two close to the west end, and two others, something larger, lying off to the southward. I call these the ISLES OF ST. FRANCIS; in the persuasion that the central one is that named St. Francis by Nuyts. Independently of the eight isles and a rock, surrounding this Isle St. Francis, I set from the north-east point three other islands. The first, named Lacy's Isle, bore N. 28° E., seven miles; and two miles from it to the north-west there is an islet and a separate rock above water surrounded with breakers, the same near which we had tacked at half-past four on the preceding evening. The second was called Evans' Isle, and bore N. 49° E. eleven miles, and the third to which the name of Franklin was given, bore N. 81° E. sixteen miles. All these are much inferior in magnitude to the central island of St. Francis. For several days before anchoring here we had observed large flocks of sooty petrels; and I found the surface of the island, where it was sandy and produced small shrubs, to be full of their burrows. Penguins, similar to those of Furneaux's Islands, had their burrows nearer to the water-side. A small species of kangaroo, was also found, and at some preceding season the island had been frequented by geese; but at this time, the vegetation being almost burnt up, they seemed to have quitted it from want of food. The heat was, indeed, such as to make walking a great fatigue; and this was augmented by frequently sinking into the bird holes and falling upon the sand. The thermometer stood at 98° in the shade, whilst it was at 78° on board the ship.

Where the surface is not of sand it consists of calcareous rock, mostly in loose pieces; but the stone which forms the basis of the island is heavy and of a close grain, and was judged to be porphyry. In the crevices of a low calcareous cliff, at the south-east side of the bay, I found some thin cakes of good salt, incrusted upon a stone containing laminae of quartz.

A party was sent on shore at dusk to collect petrels, and in less than two hours returned with sufficient to give four birds to every man in the ship. Early in the morning [THURSDAY 4 FEBRUARY 1802] the boats were again sent upon the same errand, and to haul the seine; but the birds were gone off to sea for the day, and no fish were caught. A small kangaroo was brought off, as also a yellow snake, which was the second killed on this island. The great heat deterred the naturalists from going on shore this morning, for the very little variety in the vegetable productions presented no inducement to a repetition of their fatigue. I landed to see what further could be discovered of the neighbouring islands; and we then prepared to get under way so soon as the breeze set in from the south-eastward, which it usually did about noon, after a few hours of calm or of light airs.

The small bay in the Isle St. Francis, which I call Petrel Bay, affords excellent shelter for two or three ships; but no fresh water, not even to rinse our mouths, could be found at this time; and a few scattered bushes were the nearest approach to wood upon the island. Petrels, penguins, and a few hair seals may be procured, and probably some geese in the wet season.

I had hitherto observed upon this coast that the south-east and east winds produced the same effect upon the barometer as at the Cape of Good Hope, in keeping the mercury high, commonly at or above 30 inches and the more fresh was the wind, the higher it stood; but within the last few days the barometer was much lower with the same winds, and at this time was at 29.74. The dense haze which prevailed might possibly have caused the change, but I suspected another reason for it. Winds coming off the land, I had remarked, had a tendency to depress the mercury, and sea winds to make it rise, though no change took place in the weather; and it therefore seemed probable, as the trending of the coast beyond these islands was unknown, that the south-east and east winds came off the land, and not from the sea, as before; in which case the unknown coast would be found trending to the southward, a conjecture which, it will be seen, was verified. That there was no entrance to a strait, nor any large inlet near these islands, was almost demonstrated by the insignificance of the tides; for neither in Fowler's Bay nor at this Isle St. Francis could any set be perceived; nor was there any rise by the shore worthy of notice.

At half-past one we left Petrel Bay; and having passed between the small isles to the north-east, steered for Evans' Island, and toward the Isles of St. Peter, which were expected to lie beyond it. At five o'clock, we passed between Evans' Island and some rocks above water, with breakers round them, lying three miles to the eastward. An island, equally high with that of St. Francis, was then seen to the north, and low land extended from it to N. 45° E., which had some appearance of being part of the main. We steered for these lands; and seeing an opening between them at sunset, I attempted it in the hope of getting anchorage for the night; but the water shoaled suddenly, from 4 fathoms to sixteen feet upon rocks, and obliged me to veer on the instant. We then stood back to the southward till eight o'clock, and nothing being perceived in the way of the ship's drift, hove to for the night.

Friday 5 February 1802

The wind was north-east in the morning; and at half-past four o'clock we filled the sails and steered eastward until eight, when the central island of St. Francis bore N. 71° W., and Franklin's Isles, for there are two, besides rocks, were distant four leagues, the small opening between them bearing N. 28° W. To the south-eastward of these islands, at the distance of eleven miles, is a low projection of the main land, to which the name of Point Brown was given, in compliment to the naturalist; and four leagues further, in the same line, was a cliffy head, called Cape Bauer after the painter of natural history. Between these projections there was a wide space where no land was visible, and for which we accordingly steered on the wind veering more to the northward. The atmosphere was still hazy, more especially about the horizon, and no observations worthy of confidence could be taken for either latitude or longitude. At noon,

Franklin's Isles bore	N. 48½° to 56½° W.
Point Brown, distant four miles,	N. 34 W.
Cape Bauer, south extremity, dist. 3 leagues,	S. 50 E.

No land was yet visible ahead; and there being much refuse from the shore, as well as seaweed floating about, some hopes of finding a river were entertained. At half-past two, however, low, sandy land was seen from the mast head, nearly all round, the depth had diminished from 19 to 7 fathoms, and the water was much discoloured in streaks at less than a mile from the ship. Smokes Were rising in three different places; but as the wind was unfavourable, and there was no prospect of any opening sufficiently large to admit the Investigator, I gave up the further examination of this place, and called it STREAKY BAY.

There remained nearly forty miles of space between Point Bell and Point Brown, in which the main coast had not been seen. This it was necessary to explore; but the wind being then at north-north-east, I steered to the southward, to gain some further knowledge of the coast in that direction before dark.

West of Cape Bauer, and distant four miles, there is a low island, extensively surrounded with rocks and breakers, which I called Olive's Island. We passed between it and the cape, and observed the cliffs of the latter to be stratified, and apparently calcareous. Another cliffy and somewhat higher projection opened from it at S. 1° W., distant seven miles, the intermediate low land forming a bight four or five miles deep, which is mostly skirted by a sandy beach. This projection I named Point Westall, in compliment to the landscape painter; and at six in the evening, when it bore north-east-by-east two or three miles, we veered round to the northward. Beyond Point Westall the coast takes a more eastern direction, the first land which opened out from it being at S. 43° E.: this was a third cliffy projection, terminating another sandy bight in the coast. No hill nor anything behind the shore could be perceived, but it does not certainly follow that there are no hills in the back country, for the haze was too thick to admit of the sight extending beyond four or five leagues.

The wind having veered to east-north-east, we kept to the northward all night, under easy sail; and at daylight [SATURDAY 6 FERBRUARY 1802], the lands around us were in the following bearings:

I. St. Francis, the largest southern cliffs,	N. 80° W.
Lacy's Isle, centre,	N. 57 W.
Evans' Isle, centre,	N. 43 W.
Franklin's Isles, extremes,	N. 29° to 10 W.
Point Brown, south extremity,	N. 65 E.
Cape Bauer, north extremity,	S. 78 E.
Olive's Island, centre,	S. 67 E.
Cliffy Head beyond Point Westall,	S. 45 E.

All sail was made to fetch between Franklin's Isles and Point Brown, in order to follow the course of the main land as close as possible; but finding, after several tacks, the impossibility of weathering the isles, we bore away; and at noon hauled up north-north-east round them. The wind was light at east, and the weather fine over head; but there was so dense a haze below that, the true horizon could not be distinguished from several false ones, and we had six or seven different latitudes from as many observers: those taken by me to the north and south differed 19 minutes. This dense haze, from its great refractive power, altered the appearance of objects in a surprising manner: a sandy beach seemed to be a chalky cliff, and the lowest islands to have steep shores. The thermometer stood, at this time, at 82° and the barometer at 29.60 inches.

On the north side of Point Brown the shore formed a large open bay, into which we hauled up as much as the wind would permit, passing near to a reef of rocks and breakers, two miles to the north-north-east of Franklin's Isles. At half-past two the water had shoaled to 5 fathoms; and not being able to distinguish any inlet, we then bore away westward along the land. The number of smokes rising from the shores of this wide, open place induced me to give it the name of SMOKY BAY.

At four o'clock we passed the small opening which had been unsuccessfully attempted in the evening of the 4th, and hauled up northward under the lee of the island forming its western side. The mainland then came in sight ahead; but between it and the islands was a space five or six miles wide, which had the appearance of being the entrance to a river. No land was visible to the north-east; and besides quantities of grass and branches of trees or bushes floating in the water, there was a number of long, gauze-winged insects topping about the surface, such as frequent fresh-water lakes and swamps. In order to form a judgment of how much fresh was mixed with the salt water, or whether any, I had some taken up for the purpose of ascertaining its specific gravity; but before the experiment could be made, the depth diminished to 3 fathoms, and low land was distinguished nearly all round. We then veered ship; and at seven o'clock came to an anchor in 6 fathoms, off a small beach on the north side of the western and smallest island, being sheltered at all points except between S. 58° and N. 80° W.

The specific gravity of the water taken up proved to be 1.034, or .008 greater than the water of the Southern Indian Ocean, westward of the Island Amsterdam, although the temperature in which it was weighed was higher by 14°. This circumstance, with the shallowness of the inlet and the land having been seen to close round so nearly, made me give up the intention of attempting to proceed any higher up, since no river of importance was to be expected.

Great flocks of sooty petrels were observed coming in from sea to the island, and at the first dawn next morning [SUNDAY 7 FEBRUARY 1802] a boat was sent to collect a quantity of them, and to kill seals; but the birds were already moving off, and no more than four seals, of the hair kind, were procured. The botanists preferred going on shore to the more eastern land, which, though low, was much more extensive than the island nearer to the ship; and in fact it was not yet ascertained whether it were not a part of the main. I went to the higher island with a theodolite to take bearings; and as the survey had shown that no dependence was to be placed in any observations taken on board the ship during the last five days, I took with me the necessary instruments for determining the latitude and longitude.

Granite was found to compose the rocks of the shore, and seemed to be the basis of the island; but it was covered with a crust of calcareous stone, in some places fifty feet thick. The soil at the top was little better than sand, but was overspread with shrubs, mostly of one kind, a whitish velvety plant--(artriplex reniformis of Brown),[1] nearly similar to what is called at Port Jackson, Botany Bay greens. Amongst these the petrels had everywhere undermined; and from the excessive heat of the sun, the reflection from the sand, and frequently stepping up to the mid-leg in the burrows, my strength was scarcely equal to reaching the highest hill near the middle of the island. I had no thermometer, but judged the temperature could scarcely be less than 120°; and there was not a breath of air stirring. My fatigue was, however, rewarded by an extensive set of bearings, and I overlooked the lower and larger island to the eastward, and saw the water behind it communicating with Smoky Bay. That low land and the island upon which I stood, being the north-easternmost of this archipelago, must, I conceive, be the ISLES OF ST. PETER in Nuyts' chart, notwithstanding their relatively small distance from those of St. Francis. The bay to the northward, between these islands and the mainland, I named DENIAL BAY, as well in allusion to St. Peter as to the deceptive hope we had formed of penetrating by it some distance into the interior country. The bearings most essential to the survey, taken from this station were these,

Point Brown, sandy hillocks on it,	S. 52° 0' E.
Franklin's Isles, the extremes,	S. 49° 15' to 33 45 E.
Evans' Isle, centre,	S. 23 0 W.
Isles of St. Francis, southernmost,	
the centre	S. 34 0 W.
do., the largest extremes,	S. 38 0 to 46 20 W.
Lacy's Isle, centre,	S. 51 0 W.
Purdie's Isles, the easternmost,	N. 83 15 W.
Lound's Isle, centre,	N. 76 30 W.
Point Bell, the hill on it,	N. 73 0 W.
Point Peter, across Denial Bay,	N. 12 45 W.

On returning to the shore to complete my observations, a flock of teal presented themselves, and four were shot. There were also pied shags, and gulls of three species; and in the island were seen many crows, a green paroquet, and two smaller birds. A black snake, of the common size, was killed, but its form did not bespeak it to be venomous. After observing the sun's altitude at noon, I returned on board with the intention of getting the ship under way, to examine more closely a bight in the coast near Point Bell; and then of returning to Petrel Bay in the Isle St. Francis, in order to obtain better observations for a base to my chart of this archipelago. At two o'clock, Mr. Brown and his party returned from the eastern island, bringing four kangaroos, of a different species to any before seen. Their size was not superior to that of a hare, and they were miserably thin, and infested with insects. No other than calcareous rock was seen upon the eastern island. It seemed to afford neither wood nor water, nor were there any marks of its having been visited by the natives of the continent; in which respect it resembled the western island, as it also did in its vegetation, and in being frequented by the sooty petrel. Mr. Brown's pocket thermometer stood at 125° when placed on the sand, and 98° in the shade; whilst on board the ship the height was only 83°.

The sun was too high at noon for its altitude to be taken from an artificial horizon with a sextant; but by laying down upon the beach I obtained it from the sea horizon tolerably free from the refractive errors caused by the haze. The latitude of the north side of the western Isle of St. Peter, thus observed, was 32° 21¼' south, and the longitude by time-keepers, corrected as usual, 133° 29' east. There was no set of tide past the ship; but from eight o'clock to noon the water had risen about a foot by the shore.

The anchor was weighed on the return of the botanists, and we steered westward past the small island named Lound's, and as far as Purdie's Isles. when, having seen the whole line of the coast behind them, we hauled to the southward at six o'clock for Petrel Bay; and at one in the morning [MONDAY 8 FEBRUARY 1802] came to, in 13 fathoms, near our former anchorage.

It was here confirmed by satisfactory observations on shore that our former latitudes and longitudes taken on board the ship were erroneous; and the consequent necessity of reconstructing my chart of these islands induced me to remain at anchor the rest of the day. A boat was sent to fish with hook and line, and had some success; and at dusk a sufficient number of sooty petrels were taken from the burrows to give nine to every man, making, with those before caught, more than twelve hundred birds. These were inferior to the teal shot at the western Isle of St. Peter, and by most persons would not be thought eatable on account of their fishy taste, but they made a very acceptable supply to men who had been many months confined to an allowance of salt meat.

The latitude of our anchorage in Petrel Bay proved to be 32° 33 1/3' south, and corrected longitude, by time-keepers, 133° 15½' east. The variation of the compass on the binnacle, with the ship's head south-eastwardly, but the exact point not noted, was 2° 23' west. Other azimuths, taken five leagues to the north-westward, with the head south-half-west, gave 0° 19' east; and six leagues to the eastward, the head being north half-west, we had 0° 16' east. All these observations, being corrected, and supposing the ship's head in the first case to have been south-east-half-east, as is probable, would agree in showing that the true and magnetic meridians exactly coincided at the Isles of St. Francis in 1802.

Being about to quit this archipelago, it may be expected that I should make some general remarks upon it. The basis stone of the islands where we landed, and that of the others, as also of the projecting parts of the main, appeared to be similar, was either porphyry or granite; but this was generally covered with a stratum, more or less thick, of calcareous rock. The and sterility of the two largest islands has been already mentioned; and yet they appeared superior to any of the smaller isles, where there was no probability that the small kangaroos could exist in the dry season. The surface of the continent seemed to be almost equally destitute of vegetable soil to cover the sand and rock; and from the hot winds off the land, which we felt in Streaky and Smoky Bays, it would seem that this aridity prevails to a considerable distance in the interior. There are, however, some grounds to believe that a lake or run of fresh water exists not far from Denial Bay: the flock of teal seen upon the western Isle of St. Peter, and the number of winged, fresh-water insects skimming the surface of that bay, are the grounds to which I allude.

My examination of this group of islands was tolerably minute to be done wholly in a ship; but much still remained, which boats would best accomplish, to make the survey complete, especially in the bays of the main land. No more than a general examination was prescribed by my instructions at this time, and I therefore left the minute parts for a second visit, when the ship would be accompanied by the Lady Nelson tender.

Upon the identity of the particular islands composing this group, as compared with the chart of Nuyts' discovery, there may possibly be some difference of opinion, but there can be no doubt that the group generally is the same with that laid down by the Dutch navigator; and I therefore distinguish it from others upon this coast by the title of NUYTS' ARCHIPELAGO. Besides the nine Isles of St. Francis and two of St. Peter, and several distinct rocks and patches of reef, it contains Sinclair's four Rocks, Purdie's Isles, Lound's Isle, Lacy's and Evans' Islands, Franklin's Isles, and Olive's Island; all of which are named after young officers of the Investigator. The state of navigation in 1627 does not permit the expectation of any exact coincidence between the islands laid down by the Dutch and those in my chart; if a few leading features of resemblance be found, this is all that can be fairly required; and these I shall endeavour to trace. The Cape marked A (see the copy of the Dutch chart from Thevenot), the point B, and the western reefs, I conceive to be clearly identified in Cape Nuyts, Point Fowler, and Nuyts' Reefs, although there be a difference of near half a degree in latitude. The next leading mark is the line of islands marked 1, 2, to 5, extending south-south-east from the furthest extremity of the main land. I found no islands corresponding to the first three of these; but the main coast there trends south-east, and there are cliffy projections upon it which might appear like islands to a ship so far distant as not to raise the intermediate beaches. I conceive then, that the island marked 3, is the projecting point which I have named Point Bell; and that 1 and 2 are the two cliffy projections further northward. The island marked 4 will be the largest of Purdie's Isles; and in looking on, nearly in the same line, we find 5 in Lacy's Island. The island 6, or St. Francis, should lie to the west-south-west, or perhaps south-west, for since the line of the five islands is two points too much to the right, this bearing may be the same. To the south-west-by-south the large Isle St. Francis is found, in the centre of eight smaller isles which Nuyts has not distinguished. The islands 8, 9, and 10, are to be sought to the east-north-east of 5, or Lacy's Island, or rather to the north-east, two points to the left; and there we find, though not very exactly, Evans' Island and the two Isles of St. Peter. Island 7 should be to the north-west of 8, and in a direction between 4 and 9; and in that position is Lound's small Isle.

This explanation, I am aware, may be disputed, because it leaves Franklin's Isles unnoticed; and it may be objected, that had Lound's Isle been seen, the main land north of it would have been seen also. That Nuyts passed to the southward of all the islands laid down in his chart seems improbable, since he distinguished only one of the Isles of St. Francis; but if this be supposed, then 7 and 8 might be Evans' and Franklin's Isles, and 9 and 10 would be Point Brown and Cape Bauer, which lie to the south-east, instead of north~east; and in this case the islands which I suppose to be St. Peter's, and that of Lound, will not have been seen. The question is, in fact, of no importance, other than what arises from a desire to do justice to the Dutch navigator; and on this head, I trust there can be no accusation. My opinion coincides with the first explanation; and unless an island exist to the south-west of St. Francis, and I am tolerably certain that none lies within five leagues, a correspondence more free from objections cannot easily be pointed out.

Note

[1] *Prod. flor. Nov. Holl. p. 406.*

Chapter Six

South Coast. From Nuyts' Archipelago.

Tuesday 9 February 1802

At daybreak in the morning of Feb. 9, when the anchor was weighed from Petrel Bay to prosecute the examination of the unknown coast, we were unexpectedly favoured with a refreshing breeze from the westward; and our course was directed for Cape Bauer. At noon, the latitude from mean of observations to the north and south, which differed only 1', was 32° 43' 17"; but although our distance from the land could not be more than three leagues, no part of it was distinguishable; the haze was very thick, but it was of a different nature, and had none of that extraordinary refractive power which the atmosphere possessed during the prevalence of the eastern winds. At one o'clock, Olive's Island was indistinctly perceived; and at two we came in with Point Westall, and then steered south-south-eastward along the coast at the distance of four or five miles. At six, a bold cliffy head, which I named CAPE RADSTOCK, in honour of Admiral Lord Radstock, bore N. 75° E., six or seven miles; and the land seemed there to take another direction, for nothing beyond it could be perceived. The wind was at west-south-west; and we kept on the starboard tack till eight o'clock, and then stood off for the night.

Wednesday 10 February 1802

At five in the morning we steered for the land; and soon afterward Cape Radstock was in sight, bearing N. 57° E., five leagues. The latitude of this cape is 33° 12' south, and longitude 134° 15' east. Other cliffy heads came in sight as we advanced eastward; and at seven, the appearance of an opening induced me to steer close in; but it proved to be a bight full of rocks, with low land behind. The line of the projecting parts of the coast is nearly east from Cape Radstock for four leagues; and at the end of them is a cliffy point which received the name of Point Weyland. Round this point an opening was seen of so promising an appearance that I bore away north and north-east for it, although land was in sight as far as east-south-east. Before noon the greater part of the open space was found to be occupied by low land; and no more of the opening remained than a small inlet through the beach, leading, apparently, into a lagoon, the water of which was distinguished from the mast head. This inlet was fit only to receive boats; and therefore we hauled the wind to the southward, when the sandy shore near it was distant two-and-half miles on one side, and Point Weyland one mile and a half on the other. The latitude of this point is 33° 14' south, and longitude 134° 32' east. As the day advanced the wind veered to south-west, and there being a swell from the same quarter, we could do no more than make a south-east-by-south course, parallel with the shore. At three o'clock the mainland was seen to extend out beyond what the ship could fetch; there were besides two islands lying still further out, and a third was perceived in the offing, almost directly to windward. The two first received the name of Waldegrave's Isles, and the latter with some rocks near it were called Top-gallant Isles. Our distance from the sandy shore was then barely a league; and coming into 7 fathoms water soon afterward, we tacked, hoping to weather Cape Radstock; but finding this to be impossible, were constrained to pass the night in working to windward in the bay. The weather was squally with rain, but our situation made it necessary to carry all possible sail; and we had the satisfaction, at daylight [THURSDAY 11 FEBRUARY 1802], to find the ship had gained considerably. It then blew a strong breeze at south-west-by-south, and we stretched in under Waldegrave's Isles; and finding the water become smooth, the anchor was let go in 7 fathoms, on a bottom of calcareous sand, at half a mile from the north-east end of the inner and largest island. We were here sheltered from the present wind, but exposed from west-by-south to north-north-west; the master was therefore immediately sent to sound the opening of one mile wide between the island and the main, by which alone we could hope to escape, should the wind shift to the north-westward and blow strong; but the opening proved to be full of rocks and breakers.

The press of sail carried in the night had so much stretched the rigging that it required to be set up, fore and aft. Whilst this was doing on board, the naturalists landed upon the island; where I also went to take bearings with a theodolite, and observations for the latitude and longitude. The island is about two miles long, and connected by rocks with the small outer isle; and they extend four or five miles from a projecting part of the main, in a west direction. These islands form the southern boundary, as Cape Radstock does the north point of a great open bay, which, from the night we passed in it, obtained the name of ANXIOUS BAY.

I found the island to bear a great resemblance to the western Isle of St. Peter, in its cliffy shores, granitic basis and super-stratum of calcareous stone; in its vegetable productions, and in its surface being much excavated by the burrows of the sooty petrels. It had also been frequented by geese at some preceding season of the year, and there were marks of its having been a breeding place for them; but at this time the vegetation was too much dried up to afford any subsistence. Crows of a shining black colour were numerous; and in two which I shot the bill was surrounded at the base with small feathers, extending one-fourth of the length towards the extremity. There were no appearances of the island having been before visited either by Europeans or Indians, and a single rat was the sole quadruped seen; but a few hair seals were killed upon the shore. Mr. Brown remarked that this was the first island where not a single novelty in natural history had presented itself to his observation.

South Coast. Investigator's Group.

From the highest part of the island I saw two patches of breakers, lying near three miles out from the western island; and beyond the Top-gallant Isles in the offing, there was a piece of land of more considerable extent, which the haze did not allow of being well defined. No part of the main coast was visible from hence, beyond the projection close to

Waldegrave's Isles; but on changing my station to the southward, land opened from it at the distance of three or four leagues. The principal bearings taken were as follow:

Point Weyland, distant 7 or 8 leagues,	N. 24° 10' W.
Top-gallant Isles, centre of the largest,	S. 52 20 W.
Southmost rock, like a ship under sail,	S. 48 5 W.
Further land, the east side,	S. 57° 40' to 69 10 W.
Southern extreme of the coast,	S. 49 40 E.

A squall passed over as the sun came to the meridian, and deprived me of an observation for the latitude; but the centre of Waldegrave's largest Isle was afterwards found to be in 33° 35½' south, and the longitude by my observations on shore for the time keepers, was 131° 44' east.

There were strong squalls during the night, with rain, but the wind being off the land, the ship rode easy with a whole cable. At daylight [FRIDAY 12 FEBRUARY 1802] the weather was more moderate, and we stretched out for the distant piece of land in the offing. At noon it was seven miles to windward, and seen to be an island of about five miles in length; and being near enough at dusk to observe that it afforded shelter, and that there were no apparent dangers, we continued to beat up, and got to anchor at half-past nine, in 7 fathoms, fine sand; the nearest beach being distant half a mile, and the island extending from S. 85° E. to 67° W.

Saturday 13 February 1802

In the morning we were surprised to see breaking water about one mile from the ship, and as much from the shore. It was not far from the place where the last tack had been made in the evening, and the master found no more than six feet water close to it; so that we were fortunate in having escaped. The botanical gentlemen landed early; and I followed them to make the usual observations for the survey.

From my first station, at the north-east end of the island, the largest of the Top-gallant Isles bore S. 67° E., four or five miles. It is of little extent, but high and cliffy; and there are three rocks on its south side resembling ships under sail, from which circumstance this small cluster obtained its present name. To the south-west I distinguished several small islands, of which the northernmost and largest is remarkable from two high and sharp-pointed peaks upon it, lying in latitude 33° 57' and longitude 134° 13'. This cluster, as it appeared to be, received the name of Pearson's Isles; but it is possible that what seemed at a distance to be divided into several may form two or three larger islands, or even be one connected land. Another island, about one mile long and of moderate height, was discovered bearing S. 72° W., about four leagues. It was surrounded with high breakers, as was a smaller isle near it; and the two were called Ward's Isles. These three small clusters, with Waldegrave's Isles, and this larger island, which was named Flinders', after the second lieutenant, form a group distinct from Nuyts' Archipelago; and I gave it the name of the INVESTIGATOR'S GROUP.

The form of Flinders' Island is nearly a square, of which each side is from three to five miles in length. Bights are formed in the four sides; but that to the north seems alone to afford good anchorage. In its composition this island is nearly the same as that of Waldegrave's largest isle; but between the granitic basis and the calcareous top there is a stratum of sand stone, in some places twenty feet thick. The vegetation differed from that of other islands before visited, in that the lower lands were covered with large bushes; and there was very little either of the white, velvety shrub (atriplex) or of the tufted, wiry grass. A small species of kangaroo, not bigger than a cat, was rather numerous. I shot five of them, and some others were killed by the botanists and their attendants, and found to be in tolerably good condition. We were now beginning to want a supply of water, and the northern part of the island was sought over carefully for it; but the nearest approach to success was in finding dried-up swamps in which the growing plants were tinged red, as if the water had been brackish. No other trees than a few small casuarinas, at a distance from the anchorage, were seen upon the island; but wood for fuel might with some difficulty be picked out from the larger bushes growing near the shore. The beaches were frequented by seals of the hair kind. A family of them consisting of a male, four or five females, and as many cubs was lying asleep at every two or three hundred yards. Their security was such that I approached several of these families very closely; and retired without disturbing their domestic tranquillity or being perceived by them.

The latitude of the north-east sandy cove in Flinders' Island was found to be 33° 41' south, and longitude 134° 27½' east. The variation on board, observed by Mr. Thistle on the binnacle with the ship's head south-by-east, was 0° 6' east; which, corrected, gives 0° 44' for the variation to be allowed on the bearings taken on shore, or on board the ship with the head at north or south. The tide appeared to be as inconsiderable here as in Nuyts' Archipelago. With the present southern winds the temperature at this island was very agreeable; the thermometer stood between 65° and 68°, and the barometer at 30.08 inches, and it was rising.

Sunday 14 February 1802

In the morning of the 14th, the wind was at south-south-east. We weighed the anchor at daylight, and beat to windward the whole day; but without gaining any thing to the southward. A little before midnight, the wind having veered more to the east, we passed the Top-gallant Isles, and at noon next day [MONDAY 15 FEBRUARY 1802] were in the following situation:

Latitude observed,	33° 59½'
Longitude from bearings,	134 38
Top-gallant Isles, centre of the largest,	N. 12 W.
Pearson's Isles, the two northern peaks,	N. 83 W.

No part of the main land was visible; but the wind having veered back to the southward, in the nature of a sea breeze., we were then standing eastward; and in two hours several smokes were seen, and soon afterward the land. At six o'clock, a very projecting point of calcareous cliffs, distant five miles, was the southernmost visible extreme. It was named Point Drummond, in compliment to captain Adam Drummond of the navy; and lies in 34° 10' south and 135° 13' east.
The coast from Waldegrave's Isles to Point Drummond runs waving in a south-eastern direction, and forms bights and broad, cliffy heads. It appeared to be of moderate elevation, and barren; but the further parts of it could not be well distinguished on account of the haze.
We tacked from the shore at six o'clock, when the following bearings were taken;

Point Drummond,	S. 14° E.
A broad cliffy projection, the north end,	N. 11 W.
---- south end, distant 4 or 5 miles,	N. 26 E.
A rocky islet, distant three leagues,	N. 41 W.

This islet lies four miles from the main land, and nothing was seen to prevent a ship passing between them.
Soon after we had tacked, the wind veered gradually round from the south to east; and having steered southward under easy sail till midnight, we then hove to. A heavy dew fell, which had not before been observed upon this part of the coast.

Tuesday 16 February 1802

At daylight, Point Drummond was seven miles distant to the north-by-east. The shore, after falling back four or five miles from it, trended northward; but there was other land further out, and we steered for the opening between them, passing a rocky islet five miles from Point Drummond and nearly as much from the eastern shore. At eight o'clock we found ourselves in a bay whose width, from the outer western point of entrance, named Point Sir Isaac, to the shore on the east side, was near three leagues. It extended also far into the south-south-east but the depth diminished, in less than half an hour, to 4 fathoms, although the head of the bay was still six or seven miles distant. We were then two miles from the eastern shore, with Point Sir Isaac bearing N. 67° W.; and hoping to find deeper water in that direction, hauled to the westward; but coming into 3 fathoms, were obliged to tack, and the wind veering round from the sea, we worked to windward in the entrance of the bay.
The situation of Point Sir Isaac is 34° 27' south, and from observations of the moon with stars on each side, in 135° 13' east; but by the time-keepers corrected, which I prefer, the longitude is 135° 10' east. The basis of the point seemed to be granitic, with an upper stratum of calcareous rock, much similar to the neighbouring isles of the Investigator's Group. Its elevation is inconsiderable, and the surface is sandy and barren, as is all the land near it on the same side. The large piece of water which it shelters from western winds I named COFFIN'S BAY, in compliment to the present vice-admiral Sir Isaac Coffin, Bart.; who, when resident commissioner at Sheerness, had taken so zealous a part in the outfit of the Investigator. Coffin's Bay extends four or five leagues to the south-eastward from Point Sir Isaac; but I do not think that any stream more considerable than perhaps a small rill from the back land falls into it, since sandy cliffs and beach were seen nearly all round. On the east side of the entrance the shore rises quickly from the beach to hills of considerable height, well covered with wood. The highest of these hills I call Mount Greenly; its elevation is between six and eight hundred feet, and it stands very near the water-side.

Many smokes were seen round Coffin's Bay, and also two parties of natives, one on each side; these shores were therefore better inhabited than the more western parts of the South Coast; indeed it has usually been found in this country that the borders of shallow bays and lagoons, and at the entrances of rivers, are by far the most numerously peopled. These natives were black and naked, differing in nothing that we could perceive from those of King George's Sound before described.

In the evening the wind veered to the southward; and at sunset we passed Point Sir Isaac at the distance of half a mile. Our course was then directed to the south-west, towards two high pieces of land which appeared in the offing, and obtained the name of Greenly's Isles. The ship was hove to at midnight; but on seeing the islands to leeward at two in the morning [WEDNESDAY 17 FEBRUARY 1802], we filled; and at three, tacked towards the main land. At day-light a rocky point which lies ten or eleven miles to the south-south-west of Point Sir Isaac, and is called Point Whidbey, was distant two miles; and the peak upon the southernmost of Greenly's Isles bore S. 66° W., four or five leagues. At S. 18° E., seven or eight miles from Point Whidbey, lies an island one mile in length, the middlemost and largest of seven, which I named WHIDBEY'S ISLES, after my worthy friend the former master-attendant at Sheerness. The basis of these isles appeared to be granitic, but the more elevated are covered with a thick crust of calcareous rock; and in the middlemost this upper stratum is perforated, admitting the light through the island.

The two easternmost of Whidbey's Isles are close to a low projection of the main land which was named Point Avoid. It lies eleven or twelve miles to the east-south-east of Point Whidbey; and the shore between them forms so deep a bight that the peninsula between it and Coffin's Bay seems to be there not more than two or three miles broad. At the head of this bight is a low, rocky island, and there are rocks and breakers on each side of the entrance; on which account, and from its being exposed to the dangerous southern winds, I named it AVOID BAY.

Having a wind at south-east-by-south, we beat up all the morning off the entrance of this bay, taking bearings of the different islands and points, and of Mount Greenly which was visible over the peninsula, to fix their relative positions.

At noon, our Latitude, observed to the N. and S., was	34° 43' 32"
Longitude by time keepers,	135 3 35
Greenly's Isles, the peak, bore	N. 74 W.
Whidbey's Isles, three westernmost,	S. 36° 60 W.
---- middlemost, north end dist. 2 miles,	N. 81 E.
---- two near Point Avoid,	N. 81 E.
Mount Greenly, over the peninsula,	Not distinct.
Point Whidbey, distant 7 miles,	N. 2 E.

At dusk in the evening, having weathered Whidbey's Isles, we tacked near Point Avoid and stretched off to sea; but on coming in with the land at daylight of the 18th [THURSDAY 18 FEBRUARY 1802], it appeared that nothing was gained, our situation being then in the same bight to the eastward of the point.

The shore of the bight is sandy and low, and trends from Point Avoid about five miles to the east; after which it takes a more southern direction and becomes higher, and the projecting parts of the waving coast line are cliffy. Behind the shore the land rises to a moderate height, is destitute of vegetation, and of a yellow colour, but whether from the surface being of bare rock, or of sand, could not be distinguished.

In stretching off again, with the wind at east-south-east, we passed near to a small circular reef, lying nine miles from Point Avoid and six from the nearest shore. Azimuths taken at this time with three compasses on the binnacle, and the ship's head at south (magnetic), gave the mean variation 1° 12' east; but with the surveying compass alone it was 1° 39' east, which is what I allowed in the survey. On the preceding day the two guns upon the quarter-deck, nearest to the binnacle, had been struck down into the after-hold, from a persuasion that the differences so often found in the variations and bearings when on different tacks must arise from some iron placed too near the compasses. Strict search had been repeatedly made for sail needles, marline-spikes, or other implements of iron which might have been left in or about the binnacle, but I could fix on nothing unless it were the guns; for it is to be observed that, notwithstanding the constancy of the differences, the idea of any regularly acting cause to derange the needle had not yet fixed itself in my mind. The perfection to which naval science had arrived did not allow me to suppose, that if a constant and unavoidable attraction existed in ships, it would not have been found out, and its laws ascertained; yet no longer than three days before, differences had been observed sufficient, one would think, to have convinced any man that they were produced by some regular cause. Off Point Drummond, about fifteen leagues to the north of where the variation 1° 39' east was observed with the ship's head at south, both azimuths and an amplitude had been taken with the same compass. The first gave 1° 33' west, the head being south-east-by-east; and after we had tacked, and the head was south-west-by-west, the amplitude gave 3° 56' east! I did not yet see that as the ship's head was as much on the east side of the magnetic meridian in one case as it was to the west in the other, so was the variation as much too far west then as it was too far east afterward. Differences like this, of 5½°, which had frequently occurred, seemed to make accuracy in my survey unattainable from not knowing what variation to allow on the several bearings. The guns were removed in the hope to do away the differences, but they still continued to exist, nearly in the same proportion as before; and almost in despair, I at length set about a close examination of all the circumstances connected with them, in order to ascertain the cause, and if possible to apply a remedy; but it was long, and not without an accumulation of facts, before I could arrive at the conclusions deduced and explained in the Appendix No. II to the second volume.

We tacked towards the land soon after noon; and being within five miles of it at three o'clock, stood off again. The furthest extreme of the main land was a sloping low point, distant about three leagues; but two or three miles beyond it, to the south, was a small island to which I gave the name of Liguanea. Some of Whidbey's Isles were still to be distinguished, and the bearings taken just before tacking were as under:

Inner island near Point Avoid,	N. 31° W.
Nearest part of the cliffs,	E. N. E.
The sloping low point,	S. 71 E.
Liguanea Island, highest part,	S. 57 E.

At seven in the evening, we came in with the land a little further to windward, and tacked at a mile and a half from a patch of breakers which lie N. 72° W. three or four miles from the sloping low point. This point was still the furthest part of the main land visible, the coast seeming from thence to take a more eastern direction.

Friday 19 February 1802

In the afternoon of the 19th when the wind had returned to the south, we passed to windward of Liguanea Island, and saw it surrounded with many breakers on its south and west sides. The sloping low point was also visible; and three miles further eastward there was a steep head, with two high rocks and one lower near it, of which Mr. Westall made a sketch. (Atlas Plate XVII. View 7.) This projection I named CAPE WILES, after a worthy friend at Liguanea, in Jamaica; it lies in latitude 34° 57' south, and longitude 135° 38½' east. Before dark we got sight of a hill situate upon a projecting cape, thirteen miles to the east-south-east of Cape Wiles, and observed the intermediate coast to form a large bight or bay, which I proposed to examine in the morning; and for that purpose we stood off and on during the night, with the wind from the southward.

Saturday 20 February 1802

At daylight of the 20th the hill on the east side of the bight bore N. 68° E. five or six miles, and an island, named Isle Williams, was seen to lie two miles from it to the south-east. We steered north-west soon afterward, up the bight; but in an hour were able to see the land all round, and that this place, which, I called SLEAFORD BAY, was dangerous with the wind at south-east, as it was then blowing. We therefore braced up, to work out; and at noon, our situation, with that of the surrounding lands, was as follows:

Latitude, observed to the north and south,	35° 2' 33"
Longitude by time keepers,	135 44
Liguana Isle, the centre nearly,	N. 67 W.
Cape Wiles, centre of the cliffs,	N. 38 W.
Hill on the east side of Sleaford Bay,	N. 77 E.
Isle Williams,	E. 2 N.

In the afternoon the wind favoured us by veering to south-by-west, and the passage between the projection of the hill and Isle Williams, (Atlas Plate XVII. View 8.) seeming to be clear, we steered through it with good soundings, the least being 12 fathoms, upon rippling water. Three miles further the main land formed a point, and took the uncommon direction of N. 15° W.; but to the eastward, there was a large piece of land, whether island or main we could not tell, and several small islands lay between. The opening was four miles wide; and we steered into it, passing through ripplings of tide with irregular soundings. No land could be seen to the north-east, but the night was coming on; and as the eastern land sheltered us from the present wind, we ran within half a mile of the shore and anchored in 3½ fathoms. The master was sent to sound about the ship; and finding we had not a sufficient depth for swinging toward the shore, the anchor was tripped and let go further out, in 7 fathoms, on a sandy bottom. No part of the eastern land was visible beyond the bearing of N. 76° E., distant one mile and a half; and the furthest extreme of what we could be certain was main land bore N. 17° W.

A tide from the north-eastward, apparently the ebb, ran more than one mile an hour; which was the more remarkable from no set of tide, worthy to be noticed, having hitherto been observed upon this coast. No land could be seen in the direction from whence it came; and these circumstances, with the trending of the coast to the north, did not fail to excite many conjectures. Large rivers, deep inlets, inland seas, and passages into the Gulph of Carpentaria, were terms frequently used in our conversations of this evening; and the prospect of making an interesting discovery seemed to have infused new life and vigour into every man in the ship.

Sunday 21 February 1802

Early in the morning I went on shore to the eastern land, anxious to ascertain its connexion with or separation from the main. There were seals upon the beach, and further on, numberless traces of the kangaroo. Signs of extinguished fire existed everywhere; but they bespoke a conflagration of the woods, of remote date, rather than the habitual presence of men, and might have arisen from lightning, or from the friction of two trees in a strong wind. Upon the whole I satisfied myself of the insularity of this land; and gave to it, shortly after, the name of THISTLE'S ISLAND, from the master who accompanied me. In our way up the hills, to take a commanding station for the survey, a speckled, yellow snake lay asleep before us. By pressing the butt-end of a musket upon his neck I kept him down whilst Mr. Thistle, with a sail needle and twine, sewed up his mouth; and he was taken on board alive for the naturalist to examine; but two others of the same species had already been killed, and one of them was seven feet nine inches in length. We were proceeding onward with our prize when a white eagle, with fierce aspect and outspread wing, was seen bounding towards us; but stopping short at twenty yards off, he flew up into a tree. Another bird of the same kind discovered himself by making a motion to pounce down upon us as we passed underneath; and it seemed evident that they took us for kangaroos, having probably never seen an upright animal in the island of any other species. These birds sit watching in the trees, and should a kangaroo come out to feed in the day-time, it is seized and torn to pieces by these voracious creatures. This accounted for why so few kangaroos were seen, when traces of them were met with at every step; and for their keeping so much under thick bushes that it was impossible to shoot them. Their size was superior to any of those found upon the more western islands, but much inferior to the forest kangaroo of the continent.

From a clear spot upon the north-western head of the island I traced the main coast to a cape bearing N. 18° W., where it was lost, but reappeared at a further distance, and extended to N. 2½° W. More to the right were three small islands, which I named Sibsey, Stickney, and Spilsby Islands, but no other land in a north-east, and none in an eastern direction. On the opposite side, six leagues out at sea, there was a small cluster of low islands, and some rocks and breakers at a less distance; these were called Neptune's Isles, for they seemed to be inaccessible to men. In the opening between Thistle's Island and the main are several small isles; and the two southernmost so much contract the entrance of the passage that one mile and a half of its breadth, between the main land and western isle, are alone safe for ships; I gave to this the name of THORNY PASSAGE. The bearings taken at this station, of most importance to the survey, were these:

Hill on the east side of Sleaford Bay,	S. 70° 50' W.
Point where the coast turns northward,	S. 73 30 W.
Hill of a conic form, on the main land,	N. 35 50 W.
Sibsey I., centre, over a nearer low rock,	N. 12 0 E.
Stickney Island, centre,	N. 26 0 E.
Spilsby Island, centre,	N. 33 0 E.
Thistle's I., west side, furthest visible part,	S. 35 30 E.
Neptune's Isles, the furthest, centre,	S. 5 30 E.
---- two nearer, the extremes,	S. 1° E to 4 0 W.

Thistle's Island is about twelve miles long, and from one to two or three in breadth, and in the middle part is high enough to be seen ten or twelve leagues from a ship's deck. The stone of the north-east end was found to be calcareous; but at the top of the north-west head, not less than two hundred feet high, there were many small pieces of granite, rounded to all appearance by attrition in the water. Some of the cliffs on the western side are white, as if composed of chalk, and the soil in general seemed to be sandy; yet the island was pretty well covered with wood, principally eucalyptus and casuarina. No water could be found; and as the ship's hold was becoming very empty, I returned on board, after observing the latitude, with the intention of running over to the main in search of it. But on comparing the longitude observed by lieutenant Flinders with that resulting from my bearings, a difference was found which made it necessary to repeat the observation on shore; and as this would prolong the time too near dusk for moving the ship, Mr. Thistle was sent over with a cutter to the mainland in search of an anchoring place where water might be procured.

The latitude of a small beach on the north end of Thistle's Island was found to be 34° 56'; and longitude, by the time-keepers corrected, 136° 3½', agreeing with thirty sets of lunar observations reduced to a place connected with this by land bearings. The strongest tides set past the ship at the rate of two miles an hour, from the north-north-east and south-south-west; the latter, which appeared to be the flood, ceasing to run at the time of the moon's passage over the meridian. It rose seven feet and a half by the lead line in the night of the 20th; and there were two tides in the twenty-four hours.

At dusk in the evening the cutter was seen under sail, returning from the main land; but not arriving in half an hour, and the sight of it having been lost rather suddenly, a light was shown and lieutenant Fowler went in a boat, with a lanthorn, to see what might have happened. Two hours passed without receiving any tidings. A gun was then fired, and Mr. Fowler returned soon afterward, but alone. Near the situation where the cutter had been last seen he met with so strong a rippling of tide that he himself narrowly escaped being upset; and there was reason to fear that it had actually happened to Mr. Thistle. Had there been daylight, it is probable that some or all of the people might have been picked up; but it was too dark to see anything, and no answer could be heard to the hallooing or to the firing of muskets. The tide was setting to the southward and ran an hour and a half after the missing boat had been last seen, so that it would be carried to seaward in the first instance; and no more than two out of the eight people being at all expert in swimming, it was much to be feared that most of them would be lost.[1]

Monday 22 February 1802

At daybreak I got the ship under way and steered across Thorny Passage, over to the main land, in the direction where the cutter had been seen; keeping an officer at the masthead, with a glass, to look out for her. There were many strong ripplings, and some uncommonly smooth places where a boat, which was sent to sound, had 12 fathoms. We passed to the northward of all these; and seeing a small cove with a sandy beach, steered in and anchored in 10 fathoms, sandy bottom; the main land extending from north-half-west, round by the west and south to east-south-east, and the open space being partly sheltered by the northern islands of the passage.

South Coast. Cape Catastrophe.

A boat was despatched in search of the lost cutter, and presently returned towing in the wreck, bottom upward; it was stove in every part, having to all appearance been dashed against the rocks. One of the oars was afterwards found, but nothing could be seen of our unfortunate shipmates. The boat was again sent away in search; and a mid-shipman was stationed upon a headland, without-side of the cove, to observe everything which might drift past with the tide. Mr. Brown and a party landed to walk along the shore to the northward, whilst I proceeded to the southern extremity of the mainland, which was now named Cape Catastrophe. On landing at the head of the cove I found several footmarks of our people, made on the preceding afternoon when looking for water; and in my way up the valley I prosecuted the same research, but ineffectually, although there were many huts and other signs that natives had resided there lately.

From the heights near the extremity of Cape Catastrophe I examined with a glass the islands lying off, and all the neighbouring shores, for any appearance of our people, but in vain; I therefore took a set of angles for the survey and returned on board; and on comparing notes with the different parties, it appeared that no further information had been obtained of our unfortunate companions.

Tuesday 23 February 1802

Next morning I went in a boat ten miles along the shore to the northward, in the double view of continuing the search and carrying on the survey. All the little sinuosities of the coast were followed, and in one place I picked up a small keg which had belonged to Mr. Thistle, and also some broken pieces of the boat but these were all that could be discovered. After taking angles at three stations on the main land, I crossed over to the northernmost and largest of the six small islands lying within Thorny passage. It is a mile and a half long, with a small islet off the north and another off its south end. These I called Taylor's Isles, in memory of the young gentleman who was in the cutter with Mr. Thistle. They lie near two miles from the main, and the depth between is from 7 to 10 fathoms, on a sandy bottom. A ship might anchor and be sheltered here, off a small beach at the north end of the largest island; but I did not find any fresh water, either there or on the opposite parts of the main land.

On returning to the ship I learned from some of the gentlemen who had been at the top of the highest hills at the back of the cove, that they had seen an inlet, going in westward, a little beyond where my excursion had terminated. Next day [WEDNESDAY 24 FEBRUARY 1802], I went up with instruments; and having climbed upon a high lump of granite, saw the water extending 40° behind the coast, and forming, apparently, an extensive port. The view taken from near the same spot by Mr. Westall shows what was visible of this fine piece of water, and the appearance of the neighbouring land. In addition to this interesting discovery, I obtained bearings of Cape Wiles, of the furthest extremity of Thistle's Island, and of a group of four islands and two rocks, five leagues beyond it to the east-south-east. The largest of these was named Wedge Island, from its shape, and the group GAMBIER'S ISLES, in honour of the worthy admiral (now lord Gambier) who had a seat at the Admiralty board when the Investigator was ordered to be fitted. This morning lieutenant Fowler had been sent to search the southern islands in Thorny Passage for any remains of our people; but he was not able to land, nor in rowing round them to see any indication of the objects of his pursuit. The recovery of their bodies was now the furthest to which our hopes extended; but the number of sharks seen in the cove and at the last anchorage rendered even this prospect of melancholy satisfaction extremely doubtful; and our want of water becoming every day more pressing, we prepared to depart for the examination of the new opening to the northward. I caused an inscription to be engraven upon a sheet of copper, and set up on a stout post at the head of the cove, which I named Memory Cove; and further to commemorate our loss, I gave to each of the six islands nearest to Cape Catastrophe the name of one of the seamen: Thistle's and Taylor's Islands have been already mentioned. Mr. Westall's view from the ship in Memory Cove, represents Thistle's Island and three of the small isles in front of it.

The reader will pardon me the observation that Mr. Thistle was truly a valuable man, as a seaman, an officer, and a good member of society. I had known him, and we had mostly served together, from the year 1794. He had been with Mr. Bass in his perilous expedition in the whale-boat, and with me in the voyage round Van Diemen's Land, and in the succeeding expedition to Glass-house and Hervey's Bays. From his merit and prudent conduct he was promoted from before the mast to be a midshipman, and afterwards a master in his Majesty's service. His zeal for discovery had induced him to join the Investigator when at Spithead and ready to sail, although he had returned to England only three weeks before, after an absence of six years. Besides performing assiduously the duties of his situation, Mr. Thistle had made himself well acquainted with the practice of nautical astronomy, and began to be very useful in the surveying department. His loss was severely felt by me; and he was lamented by all on board, more especially by

Entrance of Port Lincoln, taken from behind Memory Cove

his mess-mates, who knew more intimately the goodness and stability of his disposition.

Mr. William Taylor, the midshipman of the boat, was a young officer who promised fair to become an ornament to the service, as he was to society by the amiability of his manners and temper. The six seamen had all volunteered for the voyage. They were active and useful young men; and in a small and incomplete ship's company, which had so many duties to perform, this diminution of our force was heavily felt.

The latitude of our anchorage in Memory Cove was 34° 58' south, and longitude 135° 56½' east. The variation observed on the binnacle by lieutenant Flinders, when the ship's head was S. by W., was 2° 38' east, or corrected for one point of western deviation from the magnetic meridian, 2° 0' east. In the bearings taken on the eastern side of the high land behind the cove, the variation appeared to be 3° 20', but upon the summit it was 1° 40', being less than on board the ship.

The soil of the land round Memory Cove, and of Cape Catastrophe in general, is barren; though the vallies and eastern sides of the hills are covered with brushwood, and in the least barren parts there are small trees of the genus eucalyptus. The basis stone is granite, mostly covered with calcareous rock, sometimes lying in loose pieces; but the highest tops of the hills are huge blocks of granite. Four kangaroos, not larger than those of Thistle's Island, were seen amongst the brushwood; and traces of natives were found so recent, that although none of the inhabitants were seen, they must have been there not longer than a day before. Water does consequently exist somewhere in the neighbourhood, but all our researches could not discover it.

Before quitting Memory Cove a boat was sent to haul a seine upon the beach, which was done with such success that every man had two meals of fish and some to spare for salting. In the morning [THURSDAY 25 FEBRUARY 1802] we sailed for the new discovered inlet, and at two o'clock passed round the projection which had been set at N. 18° W. from Thistle's Island. It formed the south side of the entrance to the new opening, and is named CAPE DONINGTON. Our soundings in passing it were from 7 to 9 fathoms, and in steering south-westward we left an island four miles long, named Boston Island, on the starboard hand, and passed two islets on the other side, called Bicker Isles, which lie off Surfleet Point. On the depth of water diminishing to 5 fathoms we tacked, and presently came to an anchor on the west side of this point in 4½ fathoms, soft grey sand. We were then three miles within the entrance, and the nearest shore was a beach half a mile distant, lying under a hill which had been seen from Thistle's Island. This is a ridge of moderately high land about two miles long, but when seen to the north or south it assumes a conical form. I named it Stamford Hill; and there being a good deal of wood scattered over it, a hope was given of procuring water by digging at the foot. A boat was sent to make the experiment this evening, at the back of the beach; but the water which flowed into the pit was quite salt; and notwithstanding the many natives huts about, no fresh water could be found.

Boston Island at the entrance of the port being also woody and of some elevation, the boat was sent next morning [FRIDAY 26 FEBRUARY 1802] to search there for water; and in the mean time I landed with the botanists, and ascended Stamford Hill to ascertain the nature of this inlet and take angles. The port was seen to terminate seven or eight miles to the west-south-west; but there was a piece of water beyond it, apparently a lake or mere, from which we, might hope to obtain a supply, if no more convenient watering place could be found. Betwixt Cape Donington at the entrance, and Surfleet Point, was a large cove with a sandy beach at the head, capable of sheltering a fleet of ships, if the depth should be sufficient, as it appeared to be, to receive them; this was named Spalding Cove. Wood was not wanting there, but no stream of water could be distinguished. On the north side of the port, higher up, was a projecting piece of land, with an island lying off it nearly one mile in length. This island, which was named Grantham Island, contracts the width of that part to one mile and three-quarters; whereas above and below it the width is from two to three miles.

The eastern entrance to the port, between Boston Island and Cape Donington, is one mile and a half wide; the western entrance, betwixt the island and what was called Kirton Point, is larger, and appeared to be as deep as the first, in which we had from 7 to 9 fathoms. From Kirton Point, northward, the shore curves back to the west, and makes a semicircular sweep round the island, forming an outer bay which was named Boston Bay. It is terminated by Point Boston, a low point one mile and a half from the north end of the island; but whether the water between them be deep was not ascertained. From Point Boston the shore takes another sweep to the west and northward, and comes out again three or four leagues to the north-east, at a low but somewhat cliffy projection, to which I gave the name of Point Bolingbroke. The large bight within received the appellation of Louth Bay; and two low islands in it, of which the largest is more than a mile in length, were called Louth Isles. At Point Bolingbroke the land appeared to trend north or westward, and could no further be perceived from Stamford Hill.

Three small isles had been seen from Thistle's Island and their bearings set, and the discovery of them was now augmented by several others, forming a cluster to the eastward of Point Bolingbroke. This was called SIR JOSEPH BANKS' GROUP, in compliment to the Right Honourable president of the Royal Society, to whose exertion and favour the voyage was so much indebted.

Of the numerous bearings taken with a theodolite from the top of Stamford Hill, those which follow were the most important to the connexion of the survey.

Extreme of the land toward C. Catastrophe,	S. 17° 56' E.
Thistle's I., highest part and N. E. extr.,	S. 40° and 42 50 E.
Sir J. Banks' Group, Stickney I., centre,	N. 70 30 E.
---- Sibsey Island, centre,	N. 57 10 E.
---- Kirkby Island, centre,	N. 45 20 E.
Cape Donington, north-west extremity,	N. 37 50 E.
Point Bolingbroke, south end,	N. 29 12 E.
Boston Island, highest hill near the centre,	N. 5 10 W.
---- the extremes,	N. 15° 54' E. to 13 46 W.
A lake behind the head of the port, N. end,	S. 74 40 W.

South Coast. Port Lincoln.

The port which formed the most interesting part of these discoveries I named PORT LINCOLN, in honour of my native province; and having gained a general knowledge of it and finished the bearings, we descended the hill and got on board at ten o'clock. The boat had returned from Boston Island, unsuccessful in her search for water; and we therefore proceeded upward, steering different courses to find the greatest depth. Soon after one o'clock we anchored in 4 fathoms, soft bottom, one mile from the beach at the furthest head of the port, and something less from the southern shore.

Fresh water being at this time the most pressing of our wants, I set off the same afternoon, with a party, to examine the lake or mere discovered from Stamford Hill. The way to it was over low land covered with loose pieces of calcareous rock; the soil was moist in some places, and, though generally barren, was overspread with grass and shrubs, interspersed with a few clumps of small trees. After walking two miles we reached the lake, but to our mortification the water was brackish and not drinkable; the distance, besides, from Port Lincoln was too great to roll casks over a stony road. This piece of water was named Sleaford Mere. It is one mile broad, and appeared to be three or four in length. The shore was a whitish, hardened clay, covered at this time with a thin crust, in which salt was a component part. The sun being too near the horizon to admit of going round the mere, our way was bent towards the ship; and finding a moist place within a hundred yards of the head of the port, I caused a hole to be dug there. A stratum of whitish clay was found at three feet below the surface, and on penetrating this, water drained in, which was perfectly sweet though discoloured; and we had the satisfaction to return on board with the certainty of being able to procure water, although it would probably require some time to fill all our empty casks.

Saturday 27 February 1802

Early in the morning a party of men was sent with spades to dig pits; and the time-keepers and astronomical instruments, with two tents, followed under the charge of Mr. Flinders. I went to attend the digging, leaving orders with Mr. Fowler to moor the ship and send on shore empty casks. The water flowed in pretty freely, and though of a whitish colour, and at first somewhat thick, it was well tasted. Before the evening the observations for the rates of the time-keepers were commenced; and the gunner was installed in the command of a watering party, and furnished with axes to cut wood at such times as the pits might require to be left for replenishing.

The necessary duties being all set forward under the superintendance of proper officers, I employed the following days in surveying and sounding. The direction of the port was too remote from the meridian to obtain a base line from differences of latitude, which, when observed in an artificial horizon, and at stations wide apart, I consider to be the best; nor was there any convenient beach or open place where a base line could be measured. It was therefore attempted in the following manner: Having left orders on board the ship to fire three guns at given times, I went to the south-east end of Boston Island with a pendulum made to swing half-seconds. It was a musket ball slung with twine, and measured 9.8 inches from the fixed end of the twine to the centre of the ball. From the instant that the flash of the first gun was perceived to the time of hearing the report I counted eighty-five vibrations of the pendulum, and the same with two succeeding guns; whence the length of the base was deduced to be 8.01 geographic miles.[2] A principal station in the survey of Port Lincoln was a hill on the north side called Northside Hill, which afforded a view extending to Sleaford Mere and Bay and as far as Cape Wiles on one side, and to the hills at the beak of Coffin's Bay on the other. A great part of the bearings taken from hence crossed those from Stamford Hill very advantageously. Amongst the various excursions made by the scientific gentlemen, one was directed to Sleaford Mere, of which they made the circuit. The two southern branches were found to terminate within a hundred yards of the head of Sleaford Bay, with which the mere had been suspected to have a communication from its water being not quite fresh; but they are separated by a stony bank too high for the surf ever to pass over it. At the head of the bay a boat's sail and yard were seen floating, and no doubt had belonged to our unfortunate cutter: after being set out to sea by the tide, it had been driven up there by the late south-east winds.

Wednesday 3 March 1802

The refitment of the ship being nearly completed on the 3rd of March, lieutenant Fowler was sent round to Memory Cove in a boat, to make a final search along the shores and round the islands in Thorny Passage for the bodies of our late shipmates, which the sea might have thrown up. On the 4th [THURSDAY 4 MARCH 1802] the last turn of water was received, and completed our stock up to sixty tons; and the removal of our establishment from the shore waited only for the observation of a solar eclipse, announced in the nautical ephemeris for this day. The morning was cloudy, with rain; but towards noon the weather cleared up, and I had the satisfaction to observe the eclipse with a refracting telescope of forty-six inches focus, and a power of about two hundred. The beginning took place at 1h 12' 37.8" of apparent time, and the end at 3h 36' 11.8". So soon as the observation was concluded, the tents and astronomical in-

139

struments were carried on board, the launch was hoisted in, and everything prepared for going down the port on the following morning.

Many straggling bark huts, similar to those on other parts of the coast were seen upon the shores of Port Lincoln, and the paths near our tents had been long and deeply trodden; but neither in my excursions nor in those of the botanists had any of the natives been discovered. This morning, however, three or four were heard calling to a boat, as was supposed, which had just landed; but they presently walked away, or perhaps retired into the wood to observe our movements. No attempt was made to follow them, for I had always found the natives of this country to avoid those who seemed anxious for communication; whereas, when left entirely alone, they would usually come down after having watched us for a few days. Nor does this conduct seem to be unnatural; for what, in such case, would be the conduct of any people, ourselves for instance, were we living in a state of nature, frequently at war with our neighbours, and ignorant of the existence of any other nation? On the arrival of strangers, so different in complexion and appearance to ourselves, having power to transport themselves over, and even living upon an element which to us was impassable, the first sensation would probably be terror, and the first movement flight. We should watch these extraordinary people from our retreats in the woods and rocks, and if we found ourselves sought and pursued by them, should conclude their designs to be inimical; but if, on the contrary, we saw them quietly employed in occupations which had no reference to us, curiosity would get the better of fear; and after observing them more closely, we should ourselves seek a communication. Such seemed to have been the conduct of these Australians; and I am persuaded that their appearance on the morning when the tents were struck was a prelude to their coming down, and that had we remained a few days longer, a friendly communication would have ensued. The way was, however, prepared for the next ship which may enter this port, as it was to us in King George's Sound by captain Vancouver and the ship Elligood, to whose previous visits and peaceable conduct we were most probably indebted for our early intercourse with the inhabitants of that place. So far as could be perceived with a glass, the natives of this port were the same in personal appearance as those of King George's Sound and Port Jackson. In the hope of conciliating their good will to succeeding visitors, some hatchets and various other articles were left in their paths, or fastened to stumps of the trees which had been cut down near our watering pits.

In expressing an opinion that these people have no means of passing the water, it must be understood to be a deduction from our having met with no canoe, or the remains of any about the port; nor with any tree in the woods from which a sufficient size of bark had been taken to make one. Upon Boston Island, however, there were abundant marks of fire; but they had the appearance, as at Thistle's Island, of having been caused by some conflagration of the woods several years before, rather than of being the small fire-places of the natives.

There are kangaroos on the main land but none were caught; our efforts, both in hunting and fishing, were indeed very confined, and almost wholly unsuccessful. What has been said of the neck of land between the head of the port and Sleaford Mere may be taken as a description of the country in general; it is rocky and barren, but has a sufficient covering of grass, bushes, and small trees not to look desolate. The basis stone is granitic, with a super-stratum of calcareous rock, generally in loose pieces; but in some parts, as at Boston Island, the granite is found at the surface or immediately under the soil. Behind the beach, near our watering pits, the calcareous stone was so imperfectly formed that small shells and bits of coral might be picked out of it. This fact, with the saltness of Sleaford Mere and of a small lake on the south side of the port, accords with the coral found upon Bald Head and various other indications before mentioned to show that this part, at least, of Terra Australis cannot have emerged very many centuries from the sea, the salt imbibed by the rocks having not yet been all washed away by the rains. In the mountains behind Port Jackson, on the East Coast, at a vastly superior elevation, salt is formed in some places by the exhalation of the water which drips from the grit-stone cliffs.

Port Lincoln is certainly a fine harbour; and it is much to be regretted that it possesses no constant run of fresh water, unless it should be in Spalding Cove, which we did not examine. Our pits at the head of the port will, however, supply ships at all times; and though discoloured by whitish clay, the water has no pernicious quality, nor is it ill tasted. This and wood, which was easily procured, were all that we found of use to ships; and for the establishment of a colony, which the excellence of the port might seem to invite, the little fertility of the soil offers no inducement. The wood consists principally of the eucalyptus and casuarina.

Of the climate we had no reason to speak but in praise; nor were we incommoded by noxious insects. The range of the thermometer on board the ship was from 66° to 78° and that of the barometer from 29.4 to 30.20 inches. The weather was generally clouded, the winds light, coming from the eastward in the mornings and southward after noon. On shore the average height of the thermometer at noon was 76°.

The latitude of our tents at the head of Port Lincoln, from the mean of four meridian observations of the sun taken from an artificial horizon, was 34° 48' 25" S.

The longitude, from thirty sets of distances of the sun and stars from the moon (see Table IV of the Appendix to this volume), was 135 44 51" E.

These observations, being reduced to Cape Donington at the entrance of the port, will place it in latitude 34° 44' south, longitude 135° 56½' east.

No corresponding observation of the solar eclipse appears to have been made under any known meridian, and from the nature of circumstances, the error of the moon's place could not be observed at Greenwich; the distances would therefore seem most worthy of confidence, and are adopted; but the longitude deduced from the eclipse, as recalculated by Mr. Crosley from Delambre's solar tables of 1806, and the new lunar tables of Burckhardt of 1812, differs but very little from them: it is 135° 46' 8" east.

The rates of the time keepers, deduced from equal altitudes on, and between Feb. 27 and March 4, and their errors from mean Greenwich time, at noon there on the last day of observation, were found to be as under:

Earnshaw's No.543 slow 0h 30' 30.54" and losing 8.43" per day.
Earnshaw's No.520 slow 1h 9' 7.72" and losing 18.82" per day.

Arnold's No. 176 altered its rate prodigiously on March 1st, and on the 2nd it stopped. His watch, No. 1736, varied in its rate from 7.81" to 1.90", so that it continued to be used only as an assistant.

The longitude given by the time keepers with the King-George's-Sound rates, on Feb. 27, the first day of observation at the tents, was by

No. 543, 136° 15' 9.0" east.
520, 135 58 53.55
176, 136   1 23.95.

But by allowing a rate accelerating in arithmetic progression, from those at King George's Sound to what were obtained at this place, the mean longitude by the two first time keepers would be 135" 52' 16", or 7' 25" to the east of the lunar observations; which quantity, if the positions of the Sound and of Port Lincoln be correct, is the accumulation of their irregularity during fifty-seven days. In laying down the coasts and islands from the Sound up to Cape Wiles, the longitudes are taken from the time keepers according to the accelerated rates, corrected by an equal proportion of the error 7' 25" in fifty-seven days. From Cape Wiles to the head of Port Lincoln the survey is made from theodolite bearings and observed latitudes, without the aid of the time keepers.

The Dip of the south end of the needle, taken at the tents, was nearly the same as in K. George's Sound, being 64° 27' Variation of the theodolite at the same place, 1° 39' E.

And the bearings from different stations in the port were conformable to this variation, except at Cape Donington, where, at a station on the north-western part, it appeared to be as much as 4½° east.

The observations for the variation on board the ship, at anchor in the lower part of the port, gave 2° 23' west, when the ship's head was eastward, and 0° 53' east, at south-south-east. According to the first, which were taken by lieutenant Flinders whilst the ship lay under Stamford Hill, the true variation should be 0° 51' east; but by the second, observed by myself near Cape Donington, 2° 7' east, or nearly the same as was found in Memory Cove. Were the mean taken, it would be 1° 29', or 10' less than at the head of the port.

From Mr. Flinders` remarks upon the Tide, it appeared that the rise did not exceed three-and-half feet; and that, like Princess Royal Harbour, there was only one high water in twenty-four hours, which took place at night, about eleven hours after the moon's passage over the meridian, or one hour before it came to the lower meridian; yet at Thorny Passage, which is but a few leagues distant, there were two sets of tide in the day. This difference, in so short a space, appears extraordinary; but it may perhaps be accounted for by the direction of the entrance to the port, which is open to the north-east, from whence the ebb comes.

Friday 5 March 1802

On the 5th of March in the morning we ran down the harbour, and anchored under Cape Donington at the entrance of Spalding Cove in 7 fathoms, soft mud; the north-western extremity of the point bearing N. 16° E., one mile, and partly hiding Point Bolingbroke. In the evening, lieutenant Fowler returned from his search. He had rowed and walked along the shore as far as Memory Cove, revisited Thistle's Island, and examined the shores of the isles in Thorny Passage, but could find neither any traces of our lost people nor fragments of the wreck. He had killed two or three kangaroos upon Thistle's Island.

Saturday 6 March 1802

On the following morning I landed at Cape Donington to take some further bearings, and Mr. Evans, the acting master, was sent to sound across the entrance of Spalding Cove, and between Bicker Isles and Surfleet Point, where a small ship-passage was found. The boat was afterwards hoisted up; and our operations in Port Lincoln being completed, we prepared to follow the unknown coast to the northward, or as it might be found to trend.

Notes

[1] *This evening, Mr. Fowler told me a circumstance which I thought extraordinary; and it afterwards proved to be more so. Whilst we were lying at Spithead, Mr. Thistle was one day waiting on shore, and having nothing else to do he went to a certain old man, named Pine, to have his fortune told. The cunning man informed him that he was going out a long voyage, and that the ship, on arriving at her destination, would be joined by another vessel. That such was intended, he might have learned privately; but he added, that Mr. Thistle would be lost before the other vessel joined. As to the manner of his loss the magician refused to give any information. My boat's crew, hearing what Mr. Thistle said, went also to consult the wise man; and after the prefatory information of a long voyage, were told that they would be shipwrecked, but not in the ship they were going out in: whether they would escape and return to England, he was not permitted to reveal.*

This tale Mr. Thistle had often told at the mess table; and I remarked with some pain in a future part of the voyage, that every time my boat's crew went to embark with me in the Lady Nelson, there was some degree of apprehension amongst them that the time of the predicted shipwreck was arrived. I make no comment upon this story, but recommend a commander, if possible, to prevent any of his crew from consulting fortune tellers.

[2] *This length was founded on the supposition, that sound travels at the rate of 1142 feet in a second of time, and that 6060 feet make a geographic mile. A base of 15' 24" of latitude was afterwards obtained from observations in an artificial horizon, and of 25' 17" of longitude from the time keepers with new rates, both correct, as I believe, to a few seconds. From this long base and theodolite bearings, the first base appeared to be somewhat too short; for they gave it 8.22 instead of 8.01 miles. The length of the pendulum in the first measurement was such as to swing half seconds in England; and I had not thought it, in this case, worth attention, that by the laws of gravity and the oblate spheroid, the pendulum would not swing so quick in the latitude of 35°. I must leave it to better mathematicians to determine from the data and the true length of a geographic mile in this latitude, whether the base ought to have been 8.22 as given by the observations and bearings: it was proved to be sufficiently near for all the purposes of a common nautical survey.*

Chapter Seven

South Coast. Spencer's Gulph.

Saturday 6 March 1802

At ten in the morning of March 6 we sailed out of Port Lincoln, and skirted along the east side of Boston Island and the entrance of Louth Bay. In the afternoon we passed within two miles of Point Bolingbroke, and at six in the evening came to an anchor in 10 fathoms, off the north side of Kirkby Island, which is the nearest to the point of any of Sir Joseph Banks' Group, and had been seen from Stamford Hill. A boat was lowered down to sound about the ship, and I went on shore to take bearings of the different islands; but they proved to be so numerous that the whole could not be completed before dark.

Sunday 7 March 1802

I landed again in the morning with the botanical gentlemen, taking Arnold's watch and the necessary instruments for ascertaining the latitude and longitude. Twelve other isles of the group were counted, and three rocks above water; and it is possible that some others may exist to the eastward, beyond the boundary of my horizon, for it was not extensive. The largest island seen is four or five miles long, and is low and sandy, except at the north-east and south ends; it was called Reevesby Island, and names were applied in the chart to each of the other isles composing this group. The main coast extended northward from Point Bolingbroke, but the furthest part visible from the top of Kirkby Island was not more than four or five leagues distant; its bearing and those of the objects most important to the connection of the survey were these;

Main coast, furthest extreme,	N. 13° 40' E.
Point Bolingbroke,	N. 86 50 W.
Stamford Hill, station on the north end,	S. 45 17 W.
Thistle's Island, centre of the high land,	S. 5 37 W.

Sibsey Island, extremes,	S. 16° 27' to 13 2 W.
Stickney Island,	S. 18 30 to 22 40 E.
Spilsby Island,	S. 39 30 to 48 25 E.

Granite forms the basis of Kirkby Island, as it does of the neighbouring parts of the continent before examined; and it is in the same manner covered with a stratum of calcareous rock. The island was destitute of wood, and almost of shrubs; and although there were marks of its having been frequented by geese, none of the birds were seen, nor any other species of animal except a few hair seals upon the shore. This description, unfavourable as it is, seemed applicable to all the group, with the exception of Reevesby and Spilsby Islands, which are higher and of greater extent, and probably somewhat more productive.

The latitude of the north side of Kirkby Island, observed from an artificial horizon, was 34° 33' 1" south, and longitude by timekeepers, 136° 10' 8" east. The variation from azimuths taken on board the ship at anchor, with the head south-by-west (magnetic as usual), was 2° 40' east; which corrected to the meridian would be 2° 2' east, the same nearly as was observed in Memory Cove and at the entrance of Port Lincoln; but an amplitude taken on shore with the surveying theodolite gave 3° 57' east. This seemed extraordinary when, except at Cape Donington, no local attraction of importance had been found in the shores of Port Lincoln, where the stone is the same. It was, however, corroborated by the bearings; for that of Stamford Hill, with 3° 57' allowed, differed only 2' from the back bearing with the allowance of 1° 39'; which is a nearer coincidence than I have generally been able to obtain.

At two in the afternoon the anchor was weighed, and leaving most of Sir Joseph Banks' Group to the right, we steered northward, following the direction of the main land. The coast is very low and commonly sandy, from Boston Bay to the furthest extreme seen from Kirkby Island; but a ridge of hills, commencing at North-side Hill in Port Lincoln, runs a few miles behind it. In latitude 34° 20' this ridge approaches the water side, and in its course northward keeps nearly parallel at the distance of two or three miles. It is moderately elevated, level, destitute of vegetation, and appeared to be granitic. At half-past six, when we hauled off for the night, the shore was five or six miles distant; the furthest part bore N. N. E. ½ E., and a bluff inland mountain was set at N. 71° W., over the top of the front ridge.

The wind was moderate from the south-eastward; and at seven on the following morning [MONDAY 8 MARCH 1802], when the bluff inland mountain was bearing W. 2° N., we resumed our north-eastern course along the shore; which was distant seven miles, and had not changed its appearance. Towards noon the water shoaled to 6 fathoms at three miles from a sandy beach; a lagoon was visible from the mast head, over the beach, and a small inlet, apparently connected with it, was perceived soon afterward. A few miles short of this the ridge of hills turns suddenly from the shore, and sweeps round at the back of the lagoon, into which the waters running off the ridge appeared to be received. The corner hill, where the direction of the ridge is changed, was called Elbow Hill; and since losing sight of the bluff inland mount, it was the first distinguishable mark which had presented itself for the survey; it lies in latitude 33° 43' and longitude 136° 42'. The coast there trends nearly east-by-north, and obliged us to haul close to the wind, in soundings of 7 to 9 fathoms.

We had then advanced more than twenty-five leagues to the north-north-east from Cape Catastrope; but although nothing had been seen to destroy the hopes formed from the tides and direction of the coast near that cape, they were yet considerably damped by the want of boldness in the shores and the shallowness of the water; neither of which seemed to belong to a channel capable of leading us into the Gulph of Carpentaria, nor yet to any very great distance inland.

At two o'clock the shore again took a northern direction, but it was still very low in front, and the depth did not materially increase. Land was presently distinguished on the starbord bow and beam; and before four, an elevated part, called Barn Hill from the form of its top, bore E. 4° N. We continued to follow the line of the western shore, steering north-north-east and north; and the wind being at south, we hauled north-westward at six o'clock, intending to anchor under the shelter of the land. From 7 fathoms the depth diminished to 5, and quickly to seventeen feet; upon which we veered round, ran back into 5 fathoms, and came to an anchor three or four miles off the shore on a sandy bottom. The wind blew fresh, with rainy squalls; but a whole cable being veered out, we rode smoothly all night. The furthest land visible to the northward consisted of detached hummocks of which the highest was called Mount Young in honour of the admiral. Abreast of the ship the land rose gradually from the beach to the ridge of hills which still continued to run behind it; but at this place some back hills were visible over the ridge; and the highest of several hummocks upon the top, which served as a mark in the survey, was named Middle Mount. Observations for the time keepers were taken in the morning [TUESDAY 9 MARCH 1802] before getting under way, and the situation of the anchorage was found to be in

| Longitude, | 137° 27½' |
| Mount Young bore, | N. 11 E. |

Middle Mount,	N. 62½ W.
Low western shore, extreme,	S. 21 W.
High eastern land, about the middle,	N. 71 E.

Having obtained the observations, we steered for the outermost of the northern hummocks, with soundings gradually increasing to 12 fathoms; but shoaling on a sudden to 7, upon coral, we hauled to the wind and tacked instantly; finding, however, that the depth did not further decrease, I let the ship go entirely round, and continued the former north-eastern course, with soundings from 7 to 9 fathoms.

At noon, the furthest hummock seen from the anchorage was distant four or five miles; it stands on a projection of low sandy land, and beyond it was another similar projection to which I gave the name of Point Lowly. This was the furthest visible part of the western shore; but the eastern land there approached within seven or eight miles, and extended northward, past it, in a chain of rugged mountains, at the further end of which was a remarkable peak. Our situation and bearings at this time were as follow:

Latitude, observed to the north and south,	33° 5' 14"
Longitude by time keepers,	137 41 1/3
Middle Mount,	S. 75 W.
Mount Young,	S. 87 W.
Point Lowly, the extreme,	N. 43 E.
High peak on the eastern land,	N. 25 E.

Our prospect of a channel or strait, cutting off some considerable portion of Terra Australis, was lost, for it now appeared that the ship was entered into a gulph; but the width of the opening round Point Lowly left us a consolatory hope that it would terminate in a river of some importance. In steering for the point we came into 4 fathoms, but on hauling to the eastward found 8, although a dry sand-bank was seen in that direction. The depth afterwards diminished to 6, on which the course for Point Lowly was resumed; and we passed it at the distance of a mile and a half, in 9 fathoms water. Here the gulph was found to take a river-like form, but the eastern half of it was occupied by a dry, sandy spit and shoal water. We continued to steer upwards, before the wind; but as the width contracted rapidly, and there was much shoal water, it was under very easy sail, and with an anchor ready to be let go. At four o'clock, in attempting to steer close over to the western side, we came suddenly into 2½ fathoms; the ship was instantly veered to the eastward, and on the water deepening to 7, we let go the anchor and veered out a whole cable; for the wind blew a fresh gale right up the gulph, and between S. 4° W. and 30° E. there was no shelter from the land. At sunset a second anchor was dropped under foot.

We had reached near five leagues above Point Lowly, at the entrance of the narrow part of the gulph; but the shores were low on both sides, and abreast of the ship not so much as four miles asunder. At the back of the eastern shore was the ridge of mountains before mentioned, of which Mr. Westall made the sketch given in the Atlas (Plate XVII. View 10.); and the highest peak toward their northern extremity, afterwards called Mount Brown, bore N. 32° E. On the western side, upwards, there was moderately high, flat-topped land, whose eastern bluff bore N. 36° W., about three leagues, and there the head of the gulph had the appearance of terminating; but as the tide ran one mile an hour past the ship, we still flattered ourselves with the prospect of a longer course, and that it would end in a fresh-water river.

Wednesday 10 March 1802

Early on the following morning, Messrs. Brown, Bauer and Westall, with attendants, set off upon an excursion to the eastern mountains, intending, if possible, to ascend to the top of Mount Brown; and I went away in a cutter, accompanied by the surgeon, to explore the head of the gulph, taking with me Arnold's pocket time-keeper. After crossing the middle shoal, upon which we had 2½ fathoms in the ship, the water deepened to 10, but afterwards diminished to 2, on approaching the mangroves of the western side. Keeping then upwards, I had from 7 to 10 fathoms in the mid-channel, but found shoal water extending a mile, and sometimes more, from the shore and no possibility of landing until we came near the broad, flat-topped hill. From the eastern bluff of this hill, Mount Brown bore N. 62° 20' E., and Mount Arden, a peak nearly at the furthest extreme of the ridge, N. 18° 40' E.; and the inlet was seen to run in a serpentine form to the northward, between low banks covered with mangroves. After taking the bearings we returned to the boat and pursued our course upward along the western shore, having from 4 to 7 fathoms past the bluff; but the inlet was there less than two miles wide, and a league further on it was contracted to one mile, half of which, besides, was occupied by mud flats. These banks were frequented by ducks and other water fowl; and some time being occupied in chasing them, our distance above the ship was not so much as five leagues in a straight line, when the setting sun reminded us of looking out for a place of rest. A landing was effected with some difficulty amongst the mangroves on the eastern shore; and from a small eminence of red earth I set the ship's mast heads at S. 14° E., and Mount Brown N. 85° E.

Thursday 11 March 1802

Next morning we continued the examination upwards, carrying 4, 3, and 2 fathoms in mid-channel; but at ten o'clock our oars touched the mud on each side, and it was not possible to proceed further. I then landed and took observations in an artificial horizon for the time-keeper, which gave 4' 34" of longitude to the west of the ship, or only two seconds more than was deduced from the bearings. Mount Brown bore S. 72° E., Mount Arden N. 26° E., and my last station on the eminence of red earth S. 6° E. The inlet wholly terminated at one mile and a half to the N. 16° W.
It seemed remarkable, and was very mortifying, to find the water at the head of the gulph as salt nearly as at the ship; nevertheless it was evident that much fresh water was thrown into it in wet seasons, especially from the eastern mountains. The summits of the ridge lie from three to four leagues back from the water-side, but the greater part of that space seemed to be low, marshy land. To the northward no hill was visible, and to the westward but one small elevation of flat-topped land; all else in those directions was mangroves and salt swamps, and they seemed to be very extensive.
Two miles below the place where the observations for the time-keeper were taken was a small cliff of reddish clay on the western shore; and being near it on our return, when the sun was approaching the meridian, I landed to observe the latitude. It was 32° 27' 56" south, so that the termination of the gulph may be called in 32° 24½' without making a greater error than half a mile. Mount Brown bore from thence S. 80½° E., and its latitude will therefore be 32° 30¼' south; the longitude deduced from bearings and the time-keepers on board is 138° 0¾' east.
Our return to the ship was a good deal retarded by going after the black swans and ducks amongst the flats. The swans were all able to fly, and would not allow themselves to be approached; but some ducks of two or three different species were shot, and also several sea pies or red bills. Another set of bearings was taken on the western shore, and at ten in the evening we reached the ship, where Mr. Brown and his party had not been long arrived. The ascent of Mount Brown had proved to be very difficult, besides having to walk fifteen miles on a winding course before reaching the foot; by perseverance, however, they gained the top at five on the first evening, but were reduced to passing the night without water; nor was any found until they had descended some distance on the following day.
The view from the top of Mount Brown was very extensive, its elevation being not less than three thousand feet; but neither rivers nor lakes could be perceived, nor anything of the sea to the south-eastward. In almost every direction the eye traversed over an uninterruptedly flat, woody country; the sole exceptions being the ridge of mountains extending north and south, and the water of the gulph to the south-westward.
Mr. Brown found the stone of this ridge of craggy mountains to be argillaceous, similar to that of the flat-topped land where I had taken bearings on the west side of the inlet. It is reddish, smooth, close-grained, and rather heavy. Bushes and some small trees grown in the hollows of the rising hills; and between their feet and the mangrove swamps near the water there was some tolerably good though shallow soil.
We had seen fires upon the eastern shore opposite to Point Lowly on first entering the head of the gulph, and wherever I had landed there were traces of natives; Mr. Brown found them even to a considerable height up the side of the mountain; and it should therefore seem that the country here is as well inhabited as most parts of Terra Australis, but we had not the good fortune to meet with any of the people.
The observations taken by lieutenant Flinders fixed the position of the ship in latitude 32° 44' 41" south, and longitude by the time keepers 137° 49' 56" east. Twelve sets of distances of the sun and moon gave 137° 50' 9"; but these being all on one side, the time keepers are preferred. Azimuths observed from the binnacle, when the ship's head was between S. by E. and S. S. E., gave 0° 42' east, or 1° 37' east, nearly, for the true variation; and there was no particular attraction upon the theodolite at any of my stations on shore.
We had two flood tides in the day setting past the ship, and they ran at the strongest one mile and a half per hour; the rise appeared to be from six to eight feet, and high water to take place at two hours and a half after the moon passed the meridian. Except in the time of high water, which is considerably later than at Thorny Passage, the tides at the head have a near affinity to those at the entrance of the gulph; whence the great differences at Port Lincoln, intermediately situate, become so much the more extraordinary.

Saturday 13 March 1802

Nothing of particular interest having presented itself to detain us at the head of the gulph, we got under way in the morning of the 13th, having a light breeze from the north-westward. The western shore had been followed in going up, and for that reason I proposed to keep close to the east side in returning; but before eight o'clock the water shoaled suddenly from 4 to 2 fathoms, and the ship hung upon a mud bank covered with grass, two or three miles from the shore. A kedge anchor was carried out astern; and in half an hour we again made sail downward, in soundings from 5 to 10 fathoms near the edge of the shoal.

At noon, latitude observed to the N. and S.	32° 57' 6"
Mount Brown bore	N. 9 30 E.
Pt. Lowly south extreme dist. 7 miles,	S. 79 0 W.

The depth was then 7 fathoms; but there were banks ahead, extending to a great distance from the eastern shore, and in steering westward to pass round them, we had 3½ fathoms for the least water. It afterwards deepened to 7, and we again steered southward, but were not able to get near the land; on the contrary, the shallow water forced us further off as we proceeded. The wind was at west-southwest in the evening; and this not permitting us to lie along the edge of the bank, we came to an anchor in 7 fathoms, soft bottom; being then above four leagues from the eastern low shore, although there was only 3½ fathoms at less than a mile nearer in.

Mount Brown bore	N. 21° E.
Barn Hill,	S. 43 E.
Mount Young,	N. 66 W.

Sunday 14 March 1802

In the morning we followed the line of the great eastern shoal, and its direction permitted us to approach nearer to the land, with soundings between 8 and 4 fathoms. A little before noon, after running half an hour in less than 4 fathoms and getting within about six miles of the land, we were obliged to tack and stretch off, the wind having veered to the south-west. Our situation twenty minutes afterward, was in

Latitude, observed to the north and south,	33° 23' 49"
Longitude by time keepers,	137 47
Mount Young bore	N. 38 W.
Middle Mount, west side of the gulph,	N. 66 W.
Barn Hill, on the east side,	S. 60 E.

We beat to windward all the afternoon, and at sunset anchored in 3½ fathoms near the edge of the great bank and seven or eight miles from the land. The shore was low and sandy, but there was a ridge of hills behind it nearly similar to that on the west side of the gulph. Barn Hill lies at the back of this ridge and about twelve miles from the water; and towards the southern end of the ridge was another hill, also some distance inland, of which I shall have occasion to speak hereafter. A middle mount on the west side of the gulph, higher and further back than the one before set, was in sight from this anchorage; and the bearings taken were these:

Middle back mount,	N. 61° W.
Barn Hill on the east side,	S. 74 E.
A more southern hill,	S. 38 E.

Mount Br own was no longer visible; but it had been seen this afternoon at the distance of fifty-eight miles, and was sufficiently above the horizon to have been distinguished some miles further from a ship's deck in a perfectly clear day.

Monday 15 March 1802

On the morning of the 15th the wind had shifted to south-east; and the great bank then trending south-westward, we followed it with variable soundings between 3 and 10 fathoms. At ten o'clock the water had deepened to 15; and being then nearer to the west than to the east side of the gulph, and the wind having come more ahead, we tacked to the east-south-east; but in fifty minutes were obliged to steer westward again, having fallen into 3 fathoms on the edge of the bank. This is the narrowest part of the gulph below Point Lowly, the two shores being scarcely more than twenty miles asunder; and of this space, the great eastern bank, if the part where we last had 3 fathoms be connected with it, occupies about eleven, and the shallow water of the west side one or two miles. The soundings we had in stretching westward across the deep channel were, from the shoal, 3, 5, 7, 10, 12, 12, 12, 10, 9, 8, 7, 6, 7, 6, 5 fathoms, at nearly equal distances asunder, and the last at six miles from the western land.

After sounding across the channel we stood back, lying up south-east, and reached within five miles of the eastern shore, where the anchor was dropped in 4½ fathoms; Barn Hill bearing N. 69° E., and a cliffy projection, named Point Riley after the gentleman of that name in the Admiralty, S. 14° W., two or three leagues. This point was the furthest visible part of the eastern shore; and so low and uniform had the coast been from the head of the gulph, that this was the first mark I had found upon it for the survey. The great eastern bank, which we had already followed about sixty miles, seemed to terminate at Point Riley; and from thence southward the gulph greatly enlarges its breadth. The situation of the point is about 33° 53' south and 137° 30' E.

Tuesday 16 March 1802

We got under way at six in the morning, and the wind being from the south-eastward made a good stretch along the coast until noon. A patch of breakers then lay five miles to the south-east; but the land was ten miles distant, and some white sandy cliffs, four or five leagues from Point Riley, bore S. 52° E. The intermediate coast, as also that which extends several leagues to the north of the point, is low and sandy; but at a few miles back it rises to a level land of moderate elevation, and is not ill clothed with small trees. In the afternoon we had to beat against a southern wind; and the coast in that part being too open for anchorage, this was continued all night and the next morning [WEDNESDAY 17 MARCH 1802]; but with so little profit that the same land was still in sight at noon, and our situation found to be as follows

Latitude, observed to the north and south,	34° 15' 24"
Longitude by time keepers,	137 24½
North extreme near the sandy cliffs, dist. 6 miles,	N. 19 E.
Low red cliffs, south end dist. 6 or 7 miles,	S. 54 E.

At six in the evening, the reddish cliffs were brought to bear N. 44° E., and a long point, or an island lying off a point, bore S. 43° W. two leagues. Our distance from a cliffy islet, close under the shore, was two or three miles, but the breakers from it were only half a mile off, and the depth was 4 fathoms.

Thursday 18 March 1802

On the 18th, in the morning, we fetched to windward of the island-like point, to which I gave the name of Point Pearce, in compliment to Mr. Pearce of the Admiralty. Its latitude is 34° 28½' south and longitude 137° 21' east. On the south side of this point or island, for I could not fully ascertain its connection, the shore falls back seven or eight miles to the east, and then trends southward. It is low and very sandy, but rises gradually to a level country of the same description as that near Point Riley. At sunset the land was seen as far as south-west-by-south; and the wind favouring us a little, we made a stretch for it. A fire upon the shore served as a mark to steer by; and on approaching it at ten o'clock, the anchor was let go in 6 fathoms, upon a bottom of coarse sand and small stones, the weather being fine, and wind moderate off the land.

The howling of dogs was heard during the night, and at daylight [FRIDAY 19 MARCH 1802] the shore was found to be distant two or three miles, and was woody, rising land, but not of much elevation. A remarkable point, which I named Corny Point, bearing S 73° W. three miles, was the furthest land visible to the westward; its latitude, from meridian observations of Jupiter and the moon, is 34° 52' South, and longitude from the time-keepers 137° 6½' east. Between this point and Point Pearce, twenty-eight miles to the north-north-east, is a large bay, well sheltered from all southern winds, and none others seem to blow with much strength here. The land trends eastward about seven leagues, from Corny Point to the head of the bay; but what the depth of water may be there, or whether any fresh stream fall into it, I am not able to state; the land, however, was better wooded, and had a more fertile appearance than any before seen in the neighbourhood. I called this HARDWICKE BAY, in honour of the noble earl of that title.

Several observations for the variation of the compass had been taken whilst beating in the neighbourhood of Point Pearce. On its north side, eight miles from the shore, an amplitude with the ship's head S. W. by S. gave 4° 38' east; at

E. by N., when fourteen miles off, another gave 1° 13' east; but azimuths three or four miles nearer in, 0° 10' west; and at S. E., when six miles off, 0° 35' west. On the south side of Point Pearce, the head being S. S. W., and the land distant thirteen miles, an amplitude gave 3° 15' east. These different observations, which were all taken with the surveying compass, being corrected upon the principles and by the proportion explained in the Appendix No. II. to the second volume, will be respectively, 2° 51', 4° 21' furthest from the land, 2° 58', 1° 41' nearest the land, and 2° 1' east. The mean is 2° 46' east; which may be taken for the true variation at three or four leagues off Point Pearce in 1802; but close in with the shore, I suspect it was less by 1°, or perhaps 2°.

Having remained at anchor until the sun was high enough to admit of observations for the time keepers, we got under way at half past seven o'clock; and the coast round Corny Point being found to trend S. 27° W., nearly in the wind's eye, I stretched westward across the gulph towards Thistle's Island, in order to compare the time keepers with the longitudes of places before settled. Our latitude at noon, observed on both sides, was 34° 50' 10"; Spilsby Island, the south-eastern most of Sir Joseph Banks' Group, was seen bearing N. 56° W., and the eastern bluff of Wedge Island, the central and largest of Gambier's Isles, bore S. 16½° W. Gambier's Isles, four in number besides two peaked rocks, had been first seen from the high land behind Memory Cove. They lie nearly in the centre of the entrance to the gulph; and the latitude of Wedge Island is 35°11' south, and longitude 136° 29' east. Soon after four in the afternoon, I had the following bearings:

Wedge Island, highest part,	S. 21½° E.
Thistle's Island, highest part,	S. 29 W.
C. Catastrophe, former station on the S. E. point,	S. 53½ W.
Stamford Hill, former station at the top,	N. 86 W.
Sibsey Island, centre,	N. 33 W.
Stickney Island,	N. 11 W.
Spilsby Island,	N. 17½ E.

The longitude deduced from these bearings was 30° 22" east, from the head of Port Lincoln, and that resulting from observations for the time keepers taken in the same place, was 30° 53"; showing a difference of no more than 0' 31" to the east, since quitting the port. This quantity in a sea observation is so small and uncertain, that I considered the time keepers to have gone correctly from March 4, when the last observations in Port Lincoln had been made, up to this time; and that the lunar observations taken in the interval might be reduced back to the head of the port by their means, and used to fix its longitude without any further correction.

Besides the bearings above given, there was a rocky islet four miles distant in the S. 78° W.; part of a ledge of low rocks which extended towards the north end of Thistle's Island, and may possibly be connected with the rock set from thence. This ledge is marked dangerous, in the particular chart.

Having satisfactorily ascertained the going of the time keepers, we tacked and stretched back for the coast on the east side of the gulph; but did not get sight of it before dark. At six on the following morning [SATURDAY 20 MARCH 1802],

Corny Point, dist. 5 or 6 leagues, bore	N. 63½° E.
A cliffy head, distant 10 miles,	S. 85 E.
Furthest extreme, a cliffy point,	S. 21 E.
Wedge Island, eastern bluff,	S. 49 W.
Thistle's Island, highest part,	West.

An amplitude taken when the ship's head was south-by-east, gave variation 1° 25' east, and azimuths at south-south-east, 1° 10': the mean, reduced to the meridian, is 2° 13' east, or a few minutes more than had been found on the west side of the gulph, and half a degree less than off Point Pearce.

The tide appeared to set us along the shore to the southward, although, from what was observed at Thistle's Island, it should have been the time of flood. With its assistance, and the wind having become less unfavourable, we were enabled to make a course for the furthest land. This proved to be a cape, composed of three cliffy points, near the northern part of which lay a cluster of black rocks. The southernmost cliff bore at noon E. 4½° S. six or seven miles, and beyond it there was no main coast visible; but three small islands, with several rocks and a reef, were seen to lie as far as five miles to the southward, out from the cape.

Although the continuation of the main coast was not to be distinguished beyond the cape, yet there was land in sight at the distance of seven or eight leagues, from about south to S. 18½° W. Whether this land were an island or a part of the continent, and the wide opening to the eastward a strait or a new inlet, was uncertain; but in either case, the investigation of the gulph was terminated; and in honour of the respectable nobleman who presided at the Board of

Admiralty when the voyage was planned and ship put into commission, I named it SPENCER'S GULPH. The cliffy-pointed cape which forms the east side of the entrance, and lies in 35° 18' south and 136° 55' east, was named CAPE SPENCER; and the three isles lying off it, with their rocks, Althorp Isles.

A line drawn from the nearest part of Cape Catastrophe to Cape Spencer will be forty-eight miles long, and so much is the entrance of the gulph in width. Gambier's Isles lie not far from the middle of the line; and if we measure upward from them, the gulph will be found, without regard to the small windings, to extend one hundred and eighty-five miles into the interior of the country. For the general exactness of its form in the chart I can answer with tolerable confidence, having seen all that is laid down, and, as usual, taken every angle which enters into the construction. Throughout the whole extent of the shores the water line was almost every where distinguished; the only exceptions being small portions at the head of Hardwicke and Louth Bays, of a bight near Point Lowly, and of the low land at the back of the great Eastern Shoal.

At noon, when off Cape Spencer, the wind became variable and light, with very hazy, cloudy weather; and the mercury in my marine barometer had fallen two-tenths of an inch. At six in the evening a breeze sprung up at west-north-west; and as I expected a gale would come on, and that as usual it would veer to the south-west, we ceased to follow the coast beyond Cape Spencer, and steered for the land seen in the southern quarter. The Althorp Isles were passed at eight o'clock, at the distance of eight or nine miles; and the wind being fresh at west, we made short trips during the night between the two lands, not knowing what might be in the space to leeward. At daylight [SUNDAY 21 MARCH 1802] the ship was nearly in mid-channel, between the southern land and Cape Spencer, and nothing was seen to the eastward. It then blew a fresh gale at south-west, with much sea running; we stretched south-west under close-reefed top-sails, to get under the lee of the southern land; and at eight o'clock, when the largest Althorp Isle bore N. 32° W., it was distant six or seven miles to the south, and extended from S. 61° W. to 79° E. as far as the eye could reach. It was rather high and cliffy; but there was nothing by which to judge of its connection with the main.

At ten o'clock we were close under the land; and finding the water tolerably smooth, had shortened sail with the intention of anchoring near a small, sandy beach; but the situation proving to be too much exposed, we steered eastward along the shore under two close-reefed topsails and fore-sail, the wind blowing strong in squalls from the south-west. The furthest land seen ahead at noon was a projecting point, lower than the other cliffs; it bore E. 7° S., four leagues, and and lies in 35° 33' south and 137° 41' east. It was named Point Marsden, in compliment to the second secretary of the Admiralty; and beyond it the coast was found to trend southward into a large bay containing three coves, any one of which promised good shelter from the gale. This was called NEPEAN BAY. in compliment to the first secretary (now Sir Evan Nepean, Bart.), and we hauled up for it; but the strength of the wind was such that a headland forming the east side of the bay was fetched with difficulty. At six in the evening we came to anchor in 9 fathoms, sandy bottom, within a mile of the shore; the east extreme bearing S. 76° E., and the land near Point Marsden, on the west side of Nepean Bay, N. 61° W., six leagues. A piece of high land, seemingly unconnected, bore from N. 45° to 78° E.; but no land could be distinguished to the northward.

Neither smokes nor other marks of inhabitants had as yet been perceived upon the southern land, although we had passed along seventy miles of its coast. It was too late to go on shore this evening; but every glass in the ship was pointed there, to see what could be discovered. Several black lumps, like rocks, were pretended to have been seen in motion by some of the young gentlemen, which caused the force of their imaginations to be much admired; next morning [MONDAY 22 MARCH 1802], however, on going toward the shore, a number of dark-brown kangaroos were seen feeding upon a grass-plat by the side of the wood and our landing gave them no disturbance. I had with me a double-barrelled gun, fitted with a bayonet, and the gentlemen my companions had muskets. It would be difficult to guess how many kangaroos were seen; but I killed ten, and the rest of the party made up the number to thirty-one, taken on board in the course of the day; the least of them weighing sixty-nine, and the largest one hundred and twenty-five pounds. These kangaroos had much resemblance to the large species found in the forest lands of New South Wales, except that their colour was darker, and they were not wholly destitute of fat.

After this butchery, for the poor animals suffered themselves to be shot in the eyes with small shot, and in some cases to be knocked on the head with sticks, I scrambled with difficulty through the brushwood, and over fallen trees, to reach the higher land with the surveying instruments; but the thickness and height of the wood prevented anything else from being distinguished. There was little doubt, however, that this extensive piece of land was separated from the continent; for the extraordinary tameness of the kangaroos and the presence of seals upon the shore concurred with the absence of all traces of men to show that it was not inhabited.

South Coast. Kangaroo Island.

The whole ship's company was employed this afternoon in skinning and cleaning the kangaroos; and a delightful regale they afforded, after four months' privation from almost any fresh provisions. Half a hundred weight of heads, forequarters and tails were stewed down into soup for dinner on this and the succeeding days; and as much steaks given, moreover, to both officers and men as they could consume by day and by night. In gratitude for so seasonable a supply I named this southern land KANGAROO ISLAND.

Tuesday 23 March 1802

Next day was employed in shifting the topmasts on account of some rents found in the heels. The scientific gentlemen landed again to examine the natural productions of the island, and in the evening eleven more kangaroos were brought on board; but most of these were smaller, and seemed to be of a different species to those of the preceding day. Some of the party saw several large running birds; which, according to their description, seemed to have been the emu or cassowary.

Not being able to obtain a distinct view from any elevated situation, I took a set of angles from a small projection near the ship, named Kangaroo Head; but nothing could be seen to the north, and the sole bearing of importance, more than had been taken on board, was that of a high hill at the extremity of the apparently unconnected land to the eastward: it bore N. 39° 10' E., and was named Mount Lofty. The nearest part of that land was a low point bearing N. 60° E. nine or ten miles; but the land immediately at the back was high, and its northern and southern extremes were cliffy. I named it CAPE JERVIS, and it was afterwards sketched by Mr. Westall. (Atlas Plate XVII. View 12.)

All the cliffs of Kangaroo Island seen to the west of the anchorage had the appearance of being calcareous, and the loose stones scattered over the surface of Kangaroo Head and the vicinity were of that substance; but the basis in this part seemed to be a brown slate, lying in strata nearly horizontal, and laminae of quartz were sometimes seen in the interstices. In some places the slate was split into pieces of a foot long, or more, like iron bars, and had a shining, ore-like appearance; and the strata were then further from the horizontal line than I observed them to be elsewhere.

A thick wood covered almost all that part of the island visible from the ship; but the trees in a vegetating state were not equal in size to the generality of those lying on the ground, nor to the dead trees standing upright. Those on the ground were so abundant that in ascending the higher land a considerable part of the walk was made upon them. They lay in all directions, and were nearly of the same size and in the same progress towards decay; from whence it would seem that they had not fallen from age, nor yet been thrown down in a gale of wind. Some general conflagration, and there were marks apparently of fire on many of them, is perhaps the sole cause which can be reasonably assigned; but whence came the woods on fire? That there were no inhabitants upon the island, and that the natives of the continent did not visit it, was demonstrated, if not by the want of all signs of such visit, yet by the tameness of the kangaroo, an animal which, on the continent, resembles the wild deer in timidity. Perhaps lightning might have been the cause, or possibly the friction of two dead trees in a strong wind; but it would be somewhat extraordinary that the same thing should have happened at Thistle's Island, Boston Island and at this place, and apparently about the same time. Can this part of Terra Australis have been visited before, unknown to the world? The French navigator, La Pérouse, was ordered to explore it, but there seems little probability that he ever passed Torres' Strait.

Some judgment may be formed of the epoch when these conflagrations happened from the magnitude of the growing trees; for they must have sprung up since that period. They were a species of eucalyptus, and being less than the fallen trees, had most probably not arrived at maturity; but the wood is hard and solid, and it may thence be supposed to grow slowly. With these considerations I should be inclined to fix the period at not less than ten, nor more than twenty years before our arrival. This brings us back to La Pérouse. He was in Botany Bay in the beginning of 1788; and if he did pass through Torres' Strait, and come round to this coast, as was his intention, it would probably be about the middle or latter end of that year, or between thirteen and fourteen years before the Investigator. My opinion is not favourable to this conjecture; but I have furnished all the data to enable the reader to form his own judgment upon the cause which might have prostrated the woods of these islands.

The soil of that part of Kangaroo Island examined by us was judged to be much superior to any before seen, either upon the south coast of the continent or upon the islands near it, with the exception of some portions behind the harbours of King George's Sound. The depth of the soil was not particularly ascertained; but from the thickness of the wood it cannot be very shallow. Some sand is mixed with the vegetable earth, but not in any great proportion; and I thought the soil superior to some of the land cultivated at Port Jackson, and to much of that in our stony counties in England.

Never perhaps had the dominion possessed here by the kangaroo been invaded before this time. The seal shared with it upon the shores, but they seemed to dwell amicably together. It not unfrequently happened that the report of a gun fired at a kangaroo near the beach brought out two or three bellowing seals from under bushes considerably further from the water-side. The seal, indeed, seemed to be much the most discerning animal of the two; for its actions bespoke a knowledge of our not being kangaroos, whereas the kangaroo not unfrequently appeared to consider us to be seals.

The latitude of the landing place near Kangaroo Head from an observation in the artificial horizon, was 35° 43' 0" south; and the longitude of our anchorage by timekeepers, 137° 58' 31" east. This last, being deduced from observations only four days after the proof had of the time keepers having gone correctly since leaving Port Lincoln, should be as accurate, or very nearly so, as the longitude of that port.

The variation observed from two compasses on board, with the head south-westward, was 6° 31' east; but when the ship swung to a tide coming from east-north-east, the change in the bearings of different objects showed the variation to be about 4° less. The true variation I deduce to be 4° 13' east; which is an increase upon what was observed on the west side of Cape Spencer, of 2°; although the distance be no more than twenty-four leagues, and the previous increase from Cape Catastrophe had been almost nothing. It seems probable that the existence of magnetic bodies in the land to the north-westward, and perhaps also in Kangaroo Island and Cape Jervis, was the cause of this change in the direction of the needle.

From appearances on the shore, I judged the rise of tide to be about six feet. The flood came from the east-north-east, twice in the day, and by the swinging of the ship, ceased at two hours and a half after the moon's passage; but the time of high water was afterwards found to be later by one hour and a half.

Chapter Eight

South Coast. Investigator's Strait.

Wednesday 24 March 1802

March 24 in the morning, we got under way from Kangaroo Island in order to take up the examination of the main coast at Cape Spencer, where it had been quitted in the evening of the 20th, when the late gale commenced. The wind had continued to blow fresh from the southward, but had now moderated, and was at south-west. We steered north-westward from ten o'clock till six in the evening, and then had sight of land extending from N. 62° W. to a low part terminating at N. 17° E. distant three leagues. A hummock upon this low part was named Troubridge Hill, and at first it makes like an island. Nothing was visible to the eastward of the low land; whence I judged there to be another inlet or a strait between it and Cape Jervis. Soon after dusk the wind veered to south-by-east, on which we steered south-westward, and continued the same course until four in the morning [THURSDAY 25 MARCH 1802]; when the largest Althorp Isle being seen to the north-west, the ship was hove to, with her head eastward; and at daylight, before making sail, the following bearings were taken of the lands to the northward, but no part of Kangaroo Island was visible.

Wedge I. (of Gambier's Isles), highest part,	N. 64½° W.
Althorpe Isle, largest, distant 6 miles,	N. 83° to 78 W.
Cape Spencer, south point,	N. 44 W.
Furthest extreme of the northern land,	N. 44 E.

The wind fixed itself at south-east, and it took us two days to work back against it as far as Troubridge Hill [SATURDAY 27 MARCH 1802]. The shore is generally low and sandy; but with the exception of one very low point, it may be approached within two miles. Many tacks were made in these two days from the northern land across to Kangaroo Island, and gave opportunities of sounding the intermediate strait. From 45 fathoms, in the middle of the western entrance, the depth diminished quickly to 25, then more slowly to 20 after which it is irregular between 12 and 20 fathoms, as far as the mouth of the second inlet. Of the two sides, that of Kangaroo Island is much the deepest; but there is no danger in any part to prevent a ship passing through the strait with perfect confidence, and the average width is twenty-three miles. It was named INVESTIGATOR'S STRAIT, after the ship. The bottom is mostly broken shells, mixed with sand, gravel or coral, and appeared to hold well.

From two amplitudes taken to the north-north-west of Point Marsden, and near the middle of the strait, the variation was 1° 49' east; the ship's head being south-south-east in one case, and north-east-by-north in the other. The true variation deduced from these, is 3° 20' east; which is 1° 7' greater than at Cape Spencer, and 0° 53' less than at the anchorage near Kangaroo Head.

At noon of the 27th, the eastern wind died away; and we dropped a kedge anchor in 15 fathoms, about two miles from Point Marsden, where the following observations and bearings were taken.

Latitude, observed to the north,	35° 31' 38"

Longitude by time keepers,	137 42
Kangaroo I., furthest western extreme,	S. 82 W.
do., Point Marsden, west side,	S. 26 W.
do., innermost head up Nepean Bay,	S. 27 E.
do., furthest eastern extreme,	S. 57½ E.
Cape Jervis, south extreme,	S. 73 E.

No set of tide was observable until three o'clock, when it made gently to the north-east, towards the new inlet; and a breeze springing up at south-east soon afterward, we pursued the same course, and were well within the entrance at eight o'clock. Fires were seen ahead; but the soundings being regular, and increasing, we kept on until midnight; when the land was seen also, and we stood back for two hours. At daylight [SUNDAY 28 MARCH 1802] I recognised Mount Lofty, upon the highest part of the ridge of mountains which, from Cape Jervis, extends northward behind the eastern shore of the inlet. The nearest part of the coast was distant three leagues, mostly low, and composed of sand and rock, with a few small trees scattered over it; but at a few miles inland, where the back mountains rise, the country was well clothed with forest timber, and had a fertile appearance. The fires bespoke this to be a part of the continent.

Light airs and calms prevailed during the morning, and the ship had very little way until noon, when a breeze sprung up at south-west. Our situation was then in

Latitude, observed to the north and south,	35° 4' 13"
Longitude by time keepers,	138 23
Mount Lofty bore	N. 71 E.
Southern extreme toward Cape Jervis,	S. 17 W.
Northern extreme, trees above the water,	N. 32 E.

The situation of Mount Lofty was found from hence and from some other cross bearings, to be 34° 59' south and 138° 42' east. No land was visible so far to the north as where the trees appeared above the horizon, which showed the coast to be very low, and our soundings were fast decreasing. From noon to six o'clock we ran thirty miles to the northward, skirting a sandy shore at the distance of five, and thence to eight miles; the depth was then 5 fathoms, and we dropped the anchor upon a bottom of sand, mixed with pieces of dead coral.

Monday 29 March 1802

In the morning, land was seen to the westward, and also a hummocky mountain, capped with clouds, apparently near the head of the inlet. Azimuths with the surveying compass, taken when the ship's head was south-eastward, gave 2° 27' east variation; but an amplitude taken at the same anchorage on the preceding evening, when the head was south-by-west, showed 5° 22' east. These corrected to the meridian, will be severally 4° 43' and 4° 44' east; or half a degree more than was observed near Kangaroo Head. The observations at this anchorage and the bearings taken were as follow:

Latitude observed from the moon,	34° 36' S.
Longitude by time keepers,	138 18 E.
Mount Lofty,	S. 41½° E.
Nearest shore, distant 7 miles,	N. E. to N.
Hummock mount, highest top,	N. 12½ W.
Western land, furthest extremes,	N. 51° to S. 65 W.

There being almost no wind in the morning, we remained at anchor until nine o'clock, to set up afresh the rigging of the new top masts; and I took a boat to sound upon a rippling near the ship, but found the same depth of 5 fathoms. Very little progress was made until noon, at which time shoal water obliged us to steer westward. At three the soundings had increased from 3½ to 10 fathoms, which was the deepest water to be found; for it became shallower on approaching the western shore. After steering various northwardly courses, we anchored at sunset in 5 fathoms, sand, shells and broken coral; the shores then appeared to close round at the distance of seven or eight miles; and the absence of tide gave no prospect of finding any river at the head of the inlet.

According to lieutenant Flinders' observations, the situation of the anchorage was in

Latitude,	34° 16' 36"

Longitude by time keepers,	138 6
Mount Lofty, dist. 17 leagues, bore,	S. 35 E.
Hummock Mount, highest part,	N. 5 E.
A low sandy point, dist. 3 or 4, miles,	N. 69 E.
A low point covered with mangroves,	N. 53 W.

The variation from an amplitude, observed when the ship's head was south-eastward, was 2° 50' east; but the compass being upon a stand out of its usual place, I cannot deduce the true variation, but took it to be; 4° 40' east, nearly as found at the preceding anchorage.

Tuesday 30 March 1802

Early in the morning I went in a boat, accompanied by the naturalist, to examine more closely the head of the gulph. We carried from 4 to 3 fathoms water four miles above the ship, when it shoaled to fifteen and eight feet, which brought us to mud flats, nearly dry; but by means of a small channel amongst them we got within half a mile of the shore, and walked to it upon a bank of mud and sand.

It was then ten o'clock, and the tide was out; so that I judged the time of high water to be about seven hours after the moon's passage, or three hours later than at Kangaroo Island; and the ordinary rise appeared to be six or eight feet. An observation of the sun's meridian altitude from the artificial horizon showed the landing-place to be in latitude 34° 8' 52", and the uppermost water might be 30" less; whence the extent of this inlet, from Cape Jervis on the east side of the entrance, is 1° 30' of latitude.

Microscopic shells of various kinds, not larger than grains of wheat, were heaped up in ridges at high-water mark; further back the shore was sandy, but soon rose, in an undulating manner, to hills covered with grass; and several clumps of trees scattered over them gave the land a pleasing appearance from the water side. We set off in the afternoon for the Hummock Mount, which stands upon a northern prolongation of the hills on the west side of the inlet, and about eight miles from the water; but finding it could not be reached in time to admit of returning on board the same evening, I ascended a nearer part of the range to inspect the head of the inlet. It was almost wholly occupied by flats, which seemed to be sandy in the eastern part and muddy to the westward. These flats abounded with rays; and had we been provided with a harpoon, a boat load might have been caught. One black swan and several shags and gulls were seen.

I found the grass upon these pleasant-looking hills to be thinly set, the trees small, and the land poor in vegetable soil. The mountainous ridge on the east side of the inlet passes within a few miles of Hummock Mount, and appeared to be more sandy; but the wood upon it was abundant, and of a larger growth. Between the two ranges is a broad valley, swampy at the bottom; and into it the water runs down from both sides in rainy weather, and is discharged into the gulph, which may be considered as the lower and wider part of the valley.

This eastern ridge is the same which rises at Cape Jervis; from whence it extends northward towards Barn Hill and the ridge of mountains on the east side of Spencer's Gulph. If it joins that ridge, as I strongly suspect, its length, taking it only from Cape Jervis to Mount Arden, will be more than seventy leagues in a straight line. There are some considerable elevations on the southern part; Mount Lofty is one of them, and its height appeared nearly equal to that of Mount Brown to the north, or about three thousand feet. Another lies six or seven miles to the north-by-east of the Hummock Mount, near the head of this inlet, and seems to have been the hill set from Spencer's Gulph, at the anchorage of March 14, in the evening, when it was distant ten or eleven leagues and appeared above the lower range in front of Barn Hill.

From my station on the western hills of the new inlet, across to Spencer's Gulph, the distance was not more than thirty miles; but as I did not ascend the highest part of the range, the water to the westward could not be seen. Had the Hummock Mount been within my reach, its elevation of near fifteen hundred feet would probably have afforded an extensive view, both across the peninsula and of the country to the northward.

South Coast. Gulph of St. Vincent.

In honour of the noble admiral who presided at the Board of Admiralty when I sailed from England, and had continued to the voyage that countenance and protection of which Earl Spencer had set the example, I named this new inlet the GULPH OF ST. VINCENT. To the peninsula which separates it from Spencer's Gulph I have affixed the name of YORKE'S PENINSULA, in honour of the Right Honourable Charles Philip Yorke, who followed the steps of his above-mentioned predecessors at the Admiralty.

Wednesday 31 March 1802

On the 31st at daylight we got under way to proceed down the gulph, and having followed the eastern shore in going up, I wished to trace the coast of the peninsula in returning; but the wind being nearly at south, it could only be done partially. At two in the afternoon we tacked in 3 fathoms from the eastern shoals, and at sunset in the same depth one mile from the western side; our distance from the head of the gulph being then about ten leagues, and the furthest land of the peninsula bearing S. 3° E. The western hills come down nearly to the water-side here, and have the same pleasant appearance as at the head of the gulph, being grassy, with clumps of wood scattered over them; the coast-line is somewhat cliffy, and not so low as the eastern shore.

Thursday 1 April 1802

During the night the wind veered round to east, and at three in the morning to north-east; and a fire being seen on the eastern shore, the fore top sail was laid to the mast. At daybreak we made sail west for the land of the peninsula; and at half-past nine it was less than five miles distant, being very low and sandy. The northern extreme then in sight appeared to be the same land set in the evening at S. 3° E.; the other extreme was not far from Troubridge Hill, on the west side of the entrance to the gulph; and near it was an extensive bank, part of it dry, which I called Troubridge Shoal. The bearings taken at this time were,

Northern extreme of the west shore,	N. 2° E.
Southern extreme, distant 7 miles,	S. 42 W.
Troubridge Shoal, dry part	S. 13° W. to 9 E.
Cape Jervis, S. extreme of high land,	S. 18 E.
Mount Lofty,	N. 85 E.

We now hauled the wind to the south-east, and weathered the dry part of Troubridge Shoal; but passed amongst several patches of discoloured water in soundings from 4 to 3½ fathoms. At noon, when our latitude observed on both sides was 35° 9' 38" and longitude by time keepers 138° 4½', the shoal was distant three leagues to the west-north-west; Cape Jervis bore S. 12°, and Mount Lofty N. 72° E.

Our examination of the gulph of St. Vincent was now finished; and the country round it had appeared to be generally superior to that on the borders of Spencer's Gulph. Yorke's Peninsula between them is singular in its form, bearing some resemblance to a very ill-shaped leg and foot. The length of the southern part, from Cape Spencer to the sandy point near Troubridge Shoal, is about forty-five miles; and from thence northward, to where the peninsula joins the main land, about sixty miles. Its least breadth is from the head of Hardwicke Bay to the Investigator's Strait, where it appears to be not more than three leagues.

South Coast. Kangaroo Island

Having now made myself acquainted with the shores of the continent up to Cape Jervis, it remained to pursue the discovery further eastward; but I wished to ascertain previously whether any error had crept into the time-keepers' rates since leaving Kangaroo Island, and also to procure there a few more fresh meals for my ship's company. Our course was in consequence directed for the island, which was visible from aloft; but the winds being very feeble, we did not pass Kangaroo Head until eleven at night. I purposed to have run up into the eastern cove of Nepean Bay, but finding the water to shoal from 12 to 7 fathoms, did not think it safe to go further in the dark, and therefore dropped the anchor about three-quarters of a mile from the shore, and two miles to the south-west-by-west of our former anchorage.

Friday 2 April 1802

Early on the following morning a party was sent to shoot kangaroos, another to cut wood, and the naturalists went to pursue their researches. The observations taken by lieutenant Flinders, compared with those of March 24th, showed the timekeepers to have erred 2' 10" of longitude to the west in the nine days we had been absent; and they had not, consequently, lost quite so much upon a medium as the Port Lincoln rates supposed. This small error, which principally affected the Gulph of St. Vincent, has been corrected in the longitudes there specified and in the chart by an equal proportion.

The kangaroos were found to be less numerous than at the first anchoring place, and they had become shy, so that very few were killed. Those few being brought off, with a boat load of wood, we got under way at daylight next morning to prosecute the examination of the coast beyond Cape Jervis; but the timekeepers had stopped, from having been neglected to be wound up on the preceding day. We therefore came to an anchor again; and as some time would be required to fix new rates, the ship was moored so soon as the flood tide made. I landed immediately, to commence the necessary observations, and a party was established on shore, abreast of the ship, to cut more wood for the holds. Lieutenant Fowler was sent in the launch to the eastward, with a shooting party and such of the scientific gentlemen as chose to accompany him; and there being skins wanted for the service of the rigging, he was directed to kill some seals.

Sunday 4 April 1802

On the 4th I was accompanied by the naturalist in a boat expedition to the head of the large eastern cove of Nepean Bay; intending if possible to ascend a sandy eminence behind it, from which alone there was any hope of obtaining a view into the interior of the island, all the other hills being thickly covered with wood. On approaching the southwest corner of the cove, a small opening was found leading into a considerable piece of water; and by one of its branches we reached within little more than a mile of the desired sandy eminence. After I had observed the latitude 35° 50' 2" from an artificial horizon, we got through the wood without much difficulty, and at one o'clock reached the top of the eminence, to which was given the name of Prospect Hill. Instead of a view into the interior of the island, I was surprised to find the sea at not more than one and half or two miles to the southward. Two points of the coast towards the east end of the island bore S. 77° E., and the furthest part on the other side, a low point with breakers round it, bore S. 33° W., at the supposed distance of four or five leagues. Between these extremes a large bight in the south coast was formed; but it is entirely exposed to southern winds, and the shores are mostly cliffy. Mount Lofty, on the east side of the Gulph of St. Vincent, was visible from Prospect Hill at the distance of sixty-nine miles, and bore N. 40° 40' E.

The entrance of the piece of water at the head of Nepean Bay is less than half a mile in width, and mostly shallow; but there is a channel sufficiently deep for all boats near the western shore. After turning two low islets near the east point the water opens out, becomes deeper, and divides into two branches, each of two or three miles long. Boats can go to the head of the southern branch only at high water; the east branch appeared to be accessible at all times, but as a lead and line were neglected to be put into the boat, I had no opportunity of sounding. There are four small islands in the eastern branch; one of them is moderately high and woody, the others are grassy and lower; and upon two of these we found many young pelicans, unable to fly. Flocks of the old birds were sitting upon the beaches of the lagoon, and it appeared that the islands were their breeding-places; not only so, but from the number of skeletons and bones there scattered, it should seem that they had for ages been selected for the closing scene of their existence. Certainly none more likely to be free from disturbance of every kind could have been chosen than these islets in a hidden lagoon of an uninhabited island, situate upon an unknown coast near the antipodes of Europe; nor can anything be more consonant to the feelings, if pelicans have any, than quietly to resign their breath whilst surrounded by their progeny, and in the same spot where they first drew it. Alas for the pelicans! Their golden age is past; but it has much exceeded in duration that of man.

I named this piece of water Pelican Lagoon. It is also frequented by flocks of the pied shag, and by some ducks and gulls; and the shoals supplied us with a few oysters. The surrounding country is almost everywhere thickly covered with brushwood; and the soil appeared to be generally of a good quality, though not deep. Prospect Hill and the parts around it are more sandy; and there seemed to be swamps at the head of both branches of the lagoon. The isthmus which separates the southern branch from the sea is low, but rises gradually up the cliffs of the coast.

Not being able to return on board the same night, we slept near the entrance of the lagoon. It was high water by the shore, on the morning of the 5th [MONDAY 5 APRIL 1802], at six o'clock; but on comparing this with the swinging of the ship, it appeared that the tide had then been running more than an hour from the westward. The rise in the lagoon seemed to be from four to eight feet.

A few kangaroos had been obtained during my absence, as also some seal skins; but one of the sailors having attacked a large seal incautiously, received a very severe bite in the leg and was laid up. After all the researches now made in the island, it appeared that the kangaroos were much more numerous at our first landing-place, near Kangaroo Head, than elsewhere in the neighbourhood. That part of the island was clearer of wood than most others; and there were some small grass plats which seemed to be particularly attractive and were kept very bare. Not less than thirty emus or cassowaries were seen at different times; but it so happened that they were fired at only once, and that ineffectually. They were most commonly found near the longest of the small beaches to the eastward of Kangaroo Head, where some little drainings of water oozed from the rocks. It is possible that with much time and labour employed in digging, water might be procured there to supply a ship; and I am sorry to say that it was the sole place found by us where the hope of procuring fresh water could be entertained.

Having received on board a good stock of wood, the launch was hoisted in and every thing prepared for going to sea. Next morning [TUESDAY 6 APRIL 1802], so soon as the sun was sufficiently elevated to be observed in the artificial horizon, I landed to take the last set of observations for the time-keepers; after which the anchor was weighed, and we steered out of Nepean Bay with a light breeze from the south-west. Towards noon it fell calm, and finding by the land that the ship was set westward, an anchor was dropped nearly in our first place off Kangaroo Head; and Mr. Westall took the sketch given in the Atlas. (Atlas Plate XVII. View 11.)

View on the north side of Kangaroo Island

The rates of the time keepers were obtained, for the sake of expedition, from single altitudes of the sun's upper and lower limbs, taken from a quicksilver horizon with a sextant fixed on a stand; the time being noted from Arnold's watch, compared with Earnshaw's time keepers before going on shore and immediately after returning. From the altitudes of the 3rd, 4th, and 6th, in the morning, the rates of the two time keepers and their errors from mean Greenwich time, reduced to noon there on the last day, were as under.

Earnshaw's No. 543, fast 0h 0' 18.03" and losing 8.46" per day.
          No. 520, slow 0 45 29.66 and losing 18.07" per day.

In deducing these errors, the longitude given by the time keepers on our first arrival from Spencer's Gulph, which I consider to be equally good with that of Port Lincoln, was used, with a correction of -1' 20" for the change of place. The medium of the Port Lincoln rates was something greater than that now found; which corresponded with the time keepers having given the longitude of Kangaroo Head less on the second than on the first arrival. This was some proof that the letting down had not affected the rates, and tended to give me confidence in their accuracy.

The variation observed on shore, with the theodolite, was 5° 48' east.
Do. with azimuth compass, No. 1 with the theodolite, was 2° 58' east.

For this difference between the instruments, I find it difficult to account satisfactorily; but it is the same way, and nearly similar in quantity to what was observed in Lucky Bay. The true variation on board the ship, deduced from azimuths taken at anchor two miles to the north-east, and using the compasses No. 1 and 2, was as before mentioned, 4° 13', nearly the mean of the above; but the bearings taken with the theodolite at Kangaroo Head and Prospect Hill showed only 2½° east, as compared with the bearings on board the ship. There can be little doubt of the existence of magnetic substances in the lands about here, more particularly, as I think, in Yorke's Peninsula; and there will presently be occasion to notice more instances of their effect.

The approach of the winter season, and an apprehension that the discovery of the remaining unknown part of the South Coast might not be completed before a want of provisions would make it necessary to run for Port Jackson, prevented me from stopping a day longer at Kangaroo Island than was necessary to obtaining rates for the time-keepers, and consequently from examining the south and west parts of that island. The direction of the main coast and the inlets it might form were the most important points to be now ascertained; and the details of particular parts, which it would interfere too much with those objects to examine, were best referred to the second visit, directed by my instructions to be made to this coast. When, therefore, the rising of a breeze made it advisable to get under way from Kangaroo Head, which was not until two in the afternoon, we proceeded for the eastern outlet of the Investigator's Strait, in order to prosecute the discovery beyond Cape Jervis.

The wind was at south-east; and the tide being against us, but little progress was made until the evening, when it became favourable. Our soundings were irregular, and some rocky islets being seen without side of the opening, I stood in at nine o'clock, to look for anchorage at the east end of Kangaroo Island; and finding no shelter there, we ran a little to leeward into a small bay which I had observed before dark, and anchored at half past ten, in 4½ fathoms, on a bottom of hard sand. At daylight [WEDNESDAY 7 APRIL 1802], the following bearings were taken.

East point of the little bay, dist.	1½ mile, East.
West point, distant three miles,	N. 38° W.
Cape Jervis, inner low point,	N. 3 W.
Eastern extreme of the coast,	N. 65 E.

The bay is perfectly sheltered from all southern winds; and as there were several spots clear of wood near the beach, it is probable that the kangaroos, and perhaps cassowaries, might be numerous. We did not stop to land, but got under way so soon as the bearings were taken, to beat out of the strait against the south-east wind; so little was gained, however, after working all the day, that at eight in the evening the ship was still off the east end of Kangaroo Island. This part of the Investigator's Strait is not more, in the narrowest part, than seven miles across. It forms a private entrance, as it were, to the two gulphs; and I named it Back-stairs Passage. The small bay where we had anchored is called the Ante-chamber; and the cape which forms the eastern head of the bay and of Kangaroo Island, and lies in 35° 48' south and 138° 13' east, received the appellation of Cape Willoughby. Without side of the passage, and almost equidistant from both shores, there are three small, rocky islets near together, called the Pages, whose situation is in latitude 35° 46½' and longitude 138° 21' east; these are the sole dangers in Back-stairs Passage, and two of them are conspicuous. Our soundings in beating through were from 8 to 23 fathoms; and in a strong rippling of tide like breakers there was from 10 to 12, upon a bottom of stones and shells.

At eight in the evening we tacked from Cape Willoughby; and having passed to windward of the Pages, stretched on east and north-eastward until four in the morning [THURSDAY 8 APRIL 1802]. Land was then seen under the lee, and a tack made off shore till daylight, when we stood in with the wind at east-south-east. At nine the land was distant five miles, and of a very different aspect to that of Cape Jervis. As far as six leagues from the cliffy southern extremity of the Cape the land is high, rocky and much cut by gullies or ravines; a short, scrubby brush-wood covers the seaward side, and the stone appeared to be slaty, like the opposite cliffs of Kangaroo Island. But here the hills fall back from the sea, and the shore becomes very low with some hummocks of sand upon it; and the same description of coast prevailed as far as could be seen to the eastward.

Our situation at nine o'clock, when we tacked to the south, was as follows;

Longitude by time keepers,	138° 47½'
Cape Jervis, two southern parts, bore	S. 84 W.
A round hummock,	N. 85 W.
A rocky islet, under the land,	N. 62 W.
Furthest visible part of the sandy coast,	S. 87 E.

Before two in the afternoon we stretched eastward again, and at four a white rock was reported from aloft to be seen ahead. On approaching nearer it proved to be a ship standing towards us, and we cleared for action, in case of being attacked. The stranger was a heavy-looking ship, without any top-gallant masts up; and our colours being hoisted, she showed a French ensign, and afterwards an English jack forward, as we did a white flag. At half-past five, the land being then five miles distant to the north-eastward, I hove to, and learned, as the stranger passed to leeward with a free wind, that it was the French national ship Le Géographe, under the command of captain NICOLAS BAUDIN. We veered round as Le Géographe was passing, so as to keep our broadside to her, lest the flag of truce should be a deception; and having come to the wind on the other tack, a boat was hoisted out, and I went on board the French ship, which had also hove to.

As I did not understand French, Mr. Brown, the naturalist, went with me in the boat. We were received by an officer who pointed out the commander, and by him were conducted into the cabin. I requested captain Baudin to show me his passport from the Admiralty; and when it was found and I had perused it, offered mine from the French marine minister, but he put it back without inspection. He then informed me that he had spent some time in examining the south and east parts of Van Diemen's Land, where his geographical engineer, with the largest boat and a boat's crew, had been left, and probably lost. In Bass Strait captain Baudin had encountered a heavy gale, the same we had experienced in a less degree on March 21 in the Investigator's Strait. He was then separated from his consort, Le Naturaliste; but having since had fair winds and fine weather, he had explored the South Coast from Western Port to the place of our meeting without finding any river, inlet or other shelter which afforded anchorage. I inquired concerning a large island said to lie in the western entrance of Bass Strait; but he had not seen it, and seemed to doubt much of its existence.

Captain Baudin was communicative of his discoveries about Van Diemen's land; as also of his criticisms upon an English chart of Bass Strait published in 1800. He found great fault with the north side of the strait, but commended the form given to the south side and to the islands near it. On my pointing out a note upon the chart, explaining that the north side of the strait was seen only in an open boat by Mr. Bass, who had no good means of fixing either latitude or longitude, he appeared surprised, not having before paid attention to it. I told him that some other and more particular charts of the Strait and its neighbourhood had been since published; and that if he would keep company until next morning, I would bring him a copy, with a small memoir belonging to them. This was agreed to, and I returned with Mr. Brown to the Investigator.

It somewhat surprised me that captain Baudin made no enquiries concerning my business upon this unknown coast, but as he seemed more desirous of communicating information, I was happy to receive it; next morning [FRIDAY 9 APRIL 1802], however, he had become inquisitive, some of his officers having learned from my boat's crew that our object was also discovery. I then told him, generally, what our operations had been, particularly in the two gulphs, and the latitude to which I had ascended in the largest; explained the situation of Port Lincoln, where fresh water might be procured; showed him Cape Jervis, which was still in sight; and as a proof of the refreshments to be obtained at the large island opposite to it, pointed out the kangaroo-skin caps worn by my boat's crew, and told him the name I had affixed to the island in consequence. At parting the captain requested me to take care of his boat and people in case of meeting with them; and to say to Le Naturaliste that he should go to Port Jackson so soon as the bad weather set in. On my asking the name of the captain of Le Naturaliste, he bethought himself to ask mine; and finding it to be the same as the author of the chart which he had been criticising, expressed not a little surprise, but had the politeness to congratulate himself on meeting me.

The situation of the Investigator, when I hove to for the purpose of speaking captain Baudin, was 35° 40' south and 138° 58' east. No person was present at our conversations except Mr Brown; and they were mostly carried on in English, which the captain spoke so as to be understood. He gave me, besides what is related above, some information of his losses in men, separations from his consort, and of the improper season at which he was directed to explore this coast; as also a memorandum of some rocks he had met with, lying two leagues from the shore, in latitude 37° 1', and he spoke of them as being very dangerous.

I have been the more particular in detailing all that passed at this interview from a circumstance which it seems proper to explain and discuss in this place.

At the above situation of 35° 40' south and 138° 58' east, the discoveries made by captain Baudin upon the South Coast have their termination to the west; as mine in the Investigator have to the eastward. Yet Mons. Peron, naturalist in the French expedition, has laid a claim for his nation to the discovery of all the parts between Western Port in Bass Strait, and Nuyts' Archipelago; and this part of New South Wales is called Terre Napoléon. My Kangaroo Island, a name which they openly adopted in the expedition, has been converted at Paris into L'Isle Decrés; Spencer's Gulph is named Golfe Bonaparte; the Gulph of St. Vincent, Golfe Josephine; and so on along the whole coast to Cape Nuyts, not even the smallest island being left without some similar stamp of French discovery.[1]

It is said by M. Peron, and upon my authority too, that the Investigator had not been able to penetrate behind the Isles of St. Peter and St. Francis; and though he doth not say directly that no part of the before unknown coast was discovered by me, yet the whole tenor of his Chap. XV induces the reader to believe that I had done nothing which could interfere with the prior claim of the French.

Yet M. Peron was present afterwards at Port Jackson when I showed one of my charts of this coast to captain Baudin, and pointed out the limits of his discovery; and so far from any prior title being set up at that time to Kangaroo Island and the parts westward, the officers of the Géographe always spoke of them as belonging to the Investigator. The first lieutenant, Mons. Freycinet, even made use of the following odd expression, addressing himself to me in the house of governor King, and in the presence of one of his companions, I think Mons. Bonnefoy: "Captain, if we had not been kept so long picking up shells and catching butterflies at Van Diemen's Land, you would not have discovered the South Coast before us."

The English officers and respectable inhabitants then at Port Jackson can say if the prior discovery of these parts were not generally acknowledged; nay, I appeal to the French officers themselves, generally and individually, if such were not the case. How then came M. Peron to advance what was so contrary to truth? Was he a man destitute of all principle? My answer is, that I believe his candour to have been equal to his acknowledged abilities; and that what he wrote was from over-ruling authority, and smote him to the heart; he did not live to finish the second volume.

The motive for this aggression I do not pretend to explain. It may have originated in the desire to rival the British nation in the honour of completing the discovery of the globe; or be intended as the forerunner of a claim to the possession of the countries so said to have been first discovered by French navigators. Whatever may have been the object in view, the question, so far as I am concerned, must be left to the judgment of the world; and if succeeding French writers can see and admit the claims of other navigators as clearly and readily as a late most able man of that nation[2] has pointed out their own in some other instances, I shall not fear to leave it even to their decision.

Notes

[1] *The most remarkable passages on the subject are the following, under the title of Terre Napoléon.*
"De ce grand espace (the south coast of Terra Australis), la partie seule qui du Cap Leuwen s'étend aux îles St. Pierre et St. François, écoit connue lors de notre départ d'Europe. Découverte par les Hollandois en 1627, elle avoit été, dans ces derniers temps, visitée par VANCOUVER et surtout par DENTRECASTEAUX; mais ce dernier navigateur n'ayant pu lui-même s'avancer au-delà des îles St. Pierre et St. François, qui forment la limite orientale de la terre de Nuyts, et les Anglois n'ayant pas porté vers le Sud leurs recherches plus loin que le port Western, il en résultoit que toute la portion comprise entre ce dernier point et la terre de Nuyts étoit encore inconnue au moment où nous arrivions sur ces rivages." p. 316. That is on March 30, 1802. M. Peron should have said, not that the south coast from Western Port to Nuyts' Land was then unknown; but that it was unknown to them; for captain Grant of the Lady Nelson had discovered the eastern part, from Western Port to the longitude 140¼°, in the year 1800, before the French ships sailed from Europe; and on the west I had explored the coast and islands from Nuyts' land to Cape Jervis in 138° 10', and was, on the day specified, at the head of the Gulph of St. Vincent.
"Dans ce moment, le capitaine Anglois nous héla, en nous dernandant si nous n'étions pas l'un des deux vaisseaux partis de France pour faire des découvertes dans l'hemisphère Austral. Sur notre réponse affirmative, il fit aussitôt mettre une embarcation a la mer, et peu d'instans après nous le reçûmes à bord. Nous apprîmes que c'étoit le capitaine FLINDERS, celui-là même qui avoit déja fait la circonnavigation de la terre de Diémen; que son navire se nommoit the Investigator; que, parti d'Europe depuis huit mois dans le dessein de compléter la reconnoissance de la Nouvelle Hollande et des archipels du grand Océan équatorial, il se trouvoit, depuis environs trois mois, à la terre de Nuyts; que, contrarié par les vents, il n'avoit pu pénétrer, comme il en avoit eu le projet, derrière les îles St. Pierre et St. François; que, lors de son départ d'Angleterre," etc. p. 324, 325.
"En nous fournissant tous ces détails. M. FLINDERS se montra d'une grande réserve sur ses opérations particulières. Nous apprimes toutefois par quelques-uns de ses matelots, qu'il avoit eu beaucoup à souffrir de ces mêmes vents de la partie du Sud qui nous avoient êtê si favorables, et ce fut alors sur-tout que nous pûmes apprécier davantage toute la sagesse de nos propres instructions. Après avoir conversé plus d'une heure avec nous," (no person except Mr. Brown was present at my conversation with captain Baudin, as I have already said), *"le capitaine FLINDERS repartit pour son bord, promettant de revenir le lendemain matin nous apporter une carte particulière de la rivière Dalrymple, qu'il venait de publier en Angleterre. Il revint en effet, le 9 avril, nous la remettre, et bientôt après nous le quittâmes pour reprendre la suite de nos tra vaux géographiques." p. 325.*
"L'île principale de ce dernier groupe" (their Archipel Berthier) *"se dessine sous la forme d'un immense hamaçon."* (Thistle's Island seems to he here meant.) *"Indépendamment de toutes ces îles, il en existe encore plus de vingt autres disséminées aux environs de la pointe occidentale du golfe et en déhors de son entée: chacune d'elles fut désignée par un de ces noms honorables dont notre patrie s'enorgueillit à juste titre." p. 327.*
Voyage de Découverte aux Terres Australes, rédigé par M. F. Peron, Naturaliste de l'expédition, etc. Paris, 1807.]
[2] *M. DE FLEURIEU.*

Chapter Nine

South Coast. Encounter Bay

Friday 9 April 1802

I returned with Mr. Brown on board the Investigator at half past eight in the morning, and we then separated from Le Géographe; captain Baudin's course being directed to the north-west, and ours to the southward. We had lost ground during the night, and the wind was very feeble at east, so that the French ship was in sight at noon, and our situation was as follows:

Latitude observed,	35° 44'
Longitude by time keepers,	138 53
Cape Jervis bore	N. 82½ W.
Hummock at the east end of the high land,	N. 4½ E.
Nearest sandy hillock, dist. 3 or 4 leagues,	N. 65 E.

At the place where we tacked from the shore on the morning of the 8th, the high land of Cape Jervis had retreated from the waterside, the coast was become low and sandy, and its trending was north-east; but after running four or five leagues in that direction it curved round to the south-eastward, and thus formed a large bight or bay. The head of this bay was probably seen by captain Baudin in the afternoon; and in consequence of our meeting here, I distinguished it by the name of ENCOUNTER BAY. The succeeding part of the coast having been first discovered by the French navigator, I shall make use of the names in describing it which he or his country men have thought proper to apply; that is, so far as the volume published enables me to make them out; but this volume being unaccompanied with charts, and containing few latitudes and longitudes by which the capes and bays can be identified, I must be excused should any errors be committed in the nomenclature.

There was no wind from noon to two o'clock; and it appeared by the lead that the ship was drifted to the west-north-west, probably by a flood tide. On a breeze springing up from the southward we stretched in for the shore; and at six in the evening it was four miles distant, being sandy and generally very low; but there were several hillocks upon it high enough to be seen four or five leagues from a ship's deck, and one of them, more bluff than the rest, and nearly destitute of vegetation, bore N. 17° E. Next day [SATURDAY 10 APRIL 1802] at noon our situation was within three miles of the land, but very little advanced beyond that of the preceding day, our latitude being 35° 49 1/3', and the bluff hummock in sight bearing N. 22° W.

A tide or current setting along the shore appeared to retard us considerably, for at sunset we were not so much as two miles from the noon's place; the hummock then bore N. 25° W., and the furthest part of the coast south-east-by-east from the mast head.

An amplitude taken in the morning, with the ship's head west-by-south, gave 5° 11' east variation; and in the afternoon, when the land was only three miles distant and the head south-east, azimuths with the same compass gave 0° 50' west. These, corrected to the meridian in the mode I have adopted, will be severally 1° 57' and 1° 30' east; and the mean 1° 44'. The variation had therefore decreased considerably since leaving Kangaroo Island, contrary to the natural order; which proves that the quick increase on passing Yorke's Peninsula, was owing to some peculiar attraction, either in that or the neighbouring lands. Whilst beating through the Back-stairs Passage, I had observed an amplitude when the ship's head was south-south-west, which gave the extraordinary variation of 2° 41' east, or reduced to the meridian, 1° 27' east; although we were then not so much as four miles from the anchorage where it had been found 4° 13' east. Another amplitude was observed at eight leagues to the east of Cape Willoughby, when the head was north-east-half-east, and gave 2° 5' east variation, or reduced, 4° 36'. This last is correspondent with what was observed near Kangaroo Head and in the Gulph of St. Vincent; but the variation of 1° 27' in the passage is totally irregular, and must I think be ascribed to an attraction either in Cape Jervis to the north-east, or in the east end of Kangaroo Island to the south-east, or to both. When the great variation Of 4° 36' was obtained, both these lands were to the west; and when afterwards the 1° 57' and 1° 30' were observed, the nearest land was again to the eastward of the ship; and nearest in the last case.

The winds continued to be light and unfavourable; but by taking advantage of the changes in direction, and keeping further from the land, out of the tide or current, we had gained eight leagues by noon of the 11th [SUNDAY 11 APRIL 1802]. About twenty miles of coast beyond what had been set as the furthest extreme on the preceding day, was then in sight (Atlas Plate V.); and our situation and bearings were as follow:

Latitude by corrected log,	36° 11'
Longitude by time keepers.	139 29½
Northern extreme, from the mast head,	N. 10 E.
Nearest part, distant 7 or 8 miles,	N. 59 E.
A broad patch of white sand,	N. 78 E.
Southern extreme, from the mast head,	S. 66 E.

At one o'clock we bore away along the coast with a light breeze from the north-eastward; and having run five leagues, tacked to seaward soon after dark. Next morning [MONDAY 12 APRIL 1802] we again followed the coast at the distance of from five to three miles; and at noon a somewhat projecting part, which appears to be the Cape Bernouilli of the French navigators, was three or four miles distant to the east. Its latitude is 36° 33' and longitude 139° 51'; and about six miles to the south-south-east there are two low, black rocks lying close under the shore.

South Coast. Towards Cape Northumberland.

From Encounter Bay to this slight projection the coast is little else than a bank of sand, with a few hummocks on the top, partially covered with small vegetation; nor could anything in the interior country be distinguished above the bank. The shore runs waving between east-south-east and south-south-east; but to form what is called Cape Bernouilli it trends south, and then curves back south-eastward into a bight. The land then becomes better clothed with bushes and small trees; and it also differs from the more northern part in that some little risings of back land were visible.

Our soundings were more shallow along this part of the coast than before. The depth in passing Cape Bernouilli was from 8 to 12 fathoms; and on tacking out of the southern bight, at half past five in the evening, it was no more than 6, at three miles from the shore. We then saw land extending as far out as S. 29° W., which was the south head of the bight, and appears to be the Cape Jaffa of the French; but I do not find that they have given any name to the bight or bay, although much more deserving than some other sinuosities in the coast on which that honour is conferred.

This evening the variation from azimuths was 1° 25' east, taken when the ship's head was S. S. E. ½ E.; which being corrected upon the same principle as before, is 3° 0' east, and showed the variation to be now increasing, according to the regular order.

During the night, we worked up successfully against a south-south-east wind, for at six in the morning [TUESDAY 13 APRIL 1802] the low, outer extreme of Cape Jaffa bore N. 15° E., six or seven miles. The shore is sandy, but rises from the beach to a moderate elevation, and is then well clothed with small wood. About three leagues to the south of the cape is a cluster of low rocks, apparently the same of which captain Baudin had given me information; they do not, however, lie exactly in the situation expressed in his memorandum, and are not more than two miles from the land. We called them Baudin's Rocks; and since no name is applied to them in M. Peron's account of their voyage, the appelation is continued.

Four miles beyond the rocks is a point of moderate elevation; sandy, but mostly overspread with bushes. This is their Cape Lannes; and on its north side is a small bay, called the Baye de Rivoli, with a sandy shore and open to west winds. The bearings of these places, and our situation at noon, half an hour after tacking from Baudin's Rocks, were as under;

Latitude, observed to the north	37° 7¼'
Longitude by time keepers,	139 41
Cape Jaffa, extreme,	N. 2 E.
Baudin's Rocks, distant 3 miles,	N. 70 E.
Rivoli Bay, about the middle,	S. 72 E.
Cape Lannes, distant 4 or 5 miles,	S. 46 E.
Furthest extreme of the coast,	S. 38 E.

Wednesday 14 April 1802

For the last two days there had been a little current in our favour, and notwithstanding that the winds had been mostly adverse, we made some progress along the coast; but on opening out the land beyond Cape Lannes, the current took a northern direction, and at noon of this day we were no further advanced than to have that cape bearing N. 86° E. at the distance of nine or ten miles. The furthest part of the coast then visible was a peaked sandy hummock, bearing S. 68½° E. In the night, the wind came more off the land, and permitted us to make an advantageous tack to the southward; and at noon next day [THURSDAY 15 APRIL 1802], when we had reached in again with the coast, our situation was in

Latitude observed,	37° 23½'
Longitude by time keepers,	139 50
Cape Lannes, west extreme, bore	N. 13 W.
The peaked sandy hummock, dist. 5 miles,	N. 29 E.
Furthest extreme,	S. 59 E.

In the evening we got sight of a projecting and somewhat elevated part which lies ten leagues to the south-eastward of Cape Lannes, and appears to be the Cape Buffon of the French navigators. The intermediate coast is similar to that between Encounter Bay and Cape Bernouilli, with the sole difference that the hummocks upon the sandy bank are somewhat higher: nothing inland appeared above them.

The wind was again favourable in the night for making a long stretch to the southward; and it was prolonged to the next day at noon [FRIDAY 16 APRIL 1802], when our distance from the coast was judged to be ten leagues; but no part of it was in sight, and we had then got out of soundings, there being no bottom at 200 fathoms. The latitude was 37° 57' south, and longitude from six sets of distances of stars east and west of the moon, 139° 39', but by the time keepers corrected, 139° 45' east. Not more than seven or eight leagues from this situation, there should lie an island according to the account given by captain Turnbull of the Britannia south whaler, who saw it in his passage out to Port Jackson. Having thick weather at the time, he was not able to ascertain its latitude or longitude, otherwise than by the log; and as it was not in sight from our mast head, its position must be considered as very uncertain. The variations observed this day, with the same compass always on the binnacle, were as under:

By morning's amplitude, ship's head	S. E. by S. 2° 39' east.
By morning's azimuth, ship's head	S. S. E. 2 2
By evening's azimuth, ship's head	N. E. 2 2

The mean, reduced to the meridian, will be 4° 5' east. Nine leagues to the north, and half the distance nearer to the land, an amplitude had been taken with the ship's head in the meridian, which gave 4° 8' east.

On the three preceding days many tacks had been made from the shore, and I had frequently taken bearings just before the helm was put down; and so soon as the ship was round and the compass steady, they were again taken. Differences always took place; and without any exception the bearings required a greater allowance of variation to the right after tacking, when the head was westward, than before, when eastward; agreeing with the differences so frequently found in the azimuths and amplitudes, which had always been to show a greater east or less west variation when the head was on the west side of the meridian. The least average difference in any one of five sets of bearings was 5°, the greatest 6½°, and the mean 5° 54'; and according to the system adopted in correcting the variations, explained in the Appendix No. II. to the second volume, the mean difference arising from the five changes in the direction of the ship's head, should be 5° 33'.

The eastern wind died away at noon of the 16th, and the ship scarcely had steerage way until after midnight; a breeze then sprung up from the north-westward, and we steered north-east to make the land near Cape Buffon. At half-past seven [SATURDAY 17 APRIL 1802] the cape bore N. 1° W. seven miles, and was ascertained to be in nearly 37° 36' south and 140° 10' east. There is a bight in the coast on its north side where the land was not distinctly seen all round, owing probably to its being a low beach. At nine o'clock we bore away southward, keeping at the distance of two or three miles from the shore. It was the same kind of hummock-topped bank as before described; but a ridge of moderately high hills, terminated to the southward by a bluff, was visible over it, three or four leagues inland; and there was a reef of rocks lying in front of the shore. At noon, two larger rocks were seen at the southern end of the reef, and are those called by the French the Carpenters. They lie one or two miles from a sandy projection named by them Cape Boufflers; and here a prior title to discovery interferes.

On arriving at Port Jackson I learned, and so did captain Baudin, that this coast had been before visited. Lieutenant (now captain) James Grant, commander of His Majesty's brig Lady Nelson, saw the above projection, which he named Cape Banks, on Dec. 3, 1800; and followed the coast from thence through Bass Strait.[1] The same principle upon which I had adopted the names applied by the French navigators to the parts discovered by them will now guide me in making use of the appellations bestowed by captain Grant.

The termination to the west of that part of the South Coast discovered by captain Baudin in Le Géographe has been pointed out; and it seems proper to specify its commencement to the east, that the extent of his Terre Napoléon may be properly defined. The beginning of the land which, of all Europeans, was first seen by him, so far as is known, cannot be placed further to the south-east than Cape Buffon; for the land is laid down to the northward of it in captain Grant's chart, though indistinctly. The Terre Napoléon is therefore comprised between the latitudes 37° 36' and 35° 40' south, and the longitudes 140° 10' and 138° 58' east of Greenwich; making, with the windings, about fifty leagues of coast, in which, as captain Baudin truly observed, there is neither river, inlet nor place of shelter, nor does even the worst parts of Nuyts' Land exceed it in sterility.

At noon of the 17th we were in Latitude observed,	37° 47½'
Longitude by time keepers,	140 16½
Cape Buffon bore	N. 26 W.
Reef of rocks, (nearest part dist. 2½ miles)	N. 51° to S. 42 E.
Hills behind the coast,	N. 38 to N. 79 E.
Sandy hummock on West[2] Cape Banks	S. 44 E.

In the afternoon the wind veered to the southward, and we tacked from the shore, not being able to weather the Carpenters at the south end of the reef. A long swell rolled in at this time, and seemed to announce a gale from the southward, yet the wind died away in the night, and at daybreak [SUNDAY 18 APRIL 1802] a light breeze sprung up at north-west, and enabled us to close in with the land. We passed the Carpenters at the distance of four miles; but at two in the afternoon the wind again died away. A cliffy point, which proved to be the Cape Northumberland of captain Grant, was then in sight, as also were two inland mountains lying to the north-east; the nearest is his Mount Schanck, of a flat, table-like form; the further one, Mount Gambier, is peaked. The following bearings were taken whilst lying becalmed.

West C. Banks, sandy hummock, dist. 2 leagues,	N. 2° W.
Mount Schanck,	N. 70 E.
Cape Northumberland, dist. 3 or 4 leagues,	S. 82 E.

The long swell from the southward still prevailed, and the barometer was fast falling; but at seven in the evening a breeze sprung up once more from the north-west, and after stretching a little off from the shore, we laid to for the greater part of the night. At daylight [MONDAY 19 APRIL 1802] the wind was at north-north-west, and blew fresh, with squally weather. We reached in for the land; and at eight,

C. Northumberland, dist. 6 or 7 miles, bore	N. 32° W.
Mount Schanck,	N. 1 W.
Furthest extreme, obscured by haze,	S. 66 E.

Close to Cape Northumberland are two pointed rocks resembling the back fins of sharks; and on its eastern side were heavy breakers, extending more than a mile from the shore. The situation of the cape, as near as it could be ascertained, is in 38° 2' south and 140° 37½' east.
Beyond Cape Northumberland the coast was found to trend east-by-north, but curved afterwards to east-by-south; it was higher than we had lately seen and not so barren; nevertheless, the shrubs and small trees did not more than half cover the sandy surface. We pursued the round of the coast at the distance of four or five miles, having three reefs in the top-sails on account of the squally weather. At ten o'clock, in a clear interval, land was seen bearing S. 51° E.; and a thick squall with rain coming on, in which the wind shifted suddenly from north-north-west to south-west, we were forced to haul close up and let out the third reefs in order to weather the coast. A constant succession of rainy squalls prevented us from knowing how the land lay for some time, nor could an observation for the latitude be obtained; but at half-past noon our anxiety was relieved by distinguishing the furthest extreme, a bold, cliffy, cape, bearing S. 72½° E., broad on the lee bow.

South Coast. Off Cape Bridgewater.

This high projection was the Cape Bridgewater of captain Grant. A hill upon it slopes to the edge of the cliffs in which the cape is begirt toward the sea; and on the land side it descends so low that the connection of the hill with the main could not be clearly discerned. To the northward, and nearly in a line with the first, are two other hills almost equal to it in elevation. As we passed Cape Bridgewater, a second cliffy head opened at S. 73½° E., and a further round the last at N. 83° E. These are the Capes Nelson and Sir W. Grant, though differing considerably in relative position from what they are laid down in captain Grant's chart.
At two o'clock, the weather having become somewhat finer, I ventured to bear away along the coast; and presently a small island with two hummocks on it and a rock nearer to the shore were visible: these are Lawrence's Isles. The bearings of the land at four were,

C. Bridgewater, top of the hill, dist. 4 leagues,	N. 44° W.
Cape Nelson, the south-west extreme,	N. 21 W.
Cape Sir W. Grant, east part of the cliffs,	N. 12 E.
Lawrence's double Isle, dist. 3 leagues,	N. 25 E.

Before six we hauled the wind off shore; having set the double isle at N. 43° W., six or seven miles, and seen the land indistinctly as far as east-north-east.
During the night there were squalls of wind with hail and rain, but tolerably moderate weather in the intervals. At daylight [TUESDAY 20 APRIL 1802], we bore away for the land; and at half past seven, the

Hill on Cape Bridgewater bore	N. 66° W.
Lawrence's double isle,	N. 53 W.
A cliffy, flat-topped isle, west extreme,	N. 16 E.

This last is Lady Julia Percy's Isle; and when it bore N. 64° E. five miles, we steered eastward along the coast. At some distance inland, to the northward of Lady Percy's Isle, a round hill was distinguished; but the shore was scarcely perceptible through the squalls and haze: what little of it could be seen, appeared to be sandy and of moderate elevation. At eleven, the land was perceived to the eastward, and we hauled up east-south-east. Our latitude at noon, from an indifferent double altitude, was 38° 33½' and it is upon this uncertain observation, that the correctness of the neighbouring lands in the chart principally depend; I do not, therefore, specify here either the latitudes or longitudes. The coast was seen to leeward at times, and appeared to he moderately high; we ran along it at the distance of five, and from that to eight miles, clewing down the treble-reefed top sails occasionally, and setting them after the squalls were passed. At two o'clock, the land appeared to be trending south-east, which obliged us to haul up to the wind and take in close reefs; and the gale increasing, the fore and mizen top sails were handed.

It was seldom that the weather would allow of any thing being distinguished beyond two miles; and when the night came on we were quite uncertain of the trending of the coast. At eight o'clock, by favour of moon light and a short cessation of rain, land was perceived on the lee beam; it seemed to be a head of considerable elevation, and was judged to be from three to six miles off. The fore and mizen top-sails and reefed main-sail were immediately set, notwithstanding the danger to the masts; and there being much sea running, the ship was kept one point from the wind to make her go through the water. We had no chance of clearing the land on the other tack, and therefore our sole hope was that the coast might not trend any further to the southward.

Wednesday 21 April 1802

At two in the morning the strength of the gale obliged us to take in the fore and mizen top sails and main sail; and we had soundings in 45 fathoms, small stones. Our anxiety was great until daylight, when it was dissipated by not finding any land near us; and in the course of the morning the wind moderated, the barometer began to ascend, and the weather became even fine. Our latitude at noon was 39° 10½' and longitude 144° 22'; the last being 22' more than given by the log. High land was then visible astern, extending from about N. 50° to 17° W., at the supposed distance of twelve or fifteen leagues.

South Coast. Bass' Strait.

We were now entered into Bass' Strait; and the subsiding of the sea made me suspect that the large island, concerning which I had made inquiry of captain Baudin, was to windward. The south part of this island was discovered by Mr. Reid in a sealing expedition from Port Jackson; and before quitting New South Wales in 1799, I had received an account of its lying to the north-west of Hunter's Isles. It afterwards appeared that the northern part was seen in January 1801 by Mr. John Black, commander of the brig Harbinger, who gave to it the name of KING'S ISLAND.[3] Of this I was ignorant at the time; but since it was so very dangerous to explore the main coast with the present south-west wind, I was desirous of ascertaining the position of this island before going to Port Jackson, more especially as it had escaped the observation of Captain Baudin.

Our soundings in the afternoon, and until four in the morning [THURSDAY 22 APRIL 1802] when we tacked to the westward, were from 35 to 28 fathoms, sand and shells. At eight o'clock, land was seen to the south-west; and at noon our

Latitude observed was	39° 31¼'
Longitude by time keepers,	144 16
King's Island, south extreme, bore	S. 18 W.
King's Island, a middle hummock,	S. 37 W.
King's Island, northern extreme,	S. 74 W.
High main land from the mast head,	N. 23 W.

We tacked to the south-south-east at three o'clock, working up for King's Island, which was distant about five or six leagues directly to windward. In the night we lay up south, parallel with the east side of the island; but the soundings having diminished to 16 fathoms, I feared we might be approaching a reef of rocks lying off the south-east end, of which Mr. Reid had spoken. We therefore tacked to the northward at eleven o'clock; and after beating until three in the following afternoon [FRIDAY 23 APRIL 1802], got to an anchor in 9 fathoms, fine sand, under the north-east end of King's Island; the nearest part of the shore being distant a short half mile, and the extremes bearing S. 37° E. and N. 69° W.

A boat was immediately hoisted out, and I landed with the botanical gentlemen. On stepping out of the boat I shot one of those little bear-like quadrupeds called Womat; and another was afterwards killed. A seal, of a species different to any yet seen by us, was also procured; its phippers behind were double when compared to the common kinds of seal, and those forward were smaller, and placed nearer to the head; the hair was much shorter, and of a blueish, grey colour; the nose flat and broad; and the fat upon the animal was at least treble the usual quantity. I never saw the sea elephant, and possibly this might have been a young female; but there was no appearance of any trunk. A top-mast studding-sail boom, not much injured, was lying near the landing-place; and as I afterwards learned that the wreck of a vessel had been found upon the west side of the island, this boom had probably drifted from thence.

The north-east part of King's Island extends south-east-by-east, three or four leagues. The shore is mostly of sand, and behind the beach it was washed or blown up in great ridges, but partly overspread with a kind of dog grass which kept the sand together. In general the land is low; but some little eminences appeared at a distance, and at the north end of the island there is a short range of hills, moderately high and covered with wood. Granite seemed to be the basis of the shore where we landed. Behind the front ridges of sand was a brush wood, so thick as to be almost impenetrable; but whilst I was occupied in taking bearings, the botanists found some openings in the brush, and picked up so many plants as to make them desirous of a further examination. We returned on board at dusk, with our womats, the seal and a kangaroo; the last being of a middle size between the small species of the lesser islands and the large kind found at Kangaroo Island and on the continent. It appeared indeed, all along the South Coast, that the size of the kangaroo bore some proportion to the extent of land which it inhabited.

Saturday 24 April 1802

In the morning the wind blew fresh from the southward. A boat was sent on shore with Mr. Brown and his party; and at eleven o'clock, when they returned, we got under way.

A small lake of fresh water was found at a little distance behind the sandy ridges in front of the shore. This was surrounded by a good vegetable soil; and the number of plants, collected near it was greater than had before been found upon any one island. The small lake is too far from the sea side for a ship to obtain water from it conveniently; but two little streams which drained from the sand hills made it probable that fresh water might have been obtained anywhere at this time by digging. The water of these rills was tinged red, similar to that obtained at King George's Sound and to the pools I had before seen at Furneaux's Islands; and as the stone in these places is granite, and water so discoloured was not found any where else, it seems very probable that the discolouring arises from the granite and granitic sand.

Two more womats were killed this morning; and a skull was picked up which was thought to be of a small dog, but more probably was that of an opossum.

From the observations taken whilst beating up to the anchorage, the top of the highest hill at the north end of King's Island will be in latitude 39° 36½' south, and longitude 143° 54' east. The variation of the compass, taken on the binnacle with the ship's head at south, was 7° 59' east; but ten leagues to the eastward it was 11° 52', with the head west-south-west, or reduced to the meridian, 8° 43' east. The tides set one mile and a half an hour past the ship, northwest-by-west and south-east-by-east, nearly as the coast lies; that from the eastward running nearly eight hours, and turning about two hours after the moon had passed the meridian; but, which tide was the flood, or what the rise, we did not remain long enough to determine.

The time was fast approaching when it would be necessary to proceed to Port Jackson, both on account of the winter season, and from the want of some kinds of provisions. Before this took place I wished to finish as much of the South Coast as possible, and would have recommenced at Cape Bridgewater had the wind been favourable; but it still blew fresh from the southward, and all that part remained a lee shore. I determined, however, to run over to the high land we had seen on the north side of Bass' Strait, and to trace as much of the coast from thence eastward as the state of the weather and our remaining provisions could possibly allow.

In steering north-north-west from King's Island, two small isles were seen lying off the north-west side; the first opening from the northern extreme at S. 50°, and the second being clear of it at S. 36° W. These are the same which Mr. Black named New Year's Isles; and his Harbinger's Reefs were seen to extend, in patches, nearly two leagues from the north end of King's Islands; but there is, as I afterwards learned, one or more passages between the reefs, and another between them and the island.[4]

At three in the afternoon the northern land was in sight, and the highest hills of King's Island were sinking below the horizon as seen from the deck. Their distance was twenty-five miles; and consequently the elevation of them is between four and five hundred feet above the level of the sea. At five o'clock a bluff head, the most projecting part of the northern land, was distant three or four leagues; it was Captain Grants'

Cape Otway, and bore	N. 54° W.
The extremes of the land,	N. 58 W. to 23° E.

We then hauled to the wind and stood off and on; at daylight [SUNDAY 25 APRIL 1802] bore away for the land with a moderate breeze from the southward; and at eight o'clock, when Cape Otway bore N. 69° W. ten miles we steered north-eastward along the shore. On the west side of Cape Otway the coast falls back somewhat to the north, and projects again at the distance of ten or eleven miles, where it is not, as I think, more than three leagues to the east of the headland seen under the lee at eight in the evening of the 20th. From Cape Otway, eastward, the shore trends east-north-east about three leagues, to a projection called Cape Patton, and according to Captain Grant a bay is formed between them; but at three leagues off nothing worthy of being called a bay could be perceived. Beyond Cape Patton the coast took a more northern direction to a point with a flat-topped hill upon it, and further than this it was not visible.

The whole of this land is high, the elevation of the uppermost parts being not less than two thousand feet. The rising hills were covered with wood of a deep green foliage, and without any vacant spaces of rock or sand; so that I judged this part of the coast to exceed in fertility all that had yet fallen under observation.

Cape Otway lies very nearly in latitude 38° 51' south and longitude 143° 29' east. The width of the north-west entrance to Bass' Strait, between this cape on the north and King's Island to the south, is therefore sixteen leagues; and with the trifling exception of the Harbinger's Reefs, which occupy not quite two leagues of the southern part, the passage is free from danger. In such parts of it as we got soundings the depth was between 38 and 50 fathoms.

At noon, the wind had veered to the south-east, which being directly upon the shore, I did not think it prudent to follow the land too closely; and we therefore kept up nearly to the wind. In the course of the afternoon, land came in sight to the eastward; and the bearings taken at sunset were these:

Furthest extreme towards C. Otway,	S. 73° W.
Furthest connected part to the northward,	N. 18 W.
Two small distant peaks,	N. 1 W.
Bluff head, like the N. end of an island,	N. 63 E.
Extreme of the eastern land,	N. 83 E.

Between the first and last of these bearings there was a deep bight formed, at the head of which no other land than the two small peaks could be perceived.

Monday 26 April 1802

In the morning we kept close to an east-south-east wind, steering for the land to the north-eastward; and at nine o'clock captain Grant's Cape Schanck, the extreme of the preceding evening, was five leagues distant to the N. 88° E., and a rocky point towards the head of the bight bore N. 12° E. On coming within five miles of the shore at eleven o'clock we found it to be low, and mostly sandy, and that the bluff head which had been taken for the north end of an island was part of a ridge of hills rising at Cape Schanck. We then bore away westward in order to trace the land round the head of the deep bight; and a noon, the situation of the ship and principal bearings were as under:

Latitude observed,	38° 22'
Longitude by time keepers,	144 31½
Cape Schanck,	S. 68° E.
The rocky point, distant 6 or 7 miles,	N. 48 E.
Highest of two inland peaks,	N. 15 W.
A square-topped hill near the shore,	N. 28 W.
Extr. of the high land towards C. Otway,	S. 56 W.

On the west side of the rocky point there was a small opening, with breaking water across it; however, on advancing a little more westward the opening assumed a more interesting aspect, and I bore away to have a nearer view. A large extent of water presently became visible within side; and although the entrance seemed to be very narrow, and there were in it strong ripplings like breakers, I was induced to steer in at half-past one, the ship being close upon a wind and every man ready for tacking at a moment's warning. The soundings were irregular between 6 and 12 fathoms until we got four miles within the entrance, when they shoaled quick to 2¾. We then tacked; and having a strong tide in our favour, worked to the eastward between the shoal and the rocky point, with 12 fathoms for the deepest water.

In making the last stretch from the shoal the depth diminished from 10 fathoms quickly to 3, and before the ship could come round, the flood tide set her upon a mud bank and she stuck fast. A boat was lowered down to sound, and finding the deep water lie to the north-west, a kedge anchor was carried out; and having got the ship's head in that direction, the sails were filled and she drew off into 6 and 10 fathoms; and it being then dark, we came to an anchor.

South Coast. Port Phillip.

The extensive harbour we had thus unexpectedly found I supposed must be Western Port, although the narrowness of the entrance did by no means correspond with the width given to it by Mr. Bass. It was the information of captain Baudin, who had coasted along from thence with fine weather, and had found no inlet of any kind, which induced this supposition; and the very great extent of the place, agreeing with that of Western Port, was in confirmation of it. This, however, was not Western Port, as we found next morning [TUESDAY 27 APRIL 1802]; and I congratulated myself on having made a new and useful discovery; but here again I was in error. This place, as I afterwards learned at Port Jackson, had been discovered ten weeks before by lieutenant John Murray, who had succeeded captain Grant in the command of the Lady Nelson. He had given it the name of PORT PHILLIP, and to the rocky point on the east side of the entrance that of Point Nepean.

Our situation was found in the morning to be near two miles from the south shore, and the extreme towards Point Nepean bore N. 83° W., two leagues. About three miles to the north-by-west were some dry rocks, with bushes on them, surrounded with mud flats; and they appeared to form a part of the same shoal from which we had three times tacked in 2½ and 3 fathoms. The mud bank where the ship had grounded is distinct from the middle shoal; but I am not certain that it is so from the south shore, from which it is one mile distant. The Bluff Mount (named Arthur's Seat by Mr. Murray, from a supposed resemblance to the hill of that name near Edinburgh) bore S. 76° E.; but from thence the shore trended northward so far that the land at the head of the port could not be seen even from aloft. Before proceeding any higher with the ship I wished to gain some knowledge of the form and extent of this great piece of water; and Arthur's Seat being more than a thousand feet high and near the water-side, presented a favourable station for that purpose.

After breakfast I went away in a boat, accompanied by Mr. Brown and some other gentlemen, for the Seat. It was seven or eight miles from the ship; and in steering nearly a straight course for it we passed over the northern skirt of the shoal where the ship had touched; but afterwards had from 7 to 5 fathoms nearly to the shore. Having observed the latitude there from an artificial horizon, I ascended the hill; and to my surprise found the port so extensive, that even at this elevation its boundary to the northward could not be distinguished. The western shore extended from the entrance ten or eleven miles in a northern direction to the extremity of what, from its appearance, I called Indented Head; beyond it was a wide branch of the port leading to the westward, and I suspected might have a communication with the sea; for it was almost incredible that such a vast piece of water should not have a larger outlet than that through which we had come.

I took an extensive set of bearings from the clearest place to be found on the north-western, bluff part of the hill; and we afterwards walked a little way back upon the ridge. From thence another considerable piece of water was seen, at the distance of three or four leagues; it seemed to be mostly shallow; but as it appeared to have a communication with the sea to the south, I had no doubt of its being Mr. Bass's Western Port.

Arthur's Seat and the hills and vallies in its neighbourhood were generally well covered with wood; and the soil was superior to any upon the borders of the salt water which I have had an opportunity of examining in Terra Australis. There were many marks of natives, such as deserted fire-places and heaps of oyster shells; and upon the peninsula which forms the south side of the port a smoke was rising, but we did not see any of the people. Quantities of fine oysters were lying upon the beaches, between high and low water marks, and appeared to have been washed up by the surf; a circumstance which I do not recollect to have observed in any other part of this country.

Wednesday 28 April 1802

We returned on board at dusk in the evening; and at daylight the anchor was weighed with the intention of coasting round the port with the ship. The wind was at north-east, but the flood tide was in our favour; and having made a stretch toward the middle shoals, we tacked and ran east-south-east along their south side, until past eight, when, the flood having ceased, we came to in 7 fathoms. At slack water in the afternoon we again steered eastward, but were soon obliged to anchor for want of wind; and I found that this slow mode of proceeding was not at all suited to the little time for which we had provisions remaining, besides that there was much probability of getting frequently aground; the plan of examining the port with the ship was therefore abandoned.

Having left orders with Mr. Fowler, the first lieutenant, to take the ship back to the entrance, I went in a boat early next morning [THURSDAY 29 APRIL 1802] with provisions for three days, in order to explore as much of the port as could be done in that time. Round the east end of the middle shoals I carried 6 and 7 fathoms; and keeping north-eastward, had 8 and 9 fathoms at a mile or more from the shore, and 4 close past the second rocky point above Arthur's Seat. The wind being at north-west, I was obliged to land behind some rocks more than two miles short of the third point, but walked to it with my surveying instruments. This was nine miles from the Seat, and the furthest part of the shore seen from thence; further on the shore falls back more eastward, in long sandy beaches, and afterwards curves to the north-west; but it was lost to sight long before joining the land on the west side of the port. After taking angles and observing for the latitude and longitude, I rowed to windward for Indented Head, five leagues off. At the end of the first mile and a half the depth was 11 fathoms, but afterwards no bottom at 12 until within two miles of the western shore, where it was 9 fathoms. We landed at nine o'clock at night, near the uppermost part which had yet been seen.

Friday 30 April 1802

In the morning a fire was perceived two hundred yards from the tent; and the Indians appeared to have decamped from thence on our landing. Whilst I was taking angles from a low point at the north-easternmost part of Indented Head, a party of the inhabitants showed themselves about a mile from us; and on landing there we found a hut with a fire in it, but the people had disappeared, and carried off their effects. I left some strips of cloth, of their favourite red colour, hanging about the hut, and proceeded westward along the shore to examine the arm of the port running in that direction.

Three natives having made their appearance abreast of the boat, we again landed. They came to us without hesitation, received a shag and some trifling presents with pleasure, and parted with such of their arms as we wished to possess without reluctance. They afterwards followed us along the shore; and when I shot another bird, which hovered over the boat, and held it up to them, they ran down to the water-side and received it without expressing either surprise or distrust. Their knowledge of the effect of fire-arms I then attributed to their having seen me shoot birds when unconscious of being observed; but it had probably been learned from Mr. Murray.

At noon I landed to take an observation of the sun, which gave 38° 7' 6" for the latitude; my position being nearly at the northern extremity of Indented Head. Some bearings were taken from the brow of a hill a little way back; and after a dinner of which the natives partook, we left them on friendly terms to proceed westward in our examination. The water became very shallow abreast of a sandy point, whence the shore trends nearly south-west; and there being no appearance of an opening to the sea this way, I steered across the western arm, as well to ascertain its depth as with the intention of ascending the hills lying behind the northern shore. Two of the peaks upon these hills had been set from the ship's deck at sunset of the 25th, at the distance of thirty-seven miles; and as their elevation must consequently be a thousand feet, or more, I expected to obtain from thence such a view of the upper parts of the port as would render the coasting round it unnecessary.

The width of the western arm was found to be six miles; and the soundings across augmented regularly to 6 fathoms in mid channel, and then decreased in the same way; but there was less than 3 fathoms at two miles from the northern shore. That side is indeed very low and marshy, with mud banks lying along it; and we had difficulty in finding a dry place to pitch the tent, and still more to procure wood wherewith to cook the ducks I had shot upon the banks.

Saturday 1 May 1802

At day dawn I set off with three of the boat's crew for the highest part of the back hills called Station Peak. Our way was over a low plain, where the water appeared frequently to lodge; it was covered with small-bladed grass, but almost destitute of wood, and the soil was clayey and shallow. One or two miles before arriving at the feet of the hills we entered a wood where an emu and a kangaroo were seen at a distance; and the top of the peak was reached at ten o'clock. My position was then 21' of latitude from Point Nepean, in the direction of N. 28° 30' W., and I saw the water of the port as far as N. 75° E., at the distance of seven or eight leagues; so that the whole extent of the port, north and south, is at least thirty miles. The extremity of the western arm bore S. 15° 45' W., which makes the extent, east and west, to be thirty-six miles; but there was no communication with the sea on that side, nor did the western arm appear to be navigable beyond seven miles above where I had crossed it. Towards the interior there was a mountain bearing N. 11° E., eleven leagues distant; and so far the country was low, grassy and very slightly covered with wood, presenting great facility to a traveller of penetrating inland.

I left the ship's name on a scroll of paper, deposited in a small pile of stones upon the top of the peak; and at three in the afternoon reached the tent, much fatigued, having walked more than twenty miles without finding a drop of water. Mr. Lacy, the midshipman of the boat, had observed the latitude at the tent from an artificial horizon to be 38° 2' 22"; and Station Peak bore from thence N. 47° W.

In the evening we rowed back to Indented Head, and landed there soon after dark. Fires had been seen moving along the shore, but the people seemed to have fled; though we found two newly erected huts with fires in them, and utensils, which must have belonged to some of the people before seen, since there was boiled rice in one of the baskets. We took up our quarters here for the night, keeping a good watch; but nothing was seen of the Indians till we pushed off from the shore in the morning [SUNDAY 2 MAY 1802], when seven showed themselves upon a hill behind the huts. They ran down to examine their habitations, and finding every thing as they had left it, a little water excepted of which we were in want, they seemed satisfied; and for a short time three of them followed the boat.

Along the north-east and east sides of Indented Head I found the water to be shoal for nearly a mile off; but on approaching the entrance of what Mr. Murray called Swan Harbour, but which I have taken the liberty to converting into Swan Pond, it became somewhat deeper. Seeing swans there, I rowed into it after them, but found the place full of mud banks, and seldom more than three or four feet in depth. Three of the birds were caught; and at the south side of the entrance, upon the sandy peninsula, or island as it is when the tide is in, I shot some delicate teal, and found fresh water in small ponds.

The ship was lying about three miles within the mouth of the port, near to the south shore; and after I had taken bearings at two stations on the sandy peninsula, we steered a straight course for her, sounding all the way. It appeared that there was a passage up the port of a mile wide between the middle banks and the western shore, with a depth in it from 3 to 4½ fathoms. On the western extremity of the banks I had 2½ fathoms, and afterwards 5, 7, 4, 7, 8, 9, 9 to the ship.

Lieutenant Fowler had had a good deal of difficulty in getting back to the entrance of the port; owing in part to the western winds, and partly from the shoals, which do not seem to lie in any regular order. He had touched upon one of these, where there was ten feet on one side of the ship, and on the other 5 fathoms. This seems to have been a more eastern part of the same shoal upon which we had before grounded; but no danger is to be feared from these banks to a flat-floored ship.

I find it very difficult to speak in general terms of Port Phillip. On the one hand it is capable of receiving and sheltering a larger fleet of ships than ever yet went to sea; whilst on the other, the entrance, in its whole width, is scarcely two miles, and nearly half of it is occupied by the rocks lying off Point Nepean, and by shoals on the opposite side. The depth in the remaining part varies from 6 to 12 fathoms; and this irregularity causes the strong tides, especially when running against the wind, to make breakers, in which small vessels should be careful of engaging themselves; and when a ship has passed the entrance, the middle shoals are a great obstacle to a free passage up the port. These shoals are met with at four miles directly from the entrance, and extend about ten miles to the east-south-east, parallel with the south shore; they do not seem, however, to be one connected mass, for I believe there are two or three deep openings in them, though we had not time to make an examination.

No runs of fresh water were seen in any excursions; but Mr. Charles Grimes, surveyor-general of New South Wales, afterwards found several, and in particular a small river falling into the northern head of the port. Mr. Grimes was sent by governor King, in 1803, to walk round, and survey the harbour; and from his plan I have completed my chart of Port Phillip. The parts of the coast left unshaded are borrowed from him, and the soundings written at right angles are those of his companion, lieutenant Robbins.

The country surrounding Port Phillip has a pleasing, and in many parts a fertile appearance; and the sides of some of the hills and several of the vallies are fit for agricultural purposes. It is in great measure a grassy country, and capable of supporting much cattle, though better calculated for sheep. To this general description there are probably several exceptions; and the southern peninsula, which is terminated by Point Nepean, forms one, the surface there being mostly sandy, and the vegetation in many places little better than brush wood. Indented Head, at the northern part of the western peninsula, had an appearance particularly agreeable; the grass had been burned not long before, and had sprung up green and tender; the wood was so thinly scattered that one might see to a considerable distance; and the hills rose one over the other to a moderate elevation, but so gently that a plough might every where be used. The vegetable soil is a little mixed with sand, but good, though probably not deep, as I judged by the small size of the trees. The most common kinds of wood are the casuarina and eucalyptus, to which Mr. Grimes adds the banksia, mimosa and some others; but the timber is rarely sound, and is not large.

Were a settlement to be made at Port Phillip, as doubtless there will be some time hereafter, the entrance could be easily defended; and it would not be difficult to establish a friendly intercourse with the natives, for they are acquainted with the effect of fire-arms and desirous of possessing many of our conveniences. I thought them more muscular than the men of King George's Sound; but, generally speaking, they differ in no essential particular from the other inhabitants of the South and East Coasts except in language, which is dissimilar, if not altogether different to that of Port Jackson, and seemingly of King George's Sound also. I am not certain whether they have canoes, but none were seen.

In the woods are the kangaroo, the emu or cassowary, paroquets, and a variety of small birds; the mud banks are frequented by ducks and some black swans, and the shores by the usual sea fowl common in New South Wales. The range of the thermometer was between 61° and 67°; and the climate appeared to be as good and as agreeable as could well be desired in the month answering to November. In 1803, colonel Collins of the marines was sent out from England to make a new settlement in this country; but he quitted Port Phillip for the south end of Van Diemen's Land, probably from not finding fresh water for a colony sufficiently near to the entrance.

Point Nepean is in latitude 38° 18' south. The longitude from twelve sets of distances taken by lieutenant Flinders in the port, and six others by me ten days before arriving, the particulars of which are given in Table V of the Appendix to this volume, is 144° 30½' east; but these observations being mostly on one side of the moon, the corrected longitude by time keepers, 144° 38' east, is preferred.

No observations were taken in the port for the variation of the compass; but at seven leagues to the south-south-west of Point Nepean, azimuths gave 3° 41' when the ship's head was at N.E. by E. ½ E., and an amplitude at N. N. E. ½ E., 6° 48' east. The mean of these, corrected to the meridian, will be 7° 30', or half a degree less than at King's Island; I therefore take the variation in Port Phillip to have been generally, 7°, though at some stations it seemed to have been no more than 6° 30' east.

The rise of tide is inconsiderable in the upper parts of the port; near the entrance it is from three to six feet. By the swinging of the ship, which, however, varied at different anchorages, it appeared to be high water two hours and a half after the moon's passage; but at Point Nepean the time of high water by the shore is said by Mr. Grimes to be only one hour after the moon. At Western Port, Mr. Bass found high water to take place half an hour after the moon's passage, and the tide to rise from ten to fourteen feet. This great increase, in a place so near, seems extraordinary; but may perhaps be accounted for by the meeting of the tides from two entrances, whilst Port Phillip has only one, and that very narrow.

Notes

[1] *See A Voyage in the Lady Nelson to New South Wales, by James Grant. London, 1803. This voyage was published four years previously to M. Peron's book; but no more attention was paid at Paris to captain Grant's rights than to mine; his discoveries, though known to M. Peron and the French expedition in 1802, being equally claimed and named by them.*
[2] *The addition of West is made to the name, to distinguish it from Cape Banks on the East Coast, named by captain Cook. It is to be regretted, that navigators often apply names in so careless a manner as to introduce confusion into geography.*
[3] *Grant's Voyage to New South Wales, page 86.*
[4] *The New Year's Isles form a small roadsted, in which the brig Harrington from Port Jackson, commanded by Mr. W. Campbell, had rode out the south-west gale; and was lying there at this time, engaged in a sealing speculation. Bass' Strait had not been discovered much above two years, and it was already turned to purposes of various utility; a strong proof of enterprising spirit in the colonists of New South Wales.*

Chapter Ten

South Coast. Bass' Strait.

Monday 3 May 1802

On the 3rd of May at daylight the anchor was weighed to go out of Port Phillip with the last half of the ebb; and the wind being from the westward, we backed, filled and tacked occasionally, dropping out with the tide. When the entrance was cleared, and five miles distant, Mr. Westall took a view of it (Atlas Plate XVII, View 13.), which will be an useful assistance in finding this extensive but obscure port; and at eleven o'clock, when we bore away eastward to pass Cape Schanck, he sketched that cape and the ridge of hills terminating at Arthur's Seat (View 14). Cape Schanck is a cliffy head, with three rocks lying off, the outermost of which appears at a distance like a ship under sail: the latitude is 38° 29' or 30' south, and longitude 144° 53' east. It will always be desirable for vessels to get sight of this cape before they run far into the great bight for Port Phillip; and if the wind blow strong from the southward it will be unsafe to run without having seen it.

Cape Schanck is also an excellent mark for ships desiring to go into Western Port, of which it forms the west side of the principal entrance; but as there are many breakers and shoals on that side, which extend almost to mid-channel, it will be necessary to give the cape a wide berth by keeping over to Phillip Island on the starboard hand.
At noon, Cape Schanck bore N. 36° W. five or six miles; the breeze was fresh from the westward, with cloudy weather, and we steered for Point Grant, at the east side of the entrance into Western Port. There is a square-topped rock surrounded with a reef lying off the point; but the Lady Nelson has passed between them, with 3 fathoms water. On reaching within a mile of this reef, at one o'clock, I set

C. Schanck, distant 9 or 10 miles, at	N. 85° W.
A cliffy head up the entrance, distant 5 miles,	N. 16 W.
Square-topped rock,	N. 85 E.
Cape Wollamai,	S. 80½ E.

We then steered eastward along the south side of Phillip Island, and passed a needle-like rock lying under the shore. Cape Wollamai is the east end of the island, and forms one side of the small, eastern entrance to the port; and at three o'clock when it bore, N. 14° E., five or six miles, its longitude was ascertained by means of the time-keepers to be 145° 25' east: the latitude deduced from bearings is 38° 33' south. Wollamai is the native name for a fish at Port Jackson, called sometimes by the settlers light-horseman, from the bones of the head having some resemblance to a helmet; and the form of this cape bearing a likeness to the head of the fish, induced Mr. Bass to give it the name of Wollamai. We ran south-eastward along the shore, at the rate of six or seven knots, until sunset; when a steep head, supposed to be the Cape Liptrap of captain Grant, was seen through the haze, and our bearings of the land were,

Cape Wollamai, distant six leagues,	N. 49° W.
A low projection, distant seven miles,	N. 21 E.
Cape Liptrap,	S. 50 E.

We soon afterwards hauled to the wind off shore, under treble-reefed top-sails; and the gale increasing, with much swell from the south-westward, the close reefs were taken in. At midnight, tacked to the northward, and stood off and on till daybreak [TUESDAY 4 MAY 1802]; the wind being strong at west, and weather squally with rain. We then bore away for the land, which was seen to leeward; and at seven, the bearings of the principal parts were as under:

Land indistinct, apparently C. Liptrap,	N. 5° W.
Wilson's Promontory, south extreme,	S. 85 E.
A peaked I. (Rodondo of captain Grant),	S. 71 E.

Besides Rodondo, which lies about six miles to the south-by-east of the promontory, I distinguished five or six less conspicuous isles, lying along the south and west sides of this remarkable headland; these are called Glennie's Isles. To the N. 88° E. from Rodondo, and distant about two leagues, was a small island which appears to have been one of Moncur's Isles; and in steering south-eastward we got sight of the Devil's Tower, and of the high island and rocks named Sir Roger Curtis' Isles. These names were given by captain Grant in 1800; but he was not the discoverer of the places to which they are applied. They are all laid down upon my chart of 1799, on the authority of Mr. Bass; and when it is considered that this enterprising man saw them from an open boat, in very bad weather, their relative positions to Wilson's Promontory will be thought surprisingly near the truth. Unfortunately the situation of the promontory itself, owing to some injury done to his quadrant, is considerably in error, being twelve or fourteen miles wrong in latitude. A reef is mentioned by captain Grant as lying to the southward between Rodondo and Moncur's Isles; and a rock, level with the water, was seen in the same situation by the ships Gato and Castle of Good Hope, from which last it received the appropriate name of Crocodile Rock. This also was seen by Mr. Bass, and laid down in its relative situation; but in the Investigator I was not sufficiently near to get sight of this important danger.
We continued to steer south-eastward, round all these islands, having a fresh gale at west-south-west with squally weather; and at noon our situation was in

Latitude observed,	39° 35'
Longitude by time keepers,	146 30
Rodondo bore	N. 15 W.
Sir R. Curtis' Island, the peak, dist. 7 miles,	N. 46 E.
(The Devil's Tower being nearly on with the north side.)	

Two pointed rocks,	N. 57° and 62 E.

Wilson's Promontory was no longer visible; but from the best bearings I had been able to obtain in such blowing weather, its south-eastern extremity lies in latitude 39° 11½' south, and longitude 146° 24' east.

Not seeing any more islands to the southward from the masthead, we bore away east soon after noon to make Kent's Groups; and before three o'clock they both came in sight, as did an island to the northward, which seems to have been one of the small cluster discovered by Mr. John Black, and named Hogan's Group. The longitude by time keepers at this time was 146° 58' east, and the following bearings were taken:

Sir R. Curtis' Island, the peak,	N. 71° W.
Hogan's highest Island, from the mast head,	N. 5 E.
Kent's large Group, south end of the eastern I.	N. 70 E.
Small Group, dist. 6 or 7 miles, hiding the	
north-west end of the large group,	N. 52° to 45 E.

In steering past the south sides of the two groups at the distance of four to six miles, I was enabled to correct their positions; and also that of the pyramid, which was set at S. 4½° E. ten miles at four o'clock. When these lands had been laid down in the Francis and Norfolk in 1798, it was without the assistance of a time keeper, and therefore liable to considerable errors in longitude.

At five in the evening I thought myself fortunate to get a sight of Furneaux's great island through the haze; and also of a small, craggy isle which had been before fixed relatively to the inner Sister. To obtain the positions of these places by our timekeepers was to me an important object; since they were connected with the former survey of Furneaux's Islands and the north-eastern part of Van Diemen's Land. The bearings taken at five were,

Furneaux's great I., hills on the west part,	S. 48° E.
Small craggy isle,	S. 69 E.
Kent's large Group, extremes,	N. 7° to 47 W.
Small Group, the largest isle,	N. 77 W.
A small rock, not seen before,	N. 88 E.

The hills upon Furneaux's great island, which I believe, but could not certainly ascertain to have been upon the westernmost point, will therefore lie very nearly S. 48° E., from the bluff south-west end of Kent's large Group, instead of S. 38° E., as before marked. This places the great island 10' of longitude further east from the group, than was given by my run in the Francis during the night of Feb. 8, 1798.

We passed to the northward of the small new rock at the distance of three miles, and I judged it to lie four, or four-and-half leagues from the eastern side of Kent's large Group. No kind of danger was observed between them, but it was then nearly dark; and the wind being fresh and favourable, and not having more than ten days provisions in the ship, I felt it necessary to leave this and some other parts of Bass' Strait to a future examination; and we steered onward, east-north-east for Port Jackson.

Wednesday 5 May 1802

At daylight of the 5th the course was altered more northward; and at noon, land was seen from the mast head to the north-north-west, probably some of the hills at the back of the Long Beach, and distant not less than twenty leagues: our latitude was 38° 32' south and longitude 149° 35' east. The wind had then moderated and having shifted to north-west we kept close up to make Cape Howe. At four, hove to and sounded, but no bottom could be had with 90 fathoms; the land extended in patches from west-north-west distant twenty-five or more leagues to near the Ram Head at north; and consequently the hills at the back of the Long Beach must be of considerable elevation, superior to any other land near the sea in the southern, or perhaps any part of New South Wales.

Thursday 6 May 1802

On the wind shifting to the east side of north, next day, I tacked to get in with the land; being desirous of running near to as much of the coast, and correcting its longitude in our way to Port Jackson, as could be done without loss of time; but at noon the wind veered back, and our north-eastern course was resumed. The land could not then be further distant than nine or ten leagues; but no part of it was in sight, nor from the dullness of the weather could any observation be taken.

Friday 7 May 1802

After a squally night the wind fixed at west-by-north; and at daybreak of the 7th the land was visible from west to north-west, and our course was parallel to it (Atlas Plate VIII). At noon, the latitude was 36° 24' south, and longitude 151° 16' east; Mount Dromedary was in sight bearing N. 85° W., and by the difference of longitude, was distant fifty-two miles: I estimate its highest south part to lie in 36° 19' south, and 150° 11' east. The wind returned to the north-west in the afternoon, and we lost sight of the land; but becoming fairer afterwards, and the southern current not having much strength, by four next day [SATURDAY 8 MAY 1802] the heads of Port Jackson were in sight. At dusk the flag-staff upon the South Head bore west-south-west, and our distance from the shore was seven or eight miles.

I tried to beat up for the port in the night, being sufficiently well acquainted to have run up in the dark, had the wind permitted; but we were still to leeward in the morning [SUNDAY 9 MAY 1802], and Mr. Westall made a good sketch of the entrance (Atlas Plate XVIII. View 1). At one o'clock, we gained the heads, a pilot came on board, and soon after three the Investigator was anchored in Sydney Cove.

There was not a single individual on board who was not upon deck working the ship into harbour; and it may be averred that the officers and crew were, generally speaking, in better health than on the day we sailed from Spithead, and not in less good spirits. I have said nothing of the regulations observed after we made Cape Leeuwin; they were little different from those adopted in the commencement of the voyage, and of which a strict attention to cleanliness and a free circulation of air in the messing and sleeping-places formed the most essential parts. Several of the inhabitants of Port Jackson expressed themselves never to have been so strongly reminded of England as by the fresh colour of many amongst the Investigator's ship's company.

View of Port Jackson, taken from the South Head

So soon as the anchor was dropped, I went on shore to wait upon his Excellency Philip Gidley King, Esq., governor of New South Wales, and senior naval officer upon the station; to whom I communicated a general account of our discoveries and examinations upon the South Coast, and delivered the orders from the Admiralty and Secretary of State. These orders directed the governor to place the brig Lady Nelson under my command, and not to employ the Investigator on other service than that which was the object of the voyage; and His Excellency was pleased to assure me that every assistance in the power of the colony to render should be given to forward a service so interesting to his government, and to himself. The Lady Nelson was then lying in Sydney Cove; but her commander, lieutenant Grant, had requested permission to return to England, and had sailed six months before.

Besides the Lady Nelson, there were in the port His Majesty's armed vessel Porpoise, the Speedy, south-whaler, and the Margaret privateer; also the French national ship Le Naturaliste, commanded by captain Hamelin, to whom I communicated captain Baudin's intention of coming to Port Jackson so soon as the bad weather should set in. Le Géographe's boat had been picked up in Bass' Strait by Mr. Campbell of the brig Harrington, and the officers and crew were at this time on board Le Naturaliste.

May 1802

The duties required to fit the ship for prosecuting the voyage with success being various and extensive, Cattle Point, on the east side of Sydney Cove, was assigned to us by the governor for carrying on some of our employments, whilst others were in progress on board the ship and in the dockyard. On the morning after our arrival we warped to a convenient situation near the point, and sent on shore the tents, the sailmakers and sails, and the cooper with all the empty casks. Next day the observatory was set up, and the time-keepers and other astronomical instruments placed there under the care of lieutenant Flinders, who, with Mr. Franklin, his assistant, was to make the necessary observations and superintend the various duties carrying on at the same place; and a small detachment of marines was landed for the protection of the tents.

I had found the barricade of the quarter deck to stand so high, as to be not only an obstacle to beating to windward, but a great inconvenience to surveying the coast; for when the wind was on the side next to the land, there were no means of taking bearings over it but by standing on the top of the binnacle; or otherwise by removing the compass to different places, which I had found could not be done without materially changing the variation. These inconveniences being stated to the governor, his permission was obtained to reduce it so low as that it might be overlooked in all cases; and an order was given that four convict carpenters, and such other assistance from the dockyard should be furnished as was necessary.

To supply the place of the cutter we had lost at the entrance of Spencer's Gulf, I contracted for a boat to be built after the model of that in which Mr Bass made his long and adventurous expedition to the strait. It was twenty-eight feet seven inches in length over all, rather flat floored, head and stern alike, a keel somewhat curved, and the cut-water and stern post nearly upright; it was fitted to row eight oars when requisite, but intended for six in common cases. The timbers were cut from the largest kind of banksia, which had been found more durable than mangrove; and the planking was of cedar. This boat was constructed under the superintendance of Mr. Thomas Moore, master builder to the colony; and proved, like her prototype, to be excellent in a sea, as well as for rowing and sailing in smooth water. The cost at Port Jackson was no more than £30.; but this was owing to some of the materials being supplied from the public magazines.

Whilst these branches of our refitment were going on, a thorough examination was made and survey taken of all the ship's stores; as well for the purpose of sending away those unserviceable and replacing them with others so far as they could be obtained, as with a view to enable the warrant officers to pass their accounts and obtain their pay up to this time; a precaution which the nature of our voyage rendered more peculiarly necessary. After the surveys were ended, the seamen were employed in stripping and re-rigging the masts, and preparing the hold to receive a fresh stock of provisions and water; the naturalist and his assistants, as also the two painters, made excursions into the interior of the country; and my time was mostly occupied in constructing the fair charts of our discoveries and examinations upon the south coast, for the purpose of their being transmitted to the secretary of the Admiralty.

June 1802

On the 4th of June, the ship was dressed with colours, a royal salute fired, and I went with the principal officers of the Investigator to pay my respects to His Excellency the governor and captain-general, in honour of HIS MAJESTY'S birth day. On this occasion, a splendid dinner was given to the colony; and the number of ladies and civil, military, and naval officers was not less than forty, who met to celebrate the birth of their beloved sovereign in this distant part of the earth.

On the 6th, the Speedy, south-whaler, sailed for England. By Mr. Quested, the commander, I transmitted to the Admiralty an account of my proceedings upon the south coast of Terra Australis; but the charts being unfinished, were obliged to be deferred to a future opportunity. To the Astronomer Royal I sent Arnold's time keepers, No. 82 and 176, which had stopped; together with a statement of the principal astronomical observations hitherto made, and an account of Earnshaw's two time keepers, No. 543 and 520, which continued to perform well.

Captain Baudin arrived in Le Geographe on the 20th, and a boat was sent from the Investigator to assist in towing the ship up to the cove. It was grievous to see the miserable condition to which both officers and crew were reduced by scurvy; there being not more out of one hundred and seventy, according to the commander's account, than twelve men capable of doing their duty. The sick were received into the colonial hospital; and both French ships furnished with everything in the power of the colony to supply. Before their arrival, the necessity of augmenting the number of cattle in the country had prevented the governor from allowing us any fresh meat; but some oxen belonging to government were now killed for the distressed strangers; and by returning an equal quantity of salt meat, which was exceedingly scarce at this time, I obtained a quarter of beef for my people. The distress of the French navigators had indeed been great; but every means were used by the governor and the principal inhabitants of the colony, to make them forget both their sufferings and the war which existed between the two nations.[1]

July 1802

His Excellency, Governor King, had done me the honour to visit the Investigator, and to accept of a dinner on board; on which occasion he had been received with the marks of respect due to his rank of captain-general; and shortly afterward, the Captains Baudin and Hamelin, with Monsieur Peron and some other French officers, as also Colonel Paterson, the lieutenant-governor, did me the same favour; when they were received under a salute of eleven guns. The intelligence of peace, which had just been received, contributed to enliven the party, and rendered our meeting more particularly agreeable. I showed to Captain Baudin one of my charts of the south coast, containing the part first explored by him, and distinctly marked as his discovery. He made no objection to the justice of the limits therein pointed out; but found his portion to be smaller than he had supposed, not having before been aware of the extent of the discoveries previously made by Captain Grant. After examining the chart, he said, apparently as a reason for not producing any of his own, that his charts were not constructed on board the ship; but that he transmitted to Paris all his bearings and observations, with a regular series of views of the land, and from them the charts were to be made at a future time. This mode appeared to me extraordinary, and not to be worthy of imitation; conceiving that a rough chart, at least, should be made whilst the land is in sight, when any error in bearing or observation can be corrected; a plan which was adopted in the commencement, and followed throughout the course of my voyage.

Amongst our employments was that of fitting up a green house on the quarter deck, and sawing plank to make boxes for the reception of such plants as might be found by the naturalist, and thought worthy of being transported to His Majesty's botanic garden at Kew. This green house had been received at Sheerness, and stowed away in pieces; but I saw that when filled with boxes of earth, the upper works of the ship, naturally very weak, would be incapable of supporting the weight; and that in bad weather, we should be obliged to throw it over board for the safety of the ship. I therefore proposed its reduction to two-thirds of the size; and Mr. Brown being of opinion it would then contain all the plants likely to be collected in any one absence from Port Jackson, it was reduced accordingly; and the feet lowered down close to the deck. This arrangement required an alteration in the tiller, and a short one, with two arms, was fitted to the after part of the rudder head; with which expedient, and leading the main braces forward, the green house was not likely to cause much inconvenience to the working of the ship. The plants already collected on the South Coast had been landed on our arrival, in good order; and deposited in the governor's garden until such time as, the objects of the voyage being completed, we should be ready to sail for England.

The ship had never made more than three inches of water in an hour, after leaving the Cape of Good Hope; so that much caulking was not required, either within or out board. What was found necessary, was finished by the middle of July, at the same time with the barricading of the quarter deck; and the masts being then new rigged, and holds nearly completed with water and provisions, the sails were bent and the ship was painted. On the 21st, the last bag of bread and turn of water were received, the new whale boat was brought off, and we dropped down the harbour; being then ready for going to sea next morning.

In consequence of the directions given by His Majesty's principal Secretary of State for the Colonies, the Lady Nelson, a brig of sixty tons, commanded by Acting-Lieutenant John Murray, was placed under my orders, as a tender to the Investigator. This vessel was fitted with three sliding keels; and built after the plan of that ingenious officer commissioner (now vice-admiral) Schanck. When the sliding keels were up, the Lady Nelson drew no more than six feet water; and was therefore peculiarly adapted for going up rivers, or other shallow places which it might be dangerous, or impossible for the ship to enter. Mr Murray's crew was mostly composed of convicts; and having no officer in whom he could place entire confidence, I lent to him Mr Denis Lacy, one of my young gentlemen acquainted with the management of a time keeper, to act as his chief mate.

The price of fresh meat at Port Jackson was so exorbitant, that it was impossible to think of purchasing it on the public account. I obtained one quarter of beef for the ship's company, in exchange for salt meat, and the governor furnished us with some baskets of vegetables from his garden; and in lieu of the daily pound of biscuit, each man received a pound and a quarter of soft bread, without any expense to government. But with these exceptions, I was obliged to leave the refreshment of the people to their own individual exertions; assisting them with the payment due for savings of bread since leaving the Cape of Good Hope, and the different artificers with the money earned by their extra services in refitting the ship. Fish are usually plentiful at Port Jackson in the summer, but not in the winter time; and our duties were too numerous and indispensable to admit of sending people away with the seine, when there was little prospect of success; a few were, however, occasionally bought alongside, from boats which fished along the coast.

In purchasing a sea stock for the cabin, I paid £3 a head for sheep, weighing from thirty to forty pounds when dressed. Pigs were bought at 9d. per pound, weighed alive, geese at 10s. each, and fowls at 3s.; and Indian corn for the stock cost 5s. a bushel.

To complete the ship's provisions, I entered into a contract for 30,000 pounds of biscuit, 8000 pounds of flour, and 156 bushels of kiln-dried wheat; but in the meantime, the ship Coromandel brought out the greater part of the twelvemonths' provisions, for which I had applied on sailing from Spithead; and the contractor was prevailed upon to annul that part of the agreement relating to flour and wheat. The biscuit cost 33s. per hundred pounds; and considering that the colony was at short allowance, and that the French ships were to be supplied, it was a favourable price. From two American vessels which arrived, I purchased 1483 gallons of rum at 6s. 6d. per gallon; which, with what remained of our former stock was a proportion for twelve months. In other respects our provisions were completed from the quantity sent out from England; and the remaining part was lodged in the public stores, in charge of the commissary, until our return.

In addition to the melancholy loss of eight officers and men, at the entrance of Spencer's Gulf, and the previous deficiency of four in the complement, I found it necessary to discharge the man who had been bitten by a seal at Kangaroo Island, as also a marine, who was invalided; so that fourteen men were required to complete my small ship's company. Mr John Aken, chief mate of the ship Hercules, was engaged to fill the situation of master, and five men, mostly seamen, were entered, but finding it impossible to fill up the complement with free people, I applied to the governor for his permission to enter such convicts as should present themselves, and could bring respectable recommendations. This request, as every other I had occasion to make to His Excellency, was complied with; and when the requisite number was selected, he gave me an official document, containing clauses relative to these men, well calculated to ensure their good conduct. As this document may be thought curious by many readers, it is here inserted; premising, that the men therein mentioned, with the exception of two, were convicts for life.

By His Excellency Philip Gidley King, Esq., captain-general and governor in chief, in and over His Majesty's territory of New South Wales and its dependencies, etc., etc., etc.

"Whereas Captain Matthew Flinders, commander of His Majesty's ship Investigator, has requested permission to receive on board that ship the undermentioned convicts as seamen, to make up the number he is deficient. I do hereby grant Thomas Toney, Thomas Martin, Joseph Marlow, Thomas Shirley, Joseph Tuzo, Richard Stephenson, Thomas Smith, Francis Smith, and Charles Brown permission to ship themselves on board His Majesty's ship Investigator, and on the return of that ship to this port, according to Captain Flinders' recommendation of them, severally and individually, they will receive conditional emancipations or absolute pardons, as that officer may request.

"And in the interim I do, by virtue of the power and authority in me vested, grant a provisional-conditional emancipation to the said Thomas Toney, etc.; for the purpose of their being enabled to serve on board His Majesty's said ship Investigator, whilst in the neighbourhood of this territory; which conditional emancipation will be of no effect, in case any of those named herein do individually conduct themselves so ill, as to put it out of captain Flinders' power to recommend them for a conditional or absolute pardon on his return to this port.

"Given under my hand and seal at government house Sydney,
in New South Wales, this 15th day of July, in the year
of our Lord 1802.
(Signed)
Philip Gidley King, (L. S.)"

Several of these men were seamen, and all were able and healthy; so that I considered them a great acquisition to our strength. With respect to themselves, the situation to which they were admitted was most desirable; since they had thereby a prospect of returning to their country, and that society from which they had been banished; and judging from the number of candidates for the vacancies, such was the light in which a reception on board the Investigator was considered in the colony. When the master was entered, one of the men, being over the complement, was sent to the Lady Nelson, with a reserve of the privilege above granted.

I had before experienced much advantage from the presence of a native of Port Jackson, in bringing about a friendly intercourse with the inhabitants of other parts of the coast; and on representing this to the governor, he authorised me to receive two on board. Bongaree, the worthy and brave fellow who had sailed with me in the Norfolk, now volunteered again; the other was Nanbaree, a good-natured lad, of whom Colonel Collins has made mention in his Account of New South Wales.

My instructions directed me to consult with Governor King upon the best means of proceeding in the execution of the voyage; they also pointed out my return to the south coast, as the first step after refitting the ship at Port Jackson; but His Excellency was of opinion, as well as myself, that it would be unsafe to do this in the middle of the winter season; and that to remain six months in port waiting for the fine weather would be a sad waste of time; I had, besides, left very little of importance to be examined upon the south coast, a circumstance which the instructions had not contemplated. Upon all these considerations, it was decided to proceed to the northward--examine Torres' Strait and the east side of the Gulf of Carpentaria before the north-west monsoon should set in--proceed as I might be able during its continuance--and afterwards explore the north and north-west coasts; returning to Port Jackson when, and by such route as might be found most advisable, and conducive to the general purposes of the voyage.

It was probable that the north-west monsoon would not set in before the beginning of November; I therefore intended to examine such parts of the east coast of New South Wales in my way to the northward, as had been passed by

Captain Cook in the night, and were not seen in my expedition with the Norfolk sloop in 1799. The openings of Keppel and Shoal-water Bays, and the still larger of Broad Sound, I was also anxious to explore; in the hope of finding a river falling into some one of them, capable of admitting the Lady Nelson into the interior of the country. These desirable objects I expected to accomplish before the approach of the monsoon would call me into the Gulf of Carpentaria. The French ships were in no forwardness for sailing; and it was understood that Captain Baudin intended sending back Le Naturaliste to France, by the way of Bass' Strait, so soon as the season should be favourable. He had purchased a small vessel of between thirty and forty tons at Sydney, to serve him as a tender; and he told me that we should probably meet in the Gulf of Carpentaria in December or January. I understood that he meant to return to the south coast, and after completing its examination, to proceed northward, and enter the Gulf with the north-west monsoon; but it appeared to me very probable, that the western winds on the south coast would detain him too long to admit of reaching the Gulf of Carpentaria at the time specified, or at any time before the south-east monsoon would set in against him.

Before leaving Sydney Cove, I placed in the hands of governor King two copies of my chart of the south coast of Terra Australis, in six sheets; with three other sheets of particular parts, on a large scale. One copy I requested him to send with my letters to the secretary of the Admiralty, by the first good opportunity that offered; the other was to remain in his hands until my return, or until he should hear of the loss of the Investigator, when it was also to be sent to the Admiralty.

During our stay of twelve weeks at Port Jackson, there were not many days favourable to our pursuits at the observatory, the weather being dull and rainy for the greater part of the time; by watching all opportunities however, a sufficient number of observations were obtained to show the rates of the time keepers, and to answer the purposes of geography and navigation.

The Latitude of Cattle Point, from thirty meridian altitudes in an artificial horizon, of which fourteen were taken by Mr. Crosley and seven by me in 1795, and nine by lieutenant Flinders at this time, is 33° 51' 45.6" S.

Longitude from forty-four sets of distances of the sun and moon, of which the individual results are given in Table VI of the Appendix to this volume, 151° 11' 49" E.[2]

This position of Cattle Point, being reduced to the entrance of Port Jackson, will be for the Flag staff on the south head, latitude 33° 51½' south, longitude 151° 16½' east.

Ramsden's universal theodolite was set up at the observatory, and intended to be used as a transit instrument; but from the unfavourable state of the weather and my numerous occupations, it was not adjusted to the meridian; and the rates of the time keepers were therefore deduced from equal altitudes, taken with a sextant and artificial horizon in the usual way. Their errors from mean Greenwich time, at noon there July 18, and the mean rates of going in the last fifteen days, which were selected as the best, were as under:

Earnshaw's No. 543, slow 0h 16' 39.72" and losing 8.63" per day.
Earnshaw's No. 520, slow 1 18 53.00 and losing 19.52 per day.

The longitude of Cattle Point, given by the time keepers with the Kangaroo-Island rates on May 10th, the first day of observation after our arrival, was by

No. 543 151° 31' 21" east
No. 520 151 26 49 east.

The mean is 17' 16" more than deduced from the lunar observations; and when rates are used equally accelerating from those at Kangaroo Island, to what were found on first arriving at Port Jackson, the longitude by the time keepers would still be 14' 57.4" to the east; so that they appear to have gone less regularly during this passage than before. In fixing the longitudes of places between the two stations, the time keepers with their accelerated rates have been used; and the error of 14' 57.4" has been corrected by quantities proportionate to the times of observation, between April 6 at Kangaroo Island, and May 9 at Port Jackson.

The mean dip of the south end of the needle at Cattle Point was 62° 52'

Variation of the compass, observed by lieutenant Flinders on Garden Island in the following year, 8° 51' east.

No remarks were made at this time upon the tide; but it is known to be high water in Port Jackson about eight hours and a quarter after the moon's passage over and under the meridian; and the usual rise to be between four and six or seven feet. When high water takes place between three or four in the afternoon and one or two in the morning, it rises from six to eighteen inches higher than the preceding flood; and the following ebb descends a few inches lower than that which preceded the high tide.

The range of the thermometer on board the ship, was from 51° to 69°; and nearly the same on shore. The mercury in the barometer stood from 29.60 to 30.36 inches; but it was remarkable that it stood lowest in the fine weather, when the wind came from the westward off the land, and was highest in the rainy, squally weather, with the wind from the sea. According to the information communicated by colonel W. Paterson, F. R. S., commander of the troops at Port Jackson, this relation between the mercury and the weather was general here in the winter season, when the eastern winds bring rain with them; and I had frequent occasion to remark upon the South Coast, that sea winds raised the mercury in the barometer, whilst those from the land, even with fine weather, caused it to descend.

Notes

[1] These liberal proceedings, which do so much honour to governor King and the colonists, are handsomely acknowledged by M. Peron in his account of the French voyage.
[2] In 1795 and 1796 I took sixty sets of distances upon Cattle Point, an equal number on each side, which gave the longitude 151° 17' 12"; but these observations not having been calculated with great nicety, nor corrected for the errors of the lunar and solar tables, the result is not considered to be of equal authority with that given above. The present admiral D'ESPINOSA, when an officer in the voyage of Malaspina, observed an eclipse of the sun at Port Jackson, and occultations of the first and second satellites of Jupiter, from which he deduces the longitude of the town of Sydney to be 151° 12' 45" east of Greenwich; not differing more than a minute of longitude from the above forty-four sets of corrected lunar observations.

Chapter Eleven

South Coast. Winds And Currents

Before entering upon the second part of the voyage, it seems proper to give an account of the winds and currents which prevailed upon the South Coast; and to add thereto such other general information as may be useful in rendering the navigation more safe and expeditious, both along the coast and through Bass' Strait.

The rate and direction of the currents here described, are deduced from the daily positions of the ship by astronomical observation, compared with those given by a log kept in the common way, but with somewhat more than common attention. In the observations, however, there may be some errors, and a log cannot be depended upon nearer than to five miles in the distance, and half a point in the course for the twenty-four hours; and consequently this account of the currents must be taken as subject to the sum, or to the difference of the errors in the observations and log; though it is probable they may have been diminished by taking the medium of several days, which has always been done where it was possible.

Besides the difficulty there is in obtaining the exact rate and direction of a current, it is known that a continuance of the wind in any particular quarter may so far change its rate of moving, and even its direction, that at another time it may be found materially different in both. Of the probability of these changes the commander of a ship must form his own judgment, from the winds he may have previously experienced; and he will consider what is here said upon both winds and currents, as calculated and intended to give him a general notion, and no more, of what may usually be expected upon the South Coast.

Several days before making Cape Leeuwin, I experienced a current setting to the northward, at the rate of twenty-seven miles per day; but at the mean distance of forty leagues, west-south-west from the cape, the current ran north-east, twenty-two miles; and when the ship got in with the South Coast, I found it setting N. 70° E., at the average rate of twenty-seven miles per day: this was in the month of December. On approaching Cape Leeuwin in May, from the north-westward, the current for five days was ten miles to the east; but at forty leagues from the cape, it ran N. 35° E. fifteen miles; and from the meridian of the cape to past King George's Sound, the current set east, twenty-seven miles per day, nearly as it had before done in December. Captain Vancouver and admiral D'Entrecasteaux do not speak very explicitly as to the currents; but it may be gathered from both, that they also experienced a set to the eastward along this part of the South Coast.

The winds seem to blow pretty generally from the westward at Cape Leeuwin. In the summer time, they vary from north-west in the night, to south-west in the latter part of the day, though not regularly; and in the winter season this variation does not seem to take place. A long swell of the sea, called ground swell to distinguish it from the lesser, variable one of the surface, appears to come at all times from the south-westward, which indicates that the strongest and most durable winds blow from that quarter; and this was partly confirmed by our experience, for whenever it blew hard, the wind was at, or near to south-west.

It is from the superior strength and apparent prevalence of this wind, that the currents in the neighbourhood of Cape Leeuwin may be explained. The sea being driven in from the south-west, and meeting with the cape, will necessarily be divided by it, and form two currents, which will follow the directions of the land; one branch will run northward, along the west coast of Terra Australis, and the other eastward along the South Coast: our present business is to follow the latter current.

If a line be drawn from the south-western extremity of New Holland, to King's Island in Bass' Strait, it will show where the current may be expected to run strongest; though it will not be equally strong at those parts of the line which are distant from the land, as at those in its immediate vicinity. In drawing another line, from the north-eastern isles of the Archipelago of the Recherche to Cape Northumberland, we shall have what will commonly be the northern boundary of the current; for within this line the water does not seem to run in any constant direction, but is moved according as the wind may happen to blow. This was found by admiral D'Entrecasteaux; and is conformable to my experience, as I shall now explain.

It has been said, that the eastwardly current was found in May and December to run twenty-seven miles per day, from Cape Leeuwin past King George's Sound. From thence to a little beyond the Archipelago of the Recherche, keeping in with the shore, I found it to set north-east thirteen miles; and at a distance from the coast, it ran north-east-by-east sixteen miles per day, the wind being more from the south than from the northward in both cases.

In coasting from the Archipelago, all round the Great Bight and as far south-eastward as to Cape Northumberland, I had no determinate current; it generally followed the impulsion given to it by the winds, and was inconsiderable. From the middle of January to the middle of April, the winds were most prevalent from south-south-east to east-north-east; coming more from the land at night, and from the sea in the day time. They seldom had any strength; whereas the winds which occasionally blew from the westward were fresh, and sometimes became gales, veering in that case, invariably to the south-west.

On reaching Cape Northumberland I again found the eastwardly current; and from thence into Bass' Strait it ran N. 80° E., at the rate of twelve miles a day, the wind blowing strong from the south-westward in the latter part of the time.

In a subsequent run across the Great Bight in May, from the Archipelago nearly direct for Bass' Strait, the current set upon the average, N. 39° E. fourteen miles a day; appearing to be much influenced in its northern direction by the winds blowing strong from the southward. Mr. Dalrymple, in reasoning from the analogy of southern Africa, expected that the winds upon this coast would be found to blow from the northward, or off the shore, in the winter time, and this might possibly be the case if close in with the land; but at a distance from it, as just observed, the winds were from the southward.

Such an accumulation of water forcing itself through Bass' Strait, would naturally lead to the expectation of finding a strong current there, setting to the east; but on the contrary, the set in common cases was found to be rather in the opposite direction, the current appearing to be predominated by the tides, whose superior strength forced it below the surface. The flood comes from the eastward; and after making high water at Furneaux's Isles, passes on to Hunter's and King's Islands, where it meets another flood from the southward; and the high water then made seems to be nearly at the time that it is low water at Furneaux's Isles. Another flood is then coming from the east, and so on; whence a ship going eastward through the Strait, will have more tide meeting than setting after her, and be commonly astern of her reckoning. This applies more especially to the middle of the strait, and is what I there found with winds blowing across it; but the bight on the north side, between Cape Otway and Wilson's Promontory, seems to be an exception, and in fact, it lies out of the direct set of the tides. In running from Port Phillip to the Promontory I was set S. 73° E., thirty-five miles in the day; but it then blew a gale from the west and south-westward.

Although the eastwardly current be not commonly found at the surface in Bass' Strait, it is not lost. Navigators find it running with considerable strength, when passing the strait two or three degrees to the east of Furneaux's Islands; and it was this current so found, which led admiral Hunter to the first opinion of the existence of an opening between New South Wales and Van Diemen's Land.

Every thing in Bass' Strait bespeaks the strongest winds to come from the south-west; and there is reason to believe that during nine months of the year, it generally blows from some point in the western quarter. In January, February, and March, eastern winds with fine weather seem to be not uncommon; but there is no dependence to be had on them at any other season. At the eastern side of the strait and of Van Diemen's Land, it is not unusual to meet a north-east or north wind, though it seldom blows strong. The gales usually come from between south-west and south-east, and most frequently from the latter direction; which renders it hazardous to approach the coast between Cape Howe and Wilson's Promontory.

Thus, speaking generally of the south coast of Terra Australis, it may be considered that during the six or eight winter months, the winds blow almost constantly from some western point; and that gales of wind at south-west are frequent. The progress of the gales is usually this: the barometer falls to 29½ inches, or lower, and the wind rises from the north-westward with thick weather, and commonly with rain; it veers gradually to the west, increasing in strength, and the weather begins to clear up so soon as it has got to the southward of that point; at south-west the gale blows hardest, and the barometer rises; and by the time the wind gets to south or south-south-east, it becomes moderate, the weather is fine, and the barometer above 30 inches. Sometimes the wind may return back to west, or something northward, with a fall in the mercury, and diminish in strength, or die away; but the gale is not over, although a cessation of a day or two may take place. In some cases, the wind flies round suddenly from north-west to south-west; and the rainy, thick weather then continues a longer time.

Such is the usual course of the gales along the South Coast and in Bass' Strait; but on the east side of the strait the winds partake of the nature of those on the East Coast, where the gale often blows hardest between south and south-east. and is accompanied with thick weather, and frequently with heavy rain.

In the four or five summer months, the south-east and east winds appear to be most prevalent all round the Great Bight; but even there, the western winds sometimes blow at that time, and usually with considerable strength. Thus I had a strong south-west wind in the middle of February, near the Investigator's Group, and a gale from the same quarter in March, at the entrance of Spencer's Gulph; which last was felt still more severely in Bass' Strait by captain Baudin. At the two extremities of the coast, that is, in the strait and near King George's Sound, the winds blow sometimes from the west and sometimes from the eastward, in the summer; but the strongest winds are from the south-west.

It will hence appear, that the summer is alone the proper time for a ship to come upon, and still more so for exploring the south coast of Terra Australis; whether she proceed along it from west to east, as I did in the Investigator, or from east to west, as captain Baudin, seems to be almost a matter of indifference. From Cape Leeuwin to the end of the Archipelago of the Recherche, and from Cape Northumberland to Bass' Strait, it is perhaps most advantageous to proceed eastward, on account of the current; but in the intermediate and more considerable part of the coast, a western route is certainly preferable. It has also this general advantage, that the winds which are fair for running along the coast are those that blow moderately, and are accompanied with fine weather, most proper for making a survey; whereas those favourable to the opposite route frequently blow strong, and render it dangerous to keep in with the land. As to making a survey of the South Coast in the winter season, which had been judged from theoretical analogy to be the most proper time, it appears to be not only a dangerous experiment, but also one from which very little accuracy of investigation could be expected; and with as much ardour as most men for such pursuits, I should very unwillingly undertake the task.

South Coast. Sailing Directions.

These observations upon the danger of sailing along the South Coast in the winter season, are not meant to apply to the commander of a ship desirous of going eastward through Bass' Strait, and of seeing no more of the land than is necessary to assure his situation. The strait may be passed without more than very common danger, at any time of the year, provided that the navigator be certain of his latitude before approaching the longitude of 143½°; he should not, however, enter the strait in the night, unless he have previously seen the land, or be certain both of latitude and longitude. The parallel of 39°, or 39° 20', according as the wind may incline, is the best for taking a ship between King's Island and Cape Otway; and a sight of either, or preferably of both, will point out his position on the chart. The sole danger to be apprehended here, is the Harbinger's Reefs, two patches lying nearly two leagues out from the north end of King's Island; but are so far separated from it, and from each other, as to leave practicable passages between them, where the shoalest water found by the Cumberland schooner was 9 fathoms.

When the position of the ship at the entrance of the strait is ascertained, a course should be shaped for Curtis' Island, which will be visible ten or eleven leagues from the deck in fine weather; and as the distance is between forty and fifty leagues, and nothing lies in the way, a part of it may be run in the night, with a good look-out. I would afterwards pass on the south side of Kent's Groups, at not a greater distance from the largest than two leagues; and then steer east-north-east by compass, if nearly before the wind, or on either side of that course as the wind may incline; but taking care not to approach the northern Long Beach.

In case of meeting with a continuance of foul winds, the most convenient places in the strait for anchorage, when going eastward, are these:

1st. Under the north-west end of King's Island, near the New Year's Isles. Of this anchorage I know only, besides what is given in the chart, that the brig Harrington there rode out a gale from south-west, the heavy sea being broken off by the New Year's Isles; and the shelter from eastern winds must certainly be much more complete.

2nd. Port Phillip; anchoring just within the entrance, on the south side. When a fair wind comes, a ship can get out of the port by means of the strong tides.

3rd. Hunter's Isles, between Three-hummock and Barren Islands; taking care not to anchor too close to the weather shore, lest the wind change suddenly.

4th. The bight between Wilson's Promontory and Cape Liptrap, in case of necessity; but I would not recommend this place, it being very dangerous should the wind shift to south-west.

5th. Kent's large Group for brigs and lesser vessels; in one of the small sandy coves under the eastern island.

6th. Furneaux's Isles, between Clarke's and Preservation Islands. If the ship be not able to weather Clarke's Island, and pass out to the south-eastward when the fair wind comes, she may run through Armstrong's Channel, with a boat ahead and a good look-out.

This is all that it seems necessary to say for the information of a commander desirous of going eastward through Bass' Strait; and with the chart in the Atlas, (Plate VI.), it is all that a man of moderate experience and judgment will desire. I have not mentioned the entrance to the strait between King's Island and Hunter's Isles, thinking it not to be recommendable; both on account of Reid's Rocks, which lie in the passage, and whose position is not well ascertained, and also because I am not satisfied that Hunter's Isles are placed in the chart at their true distance from King's Island: the difference of longitude is from an approximation only; but the error, if any, cannot exceed eight or ten miles, and is in excess. However, with daylight and a good look-out, the strait may be safely entered by this pass, at any time that a ship can carry sail upon a wind. I entered this way in the Investigator, during the night; but what a ship on discovery may do is not to be given as an example to others, whose sole objects are expedition and safety. The outlet by the pass called Banks' Strait, between Furneaux's Islands and Cape Portland, is perfectly safe; but is out of the way for a ship bound to Port Jackson.

It has been observed that the winds are commonly favourable for making a passage to the westward, through Bass' Strait and along the South Coast, in the months of January, February, and March. I have no personal experience of such a passage, further than through the strait, though it has lately been made several times; but to those who may be desirous of doing the same, and are strangers to these parts, the following observations may be acceptable.

The first remark is, that the three months when this passage is most easy to be made, are precisely those in which it is unsafe, if not impracticable to go through Torres' Strait; and the second, that it will generally be of no avail for a ship to be in Bass' Strait before the middle of December, and if it be the middle of January it will be preferable.

Ships coming from Port Jackson, or anywhere from the north-eastward, may take a departure from Cape Howe in 37° 30½' south and 150° 5' east; but from thence, they should not steer a course more westward than south-south-west by compass, until in latitude 39° 30'; on account of the danger to be apprehended from south-east winds upon the Long Beach. Having reached 39° 30' they should steer a true west course, or west-by-south by compass, leaving the Sisters, the craggy islet, and a rock, on the larbord hand. The eastern island of Kent's large Group, which lies in 39° 30' south, 147° 19' east, and may be seen ten, or perhaps twelve leagues from the deck in fine weather, will come in sight ahead; and in passing three or four miles on the south side, the small western group will be seen, and is to be passed in the same way; as are Curtis' peaked Isles, which will then be in sight. From Curtis' Isles to the north end of King's Island, the course is nearly true west, and distance about forty-two leagues, with nothing in the way; but it is better to steer five or six leagues to the north of King's Island, if the winds permit. Should they hang to the westward of north, the course may be safely directed for Three-hummock Island; passing afterwards to the north or south of King's Island, as the winds may be most favourable.

In the case of foul winds, which, if the weather be thick or rainy, may be expected to fix at south-west and blow strong, there are many places where a ship may anchor, to wait a change; but the following appear to be the most convenient.

1st. Hamilton's Road, at the east end of Preservation Island.

2nd. On the south side of the largest Swan Isle, for small vessels, or under Isle Waterhouse.

3rd. Port Dalrymple.

4th. Various places amongst Hunter's Isles.

5th. Sea-elephant Bay, on the east side of King's Island, where there is fresh water; or under the north-east end of that island, if the wind be from south-west.

6th. Western Port, under Phillip Island; anchoring so soon as the ship is sheltered. A fair wind for going onward through the strait, will take a ship out of this port.

7th. Port Phillip.

After clearing Bass' Strait, I think it most advisable to keep at not more than ten or twenty leagues off the coast, from Cape Otway to Kangaroo Island; as the wind may there be expected more favourable, and the contrary current less strong than in steering a straight course toward Cape Leeuwin. But should the wind rise from the north-westward, with thick weather and a descent more than usually rapid in the marine barometer, a stretch off shore should immediately be made, to prepare for a south-west gale. A look-out must be kept for an island lying to the west-south-west of Cape Northumberland; it was seen by Mr. Turnbull, commander of the Britannia, south whaler, but the weather being thick, its situation was not well ascertained. According to the best information I could procure, this island lies in 38¼° south, and about 139½° or ¾ east longitude.

From Kangaroo Island, a straight course may be made for the southernmost part of the Archipelago of the Recherche; but should the winds come from the westward and not blow a gale, or be light and unsteady, I would steer more northward, nearer to the land, in the hope of having them more favourable. From the Archipelago to Cape Leeuwin it seems best to keep at a distance from the land, unless under the necessity of stopping in that neighbourhood; for the current runs strong near the shore, and with the advantage of an offing of twenty or thirty leagues, a ship may lie clear of the cape with a wind which might otherwise keep her beating for many days.

There appears to be no place of shelter against western gales, between Bass' Strait and Kangaroo Island; but there are then, besides various anchorages under that island, the bays and coves at the entrance of Spencer's Gulph; and further westward, Coffin's Bay, Petrel Bay in the island St. Francis, and Fowler's Bay near the head of the Great Bight. Afterwards come Goose-Island Bay, Thistle's Cove, and the lee of Observatory Island, all in the Archipelago of the Recherche; the cove cannot be entered in a gale, but when once secured in the south-west corner, a ship will be safe; the other two places afford very indifferent shelter from strong winds, and are indeed fit only for a temporary anchorage in moderate weather. Doubtful-Island Bay and King George's Sound afford complete shelter against western gales; but some little time would be lost in getting out of them, if a ship waited until an eastern wind set in. Some account of all these places will be found in the preceding pages of this volume; with the exception of Observatory Island, for which D'Entrecasteaux's voyage may be consulted.

Appendix

Account of the observations by which the Longitudes of places on the south coast of Terra Australis have been settled.

The lunar distances and other observations taken in the Investigator's voyage having been ordered by the Commissioners of the Board of Longitude to be recalculated by a professed astronomer, with every degree of correctness which science has hitherto been able to point out as necessary, this delicate, but laborious task was assigned to Mr. John Crosley, formerly assistant at the Royal Observatory at Greenwich; a gentleman who formed part of the expedition as far as the Cape of Good Hope, but whose ill health had then made it necessary to relinquish the voyage and return to England. The data and results of all the observations will probably be made public, by order of the Commissioners; but in the mean time, for the satisfaction of the geographer, and more especially for that of the seaman, whose life and property may be connected with the accuracy of the charts., the results of the lunar distances observed upon each coast are added in the form of an Appendix to the volume wherein that coast is described. It is by these results that the time keepers have been regulated; and the longitudes used in the construction of the charts are taken from the time keepers.

To appreciate the degree of confidence to which these results may be entitled, it is necessary to know under what circumstances the observations were taken; also the method used in the calculations, and the corrections which have been applied beyond what is usual in the common practice at sea: of these the following is a general statement.

1st. The instruments used in taking the distances, were a nine-inch sextant by Ramsden, and three sextants of eight inches radius by Troughton, the latter being made in 1801, expressly for the voyage. On board the ship, the sextant was necessarily held in the hand, and the distances were sometimes so taken on shore; but in most of the latter cases, it was fixed on a stand admitting of the sextant being turned easily in any direction. The telescopes were of the largest magnifying powers which the motion of the ship, or state of the atmosphere could admit, and each longitude is the result of a set of observations, most generally consisting of six independent sights. They were taken either by lieutenant Flinders or by myself; those by him being designated in the column of Observers by the letter F, the others by C.

2nd. Preparatory to the reduction of the apparent to the true distance, the four following corrections have been applied.

From the sun's semi-diameter, as given in the nautical almanack, 3" have been subtracted. In the almanacks of the years comprehending our observations, the semi-diameter was stated from Mayer's tables, which gave it 3" too great; owing to the imperfection of the telescope with which Mayer observed.

The semi-diameters of the sun and moon being less in the vertical, than in the horizontal direction, on account of the differences in the refraction, they have been reduced proportionally to these differences and to the angles at the points of contact in measuring the distance. This correction is called contraction of the semi-diameter.

Before using the moon's horizontal parallax in the nautical almanack, where it is calculated for the equator, it has been corrected (printed as 'diminished', and corrected in the errata) by a number of seconds depending upon the latitude of the place, and upon this assumed position: that the earth is a regular spheroid, whose polar axis is to the equatorial axis, as 320 to 321. This, and the preceding correction are unnecessary, unless where great exactness may be required.

The refraction of the heavenly bodies given in the tables, being calculated for a mean height of 50° of Fahrenheit's thermometer, and 29.6 inches of the barometer, it has been corrected for the difference between these means and what was the state of the atmosphere at the time of observation.

3rd. In reducing the apparent to the true distance, Mr. Crosley has used the method of Joseph Mendoza de Rios, Esq., F. R. S., given with his Nautical Tables, second edition, 1809; and the tables from which the corrections were taken and the computations made, are those of the same valuable work.

4th. The reduced distance, found as above, has been corrected to the spheroidal figure of the earth, according to the theory explained in the Philosophical Transactions of the Royal Society of 1797; and for doing which, rules are given by Mr. Mendoza with his Nautical Tables of 1801. This calculation is tedious, and the correction, more especially in low latitudes, too small to be necessary in common cases.

5th. In the nautical almanack the distances are given to every three hours, but the irregularities of the moon's motion being such as to cause some inequality in the different parts of this interval, the distance at the hour preceding, and at the hour following the time of observation, was found by interpolation from the two nearest given on each side; and having the distances at Greenwich for each hour, the observed distance can never fall more than half an hour from one of them; and the moon's inequalities do not then produce any sensible error in the corresponding time, as obtained from common proportion. The correction arising from this process is seldom so important as to be necessary in sea observations.

6th. The longitude deduced from a comparison of the true distance at observation with the hourly distances at Greenwich, is contained in the following tables under the head of Longitude from Nautical Almanack. But as it frequently happened, that the observation was not taken exactly in the place which it is intended to fix, this longitude is reduced to that place by the application of the difference shown by the time keepers to have existed between the two situations. In ascertaining this difference, the rates of going allowed to the time keepers are generally those found at the place which is to be fixed; whether applied to observations taken before arriving, or after quitting that place. This, however, could be done only at those stations where rates had been observed; at the intermediate points, where the result of lunar distances is given principally as an object of comparison with the time keepers, the rates allowed in the reduction are those found at the station previously quitted; but then the difference of longitude is corrected by the quantity consequent on the following supposition: that the time keepers altered their rates from those at the previous, to those at the following station, in a ratio augmenting in arithmetic progression. The difference of longitude, thus corrected when necessary, is given under the head of Reduction by time keepers; and the longitudes reduced by it to the place intended to be fixed, are taken to be of equal authority with those resulting from observations made in the place itself.

7th. But these longitudes, whether reduced to, or observed in, the place to be fixed, still require a correction which is of more importance than any of those before mentioned. The theories of the solar and lunar motions not having reached such a degree of perfection as to accord perfectly with actual observation at Greenwich, the distances calculated from those theories and given in the almanack become subject to some error; and consequently so do the longitudes deduced from them. The quantities of error in the computed places of the sun and moon, have been ascertained at Greenwich as often as those luminaries could be observed; and Mr. Pond, the astronomer royal, having permitted access for this purpose to the table of errors kept in the Observatory, Mr. Crosley has calculated the corresponding effects on the longitude, and proportioned them to the time when our observations were taken. The combined effect of the two errors forms a correction to the longitudes obtained from the sun and moon; but when the moon was observed with a star, then the moon's error alone gives the correction. But it has sometimes happened, that there were many days interval between the observations of the moon at Greenwich, and that the errors preceding and following are so extremely irregular, that no accuracy could be expected in reducing them by proportion; in these unfortunate cases, that part of the error belonging to the moon has been taken absolute, such as it was found on the day nearest to the time of observation; but the sun's error is always from proportion. These corrections, with the interval in the Greenwich observations of the moon, are given under their proper heads.

8th. The longitudes thus computed, reduced to the intended point, and corrected, are placed under each other; and the mean of the whole is taken to be the true longitude of that point, unless in certain cases where it is otherwise expressed. The mean is also given of the longitudes uncorrected for the errors of the sun and moon's places, that the reader may have an opportunity of comparing them; and some sea officers who boast of their having never been out more than 5', or at most 10', may deduce from the column of corrections in the different tables, that their lunar observations could not be entitled to so much confidence as they wish to suppose; since, allowing every degree of perfection to themselves and their instruments, they would probably be 12', and might be more than 30' wrong.

In the nautical almanacks for 1811 and 1815, the distances are computed from the new tables of Burg for the moon, and of Delambre for the sun; and it is to be hoped that the necessity of correcting for errors in the distances at Greenwich will have ceased, or be at least greatly diminished. Should the computed places of the sun and moon be happily found to agree with actual observation, and supposing that our results may be taken as the average of what practised observers with good instruments will usually obtain when circumstances are favourable, then lunar observations taken in 1814 and afterwards, may be entitled to confidence within the following limits:

From one set of distances, consisting of six independent sights, the error in longitude may be 30' on either side; but will probably not exceed 12'.

From six sets on one side of the moon, each set consisting as above, the error may be 20'; but not probably more than 8'.

Twelve sets of distances, of which six on each side of the moon, are not likely to err more than 10' from the truth; and may be expected to come within 5'.

The error in sixty sets, taken during three or four lunations, and one half on each side of the moon, will not, I think, be wrong more than 5'; and will most probably give the longitude exact to 1' or 2', This degree of accuracy is far beyond what the hopes of the first proposers of the lunar method ever extended, and even beyond what astronomers accustomed only to fixed observatories will be disposed to credit at this time; but in thinking it probable that sixty sets of lunar distances will come within 1' or 2' of the truth, when compared with correct tables, I conceive myself borne out by the following facts.

In Port Lincoln, I observed an eclipse of the sun with a refracting telescope of forty-six inches focus, and a power of about two hundred. It was recalculated by Mr. Crosley from Delambre's and Burckhardt's tables, the one made four and the other ten years afterwards. The longitude deduced from the beginning differed only 1' 31.5" from that at the end, and the mean of both only 1' 17" from thirty sets of lunar distances corrected for the errors of the tables.

The Spanish admiral D'Espinosa observed emersions of the first and second satellites of Jupiter in 1793, at Port Jackson, and also an eclipse of the sun which he recalculated by the tables of Burg. He deduces from thence the longitude of Sydney Cove to be 151° 12' 45"; and from forty-four sets of lunar distances by lieutenant Flinders, it would be 151° 11' 49" east.

At Port Louis in the Isle Mauritius, the Abbé de la Caille observed an eclipse of the sun, the transit of mercury over the sun's disk, and various occultations of Jupiter's satellites; M. d'Aprés also observed several occultations; and this place should therefore be well determined. Its longitude in the Requisite Tables is 57° 29' 15" east; and from twenty-seven sets of distances taken whilst a prisoner there, I made it, when corrected for the errors of the tables, 57° 29' 57" east.

In appreciating the degrees of accuracy to which a small or larger number of lunar distances may be expected to give the longitude, I suppose the observer to be moderately well practised, his sextant or circle, and time keeper to be good, and his calculations to be carefully made; and it is also supposed, that the distances in the nautical almanack are perfectly correct. As, however, there may still be some errors, notwithstanding the science and the labour employed to obviate them, it cannot be too much recommended to sea officers to preserve all the data of their observations; more especially of such as may be used in fixing the longitudes of places but little, or imperfectly known. The observations may then be recalculated, if requisite; the corrections found to be necessary may be applied; and the observer may have the satisfaction of forwarding the progress of geography and navigation, after having contributed to the safety of the ship, and benefit of the particular service in which he may happen to have been engaged.

TABLE I.

Longitude of the *Observatory* in Princess Royal Harbour, KING GEORGE's SOUND.

Appt. Greenwich time of the observations.	Place.	Longit. E. from Naut. Alm.	Reduction by two time keepers.	E. Longitude of the Observatory.	Correction for errors of tables.	Correction Interv. of ☾'s error.	Correct. Longit. of the Observatory.	Whence deduced.
1801 Nov.	At sea.	90 56 0	+ 27 20 49	118 16 49	− 29 45	One day.	117 47 4	☉ E. ☾ C
28 at 17 30	—	91 6 15	—	118 27 4	—	—	117 57 19	Ditto.
29 at 17 50	—	95 50 45	+ 22 39 7	118 29 52	− 29 0	Two days.	118 0 52	Ditto.
	—	95 47 45		118 26 52	—	—	117 57 52	—
30 at 17 23	—	97 51 0	+ 20 20 18	118 11 18	− 28 30	—	117 42 48	F
December.	Anchorage in Princess Royal Harbour.	118 4 30		118 4 30	− 5 30	One day.	117 59 0	☉ W. ☾ C
		118 4 30		118 4 30	—	—	117 59 0	—
11 at 17 24		118 7 30		118 7 30	—	—	118 2 0	F
		118 9 45		118 9 45	—	—	118 4 15	—
		118 1 0		118 1 0	—	—	117 55 30	—
	At Observatory.	117 56 45		117 56 45	− 9 30	One day.	117 47 15	Ditto. C
	—	117 59 15		117 59 15	—	—	117 49 45	—
12 at 21 47	—	117 55 45		117 55 45	—	—	117 46 15	F
	—	117 54 30		117 54 30	—	—	117 45 0	—
	—	117 53 45		117 53 45	—	—	117 44 15	—
	Ditto.	118 2 45		118 2 45	− 13 0	One day.	117 49 45	☉ E. ☾ C
	—	118 6 30		118 6 30	—	—	117 53 30	—
	—	117 58 0		117 58 0	—	—	117 45 0	F
	—	117 56 45		117 56 45	—	—	117 43 45	—
31 at 18 32	—	117 55 0		117 55 0	—	—	117 42 0	C
	—	118 8 0		118 8 0	—	—	117 55 0	—
	—	118 4 30		118 4 30	—	—	117 51 30	—
	—	117 50 0		117 50 0	—	—	117 37 0	F
	—	117 52 30		117 52 30	—	—	117 39 30	—
	—	117 51 0		117 51 0	—	—	117 38 0	—
1802 Jan.	On shore at Lucky Bay.	122 30 45	− 4 22 38	118 8 7	+ 6 15	One day.	118 1 52	☉ W. ☾ C
	—	122 29 30	—	118 6 52	—	—	118 0 37	—
9 at 17 56	—	122 33 15	—	118 10 37	—	—	118 4 22	—
	—	122 34 45	—	118 12 7	—	—	118 5 52	—
	—	122 38 45	—	118 16 7	—	—	118 9 52	—
	—	122 41 15	—	118 18 37	—	—	118 12 22	—

	Uncorrected	118 5 41,8	Corrected	117 58 9,9 and taken
Longitude from thirty-one sets of lunar distances,				

From observations east of the moon alone	-	117 48 3,7"
west of the moon alone	-	117 57 57

	Mean	117 58 0,3 east.

TABLE II.

Longitude of the *south point* of *Lucky Bay*, ARCHIPELAGO OF THE RECHERCHE.

Appt. Greenwich time of the observations.	Place.	Longitude E. from Naut. Alm.	Reduction by two time keepers.	East Longit. of Lucky Bay.	Correction for errors of tables.	Correction Interv. of ☾'s error.	Correct. Longit. of Lucky Bay	Whence deduced.
1802 Jan.	On the South Pt.	122 30 45		122 30 45	− 6 15	One day.	122 24 30	☉ W. ☾ C
	—	122 29 30		122 29 30	—	—	122 23 15	—
9 at 17 56	—	122 33 15		122 33 15	—	—	122 27 0	—
	—	122 34 45		122 34 45	—	—	122 28 30	—
	—	122 38 45		122 38 45	—	—	122 32 30	—
	—	122 41 15		122 41 15	—	—	122 35 0	—
	At sea.	122 0 45	− 9 30 55	122 29 50	− 8 45	As on 27th there being no other obs. until Feb. 5.	122 21 5	☉ E. ☾ C
	—	131 51 15		122 20 20	—		122 11 35	—
27 at 13 28	—	131 51 0		122 20 5	—		122 11 20	—
	—	131 47 0		122 16 5	—		122 7 20	—
	—	131 50 15		122 19 20	—		122 10 35	—
	—	131 52 45		122 21 50	—		122 13 5	—
	On shore at Fowler's Bay.	132 30 45	− 10 13 38	122 17 7	− 8 30	Ditto.	122 8 37	Ditto F
28 at 14 42	—	132 24 30		122 10 52	—	—	122 2 22	—
	—	132 19 30		122 5 52	—	—	121 57 22	—
	—	132 19 15		122 5 37	—	—	121 57 7	—

	Uncorrected	122 23 27,1	Corrected	122 15 42,1
Longitude from sixteen sets of lunar distances,				

Longitude of the *south point* from the two time keepers.

On Jan. 9 at 15h 51' of Greenwich time, and using the King-George's-Sound rates, the mean longitude was 122° 15' 48"

Correction for variation in the rates found at Pt. Lincoln,	− 0 24,1
Correction for supplemental error during 9 days,	− 1 10,2

Corrected longitude, taken preferably to that above,	122 14 13,7 east.

TABLE III.
Longitude of the *Anchorage* in FOWLER'S BAY.

Appt. Greenwich time of the observations	Place	Longitude E. from Naut. Alm.	Reduction by two time keepers	East Longit. of the Anchorage	Correction for errors of tables	Interv. of ☽'s error	Corr. Longit. of the Anchorage	Whence deduced	Observers
1802 Jan. 9 at 17 56	On shore at Lucky Bay	122 30 45	+10 13 38	132 44 23	- 8 15	One day	132 38 5	☉ W. ☽	C
		122 29 30	—	132 43 8			132 36 53		
		122 33 15	—	132 46 53			132 40 38		
		122 34 45	—	132 48 23			132 42 8		
		122 38 45	—	132 52 23			132 46 8		
		122 41 15	—	132 54 53			132 48 38		
27 at 13 28	At sea	132 0 45	+ 0 42 43	132 43 28	- 8 45	As on 27th there being no other obs. until Feb. 5.	132 34 43	☉ E. ☽	C
		131 51 15	—	132 33 58			132 25 13		
		131 51 0	—	132 33 43			132 24 58		
		131 47 0	—	132 29 43			132 20 58		
		131 50 15	—	132 32 58			132 24 13		
		131 52 45	—	132 35 28			132 26 43		
28 at 14 42	On shore at Fowler's Bay	132 30 45	—	132 30 45	- 8 30	Ditto.	132 22 15	Ditto.	F
		132 24 30	—	132 24 30			132 16 0		
		132 19 30	—	132 19 30			132 11 0		
		132 19 15	—	132 19 15			132 10 45		
February 15 at 1 26	At sea	135 8 0	- 2 27 48	132 40 12	- 19 45	Two days.	132 20 27	☉ W. ☽	C
		135 18 15	—	132 50 27			132 30 42		
		135 16 30	—	132 48 42			132 28 57		
		135 44 15	—	133 6 32	- 19 15		132 47 17	Sp. Virg. E. ☽	
		135 31 15	—	132 53 32			132 34 17		
		135 31 30	—	132 43 47			132 24 32		
Longitude from twenty-two sets of lunar distances,		Uncorrected		132 39 24		Corrected	132 28 26,7		

Longitude of the *Anchorage* from the two time keepers.

On Jan. 28 at 11h 14' of Greenwich time, and using the
King-George's-Sound rates, the mean longitude was   132° 32' 37"
Correction for variation in the rates found at Pt. Lincoln,   − 3 34,4
Correction for supplemental error during 27,8 days,   − 3 36,8

Corrected longitude, taken preferably to that above,   132 25 25,8 east.

TABLE IV.
Longitude of the *Tents*, at the head of PORT LINCOLN.

Appt. Greenwich time of the observations	Place	Longit. E. from Naut. Alm.	Reduction by two time keepers	East Longit. of the Tents	Correction for errors of tables	Interv. of ☽'s error	Correct. Longit. of the Tents	Whence deduced	Observers
1802 Feb. 15 at 1 26	At sea	135 8 0	+0 44 58	135 52 58	- 19 45	Two days.	135 33 13	* Aldeb. W. of ☽	C
		135 18 15	—	136 3 13			135 43 28		
		135 16 30	—	136 1 28				* Sp. Virg. E. of ☽	
		135 44 15	—	136 29 13	- 19 15	Ditto.	136 9 58		
		135 31 15	—	136 16 13			135 47 13		
		135 21 30	—	136 6 28				☉ E. ☽	F
26 at 19 32	At the tents	136 1 15	—	136 1 15	- 4 30	One day.	135 56 45		
		135 52 30	—	135 52 30			135 48 0		
		135 51 15	—	135 51 15			135 58 55		
March 9 at 16 36	At anchor near the head of Spencer's Gulph.	138 14 30	- 2 5	136 9 25	- 15 30	Two days.	135 53 55	☉ W. ☽	F
		138 30 0	—	136 24 55			136 9 25		
		138 18 45	—	136 8 40			135 53 10		
		138 5 0	—	135 59 55			135 44 25		
		137 59 30	—	135 54 25			135 38 55		
10 at 18 42	Ditto.	138 35 30	Ditto.	135 30 25	- 16 30	Ditto.	135 13 55	Ditto.	F
		138 2 15	—	135 57 10			135 40 40		
		138 3 45	—	135 58 40			135 42 10		
		137 55 0	—	135 49 55			135 33 25		
		137 57 15	—	135 52 10			135 35 40		
25 at 12 42	Under sail, Investigator's Strait.	137 38 30	- 1 47 34	135 50 56	- 7 15	Five days.	135 43 41	☉ E. ☽	F
		137 46 45	—	135 59 11			135 51 56		
		137 38 30	—	135 50 56			135 43 41		
		137 46 45	—	135 59 11			135 51 56		
	Ditto.	137 43 0	- 1 57 51	135 45 45	- 10 45	Ditto.	135 34 21	Ditto.	F
26 at 13 6		137 41 15	—	135 43 21			135 32 36		
		137 39 45	—	135 41 51			135 31 6		
		137 41 30	—	135 43 36			135 32 51		
		137 47 30	—	135 49 36			135 38 51		
Longitude from thirty sets of lunar distances,		Uncorrected		135 58 21,6		Corrected	135 44 51,1	and taken	

From observations west of the moon alone - -   135° 43' 56,6"
      east of the moon alone - -   135 45 45,5
          Mean   135 44 51,1 east.

Solar Eclipse of March 4, 1802, observed at the tents.
Longitude deduced from beginning - 135 46 54,
          end - 135 45 22,5
          Mean   135 46 8,2 east.

TABLE V.
Longitude of *Point Nepean* at the entrance of PORT PHILLIP.

Appt. Greenwich time of observations	Place	Longitude E. from Naut. Alm.	Reduction by two time keepers	East Longitude of Pt. Nepean	Correction for errors of tables	Interv. of ☽'s error	Correct. Longit. of Pt. Nepean	Whence deduced	Observers
1802 April. 16 at 0 42	At sea	140 6 45	+4 57 25	145 4 10	- 21 45	Four days.	144 42 25	* Antares E. of ☽	C
		140 6 15	—	145 3 40			144 41 55		
		140 10 15	—	145 7 40			144 45 55		
		140 2 15	Ditto.	144 59 40	- 21 15	Ditto.	144 38 25	* Regulus. W. of ☽	
		139 52 45	—	144 53 10			144 31 55		
		139 52 30	—	144 49 55			144 28 40		
26 at 12 34	At 1st anchor in Port Phillip.	144 45 45	+0 8 10	144 40 5	- 11 45	8½ days (April 25 to May 4.)	144 25 50	☉ E. ☽	F
		144 37 45	by survey.	144 29 35			144 17 50		
		144 46 0	—	144 37 50			144 26 5		
		144 41 30	—	144 33 20			144 21 35		
		144 42 0	—	144 34 50			144 23 5		
		144 44 0	—	144 35 50			144 24 5		
		144 41 45	—	144 38 35			144 21 50		
27 at 16 28	At 2d anchor. in do.	144 44 45	+ 0 18 25	144 40 5	- 11 15	Ditto.	144 28 50	Ditto.	F
		144 56 30	by survey.	144 48 5			144 31 50		
		144 54 45	—	144 41 20			144 30 5		
		144 56 45	—	144 43 20			144 32 5		
		145 3 0	—	144 49 35			144 38 20		
Longitude from eighteen sets of lunar distances,		Uncorrected		144 45 27,5		Corrected	144 30 35,8		

Longitude of *Point Nepean* from the two time keepers.

On April 26 at 11h 11' of Greenwich time, and using the Kanguroo-I.
rates, the mean longitude of first anchorage in Port Phillip was   144° 57' 49,5"
Difference of longitude by the survey to Point Nepean,   − 8 10
Correction for variation in the rates found at Port Jackson,   − 0 53,8
Correction for supplemental error during 21 days, - -   − 9 14,4

Corrected longitude from first set of observations,   144 39 31,3

On May 2 at 11h 46' of Greenwich time, and using the Kanguroo-I.
rates, the longitude of the ship (Pt. Nepean N. 1° W. 5½') was   144 50 5
Difference of Longitude to Point Nepean, - − 0 6
Correction for variation in the rates found at Port Jackson,   − 1 28,1
Correction for supplemental error during 27 days, - − 11 52,8

Corrected longitude from second set of observations,   144 36 38,1

Mean longitude from both sets, preferred to that above, - 144 38 4,7 east.

TABLE VI.
Longitude of *Cattle Point*, PORT JACKSON.

Appt. Greenwich time of observations	Place	Longitude E. from Naut. Alm.	Reduction by two time keepers	East Longitude of Cattle Point	Correction for errors of tables	Interv. of ☽'s error	Correct. Longit. of Cattle Point	Whence deduced	Observers
1802 April. 26 at 12 34	At 1st anchor in Port Phillip.	144 45 45	+6 29 32	151 15 17	- 11 45	8½ days (April 25 to May 4.)	151 3 32	☉ E. ☽	C
		144 37 45	(From first rates found at Pt. Jackson.)	151 7 17			150 55 32		
		144 46 0	—	151 15 32			151 3 47		
		144 41 30	—	151 11 2			150 59 17		
		144 43 0	—	151 12 32			151 0 47		
		144 42 15	—	151 11 32			151 1 47		
		144 41 45	—	151 11 17			150 59 32		
27 at 16 28	At 2d anchor. in Port Phillip.	144 53 30	+6 23 2	151 16 32	- 11 30	Ditto.	151 5 17	Ditto.	F
		144 56 30	(From ditto.)	151 19 32			151 8 17		
		144 54 45	—	151 17 47			151 6 32		
		144 56 45	—	151 19 47			151 8 32		
		145 3 0	—	151 26 2			151 14 47		
May 24 at 14 15	On Cattle Point.	151 18 45	—	151 18 45	- 11 0	Two days.	151 7 45	Ditto.	F
		151 21 45	—	151 21 45			151 10 45		
		151 17 15	—	151 17 15			151 6 15		
	Ditto.	151 11 15	—	151 11 15	- 3 15	One day.	151 8 0	Ditto.	F
		151 12 30	—	151 12 30			151 9 15		
27 at 16 28		151 8 45	—	151 8 45			151 5 30		
		151 15 0	—	151 15 0			151 11 45		
		151 10 0	—	151 10 0			151 6 45		
July 8 at 16 15	Ditto.	151 47 0	—	151 47 0	- 12 0	8½ days (July 8th to 17th.)	151 35 0	☉ W ☽	F
		151 42 0	—	151 42 0			151 30 0		
		151 39 45	—	151 39 45			151 27 45		
		151 30 30	—	151 30 30			151 18 30		
	Ditto.	151 30 30	—	151 30 30	- 10 45	Ditto.	151 19 45	Ditto.	F
9 at 16 0		151 31 30	—	151 31 30			151 20 45		
		151 31 45	—	151 31 45			151 21 0		
		151 29 30	—	151 29 30			151 18 45		
		151 29 45	—	151 29 45			151 19 0		
		151 26 30	—	151 26 30			151 15 45		
August 6 at 15 45	At anchor in Port Curtis.	151 26 45	0 8 8	151 18 37	- 10 15	Two days.	151 8 22	Ditto.	F
		151 28 30	(From last rates.)	151 20 22			151 10 7		
		151 38 45	—	151 30 37			151 20 22		
		151 34 30	—	151 26 22			151 16 7		
		151 33 30	—	151 25 22			151 15 7		
		151 27 45	—	151 19 37			151 9 22		
8 at 18 30	At anchor in Keppel Bay.	151 6 15	+0 14 6	151 20 21	- 6 30	Ditto.	151 13 51	Ditto.	F
		151 2 45	(Ditto.)	151 16 51			151 10 21		
		151 11 15	—	151 25 21			151 18 51		
		151 22 30	—	151 22 36			151 16 6		
		151 5 0	—	151 19 6			151 12 36		
		151 4 30	—	151 18 36			151 12 6		
Mean of forty-four sets:		uncorrected		151 21 14,9		Corrected	151 11 49,	and taken	
From observations east of the moon alone - 151° 5' 55,6"		west of the moon alone - 151 17 42,4		Mean 151° 11' 49" east.					

186

In addition to the tables of longitude for the south coast of Terra Australis, I subjoin, for the satisfaction of nautical and geographical readers, a table of the rates of the time keepers, to show their deviations and the errors in longitude during the several passages from one fixed point to another; commencing November 1, 1901, at the Cape of Good Hope, and ending May 9, 1902, at Port Jackson. From this table, the corrections for variation of rates and supplemental error, which have been applied to obtain the corrected longitudes by the time keepers, will be more distinctly seen.

TABLE VII.

Variations in rate and errors in longitude, made by Earnshaw's time keepers No. 543 and No. 520, between the Cape of Good Hope and Port Jackson.

Departure taken.		Rates of time keepers losing.			Variations in mean rate			Errors in long. on arriving		Daily part of supplemental errors.
Place.	Longit. East.	No. 543	No. 520	Mean.	During the passage.	Number of days.	Daily acceleration.	With rate before found.	With rate accelerated.	
Cape of G. Hope	18 25 7	6,93	15,84	10,585						
King G. Sound	117 53 10	6,46	16,72	11,590	1,005	43,7	0,0230	13 55,8 E.	8 8 E.	1 41 E.
Port Lincoln	135 44 51	8,46	18,82	13,625	2,035	57	0,0357	22 10,2	7 25	7,80
(The time keepers were let down at Kanguroo Island, previously to the following rates.)										
Kanguroo Island	137 57 11	8,46	18,07	13,265						
Port Jackson	151 11 49	9,886	17,70	13,793	0,528	34	0,01558	17 16	14 57,4	26 40
(First rates on arriving.)										

In altering their rates between one station and another, the time keepers are supposed to have done it, not suddenly, but gradually and uniformly, by the quantities marked in the column of *daily acceleration*; which quantities are the results of the variations in the mean rate *during the passage*, divided by the number of days. The daily acceleration; is not much in any case, yet it makes a material difference in the longitude after some time; and as the application of this difference has always diminished the error found on arriving at any station, it is a satisfactory proof that the accelerated rate is nearer to the true going of the time keepers on the passage, than the rate found at the commencement.

The difference of longitude produced by the acceleration at any given time, is the sum of all the terms of a series in arithmetic progression of which the daily acceleration, turned into longitude, is both the first term and common difference; and the days elapsed form the number of terms. Therefore,

Daily accel. X 15, x number of days + 1, x half number of days, = the difference of longitude in seconds.

The differences thus obtained have been applied to the errors in longitude on arriving, as given by the *rate before found*; and the result is the error which remains *with rate accelerated*.

Has the time keepers been so far perfect machines, as that the change in their rates had been altogether gradual and uniform; and were the stations, as fixed by the lunar distances, perfectly exact; then the error on arriving, *with rate accelerated*, would have been 0'0" in every case. But since neither the one nor the other may be perfect, and yet it is necessary to take one of them as being so, the difference which remains is considered to be the deviation of the time keepers from an uniformly accelerating rate; and this I call their supplemental error. It is generally impossible to fix upon the manner how, or time when this error was contracted; and therefore it is distributed equally throughout the whole passage, day by day, according to the quantities marked in the last column of the table.

To recapitulate briefly: The longitudes of places given in this first Book of the voyage, and used in the construction of the charts of the South Coast, are those resulting from the time keepers, corrected as above for the acceleration of their mean rate and the supplemental error. The exceptions are, King George's Sound, Port Lincoln, and Port Jackson, which are fixed by the lunar distances; and with the position of Simon's Town, Cape of Good Hope, constitute the basis of this chronometrical fabric.

End of Volume One.

Printed in Poland
by Amazon Fulfillment
Poland Sp. z o.o., Wrocław